COMMUNICATION THEORY:
Transmission of Waveforms
and Digital Information

COMMUNICATION THEORY:
Transmission of Waveforms
and Digital Information

D. J. SAKRISON
Department of Electrical Engineering
University of California, Berkeley

 John Wiley & Sons, Inc.   New York   London   Sydney

Library of Congress
Catalog Card Number:
67-30084   GB 471 74979X
Printed in the
United States of America

To Connie
Kara, Kirsten, and John

In lieu of time I might otherwise
have spent with them

PREFACE

This book is an introductory text in communication theory, suitable for use at the senior or first year graduate level, the distinction depending on the choice of topics and the background level of the students. It is also suitable for self-study. Its objectives are to impart a familiarity with the basic methods used to communicate information in the presence of noise, and to give a thorough grounding in the concepts and methods that are basic to analyzing different methods of communication. The book is not designed to give the reader an easy (or superficial) acquaintance with a large number of communications systems and terms. A fairly large spectrum of modulation and transmission systems is discussed, but each system is discussed only after the necessary concepts have been developed for a realistic analysis and understanding of the system. To do otherwise, I believe, is a serious mistake. For an education to have *long-range* value, it is much more important for the student to have a thorough grasp of basic concepts and methods and a limited acquaintance with different communication systems than to have a superficial knowledge of all the present transmission systems.

The only prerequisite that this book assumes is a thorough knowledge of calculus plus some elementary facts about linear differential equations. An exception to this is Section 2-6, which assumes a limited knowledge of complex variable theory. However, this section and the two that depend on it (7-4 and 10-2) are peripheral to the main body of the text. If the student already has some background in linear system theory or probability theory, the amount of time spent on Chapter 2 or 3 respectively can be greatly reduced. The book has been used in note form at the University of California, Berkeley, for a two-quarter senior course with a probability prerequisite; at the University of California, Davis, for a one-quarter senior course with a probability prerequisite; and at San Francisco State College for a one-semester senior course with no probability prerequisite.

The accompanying figure shows the prerequisite relationship among the different chapters of the book.   As can be seen, the book can be used in a variety of ways.   For example, Chapters 2 through 7 and 10 can be used for an inclusive one-term course in waveform communication; and Chapters 2 through 6 and 8 provide a one-term course covering the rudiments of waveform and digital communication.   Many other combinations are obviously possible.   At Berkeley, Chapters 2 through 6 and part of 8 are covered in one quarter and the remainder of the text, along with some additional material on channel capacity and digital encoding, in another quarter.

The mathematical level at which the course can be taught is flexible. At a number of points I mention such matters as when the interchange of order of integration is permissible, but the discussion is always parenthetical in nature and can easily be passed over by the instructor.   Discussions of this nature which can be omitted are indicated by a smaller type face. The mathematical level is not consistent throughout the book simply for pedagogical reasons.   When the logical chain of ideas is short and simple, I usually mention points of mathematical nicety; when the chain is complicated, points of mathematical nicety are often ignored in order that the student not lose sight of the logical sequence of ideas.

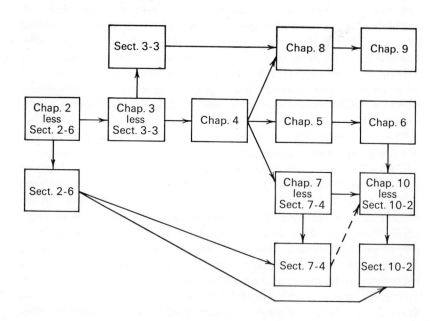

Interrelation of the Chapters.

The conceptual level of the book is not quite uniform.   Chapters 8 and 9 demand more sophistication of the reader than the remainder of the book.   However, this change of level of sophistication is not inconsistent with the normal growth experienced by a student at this level in the course of a term.

Some comments are perhaps in order on what the book does *not* cover, and why.   The emphasis of the book is on the functional operations performed by modulation and reception and not on the circuits which can achieve these operations, although frequent reference is made to the manner in which these operations can be implemented and the problems involved in implementation.   The reason for this is simply that the design of communication circuits is a topic best left to a course or book dealing primarily with electronic circuit design.   Furthermore, circuit design is a rapidly changing field, and inclusion of any great amount of such material would cause this book to become outdated unnecessarily soon.

The book makes no attempt to introduce the basic notions of strict-sense information theory, although they come into some discussions rather implicitly.   The reason for this is that while we can easily introduce the concept of a measure of information at an undergraduate level, the concept is wasted unless we discuss coding theorems.   The concepts involved in any of the interesting versions of these theorems are too subtle, in my opinion, for undergraduate consumption, at least at present.   If we regard this text as a first-year graduate book, then the inclusion of strict-sense information theory is not appropriate because this is usually taught in a separate course at the graduate level.   This dichotomy has some unfortunate consequences, but it seems here to stay.

Lastly, the book considers only additive noise channels.   While this is somewhat restrictive from a practical point of view, it is consistent with the objectives of the book.   The book is not intended to be a compendium of known results but a text in the basic methods of communication and the concepts required in their analysis.

I owe a great deal to the many people who have influenced my thinking in regard to this book.   I would like to list them, at the risk of omitting some.   First, I have been considerably influenced by the geometric interpretation of communication originated by Shannon and Kotelnikov and recently fully developed by Jack Wozencraft and Irwin Jacobs in their *Principles of Communication Engineering*.   I was particularly fortunate in being able to teach a course at M.I.T. from an early version of their notes. The influence of this and Kotelnikov's *Theory of Optimum Noise Immunity* is quite apparent in Chapters 8 and 9 of this book.   I have also benefited greatly from helpful conversations with Ralph Algazi and George Turin and received many helpful comments from James Massey, Andrew

Viterbi, Craig Rushforth, N. T. Gaarder, and Joel Smith.   I also wish to express my thanks to Mrs. Skippy Torrance, Mrs. Billie Vrtiak, and Mrs. Lynn Schell for their patience in typing a clean copy from a rather cluttered manuscript.

D. J. Sakrison
Lafayette, California

January 1968

CONTENTS

Chapter 1

Introduction

This book has two objectives. The first is to impart a basic knowledge of certain methods of communicating information in the presence of noise or interference. The second is to give the reader a thorough grounding in the *concepts* and *methods* used to analyze the problem of communicating in the presence of noise. This second objective is probably the more important, for although certain modulation methods may be technically a dead issue 10 years from now, the concepts and methods used to analyze them will be of continuous use.

The sole purpose of this chapter is to indicate briefly the scope of the problem of communication and to what extent and in what order this book treats this problem.

1-1 The Communication System

A block diagram of a general communication system is shown in Fig. 1-1. The first element in the system is the *information source*. The output of this source may be a sequence of discrete symbols or letters, in which case the source is referred to as a *digital source*. On the other hand, the source output may be a waveform or sequence of continuous valued variables, in which case the source is referred to as a *continuous source*. As an example of a digital source, consider the prices quoted at a stock exchange. These can be expressed in terms of the 10 numerals and the 26 letters of the alphabet together with punctuation marks. As an example of a continuous waveform source, consider the voltage generated by a microphone or the voltage generated by scanning a vidicon tube. Still a third example would be a sequence of temperature readings made on board a satellite. The essential feature of any of these sources, digital or continuous, is that their output is generated by a *random* or *probabilistic* mechanism. This random aspect of the source output is essential, for if the output was completely known to all before the source generated it,

1

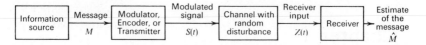

Figure 1-1   Block diagram of a communication system.

there would be no need to relay or communicate the source output to anyone.

The next link in the system is referred to variously as the encoder, modulator, or transmitter.   The term *encoder* is used dominantly when the information source is digital, and the term *modulator* is used almost exclusively when the information source is a waveform source.   The term *transmitter* is used generically.   The function of the transmitter is threefold:

1. to transform the message into an electrical signal that will propagate satisfactorily over the physical transmission channel;
2. to multiplex several information sources onto the same transmission channel;
3. to place the message information in a form that makes it immune (at least to a degree) to the random disturbances in the transmission channel.

Our emphasis in this book is on the third of these objectives, although the function that modulation can play in achieving the first two objectives is made apparent in the process.

The next link in the system is the transmission channel.   Examples of physical transmission channels are a microwave link, a telephone line, or a high-frequency ionospheric propagation link.   The essential feature of any such transmission channel is that it corrupts the transmitted signal in a *random* manner, due to random physical mechanisms in the channel itself and in the first stage of the receiver.   The following table lists types of physical transmission channels and gives a qualitative description of the type of interference encountered on the channel.

In this book, with the exception of Sec. 8-4, we consider only additive noise channels.   The reason for this is *not* that other forms of interference are not important; quite to the contrary, much of the remaining work in communications consists of obtaining a better understanding of nonadditive disturbances and how to combat such interference.   Our basic objective is to obtain a conceptual understanding of certain methods of communication and the analytical tools needed to analyze them. The problems of mathematical manipulation and tedium are minimized if we restrict ourselves to considering additive noise sources in obtaining

PHYSICAL CHANNEL	TYPE OF DISTURBANCE ENCOUNTERED
Microwave and U.H.F. relay links, 100 Mc on up, line of sight transmission. Also low-frequency groundwave propagation 20 Kc to 1.5 Mc.	Only additive noise $$Z(t) = N(t) + S(t)$$ $N(t)$ primarily noise originating in the receiver front end and from man-made and atmospheric electrical disturbances.
Wire transmission at low frequencies. Cable transmission at medium frequencies. Waveguide transmission at U.H.F.	Fixed distortion and additive noise. $Z(t) = N(t) + $ *deterministically* (non-randomly) distorted version of $S(t)$.
H.F. ionospheric skip channels, 2 Mc to 30 Mc. U.H.F. scatter channels (scattering off the ionosphere, troposphere, or needles belt).	Random distortion and additive noise. $Z(t) = N(t) + $ *randomly* distorted version of $S(t)$.

this understanding. The reader who has mastered the basic concepts and methods discussed here will be well prepared to read papers dealing with the problem of more involved forms of interference.

The last link in the communication system is the *receiver*. The receiver must process the randomly corrupted signal $Z(t)$ and attempt to construct an estimate of the original message. This estimate should be in a form suitable for direct use by the *user*.

In the text we examine different modulation systems, particularly with regard to how much bandwidth they occupy and the performance they can achieve in the presence of additive noise. At the same time, we investigate the functions that the receiver should perform in order to produce the best possible estimate of the message from the corrupted signal $Z(t)$. In studying both the modulation process and the receiver, we concentrate on the functions performed rather than on the circuitry used to achieve these functions. However, examples of circuits are occasionally given, and frequent comment is made on how certain functions can be implemented by electronic circuitry and on the problems involved in the implementation. The details of circuit design are best left to a book devoted primarily to that objective.

In the next section, the manner and sequence in which we investigate modulation and receiver design is outlined.

1-2   The Contents of the Book

In analyzing the process of communication, the principal entities with which we must deal are random signals, for communication consists essentially of a sequence of operations involving the processing of random signals.   A substantive examination of the process of communication can thus be undertaken only after we are familiar with the basic methods of describing random signals, and the first three chapters of the book are devoted to developing these methods.

This undertaking proceeds most easily in three distinct stages.   First, several methods of describing deterministic (nonrandom) signals are developed, including expansion of a function in an arbitrary orthonormal series expansion, the Fourier series expansion, the Fourier transform, and the sampling theorem.   These topics are covered in Chapter 2.   The expansion of a function in terms of a general set of orthonormal functions is a topic which is usually studied long after the Fourier series expansion. However, the general expansion is essential to the discussion of digital communication in Chapter 8, so the Fourier series is introduced as a special case of a general orthonormal expansion.

The next step is to develop the basic concepts of probability and study in detail the ways of describing the probability distribution of a set of random variables.   These topics, covered in Chapter 3, are useful in their own right in communications and are essential as preparation in studying the description of random signals.   It should be emphasized that Chapter 3 is not intended to serve as an introduction to probability theory; many basic topics from probability theory are completely ignored, and only those elements of probability that are basic to describing the communications-oriented aspects of the theory of random signals are treated thoroughly in Chapter 3.

The concepts used in the description of deterministic signals and random variables are combined in Chapter 4 to discuss the methods that are used to describe random signals.   Random signals are usually referred to as *random processes* in the literature, so this terminology is used in the remainder of this book.   Again, our discussion is not intended to be a basic introduction to the theory of random processes, but only to give a thorough introduction to the methods of describing random processes that are useful in examining the types of processing of random processes that occur in communication applications.

With the mathematical description of random processes accomplished, the balance of the book (Chapters 5 to 10) deals with using this background to examine a variety of methods of communication.

The first major area that we might consider in communication theory is the transmission of random waveform messages via a process of modulation. By a waveform message we mean a random signal which is a function that varies continuously with time; an example of a waveform message is the electrical signal generated at the output of a microphone. The signals arising from the process of modulation are usually band-pass signals; hence before considering specific modulation methods the methods used in describing band-pass random processes are discussed in Sec. 5-1. It is then natural to treat in detail the most common existing methods of modulation. The first of these is Amplitude Modulation, hereafter simply referred to as AM. The bandwidth occupancy and performance of AM in the presence of noise are analyzed in detail in Sec. 5-2, consideration being given to synchronous and envelope demodulation and Single-Sideband Amplitude Modulation (SSB-AM). The other common method of modulation is angle modulation. The basic definitions and properties of angle modulation are discussed in Sec. 6-1. The balance of Chapter 6 then focuses on a particular form of angle modulation known as Frequency Modulation (abbreviated hereafter as FM). Consideration is directed to the demodulation of FM signals, the bandwidth occupancy of FM, and the performance of FM in the presence of noise. The essential property of FM, its ability to exchange bandwidth occupancy for an improved signal-to-noise ratio, is elaborated on.

In the discussion of demodulation of either AM or FM the problem of filtering, or extracting a signal from noise, naturally arises. This problem, which is of interest in its own right in such applications as data processing as well as in demodulation, is studied in fair detail in Chapter 7. The principle underlying the optimal filtering of a signal from a randomly corrupted version is studied in Sec. 7-1 by means of a geometric analogy. This principle is then used in the balance of the chapter to determine methods of designing optimum filters. This material is then used in Sec. 7-5 to obtain the performance of AM for arbitrary message spectra, the performance calculations in Chapters 5 and 6 having been limited to idealized spectra. Placing the material in Chapter 7 after the discussion of AM and FM allows us to first obtain a familiarity with the concepts involved in modulation without worrying about the mathematical technicalities involved in filtering arbitrary message spectra. This sequence is also convenient for the reader who can only eat the cake (Chapters 5 and 6) and does not have time for the frosting (Chapter 7).

In the discussion of modulation in Chapters 5 and 6, two important points arise but are not answered in these chapters. The first point is how to generate at the receiver a local carrier in phase and frequency synchronism with the transmitted carrier for the purpose of achieving synchronous demodulation. The second point concerns angle demodulation. In Chapter 6 the performance of FM is derived under the assumption that the noise in the channel is sufficiently low, but no analytical method is given for deriving at what noise level the performance drops below the calculated value (threshold occurs). These two important points are discussed in Chapter 10, which describes the operation and performance of an important device known as the *phase lock loop*. This device is useful for generating a local carrier in synchronism with the transmitted carrier or for demodulation of angle modulated signals. Its performance as an FM demodulator is better in the threshold region than a conventional FM receiver. Section 10-3 discusses the performance of the loop in tracking a transmitted carrier and Sec. 10-4 analyzes the performance of the loop as a demodulator, *including* the point at which threshold occurs. This analysis leads to detailed performance curves for both FM and PM (Phase Modulation). Although the material in Chapter 10 is closely related to that in Chapters 5, 6, and 7, it is placed last because it is rather specialized and is less basic than the material in Chapters 8 and 9.

Our discussion up to this point has considered only information transmission in which the message is a continuously varying waveform. In contradistinction to this is a digital information source which generates one letter from a finite alphabet of letters every T seconds. The transmission of such digital information or data is rapidly becoming of increasing importance, and a person who is unfamiliar with the concepts involved in digital information transmission is truly uneducated in the field of communication. The concepts necessary for obtaining a simple geometrical interpretation of digital transmission via physical signals are developed in the first two sections of Chapter 8. The geometric interpretation used in this chapter and Chapter 9 was originated by C. E. Shannon [1] and V. A. Kotelnikov [2] and further developed by J. M. Wozencraft and I. M. Jacobs [3]. Section 8-3 analyzes the design of the optimum receiver for digital transmission in the presence of additive noise and examines how the choice of a signal set influences system performance (probability of an error). With this material as background, you will be prepared to come to grips with the concept of *channel capacity*. This important concept of being able to transmit over a noisy channel with *arbitrarily high reliability* at any rate *below* a threshold rate termed the *capacity* originated with C. E. Shannon [1]. Section 8-5 develops an understanding of the reason for the occurrence of this phenomenon and the difficulties involved in obtaining the performance promised by this phenomenon. The capacity formula and coding theorem for a channel with additive gaussian noise are stated, but the details of the proof of the theorem are omitted, being slightly beyond the mathematical scope expected of the reader.

With the background of the concepts of digital transmission in hand, the reader is prepared to cope with a class of waveform transmission methods that are distinct from those discussed in earlier chapters. These transmission methods, referred to as pulse modulation, are based on the idea of sampling a waveform at discrete sample times, transmitting only the sampled values, and reconstructing a replica of the waveform at the receiver from these sampled values. Section 9-1 isolates the total error in such a transmission system into two terms: error caused by sampling and error caused by errors in the values of the received samples. Quantitative relationships for these two sources of error are also developed at this point. The remainder of the chapter then focuses on the transmission of the samples by pulse modulation; that is, transmission in which each sample modulates an individual pulse in a sequence of pulses. Section 9-2 analyzes the performance of the most common form of pulse modulation, Pulse Amplitude Modulation (PAM), in the presence of additive noise. The geometric development of Chapter 8 is then used in Sec. 9-3 to analyze the performance of a general nonlinear pulse modulation system. Emphasis is placed on developing an understanding of why such a system has the potential for exchanging bandwidth for signal-to-noise ratio *and* why a threshold phenomenon is a necessary consequence of such a system. This development is used in Sec. 9-4 to analyze the performance of one of the most common forms of nonlinear pulse modulation, Pulse Position Modulation (PPM), including the threshold behavior. The final section in the chapter analyzes the performance of Pulse Code Modulation (PCM), a useful method of transmission in which the samples are quantized and the quantized values transmitted by digital transmission methods.

As the reader can deduce from the above discussion, the sequence in which different chapters, after the fourth, can be read is quite flexible; the interested reader can consult the preface for an elaboration of this point. At certain places throughout the book, points of mathematical detail are discussed. When these can be divorced from the main topic of discussion, they are printed in smaller type. If you are uninterested in or distracted by these details, you may skip over these portions in smaller type with no real loss of continuity.

REFERENCES

[1] Shannon, C. E., "Communication in the Presence of Noise," *Proc. IRE*, **37**, No. 1, 10–21, January, 1949.

[2] Kotelnikov, V. A., *The Theory of Optimum Noise Immunity*, McGraw-Hill Book Co., New York, 1959.

[3] Wozencraft, J. M., and I. M. Jacobs, *Principles of Communication Engineering*, John Wiley and Sons, New York, 1965; see especially Chapters 4 and 8.

Chapter 2

Description of Signals

In studying and analyzing communication systems, the principal entities that we must deal with are signals or time functions. Although a time function is defined by a rule assigning a value to the function for each instant of time of interest, such a description is not in itself always adequate for our purposes. We must be able to analyze how a signal is modified by passage through a filter or by the process of modulation. Furthermore, in Chapter 8 where we consider the transmission of digital information, it is convenient to picture signals as vectors in a Euclidean space. Our first task, therefore, is to become familiar with several ways of describing time functions so that we may more easily analyze the behavior of systems of interest.

2-1 Expansion in Orthogonal Functions

We first consider the problem of describing a time function $g(t)$ on an interval $[-T/2, T/2]$; we would like to describe this function by specifying a discrete set of coefficients. To this end, we consider a series expansion of the form

$$\hat{g}(t) = \sum_{k=1}^{N} g_k \psi_k(t) \qquad -T/2 \le t \le T/2 \qquad (2\text{-}1)$$

in which the N coefficients g_k depend only on the function $g(t)$ to be represented but *not* on time; and the N functions of time, $\psi_k(t)$, are specified independently of $g(t)$. We use the "hat" (circumflex) over $g(t)$ to denote that $\hat{g}(t)$ is to be considered an approximation to $g(t)$. If $g(t)$ is suitably well behaved, the difference between $g(t)$ and $\hat{g}(t)$ will approach zero as N approaches ∞. Further discussion of this point will be made later. In some applications the approximation using only a *finite* number of terms is of great practical importance. An example is in estimating the trajectory of an object from a noisy radar observation. The radar

9

observation fluctuates wildly due to the noise, while the actual trajectory is quite smooth. If the functions $\psi_k(t)$, $k = 1, 2, \ldots, N$, are smooth, then the function $\hat{g}(t)$ will be a good approximation to the actual trajectory.

The reader may already be familiar with an expansion of the form of Eq. 2-1 in which the $\psi_k(t)$ are sines and cosines. In many applications, such as the example above and the applications encountered in Chapter 8, it is helpful to make use of functions other than the sines and cosines, and we do not restrict ourselves to them. However, for a number of reasons that will become apparent later, it is convenient to pick expansion functions $\psi_k(t)$ having certain properties. We say that the functions $\psi_k(t)$, $k = 1, 2, 3, \ldots, N$, are *orthogonal* on the interval $[-T/2, T/2]$ if

$$\int_{-T/2}^{T/2} \psi_j(t)\psi_k{}^*(t)\, dt = 0 \qquad j, k = 1, 2, \ldots, N; j \neq k \qquad (2\text{-}2)$$

The asterisk denotes complex conjugate; allowing possibly complex valued functions for the $\psi_k(t)$ will be useful when we consider the exponential form of the Fourier series. We further say the $\psi_k(t)$ are *normalized* if

$$\int_{-T/2}^{T/2} \psi_k(t)\psi_k{}^*(t)\, dt = \int_{-T/2}^{T/2} |\psi_k(t)|^2\, dt = 1 \qquad k = 1, 2, \ldots, N \quad (2\text{-}3)$$

If the $\psi_k(t)$ satisfy both these properties, we say they are *orthonormal*; that is, the functions $\psi_k(t)$ are orthonormal if

$$\int_{-T/2}^{T/2} \psi_j(t)\psi_k{}^*(t)\, dt = \delta_{jk}$$

in which $\delta_{jk} = 0$ if $j \neq k$, and 1 if $k = j$.

We will be dealing with integrals of products of two functions so often that we adopt the following shorthand notation:

$$(x, y) = \int_{-T/2}^{T/2} x(t)y^*(t)\, dt \qquad (2\text{-}4)$$

$$\|x\|^2 = (x, x) = \int_{-T/2}^{T/2} |x(t)|^2\, dt \qquad (2\text{-}5)$$

In Chapter 8 we regard time functions as vectors in a function space; in that context we refer to (x, y) as the *inner product* of the two functions x and y (analogous to the dot product of two vectors in Euclidean space) and refer to $\|x\|$ as the norm or "length" of the function x. Note that if we regard $x(t)$ as the voltage across a 1-ohm resistor, then $\|x\|^2$, the square of the norm or length, is the energy dissipated in the resistor in the time interval $[-T/2, T/2]$. We therefore often refer to $\|x\|^2$ as the "energy" in the function $x(t)$.

Problem 2-1. Let $x(t)$ and $y(t)$ be two real-valued time functions. Show that the square of the norm of the function $x(t) + y(t)$ is the sum of the square of the norm of $x(t)$ and the square of the norm of $y(t)$ *if and only if* x and y are orthogonal (note that you must prove *two* distinct things); i.e.,

   (1) $\|x + y\|^2 = \|x\|^2 + \|y\|^2$ if $(x, y) = 0$

and

   (2) $\|x + y\|^2 = \|x\|^2 + \|y\|^2$ *only if* $(x, y) = 0$.

Note the analogy to vectors in 3-dimensional space: the Pythagorean theorem applies only to vectors which are orthogonal or perpendicular (zero dot product).

Now let us reconsider approximate representation of the function $g(t)$ by the series expansion of Eq. 2-1. We will measure the error in this approximation by

$$\epsilon = \|g - \hat{g}\|^2 = \int_{-T/2}^{T/2} |g(t) - \hat{g}(t)|^2 \, dt \tag{2-6}$$

Note that since the integrand can never be negative, this error will be zero only if $g(t)$ and $\hat{g}(t)$ are equal for all values of t.[1] Given a function $g(t)$, the question is how to choose the coefficients g_k appearing in the expansion so as to minimize this approximation error. We will assume that the $\psi_k(t)$ are orthonormal. Then by expanding the expression for the error we obtain

$$\epsilon = \int_{-T/2}^{T/2} \left[g(t) - \sum_{j=1}^{N} g_j \psi_j(t) \right] \left[g(t) - \sum_{k=1}^{N} g_k \psi_k(t) \right]^* dt$$

$$= \int_{-T/2}^{T/2} |g(t)|^2 \, dt - \sum_{j=1}^{N} g_j \int_{-T/2}^{T/2} \psi_j(t) g^*(t) \, dt$$

$$- \sum_{k=1}^{N} g_k^* \int_{-T/2}^{T/2} \psi_k^*(t) g(t) \, dt + \sum_{j,k=1}^{N} g_j g_k^* \int_{-T/2}^{T/2} \psi_j(t) \psi_k^*(t) \, dt$$

$$= \|g\|^2 - \sum_{k=1}^{N} [g_k^*(g, \psi_k) + g_k(g, \psi_k)^*] + \sum_{k=1}^{N} |g_k|^2 \tag{2-7}$$

in which we have used the orthonormality of the ψ_k. We now wish to find the minimum of the right-hand side of Eq. 2-7 with respect to the g_k. Since the g_k are complex-valued, we cannot simply take partial derivatives

---

[1] Actually ϵ can be zero if $g(t)$ and $\hat{g}(t)$ differ for a set of time points of total length zero (such as a single point or a finite number of points). For all practical engineering purposes we can regard two such functions as equal.

with respect to the g_k, but must resort to somewhat of a gimmick.   Adding and subtracting the quantity

$$\sum_{k=1}^{N} |(g, \psi_k)|^2$$

from the right hand side of Eq. 2-7 then yields

$$\epsilon = \|g\|^2 - \sum_{k=1}^{N} |(g, \psi_k)|^2$$

$$+ \sum_{k=1}^{N} \{|(g, \psi_k)|^2 - g_k{}^*(g, \psi_k) - g_k(g, \psi_k)^* + |g_k|^2\}$$

$$= \|g\|^2 - \sum_{k=1}^{N} |(g, \psi_k)|^2 + \sum_{k=1}^{N} |g_k - (g, \psi_k)|^2 \qquad (2\text{-}8)$$

The first two terms on the right-hand side of this equation are independent of the coefficients g_k, and the third term is obviously minimized by setting

$$g_k = (g, \psi_k) = \int_{-T/2}^{T/2} g(t)\psi_k{}^*(t)\, dt \qquad (2\text{-}9)$$

These minimum error coefficients are referred to as *Fourier coefficients*. From Eq. 2-8 the approximation error using these coefficients is obviously

$$\epsilon_{\min} = \|g\|^2 - \sum_{k=1}^{N} |(g, \psi_k)|^2$$

$$= \|g\|^2 - \sum_{k=1}^{N} |g_k|^2 \qquad (2\text{-}10)$$

Note that Eq. 2-9 gives a simple *explicit* expression for the g_k and that this expression is independent of N, the number of terms used in the representation; this convenience is due solely to the orthogonality of the $\psi_k(t)$.

Problem 2-2.   Refer to Eq. 2-7 and assume that all the g_k and $\psi_k(t)$ are real valued. Do *not* assume that the $\psi_k(t)$ are orthogonal and find the set of equations that determine the g_k which minimize ϵ by setting

$$\frac{\partial \epsilon}{\partial g_k} = 0 \qquad k = 1, 2, \ldots, N$$

Note that in order to find the N g_k, we must then solve a set of N *simultaneous* equations [unless the $\psi_k(t)$ are orthogonal, in which case the equations simplify].

Let us now assume that we use an infinite set of functions

$$\psi_k(t) \qquad k = 1, 2, 3, \ldots$$

In this situation our concern is under what conditions the function $\sum_{k=1}^{\infty} g_k \psi_k(t)$ will actually be equal to $g(t)$; that is, under what conditions the error term

$$\epsilon_N = \left\| g(t) - \sum_{k=1}^{N} g_k \psi_k(t) \right\|^2 = \|g\|^2 - \sum_{k=1}^{N} |g_k|^2 \qquad (2\text{-}11)$$

approaches zero as N approaches ∞. If the set of $\psi_k(t)$ is such that

$$\operatorname*{Lim}_{N \to \infty} \epsilon_N = 0 \qquad (2\text{-}12)$$

for *any* function $g(t)$ such that

$$\int_{-T/2}^{T/2} |g(t)|^2 \, dt < \infty$$

we say that the set of $\psi_k(t)$ is *complete* on $[-T/2, T/2]$. Equation 2-12 implies that any function of finite energy can be represented without error in terms of the ψ_k's. Note that when the ψ's are a complete set we have "equality" between $g(t)$ and

$$\hat{g}(t) = \sum_{k=1}^{\infty} g_k \psi_k(t)$$

in the sense that there is no energy in the error $g(t) - \hat{g}(t)$. There may be a number of points, t_j, at which $g(t)$ is discontinuous (takes a jump). At such a point it may be that

$$g(t_j) \neq \sum_{k=1}^{\infty} g_k \psi_k(t_j) = \hat{g}(t_j)$$

However, the points at which this can happen can constitute only a negligible set of the points in the interval $[-T/2, T/2]$; for almost all points[1] in this interval Eq. 2-12 will require that $g(t)$ be equal to $\hat{g}(t)$.

The question of determining whether a given set of orthonormal functions $\psi_k(t)$ is complete or not is a difficult problem in mathematical analysis that will not concern us here. When we make use of certain complete sets of orthonormal functions (such as a Fourier sine-cosine series) we will simply state their completeness without proof, and indicate where the interested reader may find a discussion and proof of such completeness.

---

[1] The phrase "almost all points" mathematically refers to all points except a set of total length zero.

Parseval's Theorem

If the set of functions $\psi_k(t)$, $k = 1, 2, 3, \ldots$, is *complete* and *orthonormal*, then from Eqs. 2-11 and 2-12 we have

$$\|g\|^2 = \int_{-T/2}^{T/2} |g(t)|^2 \, dt = \sum_{k=1}^{\infty} |g_k|^2 \qquad (2\text{-}13)$$

This equation is referred to as *Parseval's theorem*. Observe that

$$\int_{-T/2}^{T/2} |g_k \psi_k(t)|^2 \, dt = |g_k|^2 \int_{-T/2}^{T/2} |\psi_k(t)|^2 \, dt = |g_k|^2 \qquad (2\text{-}14)$$

so that $|g_k|^2$ represents the energy in the component function $g_k\psi_k(t)$. The quantity $\|g\|^2$ is the energy in the function $g(t)$ which we have expressed as a linear combination of the component functions $g_k\psi_k(t)$. Thus, in words, Parseval's theorem states: *the total energy in the function $g(t)$ is equal to the sum of the energies in each of the component functions $g_k\psi_k(t)$.*

Problem 2-3. Verify that Parseval's theorem is a direct consequence of the orthogonality (and completeness) of the ψ_k and is not true if the ψ_k are not orthogonal.

2-2   Fourier Series

We now consider expansion in a particular set of functions, the well-known Fourier sine-cosine series. We may take the $\psi_k(t)$ to be

$$\psi_k(t) = \begin{cases} \cos\left(\dfrac{k-1}{2}\Omega t\right) & k \text{ odd} \\[2ex] \sin\left(\dfrac{k}{2}\Omega t\right) & k \text{ even} \end{cases} \qquad k = 1, 2, 3, \ldots$$

in which $\Omega = (2\pi/T)$. Our series expansion

$$g(t) = \sum_{k=1}^{\infty} g_k \psi_k(t) \qquad -T/2 \leq t \leq T/2$$

could also be written in the form

$$g(t) = \sum_{k=0}^{\infty} a_k \cos(k\Omega t) + \sum_{k=1}^{\infty} b_k \sin(k\Omega t) \qquad -T/2 \leq t \leq T/2 \quad (2\text{-}15)$$

It is easily verified by evaluation of elementary integrals that this set of ψ_k is *orthogonal* (although *not normalized*). It is also well known (although not easily proven) that this set is *complete*. For a proof of this, refer to Courant [1] and Birkhoff and Rota [2].

Rather than use the sine-cosine form of the Fourier series, we use the exponential form, which is more convenient for our purposes.   Inasmuch as[1]

$$\sin k\Omega t = \frac{1}{2j} [e^{jk\Omega t} - e^{-jk\Omega t}] \tag{2-16}$$

and

$$\cos k\Omega t = \frac{1}{2} [e^{jk\Omega t} + e^{-jk\Omega t}] \tag{2-17}$$

it is apparent that any function which can be represented in the series expansion of Eq. 2-15 could also be represented in the expansion

$$g(t) = \sum_{k=-\infty}^{\infty} c_k e^{jk\Omega t} \qquad -T/2 \le t \le T/2 \tag{2-18}$$

so that this set of complex exponential functions is also complete.   For convenience the index k ranges over $0, \pm 1, \pm 2, \ldots$, instead of arranging the functions so that the index runs over $0, +1, +2, \ldots$, as previously assumed.   It is easily verified that these complex exponential functions are orthogonal since

$$(e^{jk\Omega t}, e^{jm\Omega t}) = \int_{-T/2}^{T/2} e^{jk\Omega t}(e^{jm\Omega t})^* \, dt$$

$$- \int_{-T/2}^{T/2} e^{j(k-m)\Omega t} \, dt$$

$$= T\delta_{km} \tag{2-19}$$

From this equation we see that these exponential functions are not normalized; however, dividing each function by $\sqrt{T}$, the resulting set of functions

$$(1/\sqrt{T})e^{jk\Omega t} \qquad k = 0, \pm 1, \pm 2, \ldots$$

will be orthogonal since

$$(e^{jk\Omega t}/\sqrt{T}, e^{jm\Omega t}/\sqrt{T}) = \frac{1}{T}(e^{jk\Omega t}, e^{jm\Omega t}) = \delta_{km} \tag{2-20}$$

Thus if we expand $g(t)$ in the form

$$g(t) = \sum_{k=-\infty}^{\infty} g_k(1/\sqrt{T})e^{jk\Omega t} \qquad -T/2 \le t \le T/2 \tag{2-21}$$

---

[1] The symbol j in these equations is the familiar engineering notation for the square root of minus one.

Then from Eq. 2-9 the coefficients g_k will be given by

$$g_k = \left(g, \frac{1}{\sqrt{T}} e^{jk\Omega t}\right) = \frac{1}{\sqrt{T}} \int_{-T/2}^{T/2} g(t) e^{-jk\Omega t}\, dt \qquad (2\text{-}22)$$

Upon comparing Eqs. 2-18 and 2-21, we see that the coefficients c_k in Eq. 2-18 must be given by

$$c_k = \frac{1}{\sqrt{T}} g_k = \frac{1}{T} \int_{-T/2}^{T/2} g(t) e^{-jk\Omega t}\, dt \qquad (2\text{-}23)$$

It should be noted from Eqs. 2-22 and 2-23 that if $g(t)$ is a real-valued function of time, then

$$g_{-k} = (g_k)^*; \qquad c_{-k} = (c_k)^* \qquad (2\text{-}24)$$

and that Parseval's Theorem for the exponential series assumes the form

$$\|g\|^2 = \sum_{k=-\infty}^{\infty} |g_k|^2 = T \sum_{k=-\infty}^{\infty} |c_k|^2 = \frac{1}{T} \sum_{k=-\infty}^{\infty} |(g, e^{jk\Omega t})|^2 \quad (2\text{-}25)$$

Response of a Linear System to a Periodic Input

So far we have assumed either that the function $g(t)$ was defined only on the time interval $[-T/2, T/2]$ or that our interest in the function was confined to this interval; our series representation was then intended to be valid only in this interval. Note, however, that since the functions $e^{jk\Omega t}$, $k = 0, \pm 1, \pm 2, \ldots$, are all periodic with shortest common period T, the function

$$\frac{1}{\sqrt{T}} \sum_{k=-\infty}^{\infty} g_k e^{jk\Omega t}$$

is periodic with period T. Thus, if our original function $g(t)$ is periodic with period T, the series representation will be valid for all time

$$g(t) = \frac{1}{\sqrt{T}} \sum_{k=-\infty}^{\infty} g_k e^{jk\Omega t} \qquad \begin{array}{l} \text{all } t \text{ if } g(t) \text{ periodic with} \\ \text{period } T; \ \Omega = 2\pi/T \end{array} \qquad (2\text{-}26)$$

It should also be noted that, if $g(t)$ is periodic with period T, then the coefficient g_k (or c_k) can be evaluated by integration over *any* interval of duration T; i.e.,

$$g_k = \frac{1}{\sqrt{T}} \int_{\tau-T/2}^{\tau+T/2} g(t) e^{-jk\Omega t}\, dt \qquad \begin{array}{l} k = 0, \pm 1, \pm 2, \ldots \\ \tau \text{ arbitrary} \end{array} \qquad (2\text{-}27)$$

Problem 2-4. Let $x(t)$, $y(t)$, and $z(t)$ be three periodic time functions with period T and Fourier Expansions

$$x(t) = \frac{1}{\sqrt{T}} \sum_{k=-\infty}^{\infty} x_k e^{jk\Omega t}$$

$$y(t) = \frac{1}{\sqrt{T}} \sum_{k=-\infty}^{\infty} y_k e^{jk\Omega t}$$

$$z(t) = \frac{1}{\sqrt{T}} \sum_{k=-\infty}^{\infty} z_k e^{jk\Omega t}$$

(a) Let $z(t) = \dfrac{1}{\sqrt{T}} \displaystyle\int_{-T/2}^{T/2} x(t-\tau)y(\tau)\,d\tau$

show that $z_k = x_k y_k$

(b) Let $z(t) = x(t)y(t)$

show that $z_k = \dfrac{1}{\sqrt{T}} \displaystyle\sum_{k=-\infty}^{\infty} x_{k-m} y_m$

Now consider a periodic input $x(t)$ with the Fourier series representation

$$x(t) = \frac{1}{\sqrt{T}} \sum_{k=-\infty}^{\infty} x_k e^{jk\Omega t} \tag{2-28}$$

and let this signal be the input to a *linear time-invariant*[1] system described by the differential equation

$$\left\{ \sum_{k=0}^{n} b_k \frac{d^k}{dt^k} \right\} y(t) = \left\{ \sum_{k=0}^{m} a_k \frac{d^k}{dt^k} \right\} x(t) \tag{2-29}$$

and the initial conditions

$$\left. \frac{d^k}{dt^k} y(t) \right|_{t=-T_0} = 0 \qquad k = 0, 1, \ldots, n-1 \tag{2-30}$$

The function $y(t)$ then represents the output of the system when the system starts from rest; that is, from zero initial conditions. We wish to find an expression for the output of the system. For convenience let us use the following shorthand notation for the polynomials associated with the differential equation

$$A(s) = \sum_{k=0}^{m} a_k s^k; \qquad B(s) = \sum_{k=0}^{n} b_k s^k$$

Consider first the response of the system to the input

$$x_\omega(t) = \begin{cases} 0 & t < -T_0 \\ e^{j\omega t} & t \geq -T_0 \end{cases} \tag{2-31}$$

---

[1] These terms are defined in detail in the following section. The present discussion is to motivate and set the stage for the discussion of linear systems.

Let the function $y_\omega(t)$ be defined as

$$y_\omega(t) = \begin{cases} 0 & t < -T_0 \\ \dfrac{A(j\omega)}{B(j\omega)} e^{j\omega t} + \displaystyle\sum_{k=1}^{n} M_k e^{s_k(t+T_0)} & t \geq -T_0 \end{cases} \qquad (2\text{-}32)$$

in which the s_k are the n-roots (which we have assumed distinct for convenience) of the equation

$$B(s) = 0$$

and the constants M_k are determined so that the initial conditions are satisfied

$$\left. \frac{d^q}{dt^q} y_\omega(t) \right|_{t=-T_0} = 0 \qquad q = 0, 1, \ldots, n-1$$

The function $y_\omega(t)$ given by Eq. 2-32 is the response of the system to $x_\omega(t)$ since by the choice of the M_k it satisfies the initial conditions *and* $x_\omega(t)$ and $y_\omega(t)$ satisfy the differential equation 2-29. This later fact can be ascertained just by substituting from Eqs. 2-31 and 2-32 into Eq. 2-29. It can be shown by straightforward but tedious calculation that the M_k satisfying the initial conditions are bounded in magnitude for all values of T_0. The system is stable[1] if

$$\mathrm{Re}\,\{s_k\} < 0 \qquad k = 1, 2, \ldots, n$$

In this case the homogeneous solution goes to zero as T_0 approaches ∞

$$\lim_{T_0 \to \infty} \sum_{k=1}^{n} M_k e^{s_k T_0} e^{s_k t} \equiv 0 \qquad (2\text{-}33)$$

Thus, if we apply the input

$$x_\omega(t) = e^{j\omega t} \qquad \textit{all } t$$

and the system is stable, the only response will be the particular solution

$$y_\omega(t) = \frac{A(j\omega)}{B(j\omega)} e^{j\omega t}$$

Thus, by the linearity of the system, the response to the input $x(t)$ of Eq. 2-28 will be

$$y(t) = \frac{1}{\sqrt{T}} \sum_{k=-\infty}^{\infty} x_k \frac{A(jk\Omega)}{B(jk\Omega)} e^{jk\Omega t} \qquad (2\text{-}34)$$

---

[1] Again, this term will be discussed fully in the following section.

Thus the Fourier coefficients of the output are

$$y_k = x_k \left[\frac{A(jk\Omega)}{B(jk\Omega)}\right] \qquad k = 0, \pm 1, \pm 2, \ldots$$

the coefficients of the input multiplied by the ratio $A(jk\Omega)/B(jk\Omega)$.

Let us summarize the above facts.   The response of the given linear time-invariant system to the input

$$x_\omega(t) \equiv e^{j\omega t} \qquad \text{all } t$$

was exactly of the same form as the input and differed only by the constant multiplier $A(j\omega)/B(j\omega)$ (note that this multiplier depends only on the frequency ω and *not on the time t*).   This *preservation of form*, which characterizes linear systems with exponential inputs, coupled with the completeness of the exponential functions is what makes the set of exponential functions uniquely suitable for analyzing signals passing through linear systems.   An arbitrary periodic input can be represented as a combination of exponential functions; with the input in this form the output can be written in the same form by inspection.   In the next section a more exhaustive discussion of linear systems is given.   In Sec. 2-4 we then extend the useful Fourier representation of input and output signals to nonperiodic functions.

It is worth emphasizing one point before leaving the present discussion. The exponential form of the Fourier series is used rather than the sine-cosine form because of the preservation of form of exponential signals passed through linear systems.   The reader should note that the exponential Fourier series contains terms with negative as well as positive frequencies.   These negative frequencies have no physical significance; the reader is quite aware that the sinusoidal signals generated by a signal generator are of positive frequency.   The negative frequencies in the exponential Fourier series arise because mathematically we chose in Eqs. 2-16 and 2-17 to represent sines and cosines of positive frequencies by exponential signals of positive *and negative* frequencies.

2-3   Linear Systems—Time Domain Description

One of our main concerns with time functions or signals is to study how they are affected by passage through physical systems such as electrical filters.   In this section we therefore turn temporarily away from the Fourier representation of signals to discuss some of the properties of systems that are pertinent to signal representation.

By a *system* we refer to any physical device which has an input time function $x(t)$ whose action upon the device causes an output time function

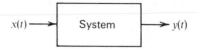

Figure 2-1   Block diagram symbolism representing input-output relation of a system.

$y(t)$.   This behavior is symbolized by the block diagram shown in Fig. 2-1. We adopt the notation $x(t) \rightarrow y(t)$ as a shorthand notation for "the input $x(t)$ causes the output $y(t)$."

Linear and Time Invariant Systems

We say that a system is *linear* if for *any* pair of input-output functions

$$x_1(t) \rightarrow y_1(t); \qquad x_2(t) \rightarrow y_2(t)$$

the input $[a\,x_1(t) + b\,x_2(t)]$ yields the output $[a\,y_1(t) + b\,y_2(t)]$ for *any* real numbers a and b.

We say that a system is *time invariant* if for *any* $x(t)$ the input-output pair

$$x(t) \rightarrow y(t)$$

implies that for the input $x(t + \tau)$ the input-output pair is

$$x(t + \tau) \rightarrow y(t + \tau)$$

for *all* values of the time shift τ.

The defining property of a linear system is referred to as the *superposition* property because it states that if we simultaneously apply a superposition (or linear combination) of any two possible inputs to a linear system, the resulting output is the superposition of the corresponding individual outputs.   The time invariance property in words simply means that an experimenter will observe the same behavior of the system no matter what time of the day he starts his experiment.

The Impulse Function and System Impulse Response

Now let us consider a particular input to a system; a short pulse of unit area.   Two such pulses are shown in Fig. 2-2.   The important feature of this pulse input is not its shape; either of the two pulses of Fig. 2-2 will suffice for our purposes.   The important feature of our pulse input is that it possess unit area and that its effective duration can be made as small as desired.

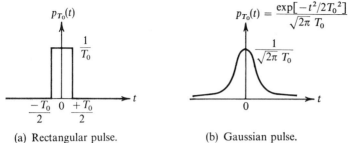

(a) Rectangular pulse.   (b) Gaussian pulse.

Figure 2-2   Pulses which approach an impulse as T_0 approaches 0.

Let us consider the essential property of the pulse of Fig. 2-2a as its width T_0 is allowed to shrink to zero. This property is brought out by considering the definite integral

$$\lim_{T_0 \to 0} \int_{-\infty}^{\infty} p_{T_0}(t)x(t + \tau) \, dt$$

in which the function $x(t)$ appearing in the integrand may be any function which is continuous at the point $t = \tau$. The limiting value of this integral is easily seen from graphical considerations. Figure 2-3a shows an arbitrary function $x(t)$ (which is continuous at $t = \tau$), Fig. 2-3b shows the function $x(t + \tau)$, and Fig. 2-3c the product function $p_{T_0}(t)x(t + \tau)$. The integral in question is just the area under this product function. As can be seen from Fig. 2-3c, as long as $x(t)$ is continuous at $t = \tau$, this area approaches $x(\tau)$ as T_0 approaches zero. This is a consequence of the mean value theorem of integral calculus (see, e.g., Courant [3], pp. 126–128). Thus we have

$$\lim_{T_0 \to 0} \int_{-\infty}^{\infty} p_{T_0}(t)x(t + \tau) \, dt = x(\tau)$$

Although this relation was deduced graphically in Fig. 2-3 for the pulse of Fig. (2-2a), the same limiting relation holds true for the pulse of Fig. (2-2b) or any pulse whose area remains unity as its width shrinks to zero. The limit of any such pulse we term the *impulse function* (or delta function or Dirac-delta function) and denote by $\delta(t)$. The defining properties of this impulse function are then

$$\delta(t) = 0 \qquad \text{all } t \neq 0 \tag{2-35}$$

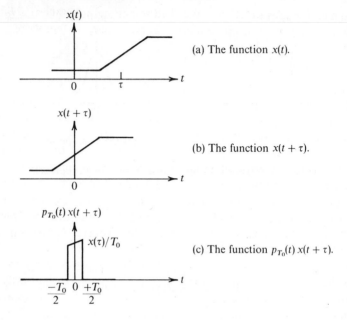

(a) The function $x(t)$.

(b) The function $x(t + \tau)$.

(c) The function $p_{T_0}(t) x(t + \tau)$.

Figure 2-3   Geometric interpretations of $\int_{-\infty}^{\infty} p_{T_0}(t)x(t + \tau)\, dt$.

and

$$\int \delta(t)x(t + \tau)\, dt = x(\tau)$$

for any function $x(t)$ continuous at $t = \tau$ and any range of integration containing $t = 0$.   (2-36)

Note that the impulse function is *not* a function in the usual sense of the word; for it is a function that is zero everywhere except at $t = 0$ where its value is unbounded.   This function has meaning only when it appears as a factor in the integrand of an integral with respect to time, and then, strictly speaking, only when the other factor in the integrand is a continuous function of time.   For convenience we often manipulate $\delta(t)$ as if it were an ordinary function, but its real role is appearing in an integral as in Eq. 2-36.

Note that the quantity defined by Eq. 2-36 is a *function* of the time shift τ.   If $x(t)$ is continuous for all t, then the quantity

$$\int_{-\infty}^{\infty} \delta(t)x(t + \tau)\, dt = x(\tau)$$

is also a continuous function.   We shall sometimes take liberties with the requirement that $x(t)$ be continuous.   In particular, we will write

$$\int_{-\infty}^{\infty} \delta(t)\delta(t + \tau)\, dt = \delta(\tau) \tag{2-37}$$

This will be justified if we regard the "function" defined by this integral not as a function in the usual sense, but as a quantity that will ultimately appear in the integrand of some integral with respect to the variable τ.

Let us now consider the response of a linear and time-invariant system to an impulse function $\delta(t)$.   We start by noting that the pulses p_{T_0} of Fig. 2-2 represent physical inputs that could be applied to a system. Consider the response to $p_{T_0}(t)$ as T_0 approaches zero.   Any physical system takes some nonzero time to respond, i.e., possesses some "inertia" and associated with these inertia effects there is a certain "response time" to the system such that if we make T_0 much less than this response time the output does not depend upon the pulse duration T_0.   If the system is linear the output will depend only on the area under the pulse [note that $p_{T_0}(t)$ has unit area for all T_0].   Thus as T_0 approaches zero and the input pulse approaches an impulse, the system response approaches a definite limit which we call the *impulse response* and denote by $h(t)$. Symbolically we have

$$\delta(t) \rightarrow h(t) \tag{2-38}$$

reading $h(t)$ is the system response to an impulse input.

If the system is time-invariant, then the response to an impulse applied at time τ must be $h(t - \tau)$; i.e.,

$$\delta(t - \tau) \rightarrow h(t - \tau) \tag{2-39}$$

so that the impulse response depends only upon $t - \tau$, the difference between the observation time (time t) and the time at which the impulse was applied (time τ).   Secondly, let us note that since we are considering a linear system, the response to an impulse of area a [note from our discussion defining $\delta(t)$ that the value associated with an impulse is its *area*] is a times the response to an impulse of unit area

$$a\delta(t - \tau) \rightarrow ah(t - \tau) \tag{2-40}$$

We will now use Eq. 2-40 to derive an expression for the response of a linear time-invariant system with impulse response $h(t)$ for an arbitrary input $x(t)$.   We begin by first approximating $x(t)$ by a staircase function composed of the pulse functions of Fig. 2-2a.   This approximation is shown in Fig. 2-4 and can be written

$$x(t) = \lim_{\Delta \to 0} \sum_{k=-\infty}^{\infty} x(k\Delta)p_\Delta(t - k\Delta)\Delta \tag{2-41}$$

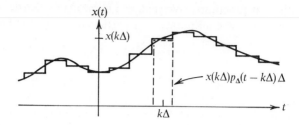

Figure 2-4   Approximation of an input signal $x(t)$ by a sequence of narrow pulses.

As Δ becomes small, then by Eq. 2-40 the response to $x(k\Delta)p_\Delta(t - k\Delta)\Delta$ must approach $x(k\Delta)h(t - k\Delta)\Delta$. Thus, applying superposition and using Eq. 2-41, $y(t)$, the output of the system, is given by

$$y(t) = \lim_{\Delta \to 0} \sum_{k = -\infty}^{\infty} x(k\Delta)h(t - k\Delta)\Delta$$

But, from calculus, recall that in the limit as Δ approaches zero the above sum is by definition the integral

$$y(t) = \int_{-\infty}^{\infty} x(\tau)h(t - \tau)\, d\tau \qquad (2\text{-}42)$$

By making a change of variable of integration, the reader can easily verify that the above equation can also be expressed in the form

$$y(t) = \int_{-\infty}^{\infty} h(\tau)x(t - \tau)\, d\tau \qquad (2\text{-}43)$$

The two equations, 2-42 and 2-43, which give the response of a system with impulse response $h(t)$ to an arbitrary input $x(t)$, are both known as the *convolution integral*. This name has meaning independently of the roles of $h(t)$ as an impulse response and $x(t)$ as a system input. For two arbitrary functions $x(t)$ and $y(t)$, the function of t defined by

$$\int_{-\infty}^{\infty} x(\tau)y(t - \tau)\, d\tau$$

is termed the *convolution of x and y* and is often denoted by the symbol

$$[x * y](t) = \int_{-\infty}^{\infty} x(\tau)y(t - \tau)\, d\tau = \int_{-\infty}^{\infty} x(t - \sigma)y(\sigma)\, d\sigma \qquad (2\text{-}44)$$

EXAMPLE. Let the two functions $x(t)$ and $y(t)$ be defined as

$$x(t) = \begin{cases} A & 0 \le t \le a \\ 0 & \text{elsewhere} \end{cases}$$

$$y(t) = \begin{cases} B & 0 \le t \le b \\ 0 & \text{elsewhere} \end{cases}$$

in which we arbitrarily assume that $a > b$.

Let us find $[x * y]$ by both analytical and graphical reasoning.   We consider the analytical approach first.   We have

$$[x * y](t) = \int_{-\infty}^{\infty} x(\tau)y(t - \tau) \, d\tau = A \int_{0}^{a} y(t - \tau) \, d\tau$$

Now $y(t - \tau)$ is nonzero and has the value

$$y(t - \tau) = B$$

only if

$$0 \le t - \tau \le b \qquad \text{or} \qquad -t \le -\tau \le b - t$$

or

$$t - b \le \tau \le t$$

There are now five possible arrangements of the pair of time instants 0 and a and the pair $t - b$ and t.

(i) $t - b > a$ or $t > b + a$
   $y(t - \tau) \equiv 0$ for $0 \le \tau \le a$ and $[x * y](t) = 0$
(ii) $t < 0$
   $y(t - \tau) \equiv 0$ for $0 \le \tau \le a$ and $[x * y](t) = 0$
(iii) $0 \le t - b < t \le a$ or $b \le t \le a$
   $[x * y] = AB \int_{t-b}^{t} d\tau = ABb$
(iv) $t - b < 0$; $0 < t < a$ or $0 < t < b$ (since $a > b$)
   $[x * y](t) = AB \int_{0}^{t} d\tau = ABt$
(v) $0 < t - b < a$; $t > a$ or $a < t < a + b$ (since $a > b$)
   $[x * y](t) = AB \int_{t-b}^{a} d\tau = AB(a + b - t)$

Summarizing the results above yields

$$[x * y] = \begin{cases} 0 & t \le 0 \\ ABt & 0 < t < b \\ ABb & b \le t \le a \\ AB(a + b - t) & a < t < a + b \\ 0 & a + b < t \end{cases}$$

The resultant function is shown in Fig. 2-5.

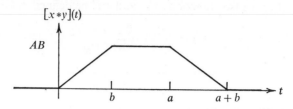

Figure 2-5   Resultant of convolution of x and y for the example.

Let us next consider how to obtain the convolution by graphical means. This is done by visualizing the functions $x(\tau)$, $y(t - \tau)$, and the product function $x(\tau)y(t - \tau)$ as functions *of* τ for different values of the time shift t.   These functions are shown in Fig. 2-6.   In graphical terms the value of the quantity $[x * y](t)$ is the area (with respect *to* τ) under the curve $x(\tau)y(t - \tau)$.   From Fig. 2-6 we can quickly deduce the result. For $t < 0$, there is no overlap of $x(\tau)$ and $y(t - \tau)$ and $[x * y](t)$ is zero. For $0 < t < b$ the area under the product function is proportional to the time shift t and $[x * y](t)$ increases linearly from 0 to ABb.   For $b < t < a$ the product function does not change with t and $[x * y](t)$ is constant. For $a < t < a + b$ the overlap decreases linearly with t and $[x * y](t)$ decreases linearly from ABb to 0.   For $t > a + b$ there is no overlap and $[x * y](t)$ is zero.   For functions with simple geometric shapes for x and y, this graphical approach is easier than the analytical approach; moreover it gives a clear interpretation to a somewhat otherwise dry and abstract definition.

Problem 2-5.   Consider two time functions $x(t)$ and $y(t)$.   Let the time functions $u(t)$ and $v(t)$ be defined by

$$u(t) = x(t - \tau_1); \qquad v(t) = y(t - \tau_2)$$

Show that

$$[u * v](t) = [x * y](t - \tau_1 - \tau_2)$$

Problem 2-6.   Let the functions $x(t)$ and $y(t)$ be given by

$$x(t) = \begin{cases} 0 & t < 0 \\ t & 0 \le t \le 1 \\ 0 & t > 1 \end{cases}$$

$$y(t) = \begin{cases} 0 & t < a \\ 1 & a \le t \le a + b \quad b > 1 \\ 0 & a + b < t \end{cases}$$

Find $[x * y](t)$ either by analytical means, graphical means, or both.

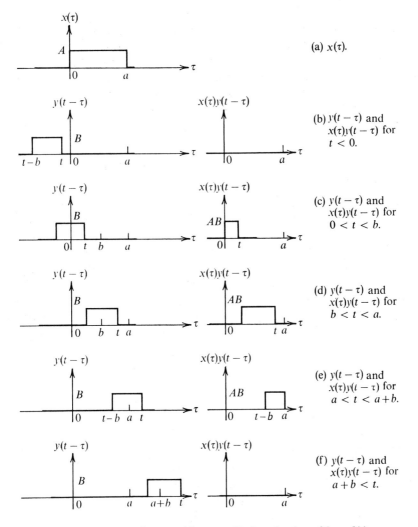

Figure 2-6   Functions used in a graphical evaluation of $[x * y](t)$.

Problem 2-7.   Let the functions $x(t)$ and $y(t)$ be given by

$$x(t) = \begin{cases} 0 & t < 0 \\ 1 & 0 \le t \le 1 \\ 0 & 1 < t \end{cases}$$

$$y(t) = \begin{cases} 0 & t < 0 \\ e^{-at} & t \ge 0 \quad a > 0 \end{cases}$$

Find $[x * y](t)$ either by analytical means, graphical means, or both.

Causal Systems and Stable Systems

The description of a linear time-invariant system in terms of its impulse response (response as a function of *time* to an impulse) and the convolution integral (an explicit rule for determining the response from the input *time* function) is termed the *time domain* description of the system. This is contrasted with the *frequency domain* description to be discussed in the following two sections. We close our discussion of the time domain description with two important properties that a system may or may not possess.

DEFINITION. We say a system is *causal* if for any time t_0 the response at time t_0 depends only on the excitation for $t \leq t_0$.

A causal system thus can have the present value of its output depend only on the past and present values of its input. Clearly all *real-time* physical systems are causal. However, a physical system which does *not* function in *real time* need not be causal. As an example, let $x(t)$, $a \leq t \leq b$, be a noisy signal that is recorded on tape. If the output is later played back, sampled, and the samples stored in a computer, then all the samples in the time range $a \leq t \leq b$ can be used to estimate the noise free value of $x(t_0)$ for t_0 a time instant within the interval. Such a system can be realized physically but is not causal.

A linear time invariant system with impulse response $h(t)$ is obviously causal if *and* only if

$$h(t) \equiv 0 \qquad t < 0 \tag{2-45}$$

We next define what we mean by a stable system.

DEFINITION. A system is *stable* if *every* bounded input yields a bounded output.

This definition of stability is sometimes specifically referred to as bounded input-bounded output stability. It is useful to be able to determine what stability implies about the impulse response of a linear time-invariant system. This point is answered by the following theorem.

Theorem. A linear, time-invariant system with impulse response $h(t)$ is stable if *and* only if

$$\int_{-\infty}^{\infty} |h(t)| \, dt < \infty \tag{2-46}$$

Proof. First, we show that if inequality 2-46 is satisfied, the system is stable. Let $x(t)$ be a bounded input

$$|x(t)| \leq M < \infty$$

Then the magnitude of the output can be bounded by

$$|y(t)| = \left| \int_{-\infty}^{\infty} h(\tau)x(t - \tau)\, d\tau \right|$$

$$\leq \int_{-\infty}^{\infty} |h(\tau)x(t - \tau)|\, d\tau$$

$$\leq \int_{-\infty}^{\infty} M\, |h(\tau)|\, d\tau < \infty$$

Thus inequality 2-46 guarantees that the system is stable. To show that the system is *not* stable if this inequality is not satisfied, consider the input

$$\begin{aligned} x(t) &= \mathrm{sgn}\,[h(t_1 - t)] \\ &= +1 \qquad \text{if } h(t_1 - t) > 0 \\ &= -1 \qquad \text{if } h(t_1 - t) < 0 \end{aligned} \qquad (2\text{-}47)$$

Clearly $x(t)$ is bounded. The response to this input at time t_1 is

$$y(t_1) = \int_{-\infty}^{\infty} h(\tau)x(t_1 - \tau)\, d\tau$$

$$= \int_{-\infty}^{\infty} h(\tau)\, \mathrm{sgn}\, h[t_1 - (t_1 - \tau)]\, d\tau$$

$$= \int_{-\infty}^{\infty} |h(\tau)|\, d\tau$$

Thus, for the bounded input of Eq. 2-47, the output at time t_1 is not bounded unless inequality 2-46 holds.

If the system is described by the differential equation

$$B(d/dt)\,y(t) = A(d/dt)\,x(t) \qquad (2\text{-}48)$$

in which

$$A(s) = \sum_{k=0}^{m} a_k s^k ; \qquad B(s) = \sum_{k=0}^{n} b_k s^k$$

then for $t > 0$ the impulse response will be of the form

$$h(t) = \sum_{k=1}^{n} M_k e^{s_k t} \qquad t > 0$$

in which the s_k are the roots of the equation

$$B(s) = 0$$

which for simplicity we have assumed are distinct. Note that the system is then stable if and only if $\mathrm{Re}\,\{s_k\} < 0$ for all $k = 1, 2, \ldots, n$.

2-4   The Fourier Transform

Having in hand some of the necessary concepts used to describe linear systems, we now return to the topic of Sec. 2-2: the representation of signals by combinations of exponential signals and the utility of this representation in analyzing the passage of signals through linear systems. We wish to generalize the Fourier series representation to a representation valid for nonperiodic signals defined for all time. We do this by re-considering the two equations

$$g(t) = \sum_{k=-\infty}^{\infty} \frac{1}{\sqrt{T}} g_k e^{jk\Omega t} \qquad -T/2 \le t \le T/2 \qquad (2\text{-}21)$$

$$g_k = \frac{1}{\sqrt{T}} \int_{-T/2}^{T/2} g(t) e^{-jk\Omega t} \, dt \qquad (2\text{-}22)$$

and letting the period T approach ∞. In doing this we will use the following modified notation:

$$\Delta f = \frac{\Omega}{2\pi} = \frac{1}{T}; \qquad f = k\Delta f = \frac{k\Omega}{2\pi}$$

and we define the function $G(f)$ by the relations

$$\Delta f G(f) = \Delta f G(k\Delta f) = \frac{g_k}{\sqrt{T}} \qquad \text{or} \qquad G(f) = \sqrt{T} g_k$$

Making this change of notation in Eqs. 2-21 and 2-22, and relabeling the coefficients, then yields

$$g(t) = \sum_{\substack{f=k\Delta f \\ k=-\infty}}^{\infty} G(f) e^{j2\pi f t} \Delta f \qquad -T/2 \le t \le T/2 \qquad (2\text{-}21')$$

and

$$G(f) = \int_{-T/2}^{T/2} g(t) e^{-j2\pi f t} \, dt \qquad (2\text{-}22')$$

If we now let T, the duration over which these equations pertain, approach ∞, the sum in the first equation approaches an integral and we have

$$g(t) = \int_{-\infty}^{\infty} G(f) e^{j2\pi f t} \, df \qquad \text{all } t \qquad (2\text{-}49)$$

$$G(f) = \int_{-\infty}^{\infty} g(t) e^{-j2\pi f t} \, dt \qquad (2\text{-}50)$$

Note what these two equations imply. Equation 2-50 states that given the time function $g(t)$, we can determine a new function $G(f)$ of the frequency variable f.   Equation 2-49 then states that given this new or transformed function $G(f)$ we can recover the original time function $g(t)$. Thus, since from $g(t)$ we can define the function $G(f)$ and from $G(f)$ we can reconstruct $g(t)$, the time function is also specified by $G(f)$; $G(f)$ can be thought of as a transformed version of $g(t)$ and is referred to as the *Fourier transform* of $g(t)$.   The time function $g(t)$ is similarly referred to as the *inverse Fourier transform* of $G(f)$.   This relation between this pair of functions is denoted in the following manner

$$G(f) = \mathscr{F}[g(t)]; \qquad g(t) = \mathscr{F}^{-1}[G(f)]$$

Our derivation of Eqs. 2-49 and 2-50 was purely formal.   However, if some restrictions are imposed on $g(t)$, then the validity of these relations can be established more rigorously.   In particular, we have

Plancherel's Theorem.   Let $g(t)$ be such that the value of

$$\int_{-\infty}^{\infty} |g(t)|^2 \, dt$$

is defined and finite.   Then

$$G(f) = \int_{-\infty}^{\infty} g(t)e^{-j2\pi ft} \, dt$$

is defined for (almost) all values[1] of f and

$$\lim_{w \to \infty} \left[\int_{-\infty}^{\infty} |g(t) - \int_{-w}^{w} G(f)e^{j2\pi ft} \, df|^2 \, dt \right] = 0$$

A proof of this may be found in Chapter 3 of reference [4].
The condition

$$\int_{-\infty}^{\infty} |g(t)|^2 \, dt < \infty$$

is only a sufficient and not a necessary condition for $g(t)$ to be Fourier transformable.   In particular, an alternate theorem states:

Theorem.   Let $g(t)$ be such that the value of

$$\int_{-\infty}^{\infty} |g(t)| \, dt$$

is defined and finite.   Then if $g(t)$ is continuous at $t = t_0$

$$\lim_{w \to \infty} \int_{-w}^{w} \left(1 - \frac{|f|}{w}\right) G(f)e^{j2\pi ft_0} \, df = g(t_0)$$

[1] By "almost all values of f" is meant for all values of f except a set of total length zero.   This phrase and its implications are not of substantial importance in engineering applications.

A rigorous proof of this theorem may be found in Chapter 2 of reference [4]; a more intuitive proof is given in Chapter 2 of reference [5]. If $g(t)$ satisfies the conditions of either of these two theorems we will refer to it as *Fourier transformable*.

Again, we should point out that the condition of this second theorem is also only a sufficient and *not* a necessary condition for the function to be Fourier transformable. The importance of the two conditions

$$\int_{-\infty}^{\infty} |g(t)|\, dt < \infty \qquad \text{or} \qquad \int_{-\infty}^{\infty} |g(t)|^2\, dt < \infty$$

stems from the fact that, in general, only if one of the two is satisfied is one guaranteed that $G(f)$ exists and that $g(t)$ can be recovered from $G(f)$ by means of Eq. 2-49. Furthermore, there are many properties associated with the transform pair of functions $g(t)$ and $G(f)$ that are guaranteed to hold only if one of the above two conditions is met. However, there are many "functions" of engineering interest, such as the impulse function $\delta(t)$ and the function $1/t$, which do not satisfy either of these two conditions, yet have Fourier transforms in a somewhat restricted sense. This point is the subject of the theory of distributions, and is discussed by a number of books such as the one by Lighthill [6]. This topic is beyond the level of this book. At this point we can only state that when taking the Fourier transforms of such functions we must use a mixture of care and suspicion and always check to see that any conclusions based on the use of such transforms seem reasonable.

The utility of the Fourier transform lies in the ease with which it allows us to describe the behavior of linear, time-invariant, stable systems. To show why this is so, let us start by considering the response of such a system to an exponential input. We do not restrict ourselves in this section to systems described by a differential equation, but consider an arbitrary linear, time-invariant, stable system with impulse response $h(t)$. The response to an exponential input

$$x_f(t) \equiv e^{j2\pi ft} \tag{2-51}$$

is

$$y_f(t) = \int_{-\infty}^{\infty} h(\tau)e^{j2\pi f(t-\tau)}\, d\tau$$

$$= e^{j2\pi ft} \int_{-\infty}^{\infty} h(\tau)e^{-j2\pi f\tau}\, d\tau \tag{2-52}$$

Now, since we assumed the system was stable,

$$\int_{-\infty}^{\infty} |h(\tau)|\, d\tau < \infty$$

and $h(\tau)$ is Fourier transformable with a transform which we denote by $H(f)$. We see that the coefficient of $e^{j2\pi ft}$ in the right-hand side of Eq. 2-52 is just $H(f)$. Thus Eq. 2-52 may be rephrased as

$$y_f(t) = H(f)e^{j2\pi ft} \qquad (2\text{-}52')$$

Thus we again have our *preservation of form* property (deduced in Sec. 2-2 for a system described by a differential equation): *the response to an exponential time function of arbitrary frequency f*

$$x_f(t) \equiv e^{j2\pi ft}$$

is the same exponential time function multiplied by a constant coefficient

$$y_f(t) = H(f)e^{j2\pi ft}$$

Note that the coefficient multiplying this exponential signal

$$H(f) = \mathscr{F}[h(t)]$$

depends only on the *frequency f* and not on *time*; this function is referred to as the *transfer function* of the system. Note that by the above argument an alternate definition {as opposed to $H(f) = \mathscr{F}[h(t)]$} of the transfer function is

$$H(f) = \frac{\text{system output}}{\text{system input}}\bigg|_{\text{input } x(t) = e^{j2\pi ft}} \qquad (2\text{-}53)$$

Now consider as an input an arbitrary signal which is Fourier transformable and may thus be expressed as

$$x(t) = \int_{-\infty}^{\infty} X(f)e^{j2\pi ft}\, df \qquad (2\text{-}54)$$

or, in the limiting form of Eq. 2-21',

$$x(t) = \lim_{\Delta f \to 0} \sum_{\substack{f = k\Delta f \\ k = -\infty}}^{\infty} X(f)e^{j2\pi ft}\, \Delta f \qquad (2\text{-}55)$$

By the linearity of the system, the response to this combination of exponential inputs would be

$$y(t) = \lim_{\Delta f \to 0} \sum_{\substack{f = k\Delta f \\ k = -\infty}}^{\infty} X(f)H(f)e^{j2\pi ft}\, \Delta f$$

$$= \int_{-\infty}^{\infty} X(f)H(f)e^{j2\pi ft}\, df \qquad (2\text{-}56)$$

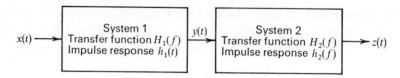

Figure 2-7   Cascade system.

The Fourier transform of the output is thus given by

$$Y(f) = X(f)H(f) \qquad (2\text{-}57)$$

The behavior of a linear time-invariant system is thus expressed quite simply in the transform domain: the transform of the output is the product of the input transform times the system transfer function. Note that this simple relation results from the Fourier transform representation of an arbitrary signal as a *linear* combination of *exponential signals* together with the *preservation of form* property of exponential signals and linear, time-invariant systems.

Our derivation above has been somewhat *ad hoc*, and is presented primarily to convey a feeling as to why the Fourier representation of a time-function as a combination of exponential functions is so convenient. A rigorous derivation of Eq. 2-57 is given in the next section under property I.

To fully appreciate the simplicity of the relation given by Eq. 2-57, we must consider combinations of systems.

Problem 2-8.   Consider the cascade system shown in Fig. 2-7.
 (a) Find the transfer function relating $Z(f)$ to $X(f)$.
 (b) Find the impulse response relating $z(t)$ to $x(t)$.

Problem 2-9.   Consider the feedback system shown in Fig. 2-8.
 (a) Find the transfer function relating $Z(f)$ to $X(f)$.
 (b) Can you find an explicit expression for the impulse response relating $z(t)$ to $x(t)$?

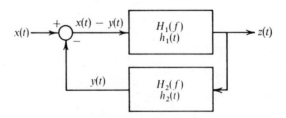

Figure 2-8   Feedback system.

2-5 Properties of the Fourier Transform

The utility of the Fourier transform stems from the ease with which it allows us to deduce properties of systems used to process signals. This utility is considerably enhanced if we are thoroughly familiar with certain properties of the transform which are now discussed.

We use the notation

$$g(t) \leftrightarrow G(f)$$

to denote that $g(t)$ and $G(f)$ are a Fourier transform pair, that is,

$$G(f) = \mathcal{F}[g(t)] = \int_{-\infty}^{\infty} g(t)e^{-j2\pi ft}\, dt \qquad (2\text{-}50)$$

and

$$g(t) = \mathcal{F}^{-1}[G(f)] = \int_{-\infty}^{\infty} G(f)e^{j2\pi ft}\, df \qquad (2\text{-}49)$$

Property A: Linearity

Let

$$g_1(t) \leftrightarrow G_1(f); \qquad g_2(t) \leftrightarrow G_2(f)$$

then

$$ag_1(t) + bg_2(t) \leftrightarrow aG_1(f) + bG_2(f)$$

for all constants a and b. The proof of this follows simply from the linearity of the integrals of Eqs. 2-49 and 2-50.

Property B: Symmetry

If $g(t) \leftrightarrow G(f)$, then $G(t) \leftrightarrow g(-f)$. Note that in Eqs. 2-49 and 2-50 t and f are arbitrary independent variables; therefore, we can replace f with t and t with $-f$; under this change of variables these two equations become

$$G(t) = \int_{-\infty}^{\infty} g(-f)e^{j2\pi ft}\, df = \mathcal{F}^{-1}[g(-f)] \qquad (2\text{-}50')$$

$$g(-f) = \int_{-\infty}^{\infty} G(t)e^{-j2\pi ft}\, dt = \mathcal{F}[G(t)] \qquad (2\text{-}49')$$

Property C: Time Scaling

Let $g(t) \leftrightarrow G(f)$. Then

$$g(at) \leftrightarrow \frac{1}{|a|} G(f/a)$$

To demonstrate this we take $\mathcal{F}[g(at)]$ and set $\tau = at$.

$$\mathcal{F}[g(at)] = \int_{-\infty}^{\infty} g(at)e^{-j2\pi ft}\, dt = \int_{T_1}^{T_2} g(\tau)e^{-j(2\pi f\tau/a)}\left(\frac{dt}{d\tau}\right) d\tau$$

if $a > 0, T_1 = -\infty, T_2 = +\infty, dt/d\tau = +|(1/a)|$
if $a < 0, T_1 = +\infty, T_2 = -\infty, dt/d\tau = -|(1/a)|$

in either case

$$\mathcal{F}[g(at)] = \frac{1}{|a|}\int_{-\infty}^{\infty} g(\tau)e^{-j(2\pi f/a)\tau}\, d\tau = \frac{1}{|a|}\, G(f/a)$$

Let us examine an example applying this property. Consider scanning across one line of a TV screen. We denote the brightness as a function of horizontal position by $g(x)$. Now, although we have described the Fourier transform as a transform from a function of time t (in seconds) to a function of a frequency f (in cycles per second), the definition can apply equally well from a function of position x (in meters) to a function of reciprocal wavelength ν (in cycles per meter). Let this transform pair be

$$g(x) \leftrightarrow G(\nu)$$

Now let $u(t) = g(tv)$ denote the time signal generated by scanning across the screen with constant velocity v. We know from the above property that

$$u(t) = g(tv) \leftrightarrow \frac{1}{|v|}\, G(f/v) = U(f)$$

From this relationship we see that the bandwidth occupied by $u(t)$ is directly proportional to the scan velocity v. For, if $|G(\nu)|$ is down to $1/\sqrt{2}$ of its maximum value at $\nu = \nu_0$, then $|U(f)|$ is down to $1/\sqrt{2}$ of its maximum value at $f/v = \nu_0$ or $f = v\nu_0$.

Property D: Time Shifting

If $x(t) \leftrightarrow X(f)$, then

$$x(t - t_0) \leftrightarrow X(f)e^{-j2\pi ft_0}$$

Proof. Let $\tau = t - t_0$, then

$$\mathcal{F}[x(t - t_0)] = \int_{-\infty}^{\infty} x(t - t_0)e^{-j2\pi ft}\, dt = \int_{-\infty}^{\infty} x(\tau)e^{-j2\pi f(\tau + t_0)}\, d\tau$$

$$= e^{-j2\pi ft_0}\int_{-\infty}^{\infty} x(\tau)e^{-j2\pi f\tau}\, d\tau = e^{-j2\pi ft_0}\,\mathcal{F}[x(t)]$$

Note that a word of caution is in order; let $u(t)$ denote the unit step function

$$u(t) = \begin{cases} 0 & t < 0 \\ 1 & t \geq 0 \end{cases} \qquad (2\text{-}58)$$

Then if $g(t)$ is Fourier transformable, so is

$$x(t) = u(t)g(t)$$

If we apply the theorem to $x(t) = u(t)g(t)$, the shifted function to which the theorem applies is $u(t - t_0)g(t - t_0)$ and *not* $u(t)g(t - t_0)$. The distinction between the different possible product functions is illustrated in Fig. 2-9.

Property E: Frequency Shifting

Let $g(t) \leftrightarrow G(f)$.   Then

$$e^{j2\pi f_0 t}g(t) \leftrightarrow G(f - f_0)$$

Proof.

$$\mathscr{F}[e^{j2\pi f_0 t}g(t)] = \int_{-\infty}^{\infty} e^{j2\pi f_0 t}g(t)e^{-j2\pi ft}\, dt$$

$$= \int_{-\infty}^{\infty} g(t)e^{-j2\pi(f - f_0)t}\, dt = G(f - f_0)$$

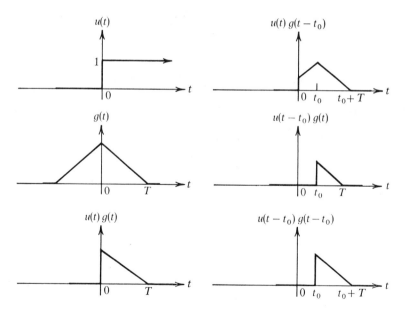

Figure 2-9   Different functions that can arise from the products of $u(t)$ and $g(t)$ and their shifted versions.

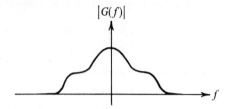

Figure 2-10   Magnitude of the Fourier transform of a low-pass signal.

EXAMPLE.   Let us consider amplitude modulation by the low-pass signal $g(t)$ of a carrier $\cos 2\pi f_0 t$.   By a low-pass signal we mean one whose Fourier transform is negligible in magnitude outside of an interval centered about zero frequency.   The signal $g(t)$ whose transform magnitude is shown in Fig. 2-10 is a low-pass signal.   The signal resulting from amplitude modulation of $\cos 2\pi f_0 t$ by $g(t)$ is

$$x(t) = [1 + kg(t)] \cos 2\pi f_0 t = \tfrac{1}{2}[1 + kg(t)][e^{j2\pi f_0 t} + e^{-j2\pi f_0 t}]$$
$$= (k/2)g(t)[e^{j2\pi f_0 t} + e^{-j2\pi f_0 t}] + \tfrac{1}{2}[e^{j2\pi f_0 t} + e^{-j2\pi f_0 t}] \qquad (2\text{-}59)$$

Now let us take a brief aside and consider the Fourier transform of a delta function,

$$\Delta(f) = \mathscr{F}[\delta(t)] = \int_{-\infty}^{\infty} \delta(t) e^{-j2\pi ft}\, dt \equiv 1 \qquad \text{all } f \qquad (2\text{-}60)$$

Care must be exercised in interpreting this transform.   Inasmuch as $\delta(t)$ is not a legitimate function, its integral is not unambiguously defined (the integral of a function which is zero except at a single point is zero). Hence, $\delta(t)$ does not satisfy the conditions of either of the theorems of Sec. 2-4 and we cannot necessarily expect to recover $\delta(t)$ from $\Delta(f)$ via the inversion integral.   The transform function $\Delta(f) \equiv 1$ has a meaning in a specialized sense, as does $\delta(t)$; the transform function has a valid interpretation when it appears multiplying the transform of any transformable function $g(t)$, the product representing the transform of the convolution of $g(t)$ with $\delta(t)$, that is, the transform of $g(t)$ itself.

Let us now reconsider Eq. 2-60; using property B (symmetry), we have for the transform of a time function which is identically one

$$\mathscr{F}[1] = \delta(-f) = \delta(f) \qquad (2\text{-}61)$$

Then by property E (frequency shifting),

$$\mathscr{F}[e^{\pm j2\pi f_0 t}] = \delta(f \mp f_0) \qquad (2\text{-}62)$$

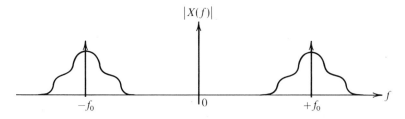

$|X(f)|$

$-f_0$

0

$+f_0$

f

Figure 2-11   Magnitude of the Fourier transform of the low-pass signal amplitude modulated by $\cos 2\pi f_0 t$.

so that by property A (linearity),

$$X(f) = \mathscr{F}[x(t)] = (k/2)[G(f - f_0) + G(f + f_0)]$$
$$+ \tfrac{1}{2}[\delta(f - f_0) + \delta(f + f_0)] \quad (2\text{-}63)$$

The magnitude of the transform of the modulated signal is sketched in Fig. 2-11 for comparison with the transform of the original low-pass signal of Fig. 2-10; the arrows at $f = \pm f_0$ indicate the presence of the impulses.

The reader may wonder at the role of negative frequencies in the Fourier transform representation of a signal when in reality we experience only positive frequencies.   This comes about because the Fourier transform mathematically represents signals as combinations of exponentials.   In such a representation, even a garden variety sinusoid of frequency f_0 has a positive and negative frequency term

$$\cos [2\pi f_0 t + \theta] = \tfrac{1}{2}[e^{j[2\pi f_0 t + \theta]} + e^{-j[2\pi f_0 t + \theta]}]$$
$$= \tfrac{1}{2}e^{j\theta}e^{j2\pi f_0 t} + \tfrac{1}{2}e^{-j\theta}e^{j2\pi(-f_0)t}$$

Negative frequency terms could be avoided if, instead of representing signals as linear combinations of exponentials, we represented them as linear combination of sines and cosines.   However, such a representation is much more cumbersome than the exponential Fourier transform.

Problem 2-10.   Let $g(t)$ be a real valued time function; we define the even and odd parts of $g(t)$ to be respectively,

$$g_e(t) = \tfrac{1}{2}[g(t) + g(-t)]; \qquad g_o(t) = \tfrac{1}{2}[g(t) - g(-t)]$$

thus

$$g(t) = g_e(t) + g_o(t); \qquad g_e(t) = g_e(-t); \qquad g_o(-t) = -g_o(t)$$

Let the transform of $g(t)$ be written

$$G(f) = G_R(f) + jG_I(f)$$

in which G_R and G_I are real-valued functions.   Show that

$$G_R(-f) = G_R(f) \qquad \text{and} \qquad G_I(-f) = -G_I(f)$$

and

$$G_R(f) = \int_{-\infty}^{\infty} g_e(t) \cos 2\pi ft\, dt = 2 \int_{0}^{\infty} g_e(t) \cos 2\pi ft\, dt$$

$$g_e(t) = \int_{-\infty}^{\infty} G_R(f) \cos 2\pi ft\, df = 2 \int_{0}^{\infty} G_R(f) \cos 2\pi ft\, df$$

$$G_I(f) = -\int_{-\infty}^{\infty} g_o(t) \sin 2\pi ft\, dt = -2 \int_{0}^{\infty} g_o(t) \sin 2\pi ft\, dt$$

$$g_o(t) = -\int_{-\infty}^{\infty} G_I(f) \sin 2\pi ft\, df = -2 \int_{0}^{\infty} G_I(f) \sin 2\pi ft\, df$$

so that

$$g(t) = 2 \int_{0}^{\infty} G_R(f) \cos 2\pi ft\, df - 2 \int_{0}^{\infty} G_I(f) \sin 2\pi ft\, df$$

Property F: Time Differentiation

Let $g(t) \leftrightarrow G(f)$ and denote

$$g^{(k)}(t) = \frac{d^k}{dt^k} g(t)$$

with

$$g^{(0)}(t) = g(t)$$

Let $g^{(k)}(t)$ be Fourier transformable for $k = 0, 1, \ldots, n$.   Then

$$\mathscr{F}[g^{(k)}(t)] = (j2\pi f)^k G(f) \qquad k = 1, 2, \ldots, n$$

Proof. Let us write the expression for $G(f)$ and evaluate the resulting integral, using integration by parts

$$G(f) = \int_{-\infty}^{\infty} g(t)e^{-j2\pi ft}\, dt$$

$$= -\frac{1}{j2\pi f} g(t)e^{-j2\pi ft} \Big|_{-\infty}^{\infty} + \frac{1}{j2\pi f} \int_{-\infty}^{\infty} g^{(1)}(t)e^{-j2\pi ft}\, dt \quad (2\text{-}64)$$

Under the conditions of the theorem, $g(t)$ is Fourier transformable and hence $\lim_{t \to \pm\infty} g(t) = 0$; thus Eq. 2-64 yields

$$G(f) = \frac{1}{j2\pi f} \cdot \mathscr{F}[g^{(1)}(t)]$$

or

$$\mathscr{F}[g^{(1)}(t)] = j2\pi f G(f) \qquad\qquad (2\text{-}65)$$

The property for $g^{(k)}(t)$, $k = 1, 2, \ldots, n$, follows by k-fold application of Eq. 2-65.

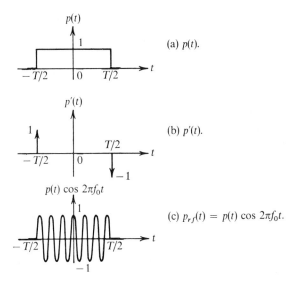

(a) $p(t)$.

(b) $p'(t)$.

(c) $p_{rf}(t) = p(t) \cos 2\pi f_0 t$.

Figure 2-12   A rectangular pulse and an RF pulse with a rectangular envelope.

EXAMPLE.   Consider the pulse shown in Fig. 2-12a.   To find the Fourier transform of $p(t)$, we note first that an impulse function integrates to a step function; that is,

$$\int_{-\infty}^{t} \delta(\tau)\, d\tau = \begin{cases} 1 & t \geq 0 \\ 0 & t < 0 \end{cases} = u(t) \tag{2-66}$$

thus, as shown in Fig. 2-12b,

$$p'(t) = \delta(t + T/2) - \delta(t - T/2) \tag{2-67}$$

Now $\mathscr{F}[\delta(t)] = 1$; thus by properties A (linearity) and D (time shifting)

$$\mathscr{F}[p'(t)] = e^{j2\pi fT/2} - e^{-j2\pi fT/2} \tag{2-68}$$

and by property F

$$\begin{aligned} \mathscr{F}[p(t)] &= \frac{1}{j2\pi f}[e^{j2\pi fT/2} - e^{-j2\pi fT/2}] \\ &= T\frac{\sin(2\pi fT/2)}{(2\pi fT/2)} \end{aligned} \tag{2-69}$$

This transform function is plotted in Fig. 2-13; since the function is always real valued we can plot the function itself and not just its magnitude. Although the delta function and its derivatives are not, strictly speaking, Fourier transformable, these functions and their transforms obey property

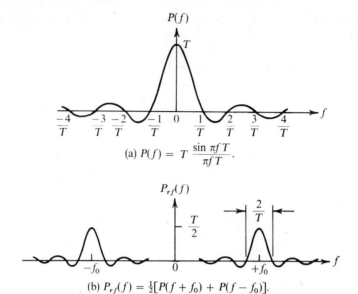

(a) $P(f) = T \dfrac{\sin \pi f T}{\pi f T}$.

(b) $P_{rf}(f) = \frac{1}{2}[P(f + f_0) + P(f - f_0)]$.

Figure 2-13   Fourier transforms of $p(t)$ and $p_{rf}(t)$.

F. For a complete discussion of this point, the reader is referred to Chapters 1 and 2 of Lighthill [6].

Consider the radio frequency pulse shown in Fig. 2-12c.

$$p_{rf}(t) = p(t) \cos 2\pi f_0 t = \tfrac{1}{2}p(t)[e^{j2\pi f_0 t} + e^{-j2\pi f_0 t}] \qquad (2\text{-}70)$$

Its transform can easily be found from property E:

$$\mathscr{F}[p_{rf}(t)] = \frac{T}{2}\left\{ \frac{\sin [2\pi(f - f_0)T/2]}{2\pi(f - f_0)T/2} + \frac{\sin [2\pi(f + f_0)T/2]}{2\pi(f + f_0)T/2} \right\} \qquad (2\text{-}71)$$

Its transform is sketched in Fig. 2-13.

EXAMPLE. Consider the ideal low-pass filter whose transfer function is given by

$$H(f) = \begin{cases} 1 & |f| \le W \\ 0 & |f| > W \end{cases} \qquad (2\text{-}72)$$

and let us find the impulse response of the filter

$$h(t) = \mathscr{F}^{-1}[H(f)]$$

This can be done by using our result from the previous example. The transfer function $H(f)$ is the same function as $p(t)$ with f replacing t and W replacing $T/2$; thus, by property B (symmetry),

$$\mathscr{F}^{-1}[H(-f)] = 2W\frac{\sin(2\pi Wt)}{(2\pi Wt)}$$

But $H(f)$ is even

$$H(-f) = H(f)$$

thus

$$\mathscr{F}^{-1}[H(f)] = h(t) = 2W\frac{\sin(2\pi Wt)}{(2\pi Wt)} \qquad (2\text{-}73)$$

Note that the impulse response of the ideal low-pass filter is nonzero for $t < 0$; thus this filter is not *causal*. This ideal filter can be approximated however, by a causal filter which incorporates a delay of T_0 seconds, where $T_0 \gg 1/W$. The impulse response of such an approximation is shown in Fig. 2-14.

Property G: Frequency Differentiation

Let $g(t) \leftrightarrow G(f)$ and the integral

$$\int_{-\infty}^{\infty} |t^n g(t)|\, dt$$

be defined and finite for $n = 1, 2, \ldots, N$.   Then

$$g(t)(-j2\pi t)^n \leftrightarrow \frac{d^n}{df^n}\, G(f) \qquad n = 1, 2, \ldots, N$$

Proof. To prove this property, we simply start with the equation for $G(f)$ and differentiate

$$\frac{dG(f)}{df} = \frac{d}{df}\int_{-\infty}^{\infty} g(t)e^{-j2\pi ft}\, dt$$

$$= \int_{-\infty}^{\infty} (-j2\pi t)g(t)e^{-j2\pi ft}\, dt = \mathscr{F}[-j2\pi tg(t)] \qquad (2\text{-}74)$$

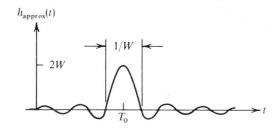

Figure 2-14 Impulse response of approximation to an ideal low-pass filter.

in which the order of differentiation and integration were interchanged to obtain the resulting equation.

Let us briefly comment on this interchange since it is a situation that we frequently face. In general, we can make the interchange

$$\frac{d}{df} \int_{-\infty}^{\infty} g(f, t)\, dt \bigg|_{f=f_0} = \int_{-\infty}^{\infty} \left[\frac{\partial}{\partial f} g(f, t)\right]_{f=f_0} dt \qquad (2\text{-}75)$$

provided that for some nonzero value of ϵ_0 there exists a function $x(t)$ such that for all ϵ, $|\epsilon| \leq \epsilon_0$

$$\left|\frac{\partial}{\partial f} g(f, t)\right|_{f=f_0+\epsilon} \leq x(t) \qquad (2\text{-}76)$$

and

$$\int_{-\infty}^{\infty} x(t)\, dt < \infty \qquad (2\text{-}77)$$

We do not expect the reader of engineering inclination to know why this result holds, nor perhaps to be greatly curious as to why it holds.[1] *However*, the reader should be aware of this result and conscious that he can obtain a completely erroneous answer by making this interchange when it is not justified.

In the situation at hand

$$\left|\frac{d}{df} g(t) e^{-j2\pi ft}\right| = |-j2\pi t g(t) e^{-j2\pi t}| = |2\pi t g(t)|$$

independent of the value of f, hence the interchange used is valid if

$$\int_{-\infty}^{\infty} |2\pi t g(t)|\, dt < \infty$$

Applying the above result N times yields the stated property.

Property H: Conjugate Functions

If $g(t) \leftrightarrow G(f)$, then

$$g^*(t) \leftrightarrow G^*(-f)$$

This property follows simply from

$$\mathcal{F}[g^*(t)] = \int_{-\infty}^{\infty} g^*(t) e^{-j2\pi ft}\, dt = \left[\int_{-\infty}^{\infty} g(t) e^{j2\pi ft}\, dt\right]^*$$

$$= \left[\int_{-\infty}^{\infty} g(t) e^{-j(-2\pi f)t}\, dt\right]^* = G^*(-f)$$

Note that if $g(t)$ is real, this property states that

$$G(-f) = G^*(f) \qquad (2\text{-}78)$$

---

[1] For the curious reader, this result follows from Taylor's theorem with remainder and the dominated convergence theorem of Lebesgue (see e.g., Burkhill [7], Chapter 3).

A further interesting consequence of this property may be obtained as follows. The symmetry property states that if $g(t) \leftrightarrow G(f)$, then $G(t) \leftrightarrow g(-f)$. Applying the symmetry property once more to the transform pair $G(t) \leftrightarrow g(-f)$, we obtain $g(-t) \leftrightarrow G(-f)$. Lastly, applying the conjugate property to this transform pair, we have

$$g^*(-t) \leftrightarrow G^*[-(-f)] = G^*(f) \qquad (2\text{-}79)$$

Thus if $g(t)$ is *real and even* so that

$$g^*(-t) = g(t)$$

we have

$$G^*(f) = G(f) \qquad (2\text{-}80)$$

so that $G(f)$ must be real. Combining Eqs. 2-78 and 2-80, we have further

$$G(f) = G(-f) \qquad (2\text{-}81)$$

so that *the transform of a real even function of time must be a real even function of frequency.*

Property I: Frequency Domain Multiplication

Let $x(t) \leftrightarrow X(f)$ and $y(t) \leftrightarrow Y(f)$.   Then if

$$\int_{-\infty}^{\infty} |x(t)|\, dt \qquad \text{and} \qquad \int_{-\infty}^{\infty} |y(t)|\, dt$$

are both defined and finite

$$[x * y](t) \leftrightarrow X(f)\, Y(f)$$

Problem 2-11.   Prove Property I.   The following hints may be useful:
(1) Write out in full the expression for $\mathscr{F}\{[x * y](t)\}$.
(2) Note that $e^{-j2\pi ft} = e^{-j2\pi f(t-\tau)}e^{-j2\pi f\tau}$.
(3) Make a suitable change of order of integration.

In regard to the interchange of order of integration, note that if any *one* of the following three conditions

$$\int_{-\infty}^{\infty}\int_{-\infty}^{\infty} |g(x, y)|\, dx\, dy < \infty \qquad (2\text{-}82)$$

$$\int_{-\infty}^{\infty} dx \int_{-\infty}^{\infty} |g(x, y)|\, dy < \infty \qquad (2\text{-}83)$$

$$\int_{-\infty}^{\infty} dy \int_{-\infty}^{\infty} |g(x, y)|\, dx < \infty \qquad (2\text{-}84)$$

is satisfied, then it is true that

$$\int_{-\infty}^{\infty} dy \int_{-\infty}^{\infty} g(x, y)\, dx = \int_{-\infty}^{\infty} dx \int_{-\infty}^{\infty} g(x, y)\, dy = \int_{-\infty}^{\infty}\int_{-\infty}^{\infty} g(x, y)\, dx\, dy \quad (2\text{-}85)$$

This result is known as *Fubini's Theorem* (see, e.g., Burkhill [7], Chapter 5). Its proof, as that of the statement of Eqs. 2-75 to 2-77, depends on a branch of mathematical analysis beyond the scope expected of the reader. Again, however, the reader should be aware of the result and conscious of the fact that an erroneous answer can result by an interchange of order of integration when it is not justified.

Property J: Time Domain Multiplication

Let $x(t) \leftrightarrow X(f)$ and $y(t) \leftrightarrow Y(f)$. If

$$\int_{-\infty}^{\infty} |X(f)| \, df \quad \text{and} \quad \int_{-\infty}^{\infty} |Y(f)| \, df$$

are both defined and finite, then

$$\mathscr{F}[x(t)y(t)] = [X * Y](f)$$

This follows directly by combining property B (symmetry) and property I (frequency domain multiplication).

EXAMPLE.   Consider finding the impulse response of the ideal band-pass filter shown in Fig. 2-15.   The student can verify directly that

$$H_{Bp}(f) = [\delta(f + f_0) + \delta(f - f_0)] * H_{Lp}(f) \tag{2-86}$$

in which $H_{Lp}(f)$ is the transfer function of the ideal low-pass filter shown in Fig. 2-15b. We have already seen that

$$2 \cos 2\pi f_0 t = [e^{j2\pi f_0 t} + e^{-j2\pi f_0 t}] \leftrightarrow \delta(f - f_0) + \delta(f + f_0) \tag{2-87}$$

and from Eq. 2-73 we have

$$2W \frac{\sin 2\pi W t}{2\pi W t} \leftrightarrow H_{Lp}(f) \tag{2-88}$$

Using property J and Eqs. 2-86 to 2-88, we thus obtain

$$\mathscr{F}^{-1}[H_{Bp}(f)] = 2W \frac{\sin 2\pi W t}{2\pi W t} \cdot 2 \cos 2\pi f_0 t$$

$$= 4W \frac{\sin 2\pi W t}{2\pi W t} \cos 2\pi f_0 t \tag{2-89}$$

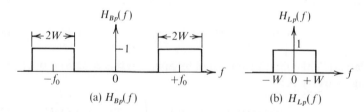

(a) $H_{Bp}(f)$ (b) $H_{Lp}(f)$

Figure 2-15   The transform functions $H_{Bp}(f)$ and $H_{Lp}(f)$.

Correlation of Two Time Functions.   Given two time functions $x(t)$ and $y(t)$, the time function formed from them by the operation

$$C_{xy}(\tau) = \int_{-\infty}^{\infty} x(t + \tau) y^*(t) \, dt \qquad (2\text{-}90)$$

is termed the *cross-correlation of x and y.*   Upon replacing the dummy variable of integration, t, with the new variable $-\sigma$, this expression becomes

$$C_{xy}(\tau) = \int_{-\infty}^{\infty} x(\tau - \sigma) y^*(-\sigma) \, d\sigma \qquad (2\text{-}91)$$

Upon comparing this expression with the definition of convolution, we see that if we define $y_r(\sigma) = y^*(-\sigma)$, then

$$C_{xy}(\tau) = [x * y_r](\tau) \qquad (2\text{-}92)$$

Note thus that $C_{xy}(\tau) \neq C_{yx}(\tau) = [x_r * y](\tau)$.

Problem 2-12.   Show that $C_{yx}(\tau) = C_{xy}^*(-\tau)$.

Property K: Correlation

Let $x(t)$ and $y(t)$ be two Fourier transformable time functions with $x(t) \leftrightarrow X(f)$ and $y(t) \leftrightarrow Y(f)$.   Then

$$\mathcal{F}[C_{xy}(\tau)] = X(f) Y^*(f)$$

This follows directly from property I (frequency domain multiplication) and Eqs. 2-79 and 2-92.   From property K we can deduce the form of Parseval's theorem that is pertinent to the Fourier transform.

Property L: Parseval's Theorem

Let $x(t)$ and $y(t)$ be two Fourier transformable time functions with $x(t) \leftrightarrow X(f)$, $y(t) \leftrightarrow Y(f)$.   Then

$$\int_{-\infty}^{\infty} x(t) y^*(t) \, dt = \int_{-\infty}^{\infty} X(f) Y^*(f) \, df$$

To show this, first note that for any transform pair $h(t) \leftrightarrow H(f)$

$$h(0) = \int_{-\infty}^{\infty} H(f) e^{j2\pi f 0} \, df = \int_{-\infty}^{\infty} H(f) \, df \qquad (2\text{-}93)$$

Parseval's theorem then follows by applying this equation to $C_{xy}(\tau)$ and using property K:

$$\int_{-\infty}^{\infty} x(t) y^*(t) \, dt = C_{xy}(0) = \int_{-\infty}^{\infty} X(f) Y^*(f) \, df \qquad (2\text{-}94)$$

Note that for $y(t) = x(t)$, this result simplifies to

$$\int_{-\infty}^{\infty} |x(t)|^2 \, dt = \int_{-\infty}^{\infty} |X(f)|^2 \, df \qquad (2\text{-}95)$$

Let us try to find the physical meaning of the form of Parseval's theorem given by Eq. 2-95. The quantity $|X(f)|^2$ is sometimes referred to as the *energy density spectrum* of the function $x(t)$. To see the justification for this term, consider the function $x(t)$ as the (real-valued) input to an ideal band-pass filter which is centered at $f = \pm f_0$ and has a bandwidth of Δ cycles per second.

$$H_{Bp} = \begin{cases} 1 & |f \pm f_0| \le \Delta/2 \\ 0 & \text{elsewhere} \end{cases}$$

This filter transfer function is shown in Fig. 2-16.

If the bandwidth, Δ, is so small that $X(f)$ is approximately constant in the intervals $|f \pm f_0| \le \Delta/2$, then the transform of the output is

$$Y(f) \approx \begin{cases} X(+f_0) & |f - f_0| \le \Delta/2 \\ X(-f_0) & |f + f_0| \le \Delta/2 \\ 0 & \text{elsewhere} \end{cases} \qquad (2\text{-}96)$$

If $y(t)$, the output, is the voltage across a 1-ohm resistor, then the energy dissipated in this resistor is

$$\int_{-\infty}^{\infty} y^2(t) \, dt = \int_{-\infty}^{\infty} |Y(f)|^2 \, df$$
$$\approx \Delta[|X(f_0)|^2 + |X(-f_0)|^2] \qquad (2\text{-}97)$$
$$= 2\Delta |X(f_0)|^2$$

since

$$|X(f_0)|^2 = |X(-f_0)|^2$$

Equation 2-97 thus states that the energy in the output of the narrow-band filter centered at $f = \pm f_0$ is equal to $|X(f_0)|^2$ times the total bandwidth

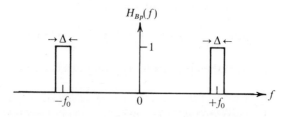

Figure 2-16   Bandpass filter used in interpreting energy density function.

occupied by the filter in cycles per second. Thus the function $|X(f)|^2$ is the density of the energy contained in $x(t)$ in joules per cycle per second.[1]

Note that from Parseval's theorem we can deduce that if one function $x(t)$ closely approximates another function $y(t)$ in the time domain, then $X(f)$ also closely approximates $Y(f)$ in the frequency domain for

$$\int_{-\infty}^{\infty} |X(f) - Y(f)|^2 \, df = \int_{-\infty}^{\infty} |x(t) - y(t)|^2 \, dt$$

EXAMPLE. Let us show how Parseval's theorem can considerably simplify certain calculations. Suppose we apply an impulse input to the ideal low-pass filter with transfer function

$$H_{Lp}(f) = \begin{cases} 1 & |f| \leq W \\ 0 & |f| > 0 \end{cases}$$

We have seen that the impulse response of this filter is

$$h_{Lp}(t) = 2W \frac{\sin 2\pi Wt}{2\pi Wt}$$

Thus the energy in the response of this filter to an impulse would be

$$E = \int_{-\infty}^{\infty} h_{Lp}^2(t) \, dt = (2W)^2 \int_{-\infty}^{\infty} \left(\frac{\sin 2\pi Wt}{2\pi Wt} \right)^2 dt$$

The evaluation of this integral directly would be difficult. However, by Parseval's theorem we have

$$E = \int_{-\infty}^{\infty} |H_{Lp}(f)|^2 \, df = \int_{-W}^{W} df = 2W$$

Problem 2-13. Let $u(t)$ denote the unit step function. Find the Fourier transforms of the functions

$$x_1(t) = u(t)e^{(-a + j2\pi f_0)t}; \qquad x_2(t) = u(-t)e^{(a + j2\pi f_0)t}$$

The quantities a and f_0 are real valued and $a > 0$. Noting that

$$\cos 2\pi f_0 t = \tfrac{1}{2}[e^{j2\pi f_0 t} + e^{-j2\pi f_0 t}]$$

use the above result to find the transform of $x_3(t) = u(t)e^{-at}\cos 2\pi f_0 t$. Also use the above result to obtain the transform of $x_4(t) = e^{-a|t|}$ all t, $a > 0$.

Problem 2-14. Let $H(x) = P(x)/Q(x)$ in which

$$P(x) = \sum_{k=0}^{M} p_k x^k; \qquad Q(x) = \sum_{k=0}^{N} q_k x^k$$

[1] The student bothered by the presence of a negative frequency term in Eq. 2-97 may wish to reinterpret Parseval's theorem in terms of the sine-cosine representation discussed in Problem 2-10.

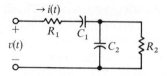

Figure 2-17   Network for Problems 2-15 and 2-16.

If $N \geq M$ and all the zeros of $Q(x)$ are distinct, it can be shown (see e.g., Ahlfors [8], pp. 43–45) that $H(x)$ can be written in the form

$$H(x) = a_0 + \sum_{k=1}^{N} \frac{a_k}{x - s_k}$$

in which the s_k are the (assumed distinct) zeros of $Q(x) = 0$.   Show that

$$a_0 = \begin{cases} \dfrac{q_N}{p_N} & \text{if } M = N \\[2mm] 0 & \text{if } M < N \end{cases} \qquad \text{and} \qquad a_n = \frac{p(s_n)}{\displaystyle\prod_{\substack{k=1 \\ k \neq n}}^{N} (s_n - s_k)} \qquad n = 1, \ldots, N$$

Problem 2-15.   The transfer function of a physical network is usually most easily obtained from the definition

$$H(f) = \left. \frac{\text{output time function}}{\text{input time function}} \right|_{\text{input} = e^{j2\pi ft}}$$

[Recall that $H(f)$ is only a function of the frequency f and not of time.]   Find the transfer function $H(f)$ for the network of Fig. 2-17 in this fashion.   Consider the voltage $v(t)$ to be the excitation and the current $i(t)$ the response.   Note also that $H(f)$ is the ratio $\mathcal{F}[i(t)]/\mathcal{F}[v(t)]$.

Problem 2-16.   Combine the results of Problems 2-13, 2-14, and 2-15 to find the impulse response of the network of Fig. 2-17 by writing a partial fraction expansion for $H(f)$, regarding $x = j2\pi f$ as the variable.   Assume for simplicity that $R_1 = R_2$ and $C_1 = C_2$.

2-6   The Laplace Transform

For most purposes in communication theory, the Fourier transform as we have described it is fully adequate for describing signals in the frequency domain. However, in Sec. 7-4 we will need to regard the frequency variable as complex valued and in Sec. 10-2 we will require another generalized form of the exponential Fourier transform.[1]

[1] These are the only two sections in this book that require the Laplace transform. You may thus omit reading this section if Secs. 7-4 and 10-2 are not of immediate interest.

Let us consider a function $x(t)$ which may or may not be Fourier transformable because the condition

$$\int_{-\infty}^{\infty} |x(t)| \, dt < \infty$$

may or may not be met. For example, $x(t) = u(t)$, a unit step is not Fourier transformable. Let us consider the function

$$x_\sigma(t) = e^{-\sigma t} x(t) \tag{2-98}$$

in which σ is real and assume that for some range of values of σ the function $x_\sigma(t)$ is Fourier transformable in that

$$\int_{-\infty}^{\infty} |x_\sigma(t)| \, dt = \int_{-\infty}^{\infty} e^{-\sigma t} |x(t)| \, dt < \infty \tag{2-99}$$

We can thus express $x_\sigma(t)$ in terms of its Fourier transform:

$$X_\sigma(f) = \int_{-\infty}^{\infty} x_\sigma(t) e^{-j2\pi f t} \, dt \tag{2-100}$$

$$x_\sigma(t) = \int_{-\infty}^{\infty} X_\sigma(f) e^{j2\pi f t} \, df \tag{2-101}$$

Let us now substitute Eq. 2-98 into Eqs. 2-100 and 2-101 and multiply both sides of Eq. 2-101 by $e^{\sigma t}$; the result is

$$X_\sigma(f) - \int_{-\infty}^{\infty} x(t) e^{-(\sigma + j2\pi f)t} \, dt \tag{2-100'}$$

$$x(t) = \int_{-\infty}^{\infty} X_\sigma(f) e^{(\sigma + j2\pi f)t} \, df \tag{2-101'}$$

It is convenient if we make some simplifications in this pair of equations. First, we define

$$\omega = 2\pi f \tag{2-102}$$

Next, we note that in the quantity

$$(\sigma + j2\pi f) = \sigma + j\omega$$

both the variables σ and ω are real valued. The quantity

$$s = (\sigma + j\omega) \tag{2-103}$$

is thus a *complex variable* whose real and imaginary parts are σ and ω, respectively. Finally, we note that the quantity $X_\sigma(f)$ can be regarded as a function of the complex variable s; we denote this function by

$$\tilde{X}(s) = X_\sigma(\omega/2\pi) \tag{2-104}$$

In terms of the above notation, Eq. 2-100' becomes

$$\tilde{X}(s) = \int_{-\infty}^{\infty} x(t)e^{-st}\, dt \qquad (2\text{-}105)$$

and Eq. 2-101' can be rewritten as

$$x(t) = \int_{-\infty}^{\infty} \tilde{X}(s)e^{st}\, df$$

$$= \frac{1}{2\pi} \int_{-\infty}^{\infty} \tilde{X}(s)e^{st}\, d\omega$$

$$= \frac{1}{2\pi j} \int_{\sigma_0 - j\infty}^{\sigma_0 + j\infty} \tilde{X}(s)e^{st}\, ds \qquad (2\text{-}106)$$
$$s = \sigma_0 + j\omega$$

Note that the integral of Eq. 2-106 is an integral along a path in the s-plane. Further note that this path must be for a value of σ_0 such that Eq. 2-99 is satisfied for $\sigma = \sigma_0$. Equation 2-105 defines a transformed function of complex frequency s for a given time function, whereas Eq. 2-106 states how this transformed function can be inverse transformed to yield the original time function. A convenient shorthand notation for this transform relationship is

$$\tilde{X}(s) = \mathscr{L}[x(t)] \qquad (2\text{-}105')$$

$$x(t) = \mathscr{L}^{-1}[\tilde{X}(s)] \qquad (2\text{-}106')$$

The operation defined by Eq. 2-105 is referred to as the *Laplace transform* and the operation of Eq. 2-106 is referred to as the *inverse Laplace transform*. As in the case of the Fourier transform, we denote a transform pair by the notation

$$x(t) \leftrightarrow \tilde{X}(s)$$

If Eq. 2-99 is satisfied for some value of σ, we say that $x(t)$ is *Laplace transformable* and the set of values of $s = \sigma + j\omega$ for which Eq. 2-99 is satisfied is known as the *region of convergence* or *domain of definition*. This region of convergence is either a vertical strip or a vertical half-plane in the complex s-plane. A typical situation is shown in Fig. 2-18.

Problem 2-17. Find the region of convergence for the time functions

$$x_1(t) = u(t)e^{-at}$$
$$x_2(t) = u(-t)e^{at} \qquad a > 0$$
$$x_3(t) = e^{-a|t|}$$

The linearity property of Fourier transforms obviously holds for Laplace transforms. Most of the other properties of the Fourier trans-

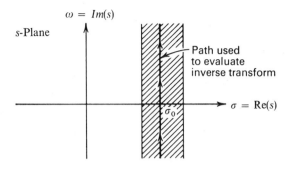

Figure 2-18 Region of convergence and path of integration in the s-plane. The shaded area denotes the region of convergence.

form that are discussed in Sec. 2-5 hold in a suitably modified form for the Laplace transform.

For the following problems, let $x(t)$ be Laplace transformable with region of convergence $\sigma_1 < \sigma < \sigma_2$ and

$$x(t) \leftrightarrow \tilde{X}(s)$$

Problem 2-18. Show that

$$x(at) \leftrightarrow \frac{1}{|a|} \tilde{X}(s/a) \qquad (2\text{-}107)$$

and find the region of convergence for $x(at)$.

Problem 2-19. Show that

$$x(t - t_0) \leftrightarrow e^{-st_0} \tilde{X}(s) \qquad (2\text{-}108)$$

and find the region of convergence for $x(t - t_0)$.

Problem 2-20. Show that

$$e^{j\omega_0 t}x(t) \leftrightarrow \tilde{X}(s - j\omega_0) \qquad (2\text{-}109)$$

and find the region of convergence for $e^{j\omega_0 t}x(t)$.

Problem 2-21. Let $dx(t)/dt$ be Laplace transformable with region of convergence $\sigma_3 < \sigma < \sigma_4$. Show that for σ in the region of convergence common to $x(t)$ and $dx(t)/dt$

$$\max (\sigma_1, \sigma_3) < \sigma < \min (\sigma_2, \sigma_4)$$

that

$$\frac{dx(t)}{dt} \leftrightarrow s\tilde{X}(s) \qquad (2\text{-}110)$$

Problem 2-22. Let $y(t)$ be Laplace transformable with region of convergence $\sigma_3 < \sigma < \sigma_4$. Show that in the region of convergence common to $x(t)$ and $y(t)$

$$\max (\sigma_1, \sigma_3) < \sigma < \min (\sigma_2, \sigma_4)$$
$$[x * y](t) \leftrightarrow \tilde{X}(s)\tilde{Y}(s) \qquad (2\text{-}111)$$

Jordan's Lemma—Inverse Transformation
by Evaluation of Residues

We now consider how to evaluate the path integral occurring in the inverse Laplace transform.   Our discussion makes use of several results from complex variable theory.   The reader not acquainted with these results should simply accept Eqs. 2-113 and 2-115 as end results.

Let us begin by considering the path of integration, P, which lies in the region of convergence together with the two semicircular paths P_1 and P_2, each of radius R.   These three paths are shown in Fig. 2-19.   It is our intention to consider the limit of the two semicircular paths as their radius R becomes infinite.

Let us note that

$$e^{st} = e^{\sigma t}e^{j\omega t}$$

so that

$$|e^{st}| = e^{\sigma t}$$

On the path P_1 as the radius R becomes large, σ is negative on all except perhaps a relatively short portion of P_1; thus, for $t > 0$, the magnitude of e^{st} becomes small over most of P_1 as R becomes large.   Similarly on P_2, σ is positive on all except perhaps a relatively short portion of P_2; thus for $t < 0$ the magnitude of e^{st} becomes small over most of P_2 as R becomes large.   We would thus expect that if $\tilde{X}(s)$ approaches zero for large values of s that the integrals

$$\int_{P_1} \tilde{X}(s)e^{st}\,ds \qquad \text{and} \qquad \int_{P_2} \tilde{X}(s)e^{st}\,ds$$

would approach zero for $t > 0$ and $t < 0$ respectively as R becomes large. This fact is indeed true and is known as Jordan's lemma.

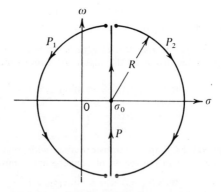

Figure 2-19   Paths of integration in the s-plane that are pertinent to Jordan's lemma.

Jordan's Lemma. If $\lim\limits_{|s| \to \infty} \tilde{X}(s) = 0$ for any angle of s, then

$$\text{for } t > 0 \qquad \lim_{R \to \infty} \int_{P_1} \tilde{X}(s)e^{st}\, ds = 0$$

and

$$\text{for } t < 0 \qquad \lim_{R \to \infty} \int_{P_2} \tilde{X}(s)e^{st}\, ds = 0$$

Our concern here is with application of this lemma to evaluating inverse transforms and we do not give the proof of the lemma here; the interested reader can find a proof of Jordan's lemma in Papoulis [5], p. 300.

Combining Jordan's lemma with Eq. 2-106 yields

$$x(t) = \begin{cases} \dfrac{1}{2\pi j} \displaystyle\int_{P+P_1} \tilde{X}(s)e^{st}\, ds & t > 0 \\[3mm] \dfrac{1}{2\pi j} \displaystyle\int_{P+P_2} \tilde{X}(s)e^{st}\, ds & t < 0 \end{cases} \tag{2-112}$$

in which P_1 and P_2 now denote semicircular paths of infinite radius.

We observe that $P + P_1$ is a closed simple *counterclockwise* path enclosing that portion of the s-plane to the *left* of the region of convergence, whereas $P + P_2$ is a closed simple *clockwise* path enclosing that portion of the s-plane to the *right* of the region of definition.

Let us now recall some basic definitions and theorems from complex variable theory. Suppose a function $G(s)$ is analytic in some neighborhood about the point s_1 except at s_1 itself. The point s_1 is termed an *isolated singularity*. If $G(s)$ has an isolated singularity at $s = s_1$ and for some integer h, $(s - s_1)^h G(s)$ is analytic *and* nonzero at $s = s_1$, then $G(s)$ is said to have a *pole of order h* at $s = s_1$. If $G(s)$ has an isolated singularity at $s = s_1$, the *residue of $G(s)$ at $s = s_1$* is defined to be the value of

$$\frac{1}{2\pi j} \int_{C_1} G(s)\, ds$$

in which C_1 is a simple counterclockwise path enclosing s_1 but no other singularities of $G(s)$. In evaluating the residue of $G(s)$ at $s = s_1$, *Cauchy's integral formula* is very useful. It states that if a function $Y(s)$ is analytic in some region and C_1 is a simple counterclockwise closed path lying in this region, then

$$\frac{d^{n-1}}{ds^{n-1}} Y(s)\bigg|_{s=s_1} = \frac{(n-1)!}{2\pi j} \cdot \int_{C_1} \frac{Y(s)}{(s-s_1)^n}\, ds$$

For a proof of this statement, consult Ahlfors [8], pp. 96–97. If $G(s)$ has a pole of order n at $s = s_1$, then applying this integral formula to the analytic function

$$Y(s) = (s - s_1)^n G(s)$$

yields

$$\text{Res}_{s=s_1} G(s) = \frac{1}{2\pi j} \int_{C_1} G(s) \, ds = \frac{1}{(n-1)!} \frac{d^{n-1}}{ds^{n-1}} [(s - s_1)^n G(s)] \Big|_{s=s_1} \quad (2\text{-}113)$$

Finally, we quote a restricted version of the *Cauchy residue theorem* that will be useful. (For a discussion of this theorem, see Sec. 5.1 of Ahlfors [8].) Let $G(s)$ be analytic in some region except at a number of isolated singularities at $s = s_k$, $k = 1, 2, \ldots, N$. Let γ be a closed path which does not pass through any of these points and let $n(k)$ be the number of net counterclockwise encirclements of the point s_k by the path γ (clockwise encirclements being counted as negative). Then

$$\frac{1}{2\pi j} \int_{\gamma} G(s) \, ds = \sum_{k=1}^{N} n(k) \, \text{Res}_{s=s_k} G(s) \quad (2\text{-}114)$$

If we now couple Eq. 2-114 with $G(s) = \tilde{X}(s)e^{st}$ together with Eq. 2-112 and the remarks following Eq. 2-112, we obtain an expression for the inversion of the Laplace transform

$$x(t) = \begin{cases} -\sum \begin{array}{l} \text{all residues of } \tilde{X}(s)e^{st} \text{ to the} \\ \text{right of region of convergence} \end{array} & t < 0 \\ +\sum \begin{array}{l} \text{all residues of } \tilde{X}(s)e^{st} \text{ to the} \\ \text{left of region of convergence} \end{array} & t > 0 \end{cases} \quad (2\text{-}115)$$

This equation, coupled with Eq. 2-113 applied for $G(s) = \tilde{X}(s)e^{st}$ allows a straightforward (although perhaps lengthy) evaluation of the inverse transform in most cases of interest.

EXAMPLE. Let $\tilde{X}(s) = \dfrac{1}{(s+1)(s-1)}$. Then $\tilde{X}(s)$ has poles of first order at $s = 1$ and $s = -1$ as its only singularities. Applying Eq. 2-113 for $n = 1$, we have

$$\text{Res}_{s=+1} \tilde{X}(s)e^{st} = (s-1)\tilde{X}(s)e^{st} \Big|_{s=1} = \frac{e^{st}}{s+1}\Big|_{s=1} = \frac{e^t}{2}$$

and

$$\text{Res}_{s=-1} \tilde{X}(s)e^{st} = (s+1)\tilde{X}(s)e^{st} \Big|_{s=-1} = \frac{e^{st}}{s-1}\Big|_{s=-1} = -\frac{e^{-t}}{2}$$

If the region of convergence is $\sigma < -1$, then from Eq. 2-115

$$x(t) = \begin{cases} -\frac{1}{2}(e^t - e^{-t}) & t < 0 \\ 0 & t > 0 \end{cases}$$

If the region of convergence is $-1 < \sigma < +1$, then

$$x(t) = \begin{cases} -\frac{1}{2}e^t & t < 0 \\ -\frac{1}{2}e^{-t} & t > 0 \end{cases}$$

Finally, if the region of convergence is $+1 < \sigma$,

$$x(t) = \begin{cases} 0 & t < 0 \\ \frac{1}{2}(e^t - e^{-t}) & t > 0 \end{cases}$$

Problem 2-23. Let $\tilde{X}(s) = 1/s^2(s + 1)$.   Find $x(t)$ if the region of convergence is

(a) $\sigma < -1$.
(b) $-1 < \sigma < 0$.
(c) $0 < \sigma$.

The One-Sided Transform—The Final Value Theorem

In finding the transient response of a system, we are usually dealing with excitations that are zero prior to some starting time, which we here take to be $t = 0$ for convenience.   If $x(t) = 0$ for $t < 0$, then we can replace the lower limit of integration in Eq. 2-105 with zero instead of $-\infty$:

$$\tilde{X}(s) = \int_{0_-}^{\infty} x(t)e^{-st}\, dt \tag{2-116}$$

By 0_- we mean any point just to the left of $t = 0$; we use this notation to indicate that any strange behavior of $x(t)$ at $t = 0$ [such as with $x(t) = \delta(t)$] is to be included fully within the integral.[1]

The Laplace transform defined by Eq. 2-116 is sometimes referred to as the *one-sided transform* since it pertains to a function which is of interest only for $t \geq 0$.   For $t \geq 0$,

$$e^{-\sigma_2 t} \leq e^{-\sigma_1 t}$$

if $\sigma_2 > \sigma_1$.   Thus, if the integral

$$\int_{0_-}^{\infty} |x(t)|e^{-\sigma_1 t}\, dt$$

is finite, then the integral

$$\int_{0_-}^{\infty} |x(t)|e^{-\sigma_2 t}\, dt$$

---

[1] In some references, the lower limit of integration is taken as 0_+ instead of 0_-. This choice of 0_+ is useful in solving transient problems in which the system configuration changes (e.g., a switch closes) at $t = 0$.

must also be finite. The region of convergence is thus the entire half-plane to the right of some line $\sigma = \sigma'$, where σ' is the largest value of σ for which the integral

$$\int_{0_-}^{\infty} |x(t)|e^{-\sigma t}\, dt$$

diverges. The function $\tilde{X}(s)$ then has its rightmost singularity on this line. The inversion relation of Eq. 2-115 becomes in this case,

$$x(t) = \begin{cases} 0 & t < 0 \\ +\sum \text{ all residues of } \tilde{X}(s)e^{st} & t > 0 \end{cases}$$

Note that if $x(t) = 0$ for $t < 0$, the differentiation property of Eq. 2-110 holds unaltered. It should be pointed out that some sources define the one-sided Laplace transform with the lower limit of integration in Eq. 2-116 as 0_+; in this case, the transform of $dx(t)/dt$ involves a term containing $x(0_+)$.

We will now discuss a transform property not previously considered which is particularly germane to the one-sided transform.

The Final Value Theorem. Let $x(t)$ be a function which is Laplace transformable and is identically zero for $t < 0$ and let $\tilde{X}(s)$ be its (one-sided) transform. Let $s\tilde{X}(s)$ have no singularities for $\sigma \geq 0$. Then

$$\lim_{t \to \infty} x(t) = \lim_{s \to 0} s\tilde{X}(s) \tag{2-117}$$

Proof. The region of convergence for $dx(t)/dt$ is to the right of the rightmost singularity of $s\tilde{X}(s)$, which by assumption is to the left of $s = 0$. Thus the region of convergence includes $\sigma > -\epsilon$ for some value of $\epsilon > 0$, and we have

$$s\tilde{X}(s) = \int_{0_-}^{\infty} \frac{dx(t)}{dt} e^{-st}\, dt; \qquad \sigma > -\epsilon$$

Now, taking the limit as s approaches zero, we have

$$\lim_{s \to 0} s\tilde{X}(s) = \lim_{s \to 0} \int_{0_-}^{\infty} \frac{dx(t)}{dt} e^{-st}\, dt = \int_{0_-}^{\infty} \lim_{s \to 0} \frac{dx(t)}{dt} e^{-st}\, dt$$

$$= \int_{0_-}^{\infty} \frac{dx(t)}{dt}\, dt = \lim_{t \to \infty} x(t) - x(0_-) \tag{2-118}$$

But $x(t)$ was assumed identically zero for $t < 0$; thus

$$\lim_{s \to 0} s\tilde{X}(s) = \lim_{t \to \infty} x(t)$$

The interchange of integration and taking the limit used in this derivation is justified by the Dominated Convergence theorem of Lebesgue (see, e.g.,

Burkhill [7], Chapter 3).   This theorem is another example of a result which is highly useful and which the reader should not be afraid to make use of, even though it is based on a branch of mathematical analysis far beyond the scope expected of the reader.   This theorem states the following.   Consider a sequence of functions $x_n(t)$, $n = 1, 2, \ldots$.   If there exists a function $g(t)$ such that $|x_n(t)| \leq g(t)$ for all t and all n and $\int_{-\infty}^{\infty} g(t)\, dt < \infty$, then

$$\lim_{n \to \infty} \int_{-\infty}^{\infty} x_n(t)\, dt = \int_{-\infty}^{\infty} \lim_{n \to \infty} x_n(t)\, dt$$

In our present case we can pick a set of points $s_n = -\frac{1}{2}(\epsilon/n)$, $n = 1, 2, \ldots$, which approach $s = 0$.   Then the set of functions

$$x_n(t) = \left|\frac{dx}{dt}\right| e^{-s_n t}$$

is bounded by $|dx/dt| e^{+(\epsilon/2)t}$.   Since the region of convergence includes $s > -\epsilon$, this function has a finite integral, and the interchange in Eq. 2-118 is valid.

The importance of the final value theorem is that it allows us to deduce the limiting behavior of a time function from its transform *without* having to go through the labor of taking the inverse transform.

Problem 2-24.   Let

$$\tilde{X}(s) = \frac{s^3 + 5s^2 + 10s + 11}{s(s + 1)(s + 2)(s + 3)(s + 4)}$$

be the one-sided transform of a time function identically zero for $t < 0$.   Find $\lim_{t \to \infty} x(t)$:

  (a) by the final value theorem.
  (b) By evaluating the inverse transform.

Problem 2-25.   Repeat the procedure of Problem 2-24 for the function

$$\tilde{X}(s) = \frac{s^3 + 5s^2 + 10s + 11}{s(s + 1)(s + 2)(s + 3)(s - 4)}$$

2-7   The Sampling Theorem

Let us now consider a real-valued signal $x(t)$ whose Fourier transform, $X(f)$, is identically zero outside the frequency band $-W \leq f \leq +W$; that is,

$$X(f) = P_W(f)X(f) \tag{2-119}$$

in which

$$P_W(f) = \begin{cases} 1 & |f| \leq W \\ 0 & |f| > W \end{cases} \tag{2-120}$$

We might expect that this limitation on the transform behavior will restrict the nature of $x(t)$ in the time domain in such a fashion as to allow a simple description of the function. This expectation is borne out in the following form.

Sampling Theorem. Let the transform of $x(t)$ be zero for $|f| > W$. Then $x(t)$ can be reconstructed for all values of time from samples taken every $1/2W$ seconds apart; specifically,

$$x(t) = \sum_{k=-\infty}^{\infty} x(k/2W) \frac{\sin [2\pi W(t - k/2W)]}{2\pi W(t - k/2W)} \qquad (2\text{-}121)$$

To prove this theorem we start by noting that $X(f)$ can be described on the interval $|f| \leq W$ by an exponential Fourier series in f of period $2W$

$$X(f) = \sum_{k=-\infty}^{\infty} X_k e^{jf(\pi/W)k} = \sum_{k=-\infty}^{\infty} X_k e^{j(2\pi k/2W)f} \qquad (2\text{-}122)$$

in which the coefficients X_k are given by

$$X_k = \frac{1}{2W} \int_{-W}^{W} X(f) e^{-j(2\pi k/2W)f} \, df \qquad (2\text{-}123)$$

Upon comparing the right-hand side of this equation with the expression for the inverse Fourier transform, we see that

$$X_k = \frac{1}{2W} x(-k/2W) \qquad (2\text{-}124)$$

Now the series expansion appearing in the right-hand side of Eq. 2-122 is only valid for $|f| \leq W$; we can obtain an expression valid for all f by multiplying this series by $P_W(f)$. Doing this, substituting from Eq. 2-124, and changing the sign of our index of summation yields

$$X(f) = \frac{1}{2W} \sum_{k=-\infty}^{\infty} x(k/2W) P_W(f) e^{-j2\pi fk/2W}$$

Now, from previous examples we have

$$\delta(t - k/2W) \leftrightarrow e^{-j2\pi fk/2W}$$

and

$$2W \frac{\sin 2\pi Wt}{2\pi Wt} \leftrightarrow P_W(f)$$

Thus, applying the frequency multiplication property, the inverse transform of $X(f)$ is

$$x(t) = \sum_{k=-\infty}^{\infty} \left(\frac{1}{2W}\right) x(k/2W) \left[\delta(t - k/2W) * \frac{\sin 2\pi Wt}{\pi t}\right]$$

$$= \sum_{k=-\infty}^{\infty} x(k/2W) \frac{\sin [2\pi W(t - k/2W)]}{[2\pi W(t - k/2W)]} \qquad (2\text{-}121)$$

The above theorem states that a band-limited function is determined by *periodic* samples taken every $1/2W$ seconds.   Actually, the sampling need not be periodic; essentially what is required is that the samples be taken at an *average* rate of $2W$ per second.   For a discussion of some nonperiodic sampling theorems, the reader is referred to Yen [9].

Problem 2-26.   Show that the functions

$$\varphi_k(t) = \frac{\sin\,[2\pi W(t - k/2W)]}{[2\pi W(t - k/2W)]} \qquad k = 0, \pm 1, \pm 2, \ldots$$

are orthogonal over the interval $-\infty < t < \infty$; in particular, show that

$$\int_{-\infty}^{\infty} \frac{\sin\,[2\pi W(t - k/2W)]}{[2\pi W(t - k/2W)]} \frac{\sin\,[2\pi W(t - m/2W)]}{[2\pi W(t - m/2W)]}\, dt = \left(\frac{1}{2W}\right)\delta_{mk} \qquad (2\text{-}125)$$

Hint: Make use of Parseval's theorem.

A practical application of the sampling theorem is pulse transmission of a waveform.   This process is shown in functional form in Fig. 2-20. Assume that we wish to transmit a function $y(t)$ whose spectrum is band-limited.   This can be accomplished by sampling $y(t)$ and generating a sequence of impulses (in practice narrow pulses) whose areas are $y(k/2W)$, $k = 0, 1, 2, \ldots$.   These pulses are then transmitted over a pulse trans-mission channel.   At the receiver, the signal $y(t)$ can be regenerated by passing this sequence of impulses through an ideal low-pass filter with impulse response $\sin 2\pi Wt/2\pi Wt$ (this noncausal filter could be approxi-mated by a causal filter with delay).

The utility of such a transmission scheme is two-fold:

(a) It allows several signals to be multiplexed over the same channel; i.e., if we can transmit pulses at a rate of $2NW$ pulses per second, we could take the samples from N signals of bandwidth W and interleave them on the pulse channel (time-division multiplex).

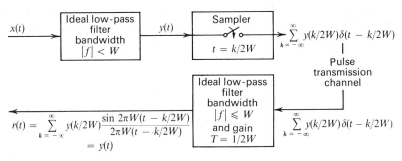

Figure 2-20   Functional block diagram of pulse transmission of a waveform.

(b) We shall see later that a variation on this type of system can be employed to trade bandwidth for signal-to-noise ratio.

Problem 2-27. The above discussion was predicated on the assumption that $y(t)$ was band-limited and we wished to transmit it. Suppose that the signal we actually wish to transmit via the above scheme is $x(t)$, and this signal is not necessarily band-limited. Assume that we are going to use the above transmission system and take $r(t)$, the output of the low-pass filter at the receiver, as an approximation of $x(t)$. Will the mean square error

$$\epsilon = \int_{-\infty}^{\infty} [r(t) - x(t)]^2 \, dt$$

be smaller if we do or do not include the low-pass filter shown between $x(t)$ and $y(t)$ in the figure; i.e., should we transmit samples of $x(t)$, or ideal-filter $x(t)$ and transmit samples of the filter output (as shown). Prove your answer conclusively. *Hint:* Note that since $r(t)$ is the output of an ideal low-pass filter, its transform is zero for $|f| > W$.

Problem 2-28. Consider the pulse transmission system discussed above and assume that $y(t)$ is the signal we wish to transmit. Suppose that, in transmission, noise is added to the pulse values and the areas of the pulses received are $r(kT) = y(kT) + n(kT)$. If we take the resulting output of the low-pass filter

$$r(t) = \sum_{k=-\infty}^{\infty} r(kT) \frac{\sin 2\pi W(t - k/2W)}{2\pi W(t - k/2W)}$$

as an approximation to $y(t)$, express the integral square error

$$\epsilon = \int_{-\infty}^{\infty} |r(t) - y(t)|^2 \, dt$$

in terms of the noise values $n(kT)$. *Hint:* Use the appropriate version of Parseval's theorem.

2-8 Multidimensional Fourier Transforms

In handling the multidimensional characteristic function associated with a number of gaussian random variables, we will need to have recourse to transforms of functions of more than a single variable. There are *no* new concepts involved in the discussion of such transforms; the only added difficulties are simply due to notation. Let $x(t_1, t_2)$ be a function of the two time variables t_1 and t_2, such that the integral

$$\int_{-\infty}^{\infty} \int_{-\infty}^{\infty} |x(t_1, t_2)| \, dt_1 \, dt_2$$

is defined and finite.

First, consider t_2 to be fixed and take the Fourier transform of the resulting function of t_1:

$$\Gamma(f_1, t_2) = \mathscr{F}_{t_1}[x(t_1, t_2)] = \int_{-\infty}^{\infty} x(t_1, t_2) e^{-j2\pi f_1 t_1} \, dt_1 \qquad (2\text{-}126)$$

Then $x(t_1, t_2)$ may be recovered from $\Gamma(f_1, t_2)$ by the inverse Fourier transform

$$x(t_1, t_2) = \int_{-\infty}^{\infty} \Gamma(f_1, t_2)e^{j2\pi f_1 t_1} \, df_1 \qquad (2\text{-}127)$$

Now for every fixed value of f_1 we can take the Fourier transform of $\Gamma(f_1, t_2)$

$$\begin{aligned}
X(f_1, f_2) = \mathscr{F}_{t_2}[\Gamma(f_1, t_2)] &= \int_{-\infty}^{\infty} \Gamma(f_1, t_2)e^{-j2\pi f_2 t_2} \, dt_2 \\
&= \int_{-\infty}^{\infty}\int_{-\infty}^{\infty} x(t_1, t_2)e^{-j(2\pi f_1 t_1 + 2\pi f_2 t_2)} \, dt_1 \, dt_2 \\
&= \mathscr{F}_{t_1 t_2}[x(t_1, t_2)]
\end{aligned} \qquad (2\text{-}128)$$

The resulting function, $X(f_1, f_2)$, is termed *the (two-dimensional) Fourier transform of* $x(t_1, t_2)$.

Note that $\Gamma(f_1, t_2)$ can be recovered from $X(f_1, f_2)$ by the inverse Fourier transform

$$\Gamma(f_1, t_2) = \mathscr{F}_{t_2}^{-1}[X(f_1, f_2)] = \int_{-\infty}^{\infty} X(f_1, f_2)e^{j2\pi f_2 t_2} \, df_2 \qquad (2\text{-}129)$$

Combining Eqs. 2-127 and 2-129, we have

$$\begin{aligned}
x(t_1, t_2) &= \mathscr{F}_{t_1, t_2}^{-1}[X(f_1, f_2)] \\
&= \int_{-\infty}^{\infty}\int_{-\infty}^{\infty} X(f_1, f_2)e^{j(2\pi f_2 t_2 + 2\pi f_1 t_1)} \, df_2 \, df_1
\end{aligned} \qquad (2\text{-}130)$$

Equations 2-128 and 2-130, respectively, comprise the direct and inverse Fourier transform relations.

The above argument can be repeated N-times: if $x(t_1, \ldots, t_N)$ is a function of N-variables satisfying

$$\int_{-\infty}^{\infty} \cdots \int_{-\infty}^{\infty} |x(t_1, \ldots, t_N)| \, dt_1 \ldots dt_N < \infty \qquad (2\text{-}131)$$

The (N-dimensional) Fourier transform is defined by

$$X(f_1, \ldots, f_N) = \int_{-\infty}^{\infty} \cdots \int_{-\infty}^{\infty} x(t_1, \ldots, t_N)e^{-j(2\pi f_1 t_1 + \cdots + 2\pi f_N t_N)} \, dt_1 \cdots dt_N$$
$$(2\text{-}132)$$

The time function $x(t_1, \ldots, t_N)$ may then be recovered by the inversion integral

$$x(t_1, \ldots, t_N) = \int_{-\infty}^{\infty} \cdots \int_{-\infty}^{\infty} X(f_1, \ldots, f_N)e^{j(2\pi f_1 t_1 + \cdots + 2\pi f_N t_N)} \, df_1, \ldots, df_N$$
$$(2\text{-}133)$$

REFERENCES

[1]   Courant, R., *Differential and Integral Calculus*, Vol. I., Interscience, New York, 1937; p. 447.
[2]   Birkhoff, G., and G. C. Rota, *Ordinary Differential Equations*, Ginn, Boston, 1962; Chapter 11.
[3]   Courant, R., *op. cit.*, pp. 126–128.
[4]   Goldberg, R. R., *Fourier Transforms*, Cambridge University Press, New York, 1961.
[5] Papoulis, A. A., *The Fourier Integral and Its Applications*, McGraw-Hill Book Co., New York, 1962.
[6]   Lighthill, M. J., *Fourier Analysis and Generalized Functions*, Cambridge University Press, New York, 1962.
[7]   Burkhill, J. C., *The Lebesque Integral*, Cambridge University Press, New York, 1963.
[8]   Ahlfors, L., *Complex Analysis*, McGraw-Hill Book Co., New York, 1953.
[9]   Yen, J. L., "On Nonuniform Sampling of Bandwidth-Limited Signals," *IRE Trans. on Circuit Theory*, **CT-3**, 252, 1956.

Chapter 3

Probability Theory

In the preceeding chapter, various methods of describing signals were discussed. Our ultimate objective is to be able to describe the random signals that occur as noise or messages in communication systems. To this end, we develop in this chapter the mathematical structure for describing probabilistic phenomena. In Chapter 4, we complete our mathematical preparation by considering the description of random signals.

3-1 The Structure of Probability Theory

The reader is quite aware of the existence of "random" phenomena in his daily life. He is aware that he does not have sufficiently precise control of his thumb to guarantee that in flipping a coin he can impart an angular momentum that will result in, say, an even number of flips. He is also aware that modern physics regards the universe to be basically random in nature when viewed at a microscopic level.

We shall not presume here to impart a further intuitive notion of the concept of randomness but trust to the reader's own background to supply, at least for the present, a vague notion of what is meant. We wish to focus our attention on the formulation of a mathematical structure to describe phenomena which are of a random nature. Let us start by observing that the purpose of a branch of applied mathematical analysis such as Probability Theory or Analytical Mechanics is to allow us to predict certain facts about the behavior of a physical system. Analytical mechanics, for instance, allows us to predict the future trajectory of an artillery shell or satellite from its initial position and velocity, or to deduce that a gyroscope will precess under certain conditions. Similarly, probability theory allows us to predict certain properties of the outcomes of a large number of dice games, and places us in an advantageous position in betting against someone who does not have a knowledge of probability theory.

However, there is one distinction between mechanics and probability theory. In mechanics, it is quite obvious what the basic structure of our theory is to be. The objects that we are to deal with are point masses, rigid bodies, and, if we get fancy, deformable bodies; the postulates that govern these objects are Newton's laws and conservation of energy and momentum. These starting points are so reasonable and useful that the beginning mechanics student accepts them without question as the logical mathematical idealizations to start with in building up an analytical structure for describing mechanical phenomena.

In probability theory this is not so. The choice of objects that we should deal with and the names that we attach to them are not immediately suggested by our physical experience. Thus, in developing an analytical theory of probability, we must first decide on the basic objects that will be useful and what postulates should govern their interrelationships. Let us note in proceeding that the basic notion in probability is that of an *experiment* with *more than one possible outcome*, and the outcome that actually occurs cannot be predicted *with certainty* before the performance of the experiment. Furthermore, *at least conceptually*, it is possible to perform this same experiment a large number of times under *identical conditions*, either sequentially or by having a large number of experiments performed simultaneously. *What we are seeking is a mathematical structure that accurately describes the outcome of a large number of such experiments.*

The Sample Space

The first objects that we shall define in setting up our mathematical structure are *sample points* and the *sample space*. A *sample point* represents a *single indecomposable outcome* of an experiment described in its most complete and basic form. We will denote a typical sample point by the letter σ.

The *sample space* consists of *all* sample points that are regarded *a priori* as *possible outcomes* for an experiment. The sample space we will denote by S.

If we are considering the experiment of flipping a coin, a useful sample space might consist of the following points:

σ_1: the coin turns up heads
σ_2: the coin turns up tails
σ_3: the coin lands on edge
σ_4: the coin rolls into an inaccessible place

For such an experiment, there is no clear choice of sample space decreed by providence; it is up to the analyst to pick a space which accurately and completely portrays the physical experiment he has in mind.

Although the notion of a sample space is conceptually simple, it can be an extremely complicated set of objects. Imagine trying to set up a sample space to describe the noise waveforms that can occur across a resistor during a given interval of time.

The Event

An *event* is an outcome that either *does* or *does not* occur when the experiment is performed. In throwing a single die, an event might be "an even number of spots turn up." In terms of our sample space, an event consists of the collection of those sample points for which the specified event occurs. In throwing a die, an obvious sample space might be:

∂_1: one turns up ∂_4: four turns up

∂_2: two turns up ∂_5: five turns up

∂_3: three turns up ∂_6: six turns up

The event "an even number turns up" would then consist of the event set or collection of points, ∂_2, ∂_4, and ∂_6; that is, whenever any one of these three points is the outcome of the experiment, the event occurs.

To emphasize that an event consists of a collection or *set* of sample points, we make use of notation that is common in set theory

$$A = \{\partial : \text{the event } A \text{ occurs when the experiment outcome}$$
$$\text{is the sample point } \partial\} \quad (3\text{-}1)$$

In words, this statement reads the *set* or *event* A consists of all those sample points ∂ such that the event A occurs when the experiment outcome is the sample point (basic indecomposable outcome) ∂.

Given two events, A and B, we can also consider the event "either A or B or both occurs." For brevity, we normally omit the "or both" and refer to this event as "A or B occurs," it being understood that if both A and B occur this also results in the event in question occurring. Mathematically, the event "A or B" consists of all those points in either the set A, or B, or both. The set theory notation for this is $A \cup B$. If we use the notation

$$\partial \in A$$

to mean the sample point ∂ belongs in the event set A, or A occurs when the basic event ∂ occurs, then

$$A \cup B = \{\partial : \partial \in A \text{ or } \partial \in B \text{ or } \partial \in \text{ both } A \text{ and } B\} \quad (3\text{-}2)$$

Given the two events A and B, it is sometimes useful to consider the event "both A and B occur (simultaneously)." Mathematically, this event set consists of all sample points that are in both the set A and the set B, or the *intersection* of A and B; hence, we denote this event by the product or intersection notation AB

$$AB = \{ \jmath : \jmath \in \text{both } A \text{ and } B \} \tag{3-3}$$

As an example, consider the tossing of a die with the sample space of the six points previously described. Let the event A be "an even number turns up" and the event B be "the number that turns up is less than (but not equal to) four." Then

$$A \cup B = \text{the number that turns up is even or less than four}$$
$$= \{ \jmath_1, \jmath_2, \jmath_3, \jmath_4, \jmath_6 \}$$

in which the notation $\{ \jmath_1, \jmath_2, \jmath_3, \jmath_4, \jmath_6 \}$ means the set or collection of the five points $\jmath_1, \jmath_2, \jmath_3, \jmath_4$, and $\jmath_6$. Similarly,

$$AB = \text{the number that turns up is both even and less than four}$$
$$= \{ \jmath_2 \}$$

It is also sometimes useful to consider the event "the event A does not occur." This event is denoted by $\overline{A}$ and sometimes referred to as the complement of A:

$$\overline{A} = \{ \jmath : \jmath \text{ is not in } A \}$$

In our example above,

$$\overline{A} = \text{an odd number turns up}$$
$$= \{ \jmath_1, \jmath_3, \jmath_5 \}$$

If we regard the sample space as a set of points in the plane, then there is an easy graphical interpretation of the relation between the sets A and B and the sets $A \cup B, AB$, and $\overline{A}$. These relationships are shown in Fig. 3-1.

We say that the events A and B are *mutually exclusive* if it is impossible for them to occur simultaneously. In terms of the event sets, this means that A and B have no sample points in common or that they are disjoint. In the graphical interpretation of Fig. 3-1, the two sets would not overlap. If we use the symbol $\varnothing$ to denote the empty set or null set (consisting of *no* points), we can then state that A and B are mutually exclusive if

$$AB = \varnothing$$

In our example above, if A is the event "the number that turns up is even" and C the event "the number that turns up is one," then A and C are disjoint.

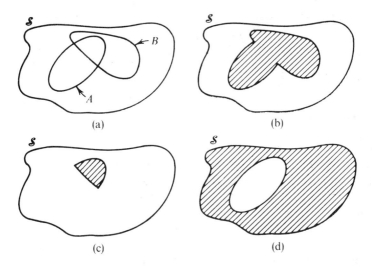

Figure 3-1 Relation between (a) the sets A and B, and the sets: (b) $A \cup B$, (c) AB, (d) $\bar{A}$.

Probability of an Event

To any event, we assign a real-valued, non-negative number which we refer to as the probability of A and denote by $P(A)$. In setting up a theory to describe a physical experiment, we assign the numbers $P(A)$ so that they represent the fraction of occurrences of the event A in a *long* sequence of independent trials of the experiment.

We have now defined and labeled all the basic objects that occur in setting up a mathematical structure to describe a random or probabilistic experiment. We next state the axioms that we take to govern these objects. After stating these axioms, we discuss their relation in modeling a "real world" random experiment.

The Axioms of Probability Theory

We take the following axioms to govern our Probability Model.

I. We list (conceptually) a *collection* of event sets. If the event sets A and B are in this collection, we require this collection to also contain the event sets $A \cup B$, AB, and $\bar{A}$. We also require this collection to contain S, the sample space consisting of all sample points.

II. To *each* set in the collection is assigned a nonnegative real number, $P(A)$, the probability of that set.

III. $P(S) = 1$.

IV. If A and B are mutually exclusive,

$$P(A \cup B) = P(A) + P(B)$$

V. If $A_1, A_2, \ldots$ is a sequence of event sets such that A_{n+1} is wholly contained in A_n and the intersection of all these events is empty

$$A_1 A_2 A_3 \ldots = \varnothing$$

then $\lim_{n \to \infty} P(A_n) = 0$.

Our reason for requiring Axioms I and II is to guarantee that all interesting events have a probability assigned to them. If the events A and B are of interest, then we certainly also wish to be sure that we can talk of the probabilities of "A or B," "A and B," and "not A."

Since we wish to interpret probability as the *ratio* of occurrences of an event in a long sequence of trials, and since the event S must occur in every trial, we must take $P(S) = 1$ in Axiom III to preserve this interpretation of frequency of occurrence. Again, Axiom IV is necessary for the preservation of this frequency interpretation. Let $n_N(A)$, $n_N(B)$, and $n_N(A \cup B)$ denote the number of occurrences of the respective events A, B, and $A \cup B$ in N trials. Then if A and B are mutually exclusive, we must have

$$n_N(A) + n_N(B) = n_N(A \cup B)$$

or

$$\frac{n_N(A)}{N} + \frac{n_N(B)}{N} = \frac{n_N(A \cup B)}{N}$$

Axiom V is required for mathematical consistency when our collection contains an infinite number of sets. We cannot comment on this point here. The interested reader is referred to Chapters 1 and 2 of Kolmogorov [1].

Conditional Probability

Before turning to a description of the types of random quantities that are of direct interest in communications, we discuss two more basic concepts, the first of which is conditional probability. It may be that from certain observations we can determine whether or not an event B occurs but cannot determine from the available observations whether or not A has occurred. We may then wish to speculate whether or not A actually occurred. It is in such a situation that the concept of conditional probability is applicable. Consider two events A and B. If the probability $P(B)$ is nonzero, we define the ratio

$$P(A \mid B) = \frac{P(AB)}{P(B)} \tag{3-4}$$

to be the conditional probability of the event A given (the occurrence of) the event B.

To interpret the empirical meaning of this probability, let us regard our frequency ratio interpretation. In a long trial of N events, the probability $P(A \mid B)$ would correspond to the ratio

$$\frac{n_N(AB)/N}{n_N(B)/N} = \frac{n_N(AB)}{n_N(B)}$$

Thus we are sorting out *those trials in which B occurred* and looking at the fraction of occurrences of A relative only to these trials. We thus focus our attention only on outcomes which give rise to event B and renormalize our probabilities [by dividing by $P(B)$] to reflect relative ratios of occurrence in this restricted situation.

Independent Events

It may be that the ratio

$$P(A \mid B) = \frac{P(AB)}{P(B)}$$

is equal to $P(A)$. This states that the ratio of occurrences of A is no different when we restrict our attention to trials in which B occurs or whether we consider all trials. In such a circumstance we regard the occurrence of A as unaffected by the occurrence of B and say that the event A is *statistically independent* of the event B. Note that the condition for this independence

$$P(A \mid B) = \frac{P(AB)}{P(B)} = P(A) \tag{3-5}$$

can be expressed

$$P(AB) = P(A)P(B) \tag{3-6}$$

Thus, if Eq. 3-5 is true,

$$P(B \mid A) = \frac{P(AB)}{P(A)} = P(B) \tag{3-7}$$

and the event B is independent of the event A. Since the independence of A on B implies the independence of B on A and vice-versa, we may simply say when Eq. 3-5, 3-6, or 3-7 holds that the events A and B are *independent* or *statistically independent*.

Consider simultaneously rolling two dice, one made from green plastic and the other from red plastic. If we let the events A and B be defined by

$$A = \text{a six turns up on the green die}$$
$$B = \text{a one turns up on the red die}$$

we would set up a probability model in which the events A and B were statistically independent, unless we had some reason to believe that the thrower had sufficient skill to affect the throw of both dice.

3-2   Random Variables and Their Probability Distributions

Random Variables

In many practical applications, it is convenient to describe the outcome of the random experiment by one or more real-valued quantities. These quantities are termed random variables. Technically, a *random variable* is a real-valued function of the sample point. In this book, random variables are denoted by capital roman letters,[1] so a typical random variable might be denoted $X(\jmath)$. We demand only of this function of the sample point $\jmath$ that it be sufficiently well behaved that the probability of the event

$$X(\jmath) \leq x$$

is defined for all (real) values of the *dummy* variable x. This dummy variable is so termed because its value is nonrandom and can be selected arbitrarily to define an event in terms of the random variable $X(\jmath)$ whose value depends on the sample point.

To take the sharp edge off this somewhat abstract definition, let us point out that in many circumstances the basic outcomes (sample points $\jmath$) may be very complex objects to describe. In such a case a simpler, and hence more useful, description might be given by one or more real-valued functions of the basic outcomes. As a concrete example, consider our experiment to be making an observation of the weather in San Francisco at 12:00 noon on a given day. Attempting to describe what constitutes a sample point (basic indecomposable outcome) for fully describing the outcome or state of such a complicated phenomenon as the weather is a hopeless task. However, we can easily think of a number of random variables that describe rather fully the state of the weather at a given time: wind speed, direction of the wind velocity, temperature, rate of precipitation, and air pressure. Note that these quantities all satisfy our definition of a random variable; for

(i) all of them are real valued.
(ii) they all depend on the exact state of the weather; i.e., they are functions of $\jmath$.

---

[1] Occasionally we depart from this and also use capital Greek letters for random variables.

(iii) they are sufficiently well-behaved physical quantities such that we are sure that it makes sense to speak of the probability of the event $X(\jmath) \leq x$ for any value of the dummy variable x.

A second example might be to consider the noise generated in a carbon resistor at some specified time instant. The basic sample point might be a description of the state of all the atomic particles in the carbon at the specified instant. Such a description would be useless for engineering purposes. Instead, we might focus our attention on the noise e.m.f. generated across the two terminals at the specified time instant. This quantity clearly satisfies our definition of a random variable; moreover, although it provides only an incomplete description of the outcome of the experiment, it is a simple description and one that is adequate for describing any effect the resistor may have on the circuit to which it is connected.

We now turn to describing the probability distribution of a random variable.

Distribution Functions

Let us consider the random variable $X(\jmath)$ and the probability of the event $X(\jmath) \leq x$. We denote this probability by

$$P\{X(\jmath) \leq x\}$$

It is apparent that this probability is a function of the *dummy* variable x. To simplify our notation we will denote this function of x by

$$F_X(x) = P\{X(\jmath) \leq x\} \qquad (3\text{-}8)$$

This function (of x) is termed the *distribution function of the random variable X*. Note that $F_X(x)$ must be a monotone nondecreasing function of x; for, if $x_2 > x_1$, $F_X(x_2) = P\{X(\jmath) \leq x_2\} = P\{X(\jmath) \leq x_1\} + P\{x_1 < X(\jmath) \leq x_2\} = F_X(x_1) + P\{x_1 < X(\jmath) \leq x_2\} \geq F_X(x_1)$. Further note that from the definition we must have $F_X(-\infty) = 0$ and $F_X(+\infty) = 1$. The subscript X denotes the random variable in question and the argument x denotes the value of the dummy variable defining the event. When possible, we match the lower case dummy variable (x above) to the capital letter (X above) representing the random variable. This is not always possible nor is it necessary. For example, $F_X(\alpha)$ unambiguously denotes the probability $P\{X(\jmath) \leq \alpha\}$. If we omit a subscript on the distribution function, *it is understood* that the random variable in question is the one *matching* the dummy variable. Thus $F(x)$ denotes the probability $P\{X(\jmath) \leq x\}$.

One further simplification in notation is possible. We write a random variable as $X(\jmath)$ to remind us that it is a function of the sample point (basic indecomposable outcome); when this reminder is unnecessary, we simply use the notation X.

If we simultaneously are considering two random variables X and Y (such as temperature and air pressure), their probability distribution is described by considering the probability of the joint event $\{X(\jmath) \leq x, Y(\jmath) \leq y\}$ as a function of the *two dummy variables* x and y. We refer to this as a *joint event* because we are simultaneously specifying two simpler events. The probability of this joint event is the *joint distribution function* of the random variables X and Y, and is written

$$F_{XY}(x, y) = P\{X(\jmath) \leq x; \; Y(\jmath) \leq y\} \tag{3-9}$$

From the definitions of $F_X(x)$ and $F_{XY}(x, y)$ as the probabilities of the events defined respectively by Eqs. 3-8 and 3-9, several properties follow immediately

$$F_X(-\infty) = 0 \tag{3-10}$$

$$F_X(+\infty) = 1 \tag{3-11}$$

$$F_{XY}(x, y) = F_{YX}(y, x) \tag{3-12}$$

$$F_{XY}(-\infty, -\infty) = 0 \tag{3-13}$$

$$F_{XY}(+\infty, +\infty) = 1 \tag{3-14}$$

$$F_{XY}(x, +\infty) = F_X(x) \tag{3-15}$$

If we are simultaneously considering n random variables $X_1, X_2, \ldots, X_n$, we denote their joint distribution function by

$$F_{X_1 X_2 \cdots X_n}(x_1, x_2, \ldots, x_n) = P\{X_1 \leq x_1, \ldots, X_n \leq x_n\} \tag{3-16}$$

Relations analogous to those of Eqs. 3-13 to 3-15 apply to this n-fold distribution function.

Probability Density Functions

An alternate description of the probability distribution of a random variable X is often useful. This is the derivative of the distribution function

$$f_X(x) = \frac{d}{dx} F_X(x) \tag{3-17}$$

which is termed the *probability density function*. Note that the differentiation in Eq. 3-17 is with respect to the *dummy* variable x. The name density function arises from the relation

$$P\{x_1 < X \leq x_2\} = F_X(x_2) - F_X(x_1)$$

$$= \int_{x_1}^{x_2} f_X(x) \, dx \tag{3-18}$$

Thus the function $f_X(x)$ expresses the *density* of the probability distribution of X.

From the definition of $f_X(x)$ and Eq. 3-11 it follows immediately that

$$\int_{-\infty}^{\infty} f_X(x)\, dx = 1 \qquad (3\text{-}19)$$

Also, as we mentioned earlier, a distribution function must always be *monotone* nondecreasing. Its derivative, or density function, must thus always be nonnegative. Thus a probability density function must always be *a nonnegative function of total area one*.

Let us consider some examples. If X is uniformly distributed (equally likely) between the two values a and b, $a < b$, and cannot occur outside this range, its density function is

$$f_X(x) = \begin{cases} \dfrac{1}{b-a} & a \le x \le b \\ 0 & \text{elsewhere} \end{cases}$$

and its distribution function given by

$$F_X(x) = \begin{cases} 0 & x \le a \\ \dfrac{x-a}{b-a} & a \le x \le b \\ 1 & x \ge b \end{cases}$$

If a random variable has the density function given by

$$f_X(x) = \frac{1}{\sqrt{2\pi}\,\sigma} \exp\left[\frac{-(x-m)^2}{2\sigma^2}\right] \qquad (3\text{-}20)$$

we say that X has a *gaussian* or *normal* distribution. We leave the interpretation of the constants m and σ to problems in a later subsection. A sketch of the form of this density function is shown in Fig. 3-2. The corresponding distribution function

$$F_X(x) = \frac{1}{\sqrt{2\pi}\,\sigma} \int_{-\infty}^{x} \exp\left[\frac{-(\tau-m)^2}{2\sigma^2}\right] d\tau \qquad (3\text{-}21)$$

cannot be expressed as any simple function of the variable x.

Problem 3-1. Show that the area under the density function of Eq. 3-20 is unity as it must be for a density function; i.e., show that

$$I = \frac{1}{\sqrt{2\pi}\,\sigma} \int_{-\infty}^{\infty} \exp\left[\frac{-(x-m)^2}{2\sigma^2}\right] dx = 1 \qquad (3\text{-}22)$$

Hint: Consider

$$I^2 = \left[\frac{1}{\sqrt{2\pi}\,\sigma} \int_{-\infty}^{\infty} \exp\left[\frac{-(x-m)^2}{2\sigma^2} \right] dx \right]^2$$

$$= \frac{1}{2\pi\sigma^2} \int_{-\infty}^{\infty} \int_{-\infty}^{\infty} \exp\left[\frac{-(x-m)^2}{2\sigma^2} \right] \exp\left[\frac{-(y-m)^2}{2\sigma^2} \right] dx\,dy$$

Although I cannot be simply evaluated, I^2 can by a suitable change of variables of integration.

If the random variable X has a distribution such that at a number of points $x_1, x_2, \ldots, x_n$, the events

$$X = x_k \qquad k = 1, 2, \ldots, n$$

have *nonzero probabilities* p_k, $k = 1, 2, \ldots, n$ (so that X is actually equal to one or more discrete values with nonzero probability) then the distribution function takes a jump of height p_k at the point x_k and the density function contains a corresponding impulse of area p_k at the point x_k. To be precise, we will define the jumps in the distribution function so that the distribution function takes on the higher value *at* the point in question (i.e., the distribution function is continuous from the right, discontinuous from the left at the point).

EXAMPLE. Suppose the random variable X is uniformly distributed between the values 0 and 1 with total probability 1/4, takes on the exact

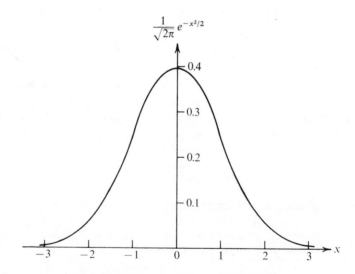

Figure 3-2   Gaussian density function for $m = 0$, $\sigma = 1$.

value 1 with probability 1/4, and is uniformly distributed between the values 1 and 2 with total probability 1/2. Then

$$f_X(x) = \begin{cases} 0 & x < 0 \\ \frac{1}{4} & 0 \le x < 1 \\ \frac{1}{4}\delta(x - 1) & x = 1 \\ \frac{1}{2} & 1 < x \le 2 \\ 0 & x > 2 \end{cases}$$

and

$$F_X(x) = \begin{cases} 0 & x < 0 \\ \frac{1}{4}x & 0 \le x < 1 \\ \frac{1}{2} + \frac{1}{2}(x - 1) & 1 \le x \le 2 \\ 1 & x > 2 \end{cases}$$

If we are simultaneously considering the two random variables X and Y, their *joint probability density function* is defined by

$$f_{XY}(x, y) = \frac{\partial^2}{\partial x \, \partial y} F_{XY}(x, y) \tag{3-23}$$

Again, $F_{XY}(x, y)$ must be monotone nondecreasing in both x and y so that $f_{XY}(x, y)$ must be nonnegative; it must also have total area unity, since

$$1 = F_{XY}(\infty, \infty) = \int_{-\infty}^{\infty} \int_{-\infty}^{\infty} f_{XY}(x, y) \, dx \, dy \tag{3-24}$$

If R denotes a region of the xy-plane, then by approximating this region by a region with rectangular edges, we could deduce by an argument similar to the one leading to Eq. 3-18 that

$$P\{X \text{ and } Y \text{ fall in } R\} = \int \int_R f_{XY}(x, y) \, dx \, dy \tag{3-25}$$

Let us note that we can obtain the density function for a single random variable from its joint density function with a second random variable. From Eq. 3-15 we have

$$F_X(x) = F_{XY}(x, \infty) = \int_{-\infty}^{x} d\sigma \int_{-\infty}^{\infty} dy \, f_{XY}(\sigma, y)$$

Differentiating both sides of this equation with respect to the dummy variable x, we obtain[1]

$$f_X(x) = \frac{\partial}{\partial x} F_X(x) = \int_{-\infty}^{\infty} dy \, f_{XY}(x, y) \tag{3-26}$$

---

[1] By the fundamental theorem of calculus $\dfrac{\partial}{\partial x} \displaystyle\int_{-\infty}^{x} f(\sigma) \, d\sigma = f(x).$

Remarks similar to those of Eqs. 3-23 to 3-26 apply to joint density functions of more than two variables.

Expectation of a Random Variable

For any random variable X, the quantity

$$E\{X\} = \int_{-\infty}^{\infty} f_X(x)x \, dx \qquad (3\text{-}27)$$

is a numerical value which we denote by the symbol $E\{X\}$ and refer to as the *expected value* of X, the *expectation* of X, or the *average* value of X. To interpret this, let us write the integral in Eq. 3-27 as the limit of an approximating sum by picking a grid of points x_k, $k = 0, \pm 1, \pm 2, \ldots$, which are spaced Δ apart

$$x_k = (k + \tfrac{1}{2})\Delta \qquad k = 0, \pm 1, \ldots$$

Then

$$
\begin{aligned}
E\{X\} &= \int_{-\infty}^{\infty} f_X(x)x \, dx \\
&= \lim_{\Delta \to 0} \sum_{k=-\infty}^{\infty} \int_{k\Delta}^{(k+1)\Delta} x_k f_X(x) \, dx \\
&= \lim_{\Delta \to 0} \sum_{k=-\infty}^{\infty} x_k P\left\{x_k - \frac{\Delta}{2} < X \le x_k + \frac{\Delta}{2}\right\} \qquad (3\text{-}28)
\end{aligned}
$$

The final sum on the right hand side of this equation can now be given a physical interpretation. Consider making a long sequence of N independent observations of the random variable X, and let $n_N(k)$ denote the number of trials for which the random variable X falls into the kth bin $x_k - \Delta/2 < X \le x_k + \Delta/2$. Then the ratio $n_N(k)/N$ approaches $P\{x_k - \Delta/2 < X_k \le x_k + \Delta/2\}$ as N becomes large. Thus $E\{X\}$ is approximated by

$$E\{X\} \approx \sum_{k=-\infty}^{\infty} x_k \left(\frac{n_N(k)}{N}\right) = \frac{1}{N} \sum_{k=-\infty}^{\infty} x_k n_N(k) \qquad (3\text{-}29)$$

The quantity on the right-hand side of this equation is the familiar "sample" average in which the sum is taken of each value of the object times the number of times that value occurred; the sum is then divided by the total number of trials or observations. This quantity is, for example, the class average of a quiz so familiar to students. In this regard, it is quite clear that the value x_k appearing in the sum and the value x appearing in the integral in Eq. 3-28 are *dummy* values or variables (as opposed to the random variable X).

Now let us consider some function $g(x)$. The quantity resulting by letting the argument be a random variable, is again a random variable,[1] which we denote by

$$G = g(X) \tag{3-30}$$

If we wished to find the expected value of G, we could find the density function $f_G(\sigma)$ and evaluate the integral

$$E\{G\} = \int_{-\infty}^{\infty} g f_G(g) \, dg \tag{3-31}$$

However, this procedure is unduly complicated. Let us consider the function $g(x)$ plotted in a two dimensional plane, as shown in Fig. 3-3. From this graphical relationship, it is clear that the probability of G falling in the dg interval about the value g_0 is equal to the probability of X falling into a number (three in the case shown) of dx intervals

$$f_G(g_0) \, dg = \sum_i f_X(x_i) \, dx_i$$

[Note that the intervals dx_i are of differing lengths, depending on $g'(x_i)$, the slope of the curve at the point x_i.] Thus the contribution

$$g_0 f_G(g_0) \, dg$$

appearing in the integral of Eq. 3-31 would be given by one or more corresponding contributions

$$\sum_i g(x_i) f_X(x_i) \, dx_i$$

---

[1] We require that the function $g(x)$ be sufficiently well behaved that the probability of the event $G = g(X) \leq \sigma$ is defined for all values of the dummy variable σ.

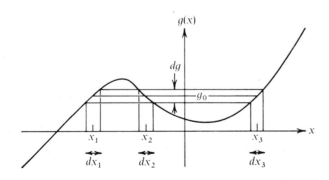

Figure 3-3 Graphical interpretation of the relation of Eq. 3-32.

appearing in the integral

$$\int_{-\infty}^{\infty} g(x)f_X(x)\, dx$$

and we have the useful result

$$E\{G\} = E\{g(X)\} = \int_{-\infty}^{\infty} gf_G(g)\, dg$$

$$= \int_{-\infty}^{\infty} g(x)f_X(x)\, dx \qquad (3\text{-}32)$$

Problem 3-2. Let X be a random variable with known density function $f_X(x)$ and let $g(X)$ be given by

$$G = g(X) = \frac{(X - a)}{b} \qquad (3\text{-}33)$$

Show that $f_G(g)$ is given by

$$f_G(g) = |b|f_X(bg + a) \qquad (3\text{-}34)$$

(a) by reasoning similar to that leading to Eq. 3-32;
(b) by noting that

$$F_G(g) = P\{G \le g\} = P\left\{\frac{(X - a)}{b} \le g\right\}$$

and differentiating both sides of the resulting equation.

Problem 3-3. Recall that we said that two events, A and B, are statistically independent if $P(AB) = P(A)P(B)$. We say that two *random variables*, X and Y, are *statistically independent* if

$$F_{XY}(x, y) = P(X \le x, Y \le y)$$
$$= P(X \le x)P(Y \le y) = F_X(x)F_Y(y)$$

for *all* x and y, $-\infty < x < \infty$, $-\infty < y < \infty$. Show that X and Y are statistically independent if and only if $f_{XY}(x, y) = f_X(x)f_Y(y)$.

In many instances it is convenient to be able to give a partial description of the probability distribution of a random variable by specifying several numbers, as opposed to completely describing the distribution by having to specify the values of its density or distribution function for all values of the dummy variable. Such a partial description of the distribution is given by one or more *moments* of the random variable. The expected value of the nth power of a random variable is referred to as its nth moment, $E\{(X)^n\}$. The first moment or expected value of X itself is commonly referred to as the *mean* of X and denoted by m_x. If the nth moment is evaluated about the mean of the random variable

$$\mu_n \overset{\Delta}{=} E\{(X - m_x)^n\} = \int_{-\infty}^{\infty} (x - m_x)^n f(x)\, dx \qquad (3\text{-}35)$$

it is referred to as the *nth central moment*. In particular, the second central moment is referred to as the *variance* of the random variable, and is denoted by

$$\text{var}\{X\} = E\{(X - m_x)^2\} = \mu_2 \tag{3-36}$$

This variance is also sometimes denoted by the symbol σ_x^2.

For two random variables, X and Y, the quantity

$$\mu_{mn} = E\{(X - m_x)^m(Y - m_y)^n\}$$
$$= \int_{-\infty}^{\infty} \int_{-\infty}^{\infty} (x - m_x)^m(y - m_y)^n f(x, y) \, dx \, dy \tag{3-37}$$

is referred to as the *mnth joint central moment* of X and Y. In particular, μ_{11} is referred to as the *covariance* of X and Y. The quantity $\rho_{xy} = \mu_{11}/\sqrt{\mu_{02}\mu_{20}}$, is termed the *correlation coefficient*. If the covariance of X and Y is zero, we say they are *uncorrelated*. Note that if X and Y are statistically independent then they are uncorrelated. The converse of this statement is not true in general.

The concepts and definitions above concerning the joint distribution functions, density functions, and joint central moments of two random variables extend in a straightforward way to more than two random variables.

Problem 3-4. Let X be a random variable with var $X < \infty$. Show that

$$P\{|X - m_x| \geq z\} \leq \frac{\text{var } X}{z^2} \tag{3-38}$$

This well known relation is referred to as the *Chebyshev inequality*. From it we see that the mean and variance of a random variable give a partial description of its probability distribution.

Problem 3-5. Let X be a random variable that takes on only positive values and let $E\{X\} < \infty$. Show that

$$P\{X > z\} \leq E\{X\}/z$$

Problem 3-6. Let Z be a random variable with a distribution determined by

$$f(z) = \begin{cases} \frac{1}{2} & -1 \leq z \leq 1 \\ 0 & |z| > 1 \end{cases}$$

and let $X = Z$; $Y = Z^2$. Show that X and Y are uncorrelated, but not statistically independent.

Problem 3-7. Consider the quantity

$$\mathscr{E}(c) = E\{(X - c)^2\}$$

Find the value of c that minimizes $\mathscr{E}(c)$.

Problem 3-8. Let the random variables Y_i, $i = 1, 2, \ldots, N$, be statistically independent and let the random variable X be defined as

$$X = \sum_{i=1}^{N} Y_i$$

Show that

$$\text{var}(X) = \sum_{i=1}^{N} \text{var}(Y_i)$$

In motivating our discussion of probability, we gave the following empirical interpretation of the probability of an event. We stated that in a long sequence of independent trials, the fraction of trials in which the event occurred would approach the probability of the event. In giving a physical interpretation of the expectation of a random variable, we used this same statement to conclude that the sample mean of a random variable computed for a large number of independent trials would approach the expected value of the random variable.

Up to this point, we have not tried to justify the statement at issue but have implicitly asked the reader to take it on faith. We are now in a position to prove the assertions made in the two interpretations discussed in the preceding paragraph. We choose to do this by means of the following two problems.

Problem 3-9. Let the random variables Y_i, $i = 1, \ldots, N$, be statistically independent and identically distributed with mean m and variance σ^2. Let us denote the sample mean of N independent trials by

$$X_N = \frac{1}{N} \sum_{i=1}^{N} Y_i \qquad (3\text{-}39)$$

Show that

$$P\{|X_N - m| \geq \epsilon\} \leq \frac{\sigma^2}{N\epsilon^2} \qquad (3\text{-}40)$$

Hint: Make appropriate use of Problems 3-4 and 3-8.

Note the interpretation of this inequality: the probability that the sample mean departs from the expectation by more than some set amount decreases in inverse proportion to the number of trials. This statement is known as the *weak law of large numbers.*

Problem 3-10. Let A denote some event that may or may not occur in the trial of an experiment and $P(A)$ denote the probability of this event. Let $n_N(A)$ denote the number of occurrences of A in N identical independent trials of the experiment. Show that

$$P\{|P(A) - n_N(A)/N| \geq \epsilon\} \leq \frac{P(A)[1 - P(A)]}{\epsilon^2 N} \qquad (3\text{-}41)$$

Hint: Let Y_i be the random variable

$$Y_i(\jmath) = \begin{cases} 1 & \text{if } A \text{ occurs in the } i\text{th trial} \\ 0 & \text{if } A \text{ does not occur in the } i\text{th trial} \end{cases}$$

Conditional Probability Distributions

Recall that for two events associated with a random experiment we defined the quantity

$$P(A \mid B) = \frac{P(AB)}{P(B)}$$

to be the conditional probability of A relative to the occurrence of B, provided that $P(B) \neq 0$.

Now let us consider two random variables X and Y; associated with them we define the two events

$$A = \{\jmath : X(\jmath) \leq x\}$$
$$B = \{\jmath : y - \Delta y < Y(\jmath) \leq y\}$$

Then

$$P\{X \leq x \mid y - \Delta y < Y \leq y\} = P(A \mid B) = \frac{P(AB)}{P(B)}$$
$$= \frac{\int_{-\infty}^{x} \int_{y-\Delta y}^{y} f_{XY}(\sigma, \tau) \, d\sigma \, d\tau}{\int_{y-\Delta y}^{y} f_{Y}(\sigma) \, d\sigma} \qquad (3\text{-}42)$$

We now assume that $f(x, y)$ and $f(y)$ are continuous at y; taking the limit of both sides of Eq. 3-42 as Δy approaches zero yields

$$P\{X \leq x \mid Y = y\} = \lim_{\Delta y \to 0} P\{X \leq x \mid y - \Delta y < Y \leq y\}$$
$$= \frac{\int_{-\infty}^{x} f_{XY}(\sigma, y) \, d\sigma}{f_{Y}(y)} \qquad (3\text{-}43)$$

For any fixed value of y, the quantity on the left-hand side of this equation considered as a function of x, has all the properties of a distribution function and is referred to as the *conditional distribution function for X given that* $Y = y$. It is denoted by $F_{X|Y}(x \mid y)$ or, more simply, $F(x \mid y)$ when the random variables match the dummy variables. It is the distribution of X that is relevant if we consider only those sample points $\jmath$ in S for which $Y(\jmath) = y$. With this distribution function, there is associated the corresponding density function

$$f(x \mid y) = \frac{d}{dx} F(x \mid y) = \frac{d}{dx} \left[\frac{\int_{-\infty}^{x} f_{XY}(\sigma, y) \, d\sigma}{f_{Y}(y)} \right]$$
$$= \frac{f_{XY}(x, y)}{f_{Y}(y)} = \frac{f(x, y)}{f(y)} \qquad (3\text{-}44)$$

As an example of the use of conditional distributions, let us consider the following problem. Suppose associated with some random experiment there are two random variables, X and Y, with a known density function for X and Y. We may consider forming the *sum random variable*.

$$Z = X + Y \qquad (3\text{-}45)$$

A physical example of such a situation might be one in which X represents the voltage across a thermocouple generated by a temperature difference. The random variable Y might be the noise e.m.f. produced by thermal agitation. The random variable Z would then be the total observed output e.m.f. of the thermocouple. We now ask, how is the density function $f(z)$ related to $f(x, y)$.

Suppose we first consider those outcomes in which $Y = y$; then $Z = X + y$ and

$$\begin{aligned}
f_{Z|Y}(z \mid y) \, dz &= P\{z - dz < Z \leq z \mid Y = y\} \\
&= P\{z - y - dz < X \leq z - y \mid Y = y\} \\
&= f_{X|Y}(z - y \mid y) \, dz
\end{aligned} \qquad (3\text{-}46)$$

Thus, using Eqs. 3-46 and 3-45,

$$\begin{aligned}
f_Z(z) &= \int_{-\infty}^{\infty} f_{ZY}(z, y) \, dy = \int_{-\infty}^{\infty} f_{Z|Y}(z \mid y) f_Y(y) \, dy \\
&= \int_{-\infty}^{\infty} f_{X|Y}(z - y \mid y) f_Y(y) \, dy = \int_{-\infty}^{\infty} f_{XY}(z - y, y) \, dy
\end{aligned} \qquad (3\text{-}47)$$

This equation yields the density for Z in terms of the known densities. If X and Y are statistically independent, this equation becomes

$$f_Z(z) = \int_{-\infty}^{\infty} f_X(z - y) f_Y(y) \, dy \qquad (3\text{-}48)$$

Problem 3-11. Given two random variables X and Y with conditional density $f_{X|Y}(x \mid y)$, the *function of y* given by

$$E\{X \mid y\} = \int_{-\infty}^{\infty} x f_{X|Y}(x \mid y) \, dx \qquad (3\text{-}49)$$

is termed the *conditional expectation of X knowing that $Y = y$*. Suppose we can observe Y but not X, and wish to estimate X by some function of Y, $g(Y)$. Show that the mean square estimation error

$$\mathscr{E} = E\{[X - g(Y)]^2\}$$

is minimized by picking the function g to be $g(y) = E\{X \mid y\}$. Make use of Problem 3-7.

Characteristic Functions

Looking at Eq. 3-48, we see that f_Z is given by the convolution of the density functions for X and Y. This suggests at least one application in which the Fourier transform of a density function might be useful. The quantity

$$M_X(v) = E\{e^{jvX}\} = \int_{-\infty}^{\infty} f_X(x)e^{jvx} \, dx \tag{3-50}$$

is referred to as the *characteristic function of the random variable X*. Note that

$$M_X(2\pi t) = \mathscr{F}^{-1}[f_X(x)] \tag{3-51}$$

(in which we think of t as the time variable and x the frequency variable) so that the density function must be given in terms of the characteristic function by

$$f_X(x) = \mathscr{F}[M_X(2\pi t)] = \int_{-\infty}^{\infty} M_X(2\pi t)e^{-j2\pi tx} \, dt$$

$$= \frac{1}{2\pi} \int_{-\infty}^{\infty} M_X(v)e^{-jvx} \, dv \tag{3-52}$$

Our derivation of Eq. 3-48 above could have been simplified by the use of characteristic functions. Assuming X and Y are statistically independent, we have

$$M_Z(v) - M_{X+Y}(v) = E\{e^{jv(X+Y)}\} = E\{e^{jvX} \, e^{jvY}\}$$

$$= E\{e^{jvX}\}E\{e^{jvY}\} = M_X(v)M_Y(v) \tag{3-53}$$

Equation 3-48 then follows directly from the time domain multiplication property. In practice, finding f_Z might be simplified by first inverse transforming f_X and f_Y and then taking the direct transform of the product $M_X(v)M_Y(v)$.

A second example of the utility of the characteristic function is its moment-generating property, given in Problem 3-12.

Problem 3-12. Show that

$$E\{(X)^n\} = (-j)^n \frac{d^n}{dv^n} M_X(v)\Big|_{v=0} \tag{3-54}$$

Problem 3-13. Let a and b be constants and let the random variable Z be related to a given random variable X by $Z = a(X - b)$. Show that

$$M_Z(v) = e^{-jvab} M_X(va) \tag{3-55}$$

Our main concern with the characteristic function will be using it to establish many useful properties of the multivariate gaussian distribution.

First we will consider the single-variate case. We defined a gaussian random variable X as one having the density function given by Eq. 3-20

$$f_X(x) = \frac{1}{\sqrt{2\pi}\,\sigma} \exp\left[\frac{-(x - m)^2}{2\sigma^2}\right] \tag{3-20}$$

We will work for convenience with the normalized random variable

$$Y = \frac{(X - m)}{\sigma} \tag{3-56}$$

whose density function is

$$f_Y(y) = \frac{1}{\sqrt{2\pi}} \exp\left\{\frac{-y^2}{2}\right\} \tag{3-57}$$

Let us find the characteristic function of Y. We could do this by evaluating the integral defining $M_Y(v)$ in terms of $f_Y(y)$. However, this integral is difficult to evaluate without making use of complex variable theory. For this reason, we derive $M_Y(v)$ by a method that requires only a knowledge of transform properties. We note first that $f_Y(y)$ satisfies the differential equation

$$\frac{d}{dy} f_Y(y) = -y f_Y(y) \tag{3-58}$$

Differentiating both sides of Eq. 3-52 with respect to x, we see that

$$\frac{d}{dx} f_X(x) = \mathscr{F}[-j2\pi t M_X(2\pi t)]$$

or

$$\mathscr{F}^{-1}\left[\frac{d}{dx} f_X(x)\right] = -j2\pi t M_X(2\pi t) \tag{3-59}$$

Similarly, differentiating both sides of Eq. 3-51 and using the time-differentiation property, we obtain

$$\frac{d}{dt} M_X(2\pi t) = \mathscr{F}^{-1}[j2\pi x f_X(x)]$$
$$= j2\pi \mathscr{F}^{-1}[x f_X(x)] \tag{3-60}$$

Taking the inverse Fourier transform of both sides of Eq. 3-58 and using the relations of Eqs. 3-59 and 3-60, we have the differential equation

$$-j2\pi t M_Y(2\pi t) = \frac{-1}{j2\pi} \frac{d}{dt} M_Y(2\pi t)$$

Upon setting $2\pi t = v$, this equation becomes

$$v M_Y(v) = -\frac{d}{dv} M_Y(v)$$

This differential equation has the solution

$$M_Y(v) = ce^{-v^2/2} \tag{3-61}$$

in which the constant c must be picked to meet a boundary condition. Now for any characteristic function

$$M_Y(0) = \int_{-\infty}^{\infty} f_Y(y)\, dy = 1 \tag{3-62}$$

Thus the constant c in Eq. 3-61 must be one, and the expression for $M_Y(v)$ is

$$M_Y(v) = e^{-v^2/2} \tag{3-63}$$

Making use of Eq. 3-55, we see that the original random variable X with the gaussian density function of Eq. 3-20 has the characteristic function given by

$$M_X(v) = e^{jvm}e^{-v^2\sigma^2/2} \tag{3-64}$$

Problem 3-14. Let the gaussian random variable X have the density function given by Eq. 3-20. Show that

$$E\{X\} = m; \quad \text{var}\{X\} = \sigma^2 \tag{3-65}$$

Problem 3-15. Let X be a gaussian random variable with mean zero and variance σ^2. Find

$$E\{(X)^n\} \quad n = 3, 4, 5, \ldots$$

Second-Order Description of a Set of Random Variables

Problem 3-7 indicates that the mean of a random variable is the "center of mass" of its probability distribution. Inequality 3-38, the Chebyshev inequality, indicates that the "spread" of the probability distribution of a random variable about its mean is bounded by its variance. Thus the mean and variance of a random variable give a simple and useful approximate description of the centering or location and the dispersion of the distribution of the random varible. This approximate description is particularly useful when an exact description of the distribution is not available or is analytically too cumbersome to work with.

This situation becomes particularly acute when we are dealing with a number of random variables, $X_1, X_2, \ldots, X_n$. When n is large, there are many instances when it is very cumbersome to exactly describe the joint probability distribution by means of the joint distribution function, joint density function, or joint characteristic function. In such a case, a useful partial description is given by the means and joint second central moments of the set of random variables.

In describing these quantities, it is often convenient to use matrix notation. The reader unfamiliar with such notation is referred to Appendix 1.

We denote the means of the random variables $X_1, X_2, \ldots, X_n$, by

$$m_k = E\{X_k\} \qquad k = 1, 2, \ldots, n \tag{3-66}$$

and the joint second central moments by

$$\lambda_{kj} = E\{(X_k - m_k)(X_j - m_j)\} \qquad k, j = 1, 2, \ldots, n \tag{3-67}$$

Let us regard the n-tuple of mean values as an n-dimensional vector $\mathbf{m}$; as a matrix we regard this vector as an n-row column vector

$$(m_1, m_2, \ldots, m_n) = \mathbf{m} \tag{3-68}$$

$$\mathbf{m} = \begin{bmatrix} m_1 \\ m_2 \\ \vdots \\ m_n \end{bmatrix} \tag{3-69}$$

The collection of second central moments we regard as the elements of an $n \times n$ matrix

$$\Lambda = \begin{bmatrix} \lambda_{11} & \lambda_{12} & \cdots & \lambda_{1n} \\ \lambda_{21} & \lambda_{22} & \cdots & \lambda_{2n} \\ \vdots & \vdots & \ddots & \vdots \\ \lambda_{n1} & \lambda_{n2} & \cdots & \lambda_{nn} \end{bmatrix} \tag{3-70}$$

We will regard n-tuples of dummy variables as n-dimensional vectors, using the form of notation of Eqs. 3-68 and 3-69. The differential of the dummy variable $\mathbf{x}$ we denote by $d\mathbf{x}$

$$d\mathbf{x} = dx_1\, dx_2 \ldots dx_n$$

The transpose of a column vector is a row vector; transposed vectors are denoted with primes

$$\mathbf{x}' = [x_1, x_2, \ldots, x_n] \tag{3-71}$$

We similarly denote the transpose of a matrix by a prime; that is, if Λ is the matrix whose k-jth element (element in the kth row and jth column) is λ_{kj}, then Λ' is the matrix whose k-jth element is λ_{jk}. The matrix Λ is *symmetric* if

$$\Lambda = \Lambda' \qquad \text{or} \qquad \lambda_{kj} = \lambda_{jk} \qquad k, j = 1, 2, \ldots, n \tag{3-72}$$

A matrix Λ is said to be *positive definite* if the (scalar) quantity $c' \Lambda c$ is positive for *all* nonzero vectors c; i.e.,

$$c' \Lambda c > 0 \qquad \text{all nonzero } c \qquad (3\text{-}73)$$

A matrix is termed *positive semi-definite* if the above condition is weakened to include equality

$$c' \Lambda c \geq 0 \qquad \text{all } c \qquad (3\text{-}74)$$

Problem 3-16. Let c denote an arbitrary vector with elements $(c_1, c_2, \ldots, c_n)$. Derive the following equations

$$E\left\{\left[\sum_{k=1}^{n} c_k(X_k - m_k)\right]^2\right\} = c' \Lambda c \qquad (3\text{-}75)$$

$$E\left\{\left[\sum_{k=1}^{n} c_k X_k\right]^2\right\} = c' \Lambda c + (m'c)^2 \qquad (3\text{-}76)$$

We may now observe the following two facts about the covariance matrix Λ defined by Eqs. 3-67 and 3-70. First, from Eq. 3-67 it follows directly that *a covariance matrix is always symmetric*. Secondly, it follows from Eq. 3-75 that *a covariance matrix is always positive semi-definite*.

Problem 3-17. Suppose that the covariance matrix of the set of random variables $\mathbf{X}$ is not positive definite but only semi-definite; i.e.,

$$c' \Lambda c \geq 0 \qquad \text{all } c$$

but there exists a c_0 for which

$$c_0' \Lambda c_0 = 0 \qquad c_0 \neq 0$$

Thus there exists a set of coefficients $c_1, c_2, \ldots, c_n$, not all zero, such that

$$E\left\{\left[\sum_{k=1}^{n} c_k(X_k - m_k)\right]^2\right\} = 0$$

(a) Verify that this can occur if one of the random variables has zero variance.
(b) Show that if all the X_k have nonzero variance, this implies that *there exists a linear relation among the random variables*; i.e. that for some choice of coefficients d_k and some index q

$$(X_q - m_q) = \sum_{\substack{k=1 \\ k \neq q}}^{n} d_k(X_k - m_k) \qquad (3\text{-}77)$$

By equality of these two random variables, we mean that their mean-square difference is zero

$$E\left\{\left[(X_q - m_q) - \sum_{\substack{k=1 \\ k \neq q}}^{n} d_k(X_k - m_k)\right]^2\right\} = 0$$

Multivariate Characteristic Functions[1]

The use of the characteristic function to describe a probability distribution is not limited to a single random variable. Associated with the set of random variables $X_1, X_2, \ldots, X_n$ is their *joint characteristic function*, defined by

$$
\begin{aligned}
M_{X_1 \cdots X_n}(\nu_1, \ldots, \nu_n) &= E\left\{ \prod_{k=1}^{n} e^{j\nu_k X_k} \right\} \\
&= E\left\{ \exp\left[j \sum_{k=1}^{n} \nu_k X_k \right] \right\} \\
&= \int_{-\infty}^{\infty} \cdots \int_{-\infty}^{\infty} \exp\left\{ j \sum_{k=1}^{n} \nu_k x_k \right\} f_{X_1 \cdots X_n}(x_1, \ldots, x_n) \\
&\quad \times dx_1 \ldots dx_n
\end{aligned}
\tag{3-78}
$$

Note that

$$
M_{X_1 \cdots X_n}(2\pi t_1, \ldots, 2\pi t_n) = \mathscr{F}^{-1}[f_{X_1 \cdots X_n}(x_1, \ldots, x_n)] \tag{3-79}
$$

The joint density function of this set of random variables can thus be obtained from the characteristic function by the multidimensional Fourier transform

$$
\begin{aligned}
f_{X_1 \cdots X_n}(x_1, \ldots, x_n) &= \mathscr{F}[M_{X_1 \cdots X_n}(2\pi t_1, \ldots, 2\pi t_n)] \\
&= \left(\frac{1}{2\pi}\right)^n \int_{-\infty}^{\infty} \cdots \int M_{X_1 \cdots X_n}(\nu_1, \ldots, \nu_n) e^{-j(\nu_1 x_1 + \cdots + \nu_n x_n)} \, d\nu_1 \ldots d\nu_n \\
\nu_k &= 2\pi t_k
\end{aligned}
\tag{3-80}
$$

There are several properties of multidimensional characteristic functions that follow almost directly from the above definition; these properties are quite useful and we state them here.

Property I.
$$
\begin{aligned}
M_{X_1 \cdots X_{k-1} X_{k+1} \cdots X_n}(\nu_1, \ldots, \nu_{k-1}, \nu_{k+1}, \ldots, \nu_n) \\
= M_{X_1 \cdots X_n}(\nu_1, \ldots, \nu_{k-1}, 0, \nu_{k+1}, \ldots, \nu_n)
\end{aligned}
\tag{3-81}
$$

Property II. The random variables $X_1, \ldots, X_n$ are all statistically independent if and only if

$$
M_{X_1 \cdots X_n}(\nu_1, \ldots, \nu_n) = \prod_{k=1}^{n} M_{X_k}(\nu_k) \tag{3-82}
$$

---

[1] The balance of this chapter is devoted to developing, in detail, the properties of the multivariate gaussian distribution. This material is essential as a prerequisite only to Chapters 8 and 9.

Property III.

$$E\{(X_1)^{n_1}\ldots(X_n)^{n_n}\}$$

$$= (-j)^N \frac{\partial^N}{\partial v_1^{n_1}\ldots\partial v_n^{n_n}} M_{X_1\cdots X_n}(v_1,\ldots,v_n)\Big|_{v_1 = v_2 = \cdots = v_n = 0}$$

$$N = \sum_{k=1}^{n} n_k \tag{3-83}$$

Problem 3-18. Show that properties I to III follow from the above definition of the multidimensional characteristic function.

3-3 The Multivariate Gaussian Distribution

In the final section of this chapter we turn our attention to describing the properties of a distribution that is extremely important in applications for two strong reasons:

(i) It is an accurate model for the random behavior of a large number of random experiments of widely differing physical origins. We will elaborate on this point in some length in Sec. 4-3.
(ii) It is a model which possesses many convenient mathematical properties.

The distribution that we have in mind is the *joint gaussian distribution*. We say that the random variables $(X_1, X_2, \ldots, X_n) = \mathbf{X}$ have a *joint gaussian distribution* if their joint characteristic function is of the form

$$M_{\mathbf{X}}(\mathbf{v}) = \exp\{j\mathbf{v}'\mathbf{m} - \tfrac{1}{2}\mathbf{v}' \Lambda \mathbf{v}\} \tag{3-84}$$

in which $\mathbf{m}$ is an arbitrary constant vector and Λ an arbitrary constant positive semidefinite symmetric matrix.

Note first that this definition of a multivariate gaussian distribution is consistent with the one-dimensional gaussian distribution, for the characteristic function associated with any single random variable X_k is

$$
\begin{aligned}
M_{X_k} &= M_{\mathbf{X}}(0, \ldots, 0, v_k, 0, \ldots, 0)\\
&= \exp\{jv_k m_k - \tfrac{1}{2}v_k{}^2\lambda_{kk}\}\\
&= \text{characteristic function of gaussian random}\\
&\qquad \text{variable with mean } m_k \text{ and variance } \lambda_{kk}.
\end{aligned}
$$

The definition of Eq. 3-84 is also self consistent in that the characteristic function of any subset of the random variables $X_1, X_2, \ldots, X_n$ also has a characteristic function of the same form as the characteristic function of Eq. 3-84 associated with the whole set.

We now wish to consider in detail some properties of the multivariate gaussian distribution.

Property I. The quantities appearing in the characteristic function in Eq. 3-84 are the mean vector and the covariance matrix of the set of random variables; i.e.,

$$E\{X_k\} = m_k \qquad k = 1, 2, \ldots, n \qquad (3\text{-}85)$$

$$E\{(X_j - m_j)(X_k - m_k)\} = \lambda_{jk} = \lambda_{kj} \qquad j, k = 1, 2, \ldots, n \qquad (3\text{-}86)$$

The proof of this property follows directly from property III of multi-dimensional characteristic functions and Eq. 3-84.

$$m_k = (-j) \frac{\partial}{\partial v_k} M_{\mathbf{X}}(\mathbf{v}) \bigg|_{\mathbf{v}=0}$$

$$E\{(X_j - m_j)(X_k - m_k)\} = E\{X_j X_k\} - m_j m_k$$

$$= (-j)^2 \frac{\partial^2}{\partial v_j \, \partial v_k} M_{\mathbf{X}}(\mathbf{v}) \bigg|_{\mathbf{v}=0} - m_j m_k$$

Note the implication of this property. Since the characteristic function of a multivariate gaussian distribution is determined by the vector **m** and the matrix Λ, we see that the *multivariate probability distribution of a set of gaussian random variables is determined completely by the means and second joint central moments of all the random variables.*

Property II. If all the random variables, $X_1, \ldots, X_n$, are *uncorrelated*

$$E\{(X_j - m_j)(X_k - m_k)\} = 0 \qquad j \neq k$$

then they are also *statistically independent*

$$f(x_1, \ldots, x_n) = \prod_{k=1}^{n} f(x_k)$$

Note that this is a special property of the gaussian distribution which does *not* apply in general. We have already given, in Problem 3-6, an example of a pair of random variables that were uncorrelated but not statistically independent.

To prove this property, we note that from property I we have by hypothesis

$$E\{(X_j - m_j)(X_k - m_k)\} = \lambda_{jk} = \delta_{jk}\lambda_{kk}$$

Thus

$$M_{\mathbf{X}}(\mathbf{v}) = \exp\left\{j\mathbf{v}'\mathbf{m} - \tfrac{1}{2}\mathbf{v}' \Lambda \, \mathbf{v}\right\} = \exp\left\{j\sum_{k=1}^{n} v_k m_k - \tfrac{1}{2}\sum_{k,m=1}^{n} v_k \lambda_{km} v_m\right\}$$

$$= \exp\left\{j\sum_{k=1}^{n} v_k m_k - \tfrac{1}{2}\sum_{k=1}^{n} v_k^2 \lambda_{kk}\right\}$$

$$= \prod_{k=1}^{n} \exp\left\{j v_k m_k - \tfrac{1}{2}v_k^2 \lambda_{kk}\right\} = \prod_{k=1}^{n} M_{X_k}(v_k)$$

Combining this equation with property II of the multidimensional characteristic function then yields the desired result.

Property III. Let $Y_1, \ldots, Y_m$ be a new set of random variables resulting from a linear transformation of the set of gaussian random variables $X_1, \ldots, X_n$

$$Y_j = \sum_{k=1}^{n} b_{jk} X_k \qquad j = 1, \ldots, m$$

or

$$\mathbf{Y} = B\mathbf{X} \tag{3-87}$$

in which B is an $m \times n$ matrix. Then the set of random variables $Y_1, \ldots, Y_m$ *also* have a *joint* gaussian distribution.

To prove this we consider the characteristic function of the Y random variables

$$M_{Y_1 \cdots Y_m}(\eta_1, \ldots, \eta_m) = M_{\mathbf{Y}}(\boldsymbol{\eta}) = E\{\exp [j\boldsymbol{\eta}'\mathbf{Y}]\}$$
$$= E\{\exp [j\boldsymbol{\eta}'B\mathbf{X}]\}$$
$$= M_{\mathbf{X}}(\boldsymbol{\nu}) \tag{3-88}$$

in which

$$\boldsymbol{\nu}' = \boldsymbol{\eta}'B \qquad \text{or} \qquad \boldsymbol{\nu} = B'\boldsymbol{\eta} \tag{3-89}$$

The last step in Eq. 3-88 results simply by recognizing

$$E\{\exp j\boldsymbol{\eta}'B\mathbf{X}\}$$

as the definition of $M_{\mathbf{X}}(B'\boldsymbol{\eta})$. Now combining Eqs. 3-84 and 3-88, we have

$$M_{\mathbf{Y}}(\boldsymbol{\eta}) = M_{\mathbf{X}}(\boldsymbol{\nu})|_{\boldsymbol{\nu}=B'\boldsymbol{\eta}}$$
$$= \exp\{j\boldsymbol{\nu}'\mathbf{m} - \tfrac{1}{2}\boldsymbol{\nu}' \Lambda \boldsymbol{\nu}\}|_{\boldsymbol{\nu}=B'\boldsymbol{\eta}}$$
$$= \exp\{j\boldsymbol{\eta}'B\mathbf{m} - \tfrac{1}{2}\boldsymbol{\eta}'B \Lambda B'\boldsymbol{\eta}\}$$
$$= \text{characteristic function of a set of gaussian random}$$
$$\text{variables with mean vector } B\mathbf{m} \text{ and covariance}$$
$$\text{matrix } B \Lambda B'. \tag{3-90}$$

Property IV. Given any set of gaussian random variables

$$\mathbf{X} = (X_1, \ldots, X_n)$$

which all have nonzero variance and which are linearly independent (i.e., there does not exist a relation among the random variables of the type given by Eq. 3-77 and hence Λ is positive definite), it is possible to form a new set of random variables $(Y_1, \ldots, Y_n)$ by a linear transformation on the X variables

$$\mathbf{Y} = B\mathbf{X}$$

in such a manner that the Y's are all statistically independent.

To prove the above property unfortunately requires two facts from matrix theory which are beyond the scope of the mathematical background assumed of the reader:

(1) Any symmetric matrix Λ can always be written in the form $\Lambda = ADA'$ in which D is a diagonal matrix and A an invertible square matrix.
(2) If Λ is positive definite all the elements of the diagonal matrix D are greater than zero.

The interested reader can find a discussion of these facts in Bellman [2].

In light of these two facts, we could pick the transformation $\mathbf{Y} = B\mathbf{X}$ discussed in Property III to have a transformation matrix $B = A^{-1}$. Then, since

$$\Lambda = ADA'$$

we have

$$D = A^{-1}\, \Lambda\, A'^{-1} = B\, \Lambda\, B' \qquad (3\text{-}91)$$

However, the right-hand side of this equation is the covariance matrix of $\mathbf{Y}$ by property III. Since the matrix D is diagonal, the Y's are uncorrelated and hence independent by property II.

Property V.   The density function of the set of gaussian random variables whose characteristic function is given by Eq. 3-84 is

$$f(\mathbf{x}) = \frac{1}{(2\pi)^{n/2}\, |\Lambda|^{\frac{1}{2}}}\, \exp\{-\tfrac{1}{2}(\mathbf{x} - \mathbf{m})'\, \Lambda^{-1}\, (\mathbf{x} - \mathbf{m})\} \qquad (3\text{-}92)$$

in which $|\Lambda|$ denotes the determinant of the covariance matrix Λ.

Conceptually, the most straightforward way of obtaining this result would be to take the multidimensional Fourier Transform of the characteristic function. However, this approach would be very difficult to actually carry out, and we proceed by a more circuitous method. We first consider the density function associated with the Y set of variables considered in Property IV. We use the notation

$$B\, \Lambda\, B' = D = \begin{bmatrix} \sigma_1{}^2 & & & 0 \\ & \sigma_2{}^2 & & \\ & & \ddots & \\ 0 & & & \sigma_n{}^2 \end{bmatrix} \qquad (3\text{-}93)$$

and

$$\mathbf{b} = B\mathbf{m} = \begin{bmatrix} b_1 \\ b_2 \\ \vdots \\ b_n \end{bmatrix} \qquad (3\text{-}94)$$

Note that $b_k = E\{Y_k\}$. In this notation the expression for $M_Y(\boldsymbol{\eta})$ is from Eq. 3-90

$$M_Y(\boldsymbol{\eta}) = \exp\{j\boldsymbol{\eta}'\mathbf{b} - \tfrac{1}{2}\boldsymbol{\eta}'D\boldsymbol{\eta}\}$$

$$= \exp\left\{\sum_{k=1}^{n} j\eta_k b_k - \tfrac{1}{2}\eta_k^2\sigma_k^2\right\}$$

$$= \prod_{k=1}^{n} \exp\{j\eta_k b_k - \tfrac{1}{2}\eta_k^2\sigma_k^2\} \tag{3-95}$$

The Y random variables are thus statistically independent gaussian random variables, the kth random variable having mean b_k and variance σ_k^2; the density function of this set of random variables must then be

$$f(\mathbf{y}) = \prod_{k=1}^{n} \frac{1}{\sqrt{2\pi}\,\sigma_k} \exp\left\{\frac{-(y_k - b_k)^2}{2\sigma_k^2}\right\} \tag{3-96}$$

Now let R_y denote some region in the y coordinates and R_x the same region described in the x coordinates; let A be the event

$$A = \{\mathfrak{a} : \mathbf{Y}(\mathfrak{a}) \in R_y\} = \{\mathfrak{a} : \mathbf{X}(\mathfrak{a}) \in R_x\}$$

then

$$P(A) = \int_{R_y} \cdots \int f_Y(y)\, dy \tag{3-97}$$

Let us now express this in terms of the x coordinates. Since

$$\frac{\partial y_m}{\partial x_j} = b_{mj}$$

the Jacobian of the transformation [3] is

$$\left|\frac{\partial y_m}{\partial x_j}\right| = |B|$$

in which the absolute magnitude of the determinant should be taken. The integral of Eq. 3-97 expressed in the x coordinates is thus [3]

$$P(A) = \int_{R_x} \cdots \int f_Y(B\mathbf{x})\,|B|\, d\mathbf{x} \tag{3-98}$$

But, since

$$P(A) = \int_{R_x} \cdots \int f_X(x)\, d\mathbf{x} \tag{3-99}$$

and since Eqs. 3-98 and 3-99 hold for an *arbitrary* region R_x, we must have

$$f_X(\mathbf{x}) = f_Y(B\mathbf{x})\,|B| \tag{3-100}$$

It should be pointed out that the reasoning following from Eq. 3-97 through Eq. 3-100 is general in the sense that it is valid for an arbitrary distribution.

Now

$$D = B \Lambda B'$$

so that, taking the determinant of both sides

$$|D| = |B| \, |\Lambda| \, |B'| = |B|^2 \, |\Lambda|$$

or

$$|B| = [|D|/|\Lambda|]^{1/2} \tag{3-101}$$

However, D is diagonal so that

$$|D| = \prod_{k=1}^{n} \sigma_k{}^2 \tag{3-102}$$

Equation 3-96 for $f_{\mathbf{Y}}(\mathbf{y})$ may thus be rewritten as

$$f_{\mathbf{Y}}(\mathbf{y}) = \frac{1}{(2\pi)^{n/2}} \prod_{k=1}^{n} \frac{1}{\sigma_k} \exp\{-\tfrac{1}{2}(\mathbf{y} - \mathbf{b})'D^{-1}(\mathbf{y} - \mathbf{b})\} \tag{3-103}$$

Combining Eqs. 3-100 through 3-103 leads finally to

$$f_{\mathbf{X}}(\mathbf{x}) = \frac{1}{(2\pi)^{n/2}} \frac{1}{|\Lambda|^{1/2}} \exp\{-\tfrac{1}{2}(B\mathbf{x} - B\mathbf{m})'D^{-1}(B\mathbf{x} - B\mathbf{m})\}$$

$$= \frac{1}{(2\pi)^{n/2}} \frac{1}{|\Lambda|^{1/2}} \exp\{-\tfrac{1}{2}(\mathbf{x} - \mathbf{m})'\Lambda^{-1}(\mathbf{x} - \mathbf{m})\} \tag{3-104}$$

Problem 3-19. Let X and Y be independent gaussian random variables with means m_x and m_y, and variances $\sigma_x{}^2$ and $\sigma_y{}^2$, respectively. Let

$$Z = X + Y$$

(a) Determine the characteristic function of Z.
(b) Determine the probability density function of Z.

Problem 3-20. Let X_1, X_2, X_3, and X_4 be random variables with a gaussian joint probability density function, and let their means all be zero. Show that

$$E(X_1 X_2 X_3 X_4) = E(X_1 X_2)E(X_3 X_4) + E(X_1 X_3)E(X_2 X_4) + E(X_1 X_4)E(X_2 X_3)$$

Hint: Make use of characteristic functions where appropriate.

Problem 3-21. Let X be a gaussian random variable with mean zero and unit variance. Let a new random variable Y be defined as follows: If $X = x$, then

$$Y = \begin{cases} x & \text{with probability } 1/2 \\ -x & \text{with probability } 1/2 \end{cases}$$

(a) Determine the joint probability density function of X and Y.
(b) Determine the probability density function of Y alone.
Note that although X and Y are both gaussian random variables, the joint probability density function of X and Y is not gaussian.

Problem 3-22.   The joint density function for two *zero mean* random variables X and Y which are gaussianly distributed is

$$f_{X,Y}(x, y) = \frac{1}{2\pi(1 - \rho^2)^{1/2}\sigma_x\sigma_y} \exp\left\{\frac{-1}{2(1 - \rho^2)}\left[\left(\frac{x}{\sigma_x}\right)^2 - \frac{2\rho xy}{\sigma_x\sigma_y} + \left(\frac{y}{\sigma_y}\right)^2\right]\right\}$$

in which

$$\sigma_x = E\{X^2\}, \qquad \sigma_y = E\{Y^2\}$$

and

$$\rho = \frac{E\{XY\}}{\sigma_x\sigma_y}$$

(a) *Sketch* lines of equidensity value for
   1. $\sigma_x = \sigma_y = 1, \quad \rho = 0$
   2. $\sigma_x = \sigma_y = 1, \quad \rho = +\frac{3}{4}$
   3. $\sigma_x = \sigma_y = 1, \quad \rho = -\frac{3}{4}$
   4. $\rho = 0, \quad \sigma_x = 5, \quad \sigma_y = 1$
(b) What does f_{XY} reduce to for $\rho = \pm 1$?   *Hint:* What is $f(x \mid y)$?

Problem 3-23.   Let X and Y be zero mean gaussian random variables with the density function given in Problem 3-22. Show that the conditional density function for X given that $Y = y$, $f_{X|Y}(x \mid y)$, is the density function of a gaussian random variable with mean $(\sigma_x/\sigma_y)\rho y$ and variance $(1 - \rho^2)\sigma_x^2$.

Problem 3-24.   Let X and Y be two arbitrary random variables with known means and joint second moments

$$m_x = E\{X\}, \qquad m_y = E\{y\}, \qquad \sigma_x^2 = E\{(X - m_x)^2\},$$
$$\sigma_y^2 = E\{(Y - m_y)^2\}, \qquad \mu_{xy} = E\{(X - m_x)(Y - m_y)\}$$

Suppose we cannot observe Y but can observe X and wish to *estimate* the value Y takes on in a given trial of an experiment from the value that X takes on.   For reasons of practicality, we may restrict this *estimate* of Y to be of the form

$$\hat{Y} = aX + b \tag{3-105}$$

(a) Find the values of a and b that minimize the mean-square estimation error

$$\mathscr{E} = E\{(Y - \hat{Y})^2\} \tag{3-106}$$

(b) For this choice of a and b, find an expression for $\mathscr{E}$.

Problem 3-25.   Reconsider Problem 3-24, assuming now that it is known that X and Y have a joint gaussian distribution.   If we make *no* restrictions on the form of our estimate (as we did in Eq. 3-105), what is the best estimate (function of X) to choose to minimize $\mathscr{E}$?   *Hint:* Make use of Problems 3-11 and 3-23.

Problem 3-26.   Prove the following inequality for two random variables X and Y:

$$E^2(XY) \leq E\{X^2\}E\{Y^2\}$$

Hint: Start with the inequality

$$E\{(X - cY)^2\} \geq 0 \qquad \text{for any value of } c$$

and make an appropriate choice for the constant c.   Note that if we apply this inequality to the random variables $|X|$ and $|Y|$, we obtain the inequality

$$E^2\{|XY|\} \leq E\{X^2\}E\{Y^2\} \tag{3-107}$$

known as the *Schwartz Inequality*.

Summary

In this chapter we have given an introduction to Probability Theory, starting from the basic structure of the theory.   However, we have single-mindedly pursued *only* those elements of the theory which are essential for the communications applications discussed in the remaining chapters. Thus our discussion is very far from complete and somewhat badly balanced.   The reader who wishes to pursue this theory in greater depth, breadth, or detail, is referred to references [1] and [4 to 7].   References [1] and [7] are directed only toward the mathematically inclined or mathematically mature reader.

REFERENCES

[1] Kolmogorov, A. N., *Foundations of the Theory of Probability*, Chelsea, New York, 1956.

[2] Bellman, R., *Introduction to Matrix Analysis*, McGraw-Hill Book Co., New York, 1960; pp. 44–54.

[3] Buck, R. C., *Advanced Calculus*, 2nd ed., McGraw-Hill Book Co., New York, 1965; pp. 296–311.

[4] Cramér, H., *The Elements of the Theory of Probability*, John Wiley and Sons, New York, 1955.

[5] Feller, W., *Probability Theory and Its Applications*, John Wiley and Sons, New York, 1960.

[6] Davenport, W., and W. Root, *Random Signals and Noise*, McGraw-Hill Book Co., New York, 1958; see especially Chapters 2, 3, 4, and 8.

[7] Cramér, H., *Mathematical Methods of Statistics*, Princeton University Press, Princeton, N. J., 1946.

Chapter 4

Random Processes

In the two preceding chapters we have discussed the description of (deterministic) signals and probability theory. In this chapter we complete our mathematical preparation by building on the material of the two preceding chapters to enable us to describe those entities of primary concern in communication: random signals.

4-1 Definitions and Description of the Probability Distribution of a Random Process

Let us consider an object of basic concern in communication; representing random signals such as the message signal generated by a microphone or the thermal noise generated across a resistor. Two things characterize our description of such signals:

1. The quantities we wish to describe are time functions defined on some observation interval $[0, T]$.
2. These signals are random in the sense that we cannot describe before the performance of the experiment what function will be observed.

Conceptually, this situation is in no way different from the basic probability model with a sample space of sample points, events that are collections of sample points, and a probability associated with each meaningful event. The distinction between this situation and a more familiar one is that *here our sample points or indecomposable outcomes are functions of time* rather than simpler quantities such as the number on a die, the angle of a rotating roulette wheel, etc. This observation might lead us to propose the following tentative definition of a random process. A *random process* is a *family of time functions* together with a *probability rule* which assigns a probability to *any* meaningful event associated with an observation of one of these functions.

This family of time functions with its associated probability rule is sometimes referred to as the *ensemble* of sample functions.

A function in this family is denoted by a function of two variables, $X(t, \partial)$, denoting that it is a function of time, t, and of which sample point ∂ is selected. For a fixed outcome of the experiment, that is, for a fixed sample point, say, ∂_k, the resulting time function $x(t, \partial_k)$ is termed a *sample function*. A sample function is sometimes written more simply as $x(t)$. Similarly, we sometimes denote the random process $X(t, \partial)$ by simply $X(t)$. If we fix t (to be, say, t_k), then the resulting quantity $X(t_k, \partial)$ varies with ∂ and is thus in fact a real-valued function of the sample point ∂, and thus is a *random variable*. This random variable $X(t_k, \partial)$ is usually denoted simply as X_{t_k}.

Although a random process is conceptually no different than more familiar random experiments (such as tossing a die), the problem *of specifying the probability distribution* is considerably more complicated. In certain simple examples, this may not be a problem. If, for example, the random variables $F(\partial)$ and $\Theta(\partial)$ have a joint density function $f(f, \theta)$, then for the random process

$$X(t, \partial) = A \cos [2\pi F(\partial)t + \Theta(\partial)] \qquad 0 \le t \le T$$

the probability of any event associated with this process is determined by the density function $f(f, \theta)$.

However, we will have to consider more general cases in which the random function may be, say, a noise signal which cannot be described by a finite number of random parameters (such as F and Θ above). In this general case it is possible to specify a countable (possibly infinite but denumerable) number of random variables with a joint distribution function; the distribution of the random process is then determined by the distribution of these random variables. This might be done as follows. Following our tentative definition of a random process, let us set up a sample space of all functions that are possible outcomes of the experiment. In engineering we are always concerned with functions which are well behaved, such as those having finite energy. On any observation interval $[0, T]$ we can represent any such function in the form

$$x(t) = \sum_{k=1}^{\infty} x_k \psi_k(t) \qquad 0 \le t \le T \qquad (4\text{-}1)$$

in which the $\psi_k(t)$ are some (*fixed*) complete orthonormal set. Thus let us consider taking our sample space to be the set of all functions which are of finite energy on the observation interval $[0, T]$. Any such function can be represented in the form of Eq. 4-1; different functions have different sets of coefficients x_k, but the $\psi_k(t)$ remain fixed. Thus any sample function in this space, $X(t, \jmath)$, can be represented as

$$X(t, \jmath) = \lim_{N \to \infty} \sum_{k=1}^{N} X_k(\jmath)\psi_k(t) \qquad (4\text{-}2)$$

the $X_k(\jmath)$ being random variables. For any value of N, the probability distribution of the function approximating $X(t, \jmath)$

$$\sum_{k=1}^{N} X_k(\jmath)\psi_k(t)$$

is determined by the joint distribution of the random variables $X_1, X_2, \ldots, X_N$.

Although the viewpoint we have taken thus far is sometimes useful and will be followed to a certain extent in Chapter 8, this view is not without pitfalls. To cite a specific example, suppose we wish to calculate the probability of the event that the random signal $X(t)$ takes on a value in a specified interval $[x_1, x_2]$ at a specified time t_0

$$x_1 \leq X(t_0, \jmath) \leq x_2$$

Such an event is quite meaningful, yet the exact value of its probability cannot be calculated from the joint distribution of the random variables $X_1, X_2, \ldots, X_N$, no matter what finite value of N is chosen.

For reasons of this nature and for reasons whose mathematical subtlety is far beyond the scope of this book, we will shift our view of a random process. We noted that the value of a random process at any specified time instant is a random variable. Furthermore, a complete observation of a random process consists of noting the value of the process for all time instants in some given observation interval. These remarks lead us to make the following formal definition of a Random Process.

— DEFINITION. A *random process* is a *collection of random variables* X_t indexed by the parameter t, t taking on all values in some specified time interval.

Following this definition and regarding a random process as a family of random variables, the probability distribution on the process is determined by the distribution on these random variables. Specifically, if for *any* value of n and *any* set of time instants $t_1, t_2, \ldots, t_n$, the distribution function

$$F(x_{t_1}, x_{t_2}, \ldots, x_{t_n}) = P\{X_{t_1} \leq x_{t_1}, X_{t_2} \leq x_{t_2}, \ldots, X_{t_n} \leq x_{t_n}\} \quad (4\text{-}3)$$

is given, then the probability of any meaningful event associated with the process can be determined.

Stationarity

Consider a resistor which has been kept in a temperature-controlled oven for an indefinitely long time.   Let $X(t)$ denote the voltage across the resistor and let A be the event defined by

$$A = (\jmath : a_j \leq X_{t_j} \leq b_j, j = 1, 2, \ldots, n\}$$

Now consider an arbitrary time shift τ; let B denote the event A observed with a shift of τ in the time origin

$$B = \{\jmath : a_j \leq X_{t_j + \tau} \leq b_j, j = 1, 2, \ldots, n\}$$

Typical events of this form are illustrated in Fig. 4-1.   Inasmuch as the conditions governing the generation of the noise signal are invariant with time, we would be somewhat surprised if shifting the time at which we made a set of observations affected the probability of any event associated with this set of observations.   In particular, for the events A and B above, we would expect to have

$$P(\text{A}) = P(\text{B})$$

These considerations lead us to the following.

DEFINITION.   A random process, $X(t, \jmath)$, is said to be *stationary* if for *any* positive integer n, *any* set of time instants $t_1, t_2, \ldots, t_n$ and *any* time shift τ, we have

$$F_{X_{t_1}, \ldots, X_{t_n}}(x_1, \ldots, x_n) = F_{X_{t_1 + \tau}, \ldots, X_{t_n + \tau}}(x_1, \ldots, x_n) \qquad (4\text{-}4)$$

that is,

$$P\{X_{t_k} \leq x_k, k = 1, 2, \ldots, n\} = P\{X_{t_k + \tau} \leq x_k, k = 1, 2, \ldots, n\} \quad (4\text{-}5)$$

Note that these equalities must hold as functions of the x_k; i.e., for all values of the x_k.

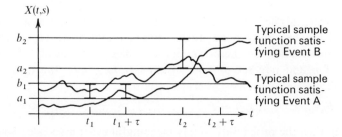

Figure 4-1   Events illustrating the concept of stationarity.

As an example, let us consider the random process consisting of a sine wave of random phase.

$$X(t, \jmath) = \sin [2\pi t + \Theta(\jmath)] \qquad (4\text{-}6)$$

in which $\Theta = \Theta(\jmath)$ is a random variable with uniform distribution

$$f(\theta) = \begin{cases} \dfrac{1}{2\pi} & 0 \le \theta \le 2\pi \\ 0 & \text{elsewhere} \end{cases} \qquad (4\text{-}7)$$

This random process is stationary. We establish this by considering the two probabilities

$$F_{X_{t_1},\dots,X_{t_n}}(x_1, \dots, x_n) = P\{\sin (2\pi t_j + \Theta) \le x_j, j = 1, 2, \dots, n\} \quad (4\text{-}8)$$

and

$$F_{X_{t_1+\tau},\dots,X_{t_n+\tau}}(x_1, \dots, x_n)$$
$$= P\{\sin (2\pi t_j + 2\pi\tau + \Theta) \le x_j, j = 1, 2, \dots, n\} \quad (4\text{-}9)$$

and showing that they are equal independent of the choice of τ, the time instants t_n, and the values of the x_n.

Let the event associated with Eq. 4-8 be denoted A and the event associated with Eq. 4-9 be denoted by B. We denote by I_A the set of all the values of θ in the interval $0 \le \theta < 2\pi$ for which the event A occurs. A typical such set is shown in Fig. 4-2a. Note that

$$P(A) = \frac{\text{length of } I_A}{2\pi}$$

Now suppose that A occurs for $\theta = \phi$; that is ϕ is in the set I_A. Then

$$\sin [2\pi t_k + \phi] \le x_k \qquad k = 1, 2, \dots, n$$

Since these inequalities may be written

$$\sin [2\pi(t_k + \tau) + \phi - 2\pi\tau] \le x_k \qquad k = 1, 2, \dots, n$$

the event B would occur for the value $\theta = \phi - 2\pi\tau$. Thus the event B occurs whenever θ takes on a value in the set $I_A(\tau)$, $I_A(\tau)$ denoting the set I_A shifted by an amount $2\pi\tau$ radians (to the left if τ is positive). This set is shown in Fig. 4-2b. We now denote by m the integer such that $m \le \tau < m + 1$.

Then let $I_A(\tau, m + 1)$ and $I_A(\tau, m)$ denote respectively the portions of $I_A(\tau)$ lying in the intervals $-(m + 1)2\pi \le \theta < -m2\pi$ and $-m2\pi \le \theta < -(m - 1)2\pi$. Since the random variable Θ takes on values in the interval $0 \le \theta < 2\pi$, let us shift the sets $I_A(\tau, m + 1)$ and $I_A(\tau, m)$ to the right by

(a)

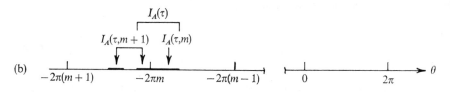

(b)

(c)

Figure 4-2   The sets used in proving the stationarity of the example:
(a) I_A;
(b) $I_A(\tau)$, $I_A(\tau, m)$, and $I_A(\tau, m + 1)$;
(c) $I_A(\tau, 0)$ and $I_A(\tau, 1)$.

$2\pi(m + 1)$ and $2\pi m$, respectively, denoting the shifted sets by $I_A(\tau, 1)$ and $I_A(\tau, 0)$. These shifted sets are shown in Fig. 4-2c. Note that they do not overlap and they both lie in the interval $0 \le \theta < 2\pi$. Since the function $\sin[2\pi t + \theta]$ is periodic in θ with period 2π, the event B occurs whenever Θ falls in the set $I_A(\tau, 1)$ or the set $I_A(\tau, 0)$. From our construction of $I_A(\tau, 1)$ and $I_A(\tau, 0)$, it is clear that

$$\text{length } I_A = \text{length } I_A(\tau, 1) + \text{length } I_A(\tau, 0)$$

Thus,

$$P(\text{A}) = \frac{\text{length } I_A}{2\pi} = \frac{\text{length } I_A(\tau, 1) + \text{length } I_A(\tau, 0)}{2\pi} = P(\text{B})$$

which completes our proof that the process of this example is stationary.

Let us make the following observation. Let $g(x)$ denote any well-behaved function, and consider the random variable $G_t = g(X_t)$. If $X(t, \sigma)$ is a stationary random process, then

$$E\{g(X_t)\} = \int_{-\infty}^{\infty} g(x) f_{X_t}(x) \, dx$$

$$= \int_{-\infty}^{\infty} g(x) f_{X_{t+\tau}}(x) \, dx = E\{g(X_{t+\tau})\} \qquad (4\text{-}10)$$

Since this must hold for any τ, we have that

$$E\{g(X_t)\} = \text{constant independent of } t \qquad (4\text{-}11)$$

for any stationary process $X(t)$ and any (well behaved) function g.

The Mean and Covariance of a Random Process

In many instances it may be that we cannot determine (by means, say, of suitable measurements) the probability distribution of a random process. A similar situation can arise even in the case of a random variable; we must sometimes content ourselves with only a partial description of the distribution of the random variable. Frequently the *mean* and *variance* of a random variable are taken to given a crude but useful description of its distribution. Similarly, when we have n random variables $X_1, X_2, \ldots, X_n$, we take the means

$$m_j = E(X_j) \qquad j = 1, 2, \ldots, n \qquad (4\text{-}12)$$

and covariances

$$\lambda_{jk} = E\{(X_j - m_j)(X_k - m_k)\} \qquad j, k = 1, 2, \ldots, n \qquad (4\text{-}13)$$

as measures of a partial description of the joint distribution of these random variables.

In the case of a random process there are corresponding quantities that give a useful partial description of the process. We define the *mean* or *mean function* of a random process $X(t)$ to be the function of time given by

$$m_x(t) = E\{X_t\} \qquad (4\text{-}14)$$

and the *covariance function* to be the function of *two time variables t and s* given by

$$L_x(t, s) = E\{[X_t - m_x(t)][X_s - m_x(s)]\} \qquad (4\text{-}15)$$

Another quantity often used is the *correlation function* or *autocorrelation function*

$$R_x(t, s) = E\{X_t X_s\} = L_x(t, s) + m_x(t)\, m_x(s) \qquad (4\text{-}16)$$

For a stationary process, these quantities assume a simpler form. The remarks leading up to Eq. 4-11 apply to the mean function,

$$m_x(t) = E\{X_t\} = E\{X_{t+\tau}\} = m_x(t + \tau) \qquad \text{all } \tau \qquad (4\text{-}17)$$

so that

$$m_x(t) = m_x = \text{a constant} \qquad (4\text{-}18)$$

for a stationary process.   Next, consider the covariance function.

$$L_x(t, s) = E\{(X_t - m)(X_s - m)\}$$
$$= \int_{-\infty}^{\infty} \int_{-\infty}^{\infty} (x - m)(y - m) f_{X_t X_s}(x, y) \, dx \, dy$$
$$= \int_{-\infty}^{\infty} \int_{-\infty}^{\infty} (x - m)(y - m) f_{X_{t+\tau} X_{s+\tau}}(x, y) \, dx \, dy \quad (4\text{-}19)$$

This holds for any value of τ.   If we set $\tau = -s$, Eq. 4-19 becomes

$$L_x(t, s) = \int_{-\infty}^{\infty} (x - m)(y - m) f_{X_{t-s} X_0}(x, y) \, dx \, dy$$
$$= L_x(t - s, 0) \quad (4\text{-}20)$$

which is a function of only the difference $t - s$.   Thus, for a *stationary* process $X(t)$, the *covariance function* is in actuality only a function of the *difference* between the *two observations times* in question.   We will denote the covariance function in the stationary case by

$$L_x(\tau) = E\{(X_{t+\tau} - m)(X_t - m)\} \quad (4\text{-}21)$$

Although it is an abuse of notation to use the same letter (L) for this function of a single variable and the function of two variables defined by Eq. 4-15, the meaning is clear.   From Eq. 4-16 it then follows that the correlation function of a stationary process, $X(t)$, is also a function of a single variable which we denote by

$$R_x(\tau) = E\{X_{t+\tau} X_t\} \quad (4\text{-}22)$$

It should be pointed out that the conditions of Eq. 4-18 and either Eq. 4-21 or 4-22 are *not* sufficient to guarantee that the process $X(t)$ is stationary.   A process which is not stationary but for which these conditions hold is said to be *stationary in the wide sense* or simply *wide-sense stationary*.

The correlation function of a wide-sense stationary process must have two properties.   First we note that it must be an even function, for

$$R_x(\tau) = E\{X_{t+\tau} X_t\} = E\{X_t X_{t+\tau}\}$$
$$= E\{X_{t-\tau} X_t\} = R_x(-\tau) \quad (4\text{-}23)$$

Secondly,

$$|R_x(\tau)| \le R_x(0) \quad \text{for all } \tau \quad (4\text{-}24)$$

This condition follows directly by writing

$$E\{[X_{t+\tau} - X_t]^2\} \ge 0 \quad (4\text{-}25)$$

and then expanding the left-hand side of the inequality. Similar remarks apply to $L_x(\tau)$,

$$L_x(\tau) = L_x(-\tau) \qquad (4\text{-}26)$$

and

$$|L_x(\tau)| \leq L_x(0) \qquad (4\text{-}27)$$

In certain situations we will be forced to consider the joint statistics of two different random processes $X(t)$ and $Y(t)$. Such a situation might arise, for example, when $X(t)$ represents an information-bearing signal appearing in the front-end of a receiver and $Y(t)$ represents the noise generated in the front-end of the receiver. In such a situation, we will find it useful to consider the *cross-correlation function between* the processes $X(t)$ and $Y(t)$:

$$R_{xy}(t, s) = E\{X_t Y_s\} \qquad (4\text{-}28)$$

Again, if the processes are *jointly stationary* (i.e., the joint distribution of the set of random variables $X_{t_1}, \ldots, X_{t_n}, Y_{s_1}, \ldots, Y_{s_m}$ is invariant to a time shift for all n and m and any choice of the time instants $t_1, \ldots, t_n$, $s_1, \ldots, s_m$) this function is a function of only a single variable. For convenience (at the expense of abusing notation) we denote this function again by

$$R_{xy}(\tau) = E\{X_{t+\tau} Y_t\} \qquad (4\text{-}29)$$

For a cross-correlation function, the property similar to that expressed by Eq. 4-24 is $R_{xy}^2(\tau) \leq R_x(0) R_y(0)$. The property corresponding to Eq. 4-23 is

$$R_{xy}(\tau) = R_{yx}(-\tau) \qquad (4\text{-}30)$$

The cross-covariance function of the two processes is also defined in the obvious way:

$$L_{xy}(t, s) = E\{[X_t - m_x(t)][Y_s - m_y(s)]\} \qquad (4\text{-}31)$$

and remarks similar to those preceding Eqs. 4-29 and 4-30 are pertinent.

EXAMPLE. Up to this point our discussion has been a sequence of definitions and formal statements of properties. To give meaning to these properties and definitions, it will be useful if we start with a physical description of a random process and derive some of its statistical properties. For this purpose, we consider a signal which takes on only the values ± 1 and switches back and forth between these two values at random event times. A typical sample function is shown in Fig. 4-3. Such a process might be generated by a facsimile signal arising from scanning a black and white picture (such as the page of a book).

We make the following assumptions concerning the nature of the event points at which the process switches from one value to the other:

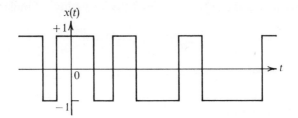

Figure 4-3   The random telegraph signal.

1. In any *infinitesimal* time interval dt, the probability of *more than one* event point occurring is zero (that is, it goes to zero faster than dt as dt approaches zero); the probability of exactly one event point occurring in any infinitesimal interval of length dt is $v\,dt$.
2. Let I_1 and I_2 be any two *disjoint* time intervals: we assume the number of event points occurring in I_1 to be statistically independent of the number occurring in I_2

We also assume that if $t = t_0$ is the start of our observation interval, then

$$P\{X_{t_0} = +1\} = P\{X_{t_0} = -1\} = \tfrac{1}{2} \qquad (4\text{-}32)$$

Semi-random ?

The process defined by these assumptions is sometimes termed the *random telegraph wave*.

Our first step in examining the probabilistic behavior of this process is to find the probability distribution for the number of event points that occur in an interval of given length.   We note that assumptions 1 and 2 are independent of the time origin; thus we have

$$
\begin{aligned}
P(k; t, t + \tau) &= P\{\text{exactly } k \text{ event points occurring} \\
&\qquad \text{between } t \text{ and } t + \tau\} \\
&= P\{\text{exactly } k \text{ event points occurring} \\
&\qquad \text{in any interval of duration } \tau\} \qquad (4\text{-}33)
\end{aligned}
$$

Since the probability of this event depends only on k and τ, we denote it by

$$P(k; t, t + \tau) = Q(k; \tau)$$

We proceed to derive the expression for $Q(k; \tau)$ by starting with $Q(0; \tau)$. Combining assumptions 1 and 2 we have

$$
\begin{aligned}
Q(0; \tau + d\tau) &= P(0; t, t + \tau + d\tau) \\
&= P(0; t, t + \tau)P(0; t + \tau, t + \tau + d\tau) \\
&= Q(0; \tau)Q(0; d\tau) \\
&= Q(0; \tau)[1 - v\,d\tau] \qquad (4\text{-}34)
\end{aligned}
$$

in which the last equality follows from

$$Q(0; d\tau) = 1 - Q(1; d\tau) = 1 - \nu \, d\tau$$

Recombining terms, we have

$$\frac{dQ(0; \tau)}{d\tau} = \frac{Q(0; \tau + d\tau) - Q(0; \tau)}{d\tau} = -\nu Q(0; \tau) \qquad (4\text{-}35)$$

The solution to this differential equation is

$$Q(0; \tau) = ce^{-\nu\tau}$$

in which c may be any constant and τ any non-negative number standing for the duration of the observation interval. However, we know that

$$Q(0; 0) = P\{0 \text{ event points in zero time}\} = 1$$

thus $c = 1$ and we have

$$Q(0; \tau) = e^{-\nu\tau} \qquad (4\text{-}36)$$

Next consider $Q(k; \tau)$. From assumptions 1 and 2 we have

$$
\begin{aligned}
Q(k; \tau + d\tau) &= P(k; t, t + \tau + d\tau) \\
&= P(k - 1; t, t + \tau)P(1; t + \tau, t + \tau + d\tau) \\
&\quad + P(k; t, t + \tau)P(0; t + \tau, t + \tau + d\tau) \\
&= Q(k - 1; \tau)Q(1; d\tau) + Q(k; \tau)Q(0; d\tau) \\
&= Q(k - 1; \tau)\nu \, d\tau + Q(k; \tau)[1 - \nu \, d\tau]
\end{aligned}
$$

Upon rearranging terms, this leads to the differential equation

$$\frac{d}{d\tau} Q(k; \tau) + \nu Q(k; \tau) = \nu Q(k - 1; \tau) \qquad (k \geq 1) \qquad (4\text{-}37)$$

with the solution [1]

$$Q(k; \tau) = ce^{-\nu\tau} + e^{-\nu\tau} \int_0^\tau \nu Q(k - 1; \zeta)e^{\nu\zeta} \, d\zeta \qquad (4\text{-}38)$$

But

$$Q(k; 0) = 0 \qquad \text{for } k \geq 1$$

thus the homogeneous solution term appearing in Eq. 4-38 must be zero and

$$Q(k; \tau) = e^{-\nu\tau} \int_0^\tau \nu Q(k - 1; \zeta)e^{\nu\zeta} \, d\zeta \qquad (4\text{-}39)$$

Starting with the expression of Eq. 4-36 for $Q(0; \tau)$ we can recursively solve for $Q(k; \tau)$ from $Q(k - 1; \tau)$. This yields the result

$$Q(k; \tau) = \frac{e^{-\nu\tau}(\nu\tau)^k}{k!}$$

$$= P\{k \text{ event points occurring in any}$$
$$\text{interval of duration } \tau\} \qquad (4\text{-}40)$$

This distribution for the number of event points is termed the *Poisson Distribution*. It is important in many physical applications; one of these, shot noise, is discussed in Section 4-3.

Now let us use this information to find the correlation function of the process. We have

$$R_x(\tau) = E\{X_t X_{t+\tau}\}$$
$$= (+1)P\{X_t \text{ and } X_{t+\tau} \text{ have the same sign}\}$$
$$+ (-1)P\{X_t \text{ and } X_{t+\tau} \text{ have different signs}\}$$
$$= (+1)P\{\text{even number of event points between } t \text{ and } t + \tau\}$$
$$+ (-1)P\{\text{odd number of event points between } t \text{ and } t + \tau\}$$
$$= +1e^{-\nu\tau} \left[\overset{k \text{ even}}{\underset{k=0}{\overset{\infty}{\sum}} \frac{(\nu\tau)^k}{k!}} - \overset{k \text{ odd}}{\underset{k=1}{\overset{\infty}{\sum}} \frac{(\nu\tau)^k}{k!}} \right]$$
$$= e^{-\nu\tau} \sum_{k=0}^{\infty} \frac{(-\nu\tau)^k}{k!}$$
$$= e^{-\nu\tau}e^{-\nu\tau} = e^{-2\nu\tau} \qquad (4\text{-}41)$$

The above equation was formulated with τ denoting the positive time duration between two observation times; that is, assuming that $t + \tau \geq t$. Since $R_x(\tau)$ is even, we have for all τ

$$R_x(\tau) = e^{-2\nu|\tau|} \qquad (4\text{-}42)$$

Lastly, using Eq. 4-32, we have for any $t \geq t_0$,

$$P\{X_t = +1\} = P\{X_{t_0} = +1\}P\{\text{even number of event points in interval}$$
$$\text{of duration } t - t_0\}$$
$$+ P\{X_{t_0} = -1\}P\{\text{odd number of event points in}$$
$$\text{interval of duration } t - t_0\}$$
$$= \tfrac{1}{2}[P\{\text{even number of event points in interval of duration}$$
$$t - t_0\}$$
$$+ P\{\text{odd number of event points in interval of}$$
$$\text{duration } t - t_0\}]$$
$$= \tfrac{1}{2} = P\{X_t = -1\} \qquad (4\text{-}43)$$

Thus,

$$E\{X_t\} = 0 = m_x(t) \qquad t \geq t_0 \tag{4-44}$$

This example illustrates how the probabilistic structure of a process can be derived starting only from fairly simple assumptions about the underlying probabilistic mechanism stated in physical terms.

Problem 4-1. Let the random variable N (which might represent the number of event points occurring in some fixed interval above) have a Poisson Distribution

$$P(N = n) = \frac{e^{-\lambda}\lambda^n}{n!} \qquad n = 0, 1, 2, \ldots \tag{4-45}$$

(a) Determine the mean and variance of N.
(b) Determine the characteristic function of N.

Problem 4-2. Let M and N be statistically independent random variables, each of which has the Poisson distribution of Problem 4-1. Find the distribution of the sum random variable $Q = M + N$.

Problem 4-3. Consider a random process whose behavior is determined by the Poisson distributed event points as in the above example. Again the value of $X(t)$ will remain constant (with *time*) between every pair of event points. The value $X(t)$ takes on between any two event points is a gaussian random variable with mean zero and variance σ^2; furthermore, this value is statistically independent of the value assumed between any other pair of event points.
(a) Find $E\{X_t\}$.
(b) Find $R_x(\tau)$.

Problem 4-4. Suppose we observe the value of a random process $X(t)$ at time t_0 and wish to predict or estimate the value of $X(t)$ at time $t_0 + \tau$, $\tau > 0$. Assume that $X(t)$ is wide-sense stationary with known mean m_x and known covariance function $L_x(\tau)$. Consider estimating $X_{t_0 + \tau}$ by an estimate of the form

$$\hat{X}_{t_0 + \tau} = aX_{t_0} + b$$

(a) Find the values of a and b as functions of the prediction time τ that minimize the mean-square prediction error

$$\mathscr{E}(\tau) = E\{(X_{t_0 + \tau} - \hat{X}_{t_0 + \tau})^2\}$$

(b) Find $\mathscr{E}(\tau)$ as a function of τ. Would you expect $\mathscr{E}(\tau)$ to increase or decrease with increasing τ in most physical situations? What sort of corresponding behavior does this imply for $L_x(\tau)$? *Hint:* Make use of Problem 3-24.

The Gaussian Random Process

We say that a random process $X(t)$ is a *gaussian random process* if, for *any n* and *any* choice of time instants $t_1, t_2, \ldots, t_n$ the random variables $X_{t_1}, X_{t_2}, \ldots, X_{t_n}$ have a joint gaussian distribution.

In Section 3-3 we saw (property I of the gaussian distribution) that the distribution of the set of gaussian random variables $X_{t_1}, X_{t_2}, \ldots, X_{t_n}$, was completely determined from the means

$$m(t_k) = E(X_{t_k}) \qquad k = 1, 2, \ldots, n$$

and covariances

$$L(t_j, t_k) = E\{[X_{t_j} - m(t_j)][X_{t_k} - m(t_k)]\} \qquad j, k = 1, 2, \ldots, n$$

However, for *any n* and *any* choice of time instants these quantities may be determined respectively from the mean function and covariance function. *Thus the distribution of a gaussian random process is completely determined by its mean and covariance functions.* As we have already noted this is not true for a general process; this is one property that makes the gaussian process particularly convenient to work with.

A second property of a gaussian process which is not true for a general process is the following: let $X(t)$ be a gaussian process with

$$E\{X_t\} = m \qquad \text{a constant}$$
$$E\{(X_t - m)(X_s - m)\} = L_x(t - s) \qquad \text{a function of } t - s$$

then $X(t)$ is stationary. This property follows directly from the first property mentioned above; the reader should verify this to his own satisfaction.

A third convenient property of gaussian random processes is that if the input to a linear filter is a gaussian process, then the output of the filter is also a gaussian process. This point is discussed in detail in Sec. 4-2.

The above properties make the gaussian process a very convenient one to work with mathematically. Moreover the gaussian process is a good model of a large number of processes of differing physical origins in which the observed random signal is the result of a superposition of a large number of individual random elements. This result is known as the *central limit theorem* which is discussed in its simplest form in Appendix 2. Shot noise, a physical example of a gaussian process is discussed in section 4-3. The widespread occurrence of physical processes for which a gaussian process is a good model, together with the ease with which the gaussian process is handled mathematically, make it very important in physical applications.

Problem 4-5. Is the process of Problem 4-3 a gaussian process? Explain. *Hint:* Make use of the results of Problem 3-23.

Ergodicity

In the case of the random telegraph wave we were able to start from a set of physical hypotheses about the process and derive many statistical properties of interest.   In some cases, we do not have sufficient information to do this and are faced with the problem of trying to measure the statistical properties of interest.

Consider simply trying to measure $m_x(t) = E\{X_t\}$.   This average is over our ensemble of possible sample functions; to evaluate it we would have to observe $x(t)$ for a large number of sample functions picked from the ensemble according to the given probability distribution and take the average of these observations.   In certain simple cases we might actually conceive of doing this.   If we were interested in estimating the average noise voltage across a resistor, we might consider placing a large number of similarly manufactured resistors in the same environment and simultaneously measuring the voltage across all of them at time t and taking the average of these measurements.   The law of large numbers (see Problem 3-8) would then dictate that our sample average over the set of resistors would approach the ensemble average m_x as the number of resistors in the set was increased. However, in general, where the source of the process is more complicated than a resistor, such a procedure would be too costly.   Reflecting on the difficulties of this procedure, we note also that the observations had to be made *simultaneously*.   However, *if* the process of interest is *stationary*, this requirement is not necessary; the observations from the different sample functions could be made at different times, and the average of these would still approach $E\{X_t\} = m_x$ (a constant) as the number of sample functions observed became large.

One is then led to ask if it would be possible to make all these observations from the same sample function.   If the times $t_1, t_2, \ldots, t_n$ are widely spaced, then we would intuitively expect the values $x(t_1), x(t_2), \ldots, x(t_n)$ to be approximately independent, so that as n grows large

$$\frac{1}{n} \sum_{k=1}^{n} x(t_k) \approx E\{X_t\} = m_x$$

Those stationary processes for which this property pertains are referred to as *ergodic*.   In particular, we make the following definition.

DEFINITION.   Let $X(t)$ be a stationary random process and let $g(t)$ denote any function of the sample function $x(t)$; for example,

$$g(t) = x(t)$$

or

$$g(t) = x^2(t)$$

or

$$g(t) = x(t)\,x(t + \tau) \qquad \tau \text{ a fixed value}$$

Consistent with past notation, we denote the random variable corresponding to observations of the process $G(t)$ at time t by G_t. Then if for *any* such function $g(t)$ and any[1] sample function from the ensemble we have

$$\lim_{T \to \infty} \frac{1}{2T} \int_{-T}^{T} g(t)\, dt = E\{G_t\} \qquad (4\text{-}46)$$

we say that the process $x(t)$ is *ergodic*.

There are two points that we should note with respect to this definition:

(1) *It makes no sense to speak of ergodicity for a nonstationary process.* In general, the ensemble average is a function of time

$$E\{G_t\} = m_g(t)$$

but does not depend on σ, the sample point. The time average of $g(t)$, which we denote by $\langle g(t) \rangle$, is a function of σ; that is, of which sample function we are observing

$$\langle g(t) \rangle = \lim_{T \to \infty} \frac{1}{2T} \int_{-T}^{T} g(t)\, dt = \langle g(t) \rangle(\sigma)$$

but is *not* a function of time. Only if $E\{G_t\} = m_g$, a constant, can we hope for the random variable $\langle g(t) \rangle(\sigma)$ to equal the constant m_g, this occurring only when the process $X(t)$ is ergodic.

(2) *Unfortunately, there is usually no simple criterion for determining whether a process is ergodic.* There are certain ergodic theorems [2], which give conditions under which we can interchange time and ensemble averages, but, except for certain simple cases, it is usually very difficult to establish if a process meets the conditions of these theorems. We are thus usually forced to consider the physical origin of the process and make a somewhat intuitive judgment as to whether it is reasonable to interchange time and ensemble averages. If it is possible for the source to "get into a rut" so that its behavior is not typical of all sources in the ensemble, then the process will certainly not be ergodic. In the special case in which the process $X(t)$ is stationary *and gaussian*, it can be shown [3] that the process is ergodic if its correlation function is continuous and absolutely integrable.

$$\int_{-\infty}^{\infty} |R_x(\tau)|\, d\tau < \infty$$

---

[1] Strictly speaking, we require that the equality of Eq. 4-46 hold for all sample functions except a set of probability zero. By a set of sample functions of probability zero, we mean that the probability of observing any function in the set in one trial of the experiment is zero; that is, it is possible but completely unlikely for such a function to occur.

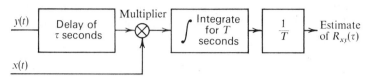

Figure 4-4   Block diagram of system for estimating $R_{xy}(\tau)$.

For a stationary ergodic process, then, the correlation function $R_x(\tau)$ can be estimated by approximating the time average

$$R_x(\tau) = \langle x(t)\, x(t + \tau)\rangle \triangleq \lim_{T \to \infty} \frac{1}{2T} \int_{-T}^{T} x(t)\, x(t + \tau)\, dt$$

We can only approximate this time average inasmuch as we cannot use an infinite observation time and, in addition, are sometimes forced to approximate the integral by a sum. For a discussion of the errors in such estimates, see Davenport and Root, pages 107 and 108, [4]. Cross-correlation functions $R_{xy}(\tau)$ may be estimated in a similar manner, provided the processes $X(t)$ and $Y(t)$ are *jointly ergodic*; that is, Eq. 4-46 holds with $g(t)$ a function of both the sample functions $x(t)$ and $y(t)$. Figure 4-4 shows in block diagram form a system suitable for estimating $R_{xy}(\tau)$.

Problem 4-6.   Consider the random process
  (i) $X(t) = a \cos [2\pi f_0 t + \Theta]$ Yes ergodic
  (ii) $X(t) = A \cos [2\pi f_0 t + \Theta]$ Not ergodic
In the first case a is a constant, in the second A is a random variable statistically independent of the random variable Θ. In both cases the random variable Θ is uniformly distributed between 0 and 2π. State in both cases whether or not the process $X(t)$ is ergodic and indicate why in each case.

4-2   Passage of a Random Process through a Linear Filter

We now wish to consider what occurs when a random process $X(t)$ is applied as an input to a linear time-invariant filter with impulse response $h(t)$. This situation is depicted in Fig. 4-5. The resulting filter output is

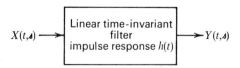

Figure 4-5   Passage of a random process through a linear filter.

also a random process; for any particular input sample function (i.e., any particular sample point $\jmath$) the resulting output sample function may be calculated as

$$Y(t, \jmath) = \int_0^\infty h(\tau) \, X(t - \tau, \jmath) \, d\tau \qquad (4\text{-}47)$$

We now wish to relate the statistical properties of the output process $Y(t)$ to those of the input process $X(t)$. Specifically, we consider the two questions:

1. How can the mean and covariance functions of Y be determined from those of X?
2. How can the complete probability distribution of the process $Y(t)$ be determined from that of $X(t)$?

Let us consider the second question first, inasmuch as we can give only a partial answer to this point. In general, it is not possible to find just the distribution of the single random variable $Y_{t'}$ (t' fixed but arbitrary) even if we know the complete distribution of the input process $X(t)$, $-\infty < t < \infty$. There is, however, one case in which it is possible to determine completely the distribution of the $Y(t)$ process; that is when the input random process is gaussian.

Theorem. Let $Y(t)$ denote the output of a linear system whose input is a gaussian random process $X(t)$. Then $Y(t)$ is a gaussian random process.

This theorem is fundamental and of great practical importance and thus deserves proof. To prove it, we consider approximating $Y(t)$ by a process $Y_{\Delta,N}(t)$ formed by an approximation to the integral of Eq. 4-47:

$$Y_{\Delta,N}(t, \jmath) = \sum_{k=0}^{N} h(k\Delta) X(t - k\Delta, \jmath)\Delta \qquad (4\text{-}48)$$

Now pick *any* n and *any* set of time instants $t_1, t_2, \ldots, t_n$ and consider the Y random variables

$$Y_{\Delta,N,t_j} \qquad j = 1, 2, \ldots, n$$

and the X random variables

$$X_{t_j - k\Delta} \qquad \begin{aligned} &j = 1, 2, \ldots, n \\ &k = 0, 1, \ldots, N \end{aligned}$$

This set of Y random variables is obtained by a linear transformation from the set of X random variables. Since $X(t)$ is a gaussian random process, this set of X random variables has a joint gaussian distribution, and hence by property III of the joint gaussian distribution, the above set of Y random variables also must have a *joint* gaussian distribution. We have thus shown that the process $Y_{\Delta,N}(t)$ which approximates $Y(t)$ is gaussian. Since this approximation can be made as close as desired by making Δ sufficiently small and N sufficiently large, the process $Y(t)$ must be gaussian.[1]

There are two points that deserve comment. First, note that when the random process $X(t)$ is gaussian, we will be able to determine completely the distribution of the process $Y(t)$ once we have a way of relating the mean and covariance functions of the Y process to those of the X process. Secondly, although our proof above was carried out for a causal time-invariant linear system, the property is true for an arbitrary linear system. The reader familiar with the concept of a time-varying impulse response can easily make the necessary changes in the proof.

We now turn to finding the mean and correlation function of the process $Y(t)$. We wish to calculate

$$m_y(t) = E\{Y_t\} = E\left\{\int_{-\infty}^{\infty} h(\tau) X(t - \tau) d\tau\right\} \qquad (4\text{-}49)$$

Let us assume that we can interchange the order of the expectation and the integration with respect to τ; then

$$m_y(t) = \int_{-\infty}^{\infty} h(\tau) E\{X_{t-\tau}\} d\tau = \int_{-\infty}^{\infty} h(\tau) m_x(t - \tau) d\tau \qquad (4\text{-}50)$$

To see when the interchange is justified, express the expectation in terms of integration with respect to the density function f_X:

$$\int_{-\infty}^{\infty} h(\tau) E\{X_{t-\tau}\} d\tau = \int_{-\infty}^{\infty} d\tau\, h(\tau) \int_{-\infty}^{\infty} dx\, x f_{X_{t-\tau}}(x)$$

the order of these two ordinary integrals can be interchanged if (see the discussion in Sec. 2-5)

$$\int_{-\infty}^{\infty} d\tau |h(\tau)| \int_{-\infty}^{\infty} dx\, |x| f_{X_{t-\tau}}(x) < \infty$$

that is, if

$$\int_{-\infty}^{\infty} |h(\tau)|\, E\{|X_{t-\tau}|\}\, d\tau < \infty \qquad (4\text{-}51)$$

Note that sufficient conditions that this inequality be satisfied are that

$$E\{|X_t|\} \le M < \infty \qquad \text{all } t$$

---

[1] We purposely did not concern ourselves with the question of convergence of the random variables Y_{Δ,N,t_j} to the random variables Y_{t_j}; this convergence will require $R_y(\tau)$ to be a continuous function of τ. Our purpose here is limited to showing the idea of the proof rather than giving a complete rigorous proof.

and the system is stable

$$\int_{-\infty}^{\infty} |h(\tau)| \, d\tau < \infty$$

These conditions are met in all meaningful communications applications.

When $m_x(t)$ is a constant, m_x, then Eq. 4-50 becomes simply

$$m_y = m_x \int_{-\infty}^{\infty} h(\tau) \, d\tau = m_x H(0) \qquad (4\text{-}52)$$

in which $H(0)$ is the d-c gain of the system.

Next consider the correlation function.

$$
\begin{aligned}
R_y(t_1, t_2) &= E\{Y_{t_1} Y_{t_2}\} \\
&= E\left\{ \int_{-\infty}^{\infty} h(\tau_1) X(t_1 - \tau_1) \, d\tau_1 \int_{-\infty}^{\infty} h(\tau_2) X(t_2 - \tau_2) \, d\tau_2 \right\} \\
&= \int_{-\infty}^{\infty} d\tau_1 \, h(\tau_1) \int_{-\infty}^{\infty} d\tau_2 \, h(\tau_2) E\{X_{t_1 - \tau_1} X_{t_2 - \tau_2}\} \\
&= \int_{-\infty}^{\infty} d\tau_1 \, h(\tau_1) \int_{-\infty}^{\infty} d\tau_2 \, h(\tau_2) R_x(t_1 - \tau_1, t_2 - \tau_2) \qquad (4\text{-}53)
\end{aligned}
$$

In this case the interchange of integration and expectation is valid as long as the system is stable and $E\{X_t^2\}$ is finite for all t. We leave it to the reader to satisfy himself on this point; this follows in a manner similar to the above discussion concerning m_y once we use the Schwartz inequality to show that

$$E\{|X_{t_1} X_{t_2}|\} \leq [E\{X_{t_1}^2\} E\{X_{t_2}^2\}]^{\frac{1}{2}}$$

The covariance function of the process $Y(t)$ can be found by combining Eqs. 4-50 and 4-53;

$$
\begin{aligned}
L_y(t_1, t_2) &= R_y(t_1, t_2) - m_y(t_1) m_y(t_2) \\
&= \int_{-\infty}^{\infty} d\tau_1 \, h(\tau_1) \int_{-\infty}^{\infty} d\tau_2 \, h(\tau_2) \\
&\qquad \times [R_x(t_1 - \tau_1, t_2 - \tau_2) - m_x(t_1 - \tau_1) m_x(t_2 - \tau_2)] \\
&= \int_{-\infty}^{\infty} d\tau_1 \, h(\tau_1) \int_{-\infty}^{\infty} d\tau_2 \, h(\tau_2) L_x(t_1 - \tau_1, t_2 - \tau_2) \qquad (4\text{-}54)
\end{aligned}
$$

Let us now consider the case in which $X(t)$ is a stationary process; then Eqs. 4-53 and 4-54 become, respectively,

$$
\begin{aligned}
R_y(t_1, t_2) &= R_y(t_1 - t_2) \\
&= \int_{-\infty}^{\infty} d\tau_1 \, h(\tau_1) \int_{-\infty}^{\infty} d\tau_2 \, h(\tau_2) R_x(t_1 - t_2 - \tau_1 + \tau_2) \qquad (4\text{-}55)
\end{aligned}
$$

and

$$L_y(t_1, t_2) = L_y(t_1 - t_2)$$
$$= \int_{-\infty}^{\infty} d\tau_1\, h(\tau_1) \int_{-\infty}^{\infty} d\tau_2\, h(\tau_2) L_x(t_1 - t_2 - \tau_1 + \tau_2) \qquad (4\text{-}56)$$

Note that if $X(t)$ is a gaussian process (so that $Y(t)$ is also) and stationary, then Eqs. 4-52 and 4-56 imply that $Y(t)$ is also stationary. This property is not limited to gaussian processes. *If $X(t)$ is stationary and the linear filter is time-invariant, then the process $Y(t)$ is also stationary.* We will not prove this statement. Its proof would roughly follow the lines followed in the proof of the gaussian property at the beginning of this section: one would approximate the Y_t variables by linear combinations of X_t variables (whose distribution is invariant to a time shift).

Power Spectral Density

Let us consider further Eq. 4-55, relating the correlation functions in the wide-sense stationary case. This equation is a repeated convolution of the correlation function R_x with the impulse response h. This immediately suggests that a simpler relation might result if we were to work in the transform domain. Accordingly, let us define the power spectral density function of the random process $X(t)$ as the Fourier transform of the correlation function R_x. This density function we denote by $S_x(f)$, so that

$$S_x(f) = \mathscr{F}[R_x(\tau)] = \int_{-\infty}^{\infty} e^{-j2\pi f\tau}\, R_x(\tau)\, d\tau \qquad (4\text{-}57)$$

Let us postpone for the moment the physical reason for the name of this function and consider the relation of $S_y(f)$ to $S_x(f)$. Using Eq. 4-55, we have

$$S_y(f) = \int_{-\infty}^{\infty} R_y(\tau)e^{-j2\pi f\tau}\, d\tau$$
$$= \int_{-\infty}^{\infty} d\tau\, e^{-j2\pi f\tau} \int_{-\infty}^{\infty} d\tau_1\, h(\tau_1) \int_{-\infty}^{\infty} d\tau_2\, h(\tau_2) R_x(\tau - \tau_1 + \tau_2)$$

Interchanging the order of the integration and writing

$$e^{-j2\pi f\tau} = e^{-j2\pi f(\tau - \tau_1 + \tau_2)}\, e^{-j2\pi f\tau_1}\, e^{j2\pi f\tau_2}$$

we have

$$S_y(f) = \int_{-\infty}^{\infty} d\tau_1\, h(\tau_1)e^{-j2\pi f\tau_1} \int_{-\infty}^{\infty} d\tau_2\, h(\tau_2)e^{+j2\pi f\tau_2}$$
$$\times \int_{-\infty}^{\infty} d\tau\, R_x(\tau - \tau_1 + \tau_2)e^{-j2\pi f(\tau - \tau_1 + \tau_2)} = H(f)H(-f)S_x(f) \qquad (4\text{-}58)$$

The interchange of integration used will be valid if the system is stable and

$$\int_{-\infty}^{\infty} |R_x(\tau)|\, d\tau < \infty$$

Noting that $h(t)$ is real and hence $H(-f) = H^*(f)$, Eq. 4-58 may be rewritten as

$$S_y(f) = |H(f)|^2 S_x(f) \qquad (4\text{-}59)$$

The relationship between the correlation functions of the input and output processes is thus quite simply expressed in the transform domain.

Now let us investigate the physical significance of the power spectral density function. To this end it is useful to consider the physical configuration shown in Fig. 4-6. Let us first note that the average power in any wide-sense stationary process [say, $X(t)$] may be expressed in terms of its correlation function or spectral density function as follows:

$$E\{X_t^2\} = R_x(0) = \int_{-\infty}^{\infty} S_x(f)\, df \qquad (4\text{-}60)$$

Now consider the power dissipated in the output of the ideal band pass filter. If the bandwidth of the filter, Δ, is sufficiently small and $S_x(f)$ a continuous function, then $S_y(f)$ is approximately

$$S_y(f) = \begin{cases} S_x(f_0) & |f \pm f_0| \le \Delta/2 \\ 0 & |f \pm f_0| > \Delta/2 \end{cases}$$

(We will show in a moment that $S_x(f)$ must be an even function of f.) The average power dissipated in the resistor in the output of the filter is thus

$$E\{Y_t^2\} = R_y(0) = \int_{-\infty}^{\infty} S_y(f)\, df = (2\Delta)S_x(f_0)$$
$$= S_x(f_0) \cdot \text{Total filter bandwidth in c.p.s.} \qquad (4\text{-}61)$$

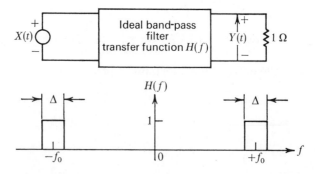

Figure 4-6   System configuration used to interpret power spectral density function.

But the filter is one which passes only those frequency components of the process $X(t)$ in a frequency band of (total two-sided) width 2Δ c.p.s. about the frequency f_0. Thus, as named, $S_x(f)$ *represents the frequency density of the average power in the process* $X(t)$ (that is, the power spectral density integrated over a band of frequencies gives the total average power in that band).

The reader should remember that the concept of power spectral density is applicable only for a wide-sense stationary process.

In closing our discussion of spectral density functions, let us note two properties of a spectral density function. First, from the discussion leading up to Eq. 4-61, it is clear that we must have

$$S_x(f) \geq 0 \qquad \text{all } f \tag{4-62}$$

Secondly, since $R_x(\tau)$ is a real valued even function of τ, the spectral density

$$S_x(f) = \mathscr{F}[R_x(\tau)]$$

must be a real even function of f from Eq. 2-81.

In Chapter 5 we will deal extensively with cross correlation functions. We will find it convenient to make use of the *cross spectral density of two processes* [say, $X(t)$ and $Y(t)$], defined by

$$S_{xy}(f) = \mathscr{F}[R_{xy}(\tau)] = \mathscr{F}[E\{X_{t+\tau}Y_t\}] \tag{4-63}$$

(Note this definition applies only if the two processes $X(t)$ and $Y(t)$ are jointly stationary.)   Since $R_{xy}(\tau) = R_{yx}(-\tau)$,

$$S_{yx}(f) = S_{xy}^*(f) \tag{4-64}$$

Note that $S_{xy}(f)$ is not necessarily real nor even, nor positive.

Problem 4-7.   Consider the system configuration shown in Fig. 4-7.   The processes $X(t)$ and $Y(t)$ are jointly stationary with known cross correlation function

$$R_{xy}(\tau) = E\{X_{t+\tau}Y_t\}$$

(a) Express the cross correlation function of the processes $U(t)$ and $V(t)$

$$R_{uv}(\tau) = E\{U_{t+\tau}V_t\}$$

in terms of $R_{xy}(\tau)$, $h_1(\tau)$, and $h_2(\tau)$.
(b) Use your answer to (a) to show that the corresponding cross spectral density is given by

$$S_{uv}(f) = H_1(f)H_2^*(f)S_{xy}(f) \tag{4-65}$$

Problem 4-8.   Let $X(t)$ be a stationary process whose power density spectrum is band-limited:

$$S_x(f) = 0 \qquad |f| > W$$

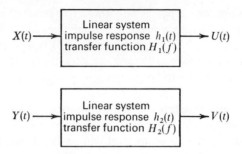

Figure 4-7   System configuration for Problem 4-7.

Since $X(t)$ contains no power outside the band $[-W, W]$, we would expect that the sampling theorem should apply in some manner. The following result, originally due to Balakrishnan [5], is true.

Let the process $X'(t)$ be defined by

$$X'(t) = \sum_{k=-\infty}^{\infty} X(k/2W) \frac{\sin 2\pi W(t - k/2W)}{2\pi W(t - k/2W)} \tag{4-66}$$

Then $X'(t)$ and $X(t)$ are equal in the mean-square sense for all time; i.e.,

$$E\{(X_t - X_t')^2\} = 0$$

Prove this statement.   *Hint:* Since $S_x(f) = \mathscr{F}[R_x(\tau)]$ is bandlimited, $\mathscr{F}[R_x(\tau - \Delta)]$ is bandlimited for any Δ (Why is this?), and we can write

$$R_x(\tau - \Delta) = \sum_{k-\infty}^{\infty} R_x(-\Delta + k/2W) \frac{\sin 2\pi W(\tau - k/2W)}{2\pi W(\tau - k/2W)} \tag{4-67}$$

Now expand $E\{(X_t - X_t')^2\}$ and use Eq. 4-67 for appropriate choices of Δ to show that the resulting terms add up to zero.

4-3   Shot Noise[1]

We now wish to give an example of how the methods we have been studying may be applied to a physical problem of interest, such as deriving the statistics of noise generated by a particular physical mechanism. We pick here one of the easier to analyze, the "shot noise" generated in a vacuum tube by the random emission of electrons from the cathode. We start first by considering the current pulse generated by a single electron passing from the cathode to the plate. We next regard the current at any time as a sum of a large number of such pulses. From this, some assumptions regarding the character of the emission times, and the central limit theorem, we then show that the current is (to a good approximation) a gaussian process.

[1] This section is based heavily on Chapter 7 of Davenport and Root [4].

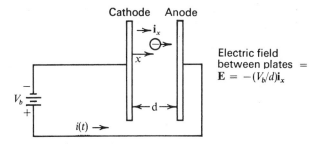

Figure 4-8   Parallel plate structure considered in study of shot noise.

We now derive the current pulse resulting from the passage of a single electron from the cathode to the plate. Inasmuch as our purpose is to demonstrate the application of certain methods to a physical problem, we pick the simplest possible configuration and physical conditions. Consider the parallel plate structure shown in Fig. 4-8. Assuming the plates are parallel and closely spaced, the electric field between the plates is uniform:

$$\mathbf{E} = -(V_b/d)\mathbf{i}_x \qquad (4\text{-}68)$$

Also we assume that the emission velocity of the electron is small compared to the velocity caused by the field; thus the position of the electron is

$$x_e(t) = \tfrac{1}{2}(t - t_e)^2\left(\frac{V_b e}{dm}\right) \qquad t_e \le t \le t_e + T \qquad (4\text{-}69)$$

in which t_e is the emission time and T the transit time:

$$T = \left(\frac{2d^2m}{V_b e}\right)^{\!1/2} \qquad (4\text{-}70)$$

Consider the current caused by the passage of the electron; the approach of the electron to the anode drives a negative charge from the plate.[1] The work that this charge does upon the battery must be equal to the work done by the battery in accelerating the electron. The work done on the

---

[1] Note that the current flowing through the battery consists of discrete charges of charge e, so that it is a fiction to speak of charge flow in Eqs. 4-72 and 4-73 in quantities less than e. In actuality, the discrete charges flowing through the battery are governed by quantum mechanical effects and the charge q in Eqs. 4-72 and 4-73 is the *average* charge flow caused by an emission from the cathode; the average being over the statistics governing the quantum mechanical conduction process. Consideration of the quantum mechanical nature of conduction is beyond the scope of this book.

electron in passing from the potential 0 at the cathode to the potential $V(x) = (x/d)V_b$ at distance x from the cathode is

$$W(x) = V(x)e = (x/d)V_be \qquad (4\text{-}71)$$

If q denotes the negative charge driven from the anode during the passage of the electron from 0 to x, the work done on the battery by q is $V_b q$. Thus we must have

$$V_b q = (x/d)V_b e \qquad (4\text{-}72)$$

or

$$i_e(t - t_e) = \frac{dq}{dt} = \frac{dx}{dt}\frac{e}{d} \qquad (4\text{-}73)$$

Differentiating Eq. 4-69 with respect to t and substituting the result into Eq. 4-73 yields

$$i_e(t - t_e) = \begin{cases} (2e/T)(t - t_e)/T & t_e \le t \le t_e + T \\ 0 & \text{elsewhere} \end{cases} \qquad (4\text{-}74)$$

The quantities t_e and T again denote the emission and transit times, respectively. The shape of this current pulse is shown in Fig. 4-9. This result was derived for a parallel plate configuration; for other configurations the shape of the pulse will vary (its area must always be e, however). Most of our results will not depend upon the pulse shape. It should also be noted that we have assumed a temperature limited situation (as opposed to a space-charge limited situation) in which the density of the electrons between the cathode and plate was sufficiently low that the field caused by the electrons was negligible with respect to the field set up by the source V_b.

We now consider the total current caused by the flow of electrons. Let K denote the number of electrons emitted between time $t - T$ and time t (note that K is a random variable). The current at time t is then

$$I_t = \sum_{k=1}^{K} i_e(t - T_k)$$

in which T_k denotes the emission time of the kth electron. Inasmuch as K and the T_k are random variables, I_t is a random variable and $I(t)$ is a

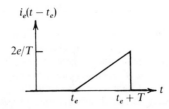

Figure 4-9   Current pulse caused by emission of electron from cathode.

random process. To derive the probability distribution of the process, we must consider the distribution of the emission times.

The assumptions we make upon the emission times are the same as those concerning the event points in the example of Sec. 4-1; namely,

1. In any *infinitesimal* time interval dt, at most one electron may be emitted; the probability of exactly one electron being emitted is νdt.
2. If I_1 and I_2 are two disjoint time intervals, the numbers of emissions in these two intervals are statistically independent.

It was shown in Sec. 4-1 that these assumptions imply a Poisson distribution for the number of emissions occurring in a time interval of given length

$$Q(k;\tau) = P\{\text{exactly } k \text{ emissions occurring in any interval of length } \tau\}$$
$$= e^{-\nu t}(\nu\tau)^k/k! \tag{4-75}$$

A necessary step in establishing that $I(t)$ is a gaussian process is to determine the distribution governing the emission times $T_1, T_2, \ldots, T_k$, conditioned by the knowledge that exactly k emissions occurred in a time interval of length T. In particular, we wish to show that, given that k emissions occur in time T, the k emission times are statistically independent uniformly distributed (over T), random variables. Toward this end let the interval of length T be divided up into m disjoint intervals of *arbitrary* lengths $\tau_1, \tau_2, \ldots, \tau_m$, with

$$\sum_{j=1}^{m} \tau_j = T \tag{4-76}$$

Let

$$P(k_1, \tau_1; \ldots; k_m, \tau_m)$$
$$= P\{k_j \text{ emissions occurring in } \tau_j, j = 1, 2, \ldots, m\} \tag{4-77}$$

and note that

$$P(k_1, \tau_1; \ldots; k_m, \tau_m; k, T) = P(k_1, \tau_1; \ldots; k_m, \tau_m) \tag{4-78}$$

in which

$$k = \sum_{j=1}^{m} k_j \tag{4-79}$$

Making use of Eq. 4-78 and assumption 2, we have for the conditional probability

$$P(k_1, \tau_1; \ldots; k_m, \tau_m \mid k \text{ in } T) = \frac{P(k_1, \tau_1; \ldots; k_m, \tau_m)}{Q(k;T)}$$

$$= \frac{\left[\prod_{j=1}^{m} Q(k_j; \tau_j)\right]}{Q(k;\tau)} \tag{4-80}$$

Using Eq. 4-75, this reduces to

$$P(k_1, \tau_1; \ldots; k_m, \tau_m \mid k \text{ in } T) = \left[\prod_{j=1}^{m} \left[\frac{e^{-\nu\tau_j}(\nu\tau_j)^{k_j}}{k_j!} \right] \right] \left[\frac{e^{-\nu T}(\nu T)^k}{k!} \right]^{-1}$$

$$= \frac{\left[\prod_{j=1}^{m} (\tau_j/T)^{k_j} \right] k!}{\prod_{j=1}^{m} k_j!} \qquad (4\text{-}81)$$

To establish that the emission times are independent uniformly distributed random variables, we now consider the following assumptions:

(a) The k event times are statistically independent.
(b) The k event times are identically distributed, the distribution being uniform over the interval of length T.

Let us compute the same probability as above on this basis.   Assume that the k electrons are marked so that they are distinguishable.   By a specific emission, we mean the emission of a given electron.   Then

$\tau_j/T = P\{$single given emission falling in the interval $\tau_j\}$

$(\tau_j/T)^{k_j} = P\{k_j$ specific emissions occurring in indistinguishable order in $\tau_j\}$

$k! = $ number of distinct ways of assigning k electrons to k emission times

$k_j! = $ number of distinct ways of assigning k_j electrons to the k_j emission times in the interval τ_j

$k!/\prod_{j=1}^{m} k_j! = $ number of ways of assigning k electrons to k emission times with exactly k_j electrons assigned in indistinguishable order to the k_j emission times in $\tau_j, j = 1, 2, \ldots, m$.

Thus, under assumptions (a) and (b), the probability of k_j emissions occurring (in indistinguishable order) in $\tau_j, j = 1, 2, \ldots, m$, given that k emissions occur in T, is

$$P(k_1, \tau_1; \ldots; k_m, \tau_m \mid k \text{ in } T) = \left[\prod_{j=1}^{m} (\tau_j/T)^{k_j} \right] \frac{k!}{\prod_{j=1}^{m} k_j!} \qquad (4\text{-}82)$$

This expression is the same as that given by Eq. 4-81 which was derived on the basis of assumptions 1 and 2.   Now $m, \tau_1, \ldots, \tau_m$ were all arbitrary; the only way in which the two expressions can agree for all such choices is if the emission times governed by assumptions 1 and 2 also obey assumptions (a) and (b).   We have thus established for a Poisson distribution of emission times that, *given that k emissions occur in time T,* the *k* emission times must all be *statistically independent uniformly distributed* (over *T*) random variables.

Now consider $I_{t,k}$, the current at time *t* under the assumption that exactly *k* emissions occurred between $t - T$ and *t*:

$$I_{t,k} = \sum_{j=1}^{k} i_e(t - T_j) \tag{4-83}$$

Note that since the T_j, $j = 1, 2, \ldots, k$, are statistically independent identically distributed random variables, the quantities $i_e(t - T_j)$ are statistically independent identically distributed random variables with mean and variance:

$$m_{i_e} = E\{i_e(t - T_k)\} = \frac{1}{T} \int_0^T i_e(t - t_k)\, dt_k = \frac{e}{T} \tag{4-84}$$

$$\sigma_{i_e}^2 = E\{i_e{}^2(t - T_k)\} - m_{i_e}^2 = \frac{1}{T} \int_0^T i_e{}^2(t - t_k)\, dt_k - \left(\frac{e}{T}\right)^2 \tag{4-85}$$

If the number of emissions, *K*, equals *k*, I_t is the sum of *k* statistically independent identically distributed random variables. If *k* is large, the central limit theorem[1] (equal components case) states that the distribution of I_t conditioned by the knowledge that $K = k$ will be approximately gaussian with mean km_{i_e} and variance $k\sigma_{i_e}^2$

$$f_{I_t|K}(i \mid k) \approx \frac{1}{\sqrt{2\pi k}\,\sigma_{i_e}} \exp\left\{-\frac{1}{2} \frac{(i - km_{i_e})^2}{k\sigma_{i_e}^2}\right\} \tag{4-86}$$

We must now take into account the fact that *K*, the number of emissions, is a random variable. The resultant density function for *I* is

$$f_{I_t}(i) = \sum_{k=0}^{\infty} Q(k; T) f_{I_t|K}(i \mid k) \tag{4-87}$$

To show that this density is approximately gaussian, we will separate this sum into two parts: one which includes the values of *K* that are highly probable and one which includes improbable values of *K*. The probability $Q(k; T)$ is Poisson with mean vT and variance vT (see Problem 4-1); thus by the Chebyshev inequality (Problem 3-4) we have that

$$\sum_{|k - vT| > \epsilon} Q(k; T) = P\{|K - vT| > \epsilon\} \le vT/\epsilon^2$$

---

[1] See Appendix 2 for a derivation of the central limit theorem.

If we set $\epsilon = (\nu T)^{\frac{2}{3}}$, then this expression becomes

$$\sum_{|k-\nu T| > \frac{\nu T}{(\nu T)^{1/3}}} Q(k;T) = P\left\{|K - \nu T| > \frac{\nu T}{(\nu T)^{\frac{1}{3}}}\right\} \le \frac{1}{(\nu T)^{\frac{1}{3}}} \qquad (4\text{-}88)$$

Thus for $\nu T \gg 1$, K departs fractionally from its mean νT only with small probability. Let us now divide up the sum of Eq. 4-87 into the two sums

$$f_{I_t}(i) = \sum_{|k-\nu T| \le \frac{\nu T}{(\nu T)^{1/3}}} Q(k;T) \qquad \underbrace{f(i/k)}_{\substack{\text{approximately gaussian with mean} \\ \approx \nu T(e/T) \text{ and variance} \approx \nu T \sigma_{i_e}^2}}$$

$$+ \sum_{|k-\nu T| > \frac{\nu T}{(\nu T)^{1/3}}} Q(k;T)f(i/k) \qquad (4\text{-}89)$$

$$\underbrace{}_{\substack{Q(k;T) \text{ terms in this sum} \\ \text{add up to less than } 1/(\nu T)^{1/3}}}$$

Thus as νT becomes very large the total area under the positive function formed by the second sum becomes negligible and the first term approaches a sum of gaussian density functions whose means and variances all approach $\nu e/T$ and $\nu T \sigma_{i_e}^2$ in the sense that the ratios of the quantities involved approach one. Thus for large values of νT, $f_{I_t}(i)$ is approximately gaussian with mean $\nu e/T$ and variance $\nu T \sigma_{i_e}^2$.

In actuality νT is quite large. Per ampere of current there are 6.25×10^{18} electrons per second. For a tube with a quiescent current ($E\{I_t\}$) of 2 ma and a transit time of 10^{-8} seconds we have $\nu T = 1.25 \times 10^8$. Thus the reasoning given above for $\nu T \gg 1$ will be applicable to most cases of practical interest.

We are not quite finished. To show that $I(t)$ is a gaussian process, we must show that the joint distribution of an arbitrary set of random variables $I_{t_1}, I_{t_2}, \ldots, I_{t_n}$ is gaussian. This requires essentially an extension of our preceding discussion to the vector case. Assume $t_1 \le t_2 \le \cdots \le t_n$ and let K denote the number of emissions in the time interval $t_1 - T$ to t_n. The random variable K is thus Poisson-distributed with both mean and variance equal to $\nu(t_n - t_1 + T)$. Then

$$I_{t_j} = \sum_{\substack{m=1 \\ t_1 - T \le T_m \le t_n}}^{K} i_e(t_j - T_m) \qquad j = 1, 2, \ldots, n \qquad (4\text{-}90)$$

in which we note that $i_e(t)$ is zero unless $0 \le t \le T$.

Let us now describe the above situation in terms of n-dimensional vectors. Let $\mathbf{I}$ be the vector whose jth component is $I_{t_j}, j = 1, 2, \ldots, n$

and $\mathbf{I}_e(T_m)$ the vector whose jth component is $i_e(t_j - T_m)$, $j = 1, 2, \ldots, n$. Then Eq. 4-90 can be expressed as

$$\mathbf{I} = \sum_{\substack{m=1 \\ t_1 - T \le T_m \le t_n}}^{K} \mathbf{I}_e(T_m) \tag{4-90'}$$

Now, if there are a fixed number, k, of emissions in the time interval $t_1 - T$ to t_n, the T_m are statistically independent identically distributed random variables; hence, the vectors $\mathbf{I}_e(T_m)$ are statistically independent, identically distributed vector random variables. Then, if $k \gg 1$, by the vector-valued version of the equal components case of the central limit theorem (see Cramér [6], pp. 285–290 and 316–317) the vector $\mathbf{I}_t$ has approximately a gaussian distribution; that is, the joint distribution of its components is approximately gaussian. The fact that the components of $\mathbf{I}_t$ have a joint gaussian distribution when K is a Poisson distributed random variable with

$$E\{K\} = \mathrm{var}\,\{K\} = \nu(t_n - t_1 + T) \gg 1$$

then follows by the same reasoning leading from Eq. 4-87 up through Eq. 4-89.

Problem 4-9. We have shown that shot noise is a gaussian random process. Since such a process is specified by its mean and autocorrelation function, we wish to find these.

(a) Let $I_t = \sum_{k=1}^{K} i_e(t - T_k)$

The quantity K, the number of emissions from $t - T$ to t, is a Poisson distributed random variable with mean νT. The T_k are statistically independent and uniformly distributed between $t - T$ and t for a fixed value of k. Find $E\{I_t\}$ (an exact expression).

(b) Is $I(t)$ stationary? Explain.

(c) Find $E\{I_t I_{t+\tau}\} = R_i(\tau)$

Hint: $I(t)$ could be generated as shown in Fig. 4-10 by passing a process $X(t)$ through a filter whose impulse response is $i_e(\tau)$, in which $X(t)$ is a process which consists of unit impulses occurring at the emission times. If you can find $R_x(\tau) = E\{X_t X_{t+\tau}\}$ you can easily find $R_i(\tau) = E\{I_t I_{t+\tau}\}$. To find $R_x(\tau)$,

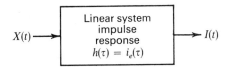

Figure 4-10   Equivalent method of generating the process $I(t)$.

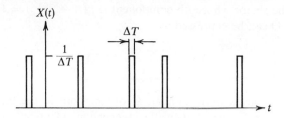

Figure 4-11   Approximation to the process $X(t)$.

consider the process shown in Fig. 4-11.   All pulses are of width ΔT and height $1/\Delta T$ and occur at Poisson distributed event points.   Assume ΔT is sufficiently small that the probability of more than one event occurring in ΔT is zero.   Find the autocorrelation function of this process and then take the limit as $\Delta T \to 0$ to get $R_x(\tau)$.

REFERENCES

[1] Birkhoff, G., and G. C. Rota, *Ordinary Differential Equations*, Ginn, Boston, 1962; Chap. 1, Sec. 5.

[2] Wiener, N., *Cybernetics*, The Technology Press, Cambridge, Mass., 1948; Chap. II.

[3] Doob, J., *Stochastic Processes*, John Wiley and Sons, New York, 1953; Chap. 11.

[4] Davenport, W., and W. Root, *Random Signals and Noise*, McGraw-Hill Book Co., New York, 1958.

[5] Balakrishnan, A. V., "A Note on the Sampling Principle for Continuous Signals," *IRE Trans. on Information Theory*, **IT-3**, No. 2, 143, 1957.

[6] Cramér, H., *Mathematical Methods of Statistics*, Princeton University Press, Princeton, N. J., 1946.

Chapter 5

Band-Pass Signals and Amplitude Modulation

In this chapter and the following one, we study the process of modulation. Modulation is a procedure in which a message signal, usually a low-pass signal, is converted into another signal prior to transmission over the communication channel. This resulting modulated signal is usually a band-pass signal centered about some carrier frequency f_0. Modulation is performed for any one or more of the following reasons:

1. Translation to a frequency band about f_0 may be necessary to yield a signal that will propagate satisfactorily through the transmission medium;
2. To place the information in the message in a form less susceptible to noise and interference;
3. To allow frequency multiplexing or simultaneous transmission of signals from several message sources in adjacent frequency bands.

In this chapter we consider amplitude modulation (AM) (including single-sideband AM), and see that although AM is useful in fulfilling the first and third objectives above, it accomplishes nothing in the way of noise protection. In Chapter 6 we consider frequency modulation (FM) which allows us to make the information less vulnerable to noise at the expense of increasing the bandwidth occupancy of the signal.

Our first concern is to develop a convenient way of describing the relationship between the message signal (modulating signal) and the resulting modulated band-pass signal. With this relationship fully understood for the case in which the modulating signal and band-pass signal are random processes, we will then be able to easily analyze the performance of amplitude modulation (AM) systems. In considering AM systems our emphasis is on analyzing the performance of the system in the presence of noise and noting the bandwidth occupancy of the system.

Although consideration is given to the effect on system performance resulting from the use of practical demodulation circuits, the emphasis is on the inherent performance capability of amplitude modulation. If the reader is interested in a thorough discussion of the analysis of various physical demodulation circuits, he should consult the treatment in Chapter III of Rowe [1].

5-1   Representation of Band-Pass Signals

Consider a (deterministic) signal $z(t)$ with Fourier transform $Z(f)$. We will say that $z(t)$ is a *band-pass* signal if $Z(f)$ is non-negligible only in some band of frequencies of total extent $2W$ about some carrier frequency $\pm f_0$. This situation is shown in Fig. 5-1. The quantity W is termed the (one-sided) *bandwidth* of the signal; if $f_0 \gg W$, we say the signal is a narrow-band signal. Conversely, we say that a signal is *low-pass* if its transform is non-negligible in a band of frequencies centered about $f = 0$.

Most of the band-pass signals that are of interest in communications are signals that have resulted by modulating some carrier signal by a low-pass information-bearing signal. We want to develop a relationship between the resulting band-pass modulated signal and the low-pass signal that results from demodulation. Toward this end, we now introduce the concept of the *Hilbert transform* of a signal. As we progress, we will see that the small amount of effort required to familiarize ourselves with this concept will greatly facilitate the handling of band-pass signals, particularly when we consider band-pass random processes and single side-band modulation.

The Hilbert Transform

Let $z(t)$ be an arbitrary real-valued signal with Fourier transform $Z(f)$. We consider a linear system which has the transfer function

$$H(f) = -j\operatorname{sgn} f = \begin{cases} -j & f > 0 \\ +j & f < 0 \\ 0 & f = 0 \end{cases} \tag{5-1}$$

Now let $\hat{z}(t)$ stand for the output of this system when the input is $z(t)$. The signal $\hat{z}(t)$ is called the Hilbert transform of $z(t)$. The process of obtaining $\hat{z}(t)$ from $z(t)$ is shown in Fig. 5-2. The system $H(f)$ can be thought of as one which phase-shifts positive frequencies by $-90°$ and negative frequencies by $+90°$. If we denote the Fourier transform of $\hat{z}(t)$ by $\hat{Z}(f)$, then

$$\hat{Z}(f) = -j(\operatorname{sgn} f)\, Z(f) \tag{5-2}$$

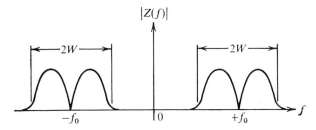

Figure 5-1   Fourier transform of band-pass signal.

Note that since $z(t)$ was assumed real, $Z(f)$ is conjugate symmetric $(Z(-f) = Z^*(f))$ and hence $\hat{Z}(f)$ is also conjugate symmetric.

$$\hat{Z}(-f) = [-j\,\text{sgn}\,(-f)]\,Z(-f) = (-j\,\text{sgn}\,f)^*\,Z^*(f) = \hat{Z}^*(f) \tag{5-3}$$

From this fact the reader can easily establish that $\hat{z}(t)$ is a real valued time function.

Next consider the Hilbert transform of the signal $\hat{z}(t)$:

$$[\hat{\hat{z}}(t)] \leftrightarrow [-j\,\text{sgn}\,f]\,\hat{Z}(f) = (-j)^2(\text{sgn}\,f)^2\,Z(f) = \begin{cases} -Z(f) & f \neq 0 \\ 0 & f = 0 \end{cases} \tag{5-4}$$

Thus Hilbert transforming twice yields (-1) times the original signal (and removes any d-c component).

$$\hat{\hat{z}}(t) = -z(t) \tag{5-5}$$

For a signal $z(t)$, we define its *pre-envelope* to be

$$z_+(t) = z(t) + j\hat{z}(t) \tag{5-6}$$

Note that $z_+(t)$ is a complex-valued signal (since $z(t)$ and $\hat{z}(t)$ are both real valued). One of the salient features of this pre-envelope is the behavior of its Fourier transform. Let

$$Z_+(f) = \mathscr{F}[z_+(t)] \tag{5-7}$$

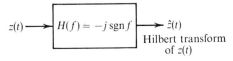

Figure 5-2   The operation of Hilbert transformation.

Then

$$Z_+(f) = Z(f) + j(-j \operatorname{sgn} f) Z(f)$$

$$= \begin{cases} 2Z(f) & f > 0 \\ Z(0) & f = 0 \\ 0 & f < 0 \end{cases} \tag{5-8}$$

so that the pre-envelope of a signal has no frequency content (its Fourier transform is zero) for negative frequencies.

Now let us consider the physical meaning of the pre-envelope. If $z(t)$ is a band-pass signal centered about frequencies $\pm f_0$, it would be convenient to express $z(t)$ in the forms

$$z(t) = x(t) \cos 2\pi f_0 t - y(t) \sin 2\pi f_0 t \tag{5-9}$$

or

$$z(t) = a(t) \cos [2\pi f_0 t + \theta(t)] \tag{5-10}$$

in which the signals $x(t)$, $y(t)$, $a(t)$, and $\theta(t)$ are all low-pass. The signals $x(t)$ and $y(t)$ are referred to as the quadrature components of the band-pass signal, and $a(t)$ and $\theta(t)$ are referred to respectively as the amplitude and phase of the signal. The relations among these signals are

$$a(t) = +\sqrt{x^2(t) + y^2(t)} \tag{5-11}$$

$$\theta(t) = \sin^{-1} [y(t)/a(t)] = \cos^{-1} [x(t)/a(t)] \tag{5-12}$$

Note that we may express $z(t)$ in the form of Eq. 5-9 or 5-10 for *any* value of the frequency f_0. The reader may know from past experience that if this value is the true center (or carrier) frequency that the function $a(t)$ would be the output of an *envelope demodulator*. We shall soon point out that the function $a(t)$ is independent of the value chosen for the frequency f_0. For this reason, $a(t)$ is referred to as the envelope of $z(t)$. For a value of f_0 equal to the center frequency (and *only* for this value), $\theta(t)$ does not contain a term that grows linearly with time. The quantities $x(t)$ and $y(t)$ may be recovered for any choice of f_0 by *synchronous demodulation*. We will elaborate on these ideas in considerable detail later.

Now let us demonstrate how the low-pass quadrature components $x(t)$ and $y(t)$ may be found. Assume that

$$z(t) \leftrightarrow Z(f)$$

in which $Z(f)$ is nonzero only for frequencies about f_0, specifically only for $|f \pm f_0| < f_0$. Then

$$z_+(t) \leftrightarrow Z_+(f)$$

in which

$$Z_+(f) = \begin{cases} 2Z(f) & f > 0 \\ 0 & f < 0 \end{cases}$$

and hence $Z_+(f)$ is nonzero only for $|f - f_0| < f_0$. Thus, by the shifting property, the signal

$$v(t) = z_+(t)e^{-j2\pi f_0 t} \qquad (5\text{-}13)$$

has a transform which is nonzero only for $|f| < f_0$; i.e., $v(t)$ is a low-pass signal. Now consider $z(t)$ expressed in terms of $v(t)$:

$$\begin{aligned} z(t) &= \text{Re}\,\{z(t) + j\hat{z}(t)\} = \text{Re}\,\{z_+(t)\} \\ &= \text{Re}\,\{v(t)e^{j2\pi f_0 t}\} \\ &= \text{Re}\,\{v(t)\}\cos 2\pi f_0 t - \text{Im}\,\{v(t)\}\sin 2\pi f_0 t \qquad (5\text{-}14) \end{aligned}$$

Since $v(t)$ is a low-pass signal, $\text{Re}\,v(t)$ and $\text{Im}\,v(t)$ are also; further, on comparing Eq. 5-14 with Eq. 5-9 we see that

$$x(t) = \text{Re}\,\{v(t)\} = \text{Re}\,\{e^{-j2\pi f_0 t}\,z_+(t)\} \qquad (5\text{-}15)$$

$$y(t) = \text{Im}\,\{v(t)\} = \text{Im}\,\{e^{-j2\pi f_0 t}\,z_+(t)\} \qquad (5\text{-}16)$$

From Eqs. 5-15 and 5-16 we have that

$$a(t) = +\sqrt{x^2(t) + y^2(t)} = |v(t)| = |e^{-j2\pi f_0 t}\,z_+(t)| = |z_+(t)| \qquad (5\text{-}17)$$

and

$$\theta(t) = \tan^{-1}\frac{\text{Im}\,[e^{-j2\pi f_0 t}\,z_+(t)]}{\text{Re}\,[e^{-j2\pi f_0 t}\,z_+(t)]} = \angle z_+(t)e^{-j2\pi f_0 t} \qquad (5\text{-}18)$$

It is shown in Sec. 5-2 that the signal

$$a(t) = |v(t)| = |v(t)e^{j2\pi f_0 t}| = |z_+(t)|$$

results from envelope demodulation (rectification and low-pass filtering) of the signal $z(t)$. For this reason, $a(t)$ is termed the *envelope* of $z(t)$ and $z_+(t)$ the *pre-envelope* of $z(t)$. Note that since $|e^{j2\pi f_0 t}| \equiv 1$, the envelope is independent of the value chosen for f_0.

Equations 5-15 and 5-16 specify how a quadrature component representation of $z(t)$ may be determined from $z_+(t)$, so that $z_+(t)$ uniquely determines this quadrature representation. One might ask conversely if this quadrature representation uniquely determines $z_+(t)$. The answer is, "Yes," as we can simply show. Assume that $z(t)$ is given by Eq. 5-14, with the transform of $v(t)$ nonzero only for $|f| < f_0$. Then

$$z(t) = \tfrac{1}{2}\{v(t)e^{j2\pi f_0 t} + v^*(t)e^{-j2\pi f_0 t}\}$$

so that the transform of $z(t)$ is given by

$$Z(f) = \tfrac{1}{2}\{V(f - f_0) + V^*(-f - f_0)\}$$

Since $V(f)$ is nonzero only for $|f| < f_0$, $Z_+(f)$ is given by

$$Z_+(f) = \begin{cases} 2Z(f) & f > 0 \\ 0 & f < 0 \end{cases} = V(f - f_0)$$

which, when expressed in the time-domain, states that $z_+(t)$ must be the same function determined by Eq. 5-13:

$$z_+(t) = v(t)e^{j2\pi f_0 t} \tag{5-13'}$$

Synchronous Demodulation

Let us now consider the manner in which the quadrature components $x(t)$ and $y(t)$ of the band-pass signal $z(t)$ may be physically obtained from the signal $z(t)$. Let the transform of $z(t)$ be as shown in Fig. 5-3a; the transform is nonzero only in a band of width $\pm W$ centered about $\pm f_0$ with $W < f_0$. The transform of $z_+(t)$, $Z_+(f)$, is then as shown in Fig. 5-3b.

We first expand upon our earlier remark about the quadrature components $x(t)$ and $y(t)$ being low-pass signals if $z(t)$ is a band-pass signal centered about frequency f_0. We then show how $x(t)$ and $y(t)$ may be physically recovered from $z(t)$. From Eq. 5-15 we can write

$$x(t) = \text{Re}\{z_+(t)e^{-j2\pi f_0 t}\} = \tfrac{1}{2}[z_+(t)e^{-j2\pi f_0 t} + z_+{}^*(t)e^{+j2\pi f_0 t}] \tag{5-19}$$

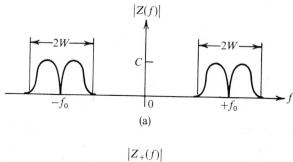

(a)

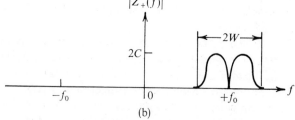

(b)

Figure 5-3   (a) Magnitude of the Fourier transform of $z(t)$.
(b) Magnitude of the Fourier transform of $z_+(t)$.

But by the properties of the Fourier transform we have

$$z_+(t) \leftrightarrow Z_+(f)$$
$$z_+(t)e^{-j2\pi f_0 t} \leftrightarrow Z_+(f + f_0)$$
$$z_+^*(t) \leftrightarrow Z_+^*(-f)$$
$$z_+^*(t)e^{+j2\pi f_0 t} \leftrightarrow Z_+^*(-f + f_0)$$

Thus

$$X(f) = \tfrac{1}{2}[Z_+(f + f_0) + Z_+^*(-f + f_0)] \qquad (5\text{-}20)$$

Inasmuch as $Z_+(f)$ is nonzero only in a band $\pm W$ centered about f_0, $Z_+(f + f_0)$ and $Z_+^*(-f + f_0)$ will both be nonzero only in a band $\pm W$ centered about $f = 0$. Hence, $X(f)$ is a low-pass function, nonzero only in a band $\pm W$ centered about $f = 0$. Similarly it can be shown that

$$y(t) = \frac{1}{2j}[z_+(t)e^{-j2\pi f_0 t} - z_+^*(t)e^{+j2\pi f_0 t}] \qquad (5\text{-}21)$$

and

$$Y(f) = \frac{1}{2j}[Z_+(f + f_0) - Z_+^*(-f + f_0)] \qquad (5\text{-}22)$$

so that $y(t)$ is also a low-pass function with a transform that is nonzero only in a band $\pm W$ centered about $f = 0$.

Now let us turn to a method for recovering $x(t)$ and $y(t)$ from $z(t)$. Consider the signal $2 \cos (2\pi f_0 t)z(t)$. Making use of Eq. 5-9, we have

$$2 \cos (2\pi f_0 t)z(t) = 2 \cos^2 (2\pi f_0 t)x(t) - 2 \cos (2\pi f_0 t) \sin (2\pi f_0 t)y(t)$$
$$= x(t) + x(t) \cos (4\pi f_0 t) - y(t) \sin (4\pi f_0 t)$$
$$= x(t) + \tfrac{1}{2}[x(t)e^{j4\pi f_0 t} + x(t)e^{-j4\pi f_0 t}]$$
$$- \frac{1}{2j}[y(t)e^{j4\pi f_0 t} - y(t)e^{-j4\pi f_0 t}]$$
$$\leftrightarrow X(f) + \tfrac{1}{2}[X(f - 2f_0) + X(f + 2f_0)]$$
$$- \frac{1}{2j}[Y(f - 2f_0) - Y(f + 2f_0)] \qquad (5\text{-}23)$$

Now the signals $X(f)$ and $Y(f)$ are nonzero only in a band $\pm W$ about 0 $(W < f_0)$. Thus, if the signal $2 \cos (2\pi f_0 t)z(t)$ is passed through a low-pass filter of bandwidth $\pm W$, the only term remaining in the output is $x(t)$. Similarly, we can show that

$$-2 \sin (2\pi f_0 t)z(t) = y(t) - \cos (4\pi f_0 t)y(t) - \sin (4\pi f_0 t)x(t)$$
$$\leftrightarrow Y(f) - \tfrac{1}{2}[Y(f - 2f_0) + Y(f + 2f_0)]$$
$$- \frac{1}{2j}[X(f - 2f_0) - X(f + 2f_0)] \qquad (5\text{-}24)$$

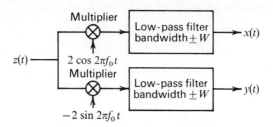

Figure 5-4   Synchronous demodulation of $z(t)$.

so that low-pass filtering of $-2 \sin (2\pi f_0 t)z(t)$ yields $y(t)$.   These remarks are summarized in Fig. 5-4 showing in functional form a circuit for obtaining $x(t)$ and $y(t)$ from $z(t)$.   This method of "detection" or "demodulation" of $z(t)$ is referred to as *synchronous detection* since it requires a carrier signal of the correct frequency and phase as an input to the demodulator.

Physical Implementation of the Hilbert Transform by Single-Sideband Amplitude Modulation

At this point let us take somewhat of an aside and point out that single-sideband amplitude modulation (SSB-AM) provides a method of physically performing the operation of taking the Hilbert transform of a signal.   Let $s(t)$ denote a (real-valued) signal whose Fourier transform is nonzero only over a band $\pm W$ centered at $f = 0$.   Suppressed carrier amplitude modulation of $2 \cos 2\pi f_0 t$ by $s(t)$ yields the signal

$$u(t) = 2s(t) \cos 2\pi f_0 t = s(t)e^{j2\pi f_0 t} + s(t)e^{-j2\pi f_0 t} \qquad (5\text{-}25)$$

with Fourier transform

$$U(f) = S(f + f_0) + S(f - f_0) \qquad (5\text{-}26)$$

The portion of the spectrum of $U(f)$ lying at frequencies $|f| > f_0$ is termed the *upper sideband* of $u(t)$; the portion of the spectrum of $U(f)$ lying at frequencies $|f| < f_0$ is termed the *lower sideband* of $u(t)$. Single-sideband modulation is obtained by filtering out one of these sidebands (say, the lower). Thus, if $z(t)$ denotes the single-sideband signal,

$$Z(f) = U(f)H_F(f) \qquad (5\text{-}27)$$

in which

$$H_F(f) = \begin{cases} 1 & f_0 \leq |f| \leq f_0 + W \\ 0 & \text{elsewhere} \end{cases} \qquad (5\text{-}28)$$

The transforms of these signals are shown in Figs. 5-5a–5-5c. Thus, if we let

$$S_+(f) = \begin{cases} 2S(f) & f > 0 \\ 0 & f < 0 \end{cases}$$

$$S_-(f) = \begin{cases} 2S(f) & f < 0 \\ 0 & f > 0 \end{cases}$$

(5-29)

the Fourier transform of the single sideband modulated signal $z(t)$ is

$$Z(f) = \tfrac{1}{2}[S_-(f + f_0) + S_+(f - f_0)] \qquad (5\text{-}30)$$

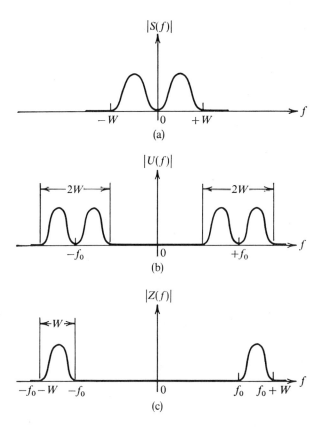

Figure 5-5   The Fourier transforms of the signals involved in single sideband modulation:

   (a) $S(f)$,   (b) $U(f)$,   (c) $Z(f)$.

Now we have shown that

$$\mathscr{F}^{-1}[S_+(f)] = s_+(t) = s(t) + j\hat{s}(t) \qquad (5\text{-}31)$$

In a similar manner it could be shown that

$$\mathscr{F}^{-1}[S_-(f)] = s_-(t) = s(t) - j\hat{s}(t) = s_+{}^*(t) \qquad (5\text{-}32)$$

Thus from Eqs. 5-30 to 5-32 we see that the single-sideband signal $z(t)$ is given by

$$
\begin{aligned}
z(t) &= \tfrac{1}{2}[s_+{}^*(t)e^{-j2\pi f_0 t} + s_+(t)e^{j2\pi f_0 t}] \\
&= \operatorname{Re}\{s_+(t)e^{j2\pi f_0 t}\} \\
&= \operatorname{Re}\{[s(t) + j\hat{s}(t)][\cos 2\pi f_0 t + j \sin 2\pi f_0 t]\} \\
&= s(t) \cos 2\pi f_0 t - \hat{s}(t) \sin 2\pi f_0 t \qquad (5\text{-}33)
\end{aligned}
$$

Thus the single-sideband modulation of $2 \cos 2\pi f_0 t$ by $s(t)$ (suppressed carrier amplitude modulation followed by filtering out the lower sidebands) results in a signal centered about f_0 whose quadrature components are $s(t)$ and $\hat{s}(t)$. As we have already seen, we can obtain $\hat{s}(t)$ by synchronously demodulating $z(t)$ by $-2 \sin 2\pi f_0 t$; that is, multiplying $z(t)$ by $-2 \sin 2\pi f_0 t$ and then low-pass filtering the resulting signal.

Problem 5-1.   In this problem we examine the process of shifting a band-pass signal to an intermediate frequency (i-f) to accomplish high selectivity filtering.   Consider the situation shown in Fig. 5-6.   Let the Fourier transforms of the signals $v(t)$, $u(t)$, and $w(t)$ be denoted by

$$V(f) = \mathscr{F}[v(t)], \qquad U(f) = \mathscr{F}[u(t)], \qquad \text{and} \qquad W(f) = \mathscr{F}[w(t)]$$

and the filters H_{rf} and H_{if} be of the form

$$
\begin{aligned}
H_{rf}(f) &= H_1{}^*(-f - f_1) + H_1(f - f_1) \\
H_{if}(f) &= H_2{}^*(-f - f_{if}) + H_2(f - f_{if})
\end{aligned}
$$

Let f_v denote the bandwidth of the signal $v(t)$, so that

$$V(f) = 0 \qquad |f| \geq f_v$$

We assume that $f_1 > 2f_{if}$, $f_{if} > f_v$, and

$$
\begin{aligned}
H_2(f) &= 0 \qquad |f| \geq f_{if} \\
H_1(f) &= 0 \qquad |f| \geq f_{if}
\end{aligned}
$$

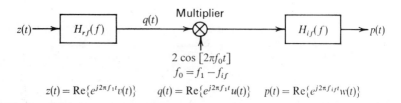

$$z(t) = \operatorname{Re}\{e^{j2\pi f_1 t}v(t)\} \qquad q(t) = \operatorname{Re}\{e^{j2\pi f_1 t}u(t)\} \qquad p(t) = \operatorname{Re}\{e^{j2\pi f_{if} t}w(t)\}$$

Figure 5-6   Block diagram of the rf filter, converter, and if filter of a communications receiver.

We wish to show that the whole operation shown in Fig. 5-6 can be replaced by a system consisting simply of a single filter in which the input is the original input shifted to a new frequency. This can be done in two simple steps.

(a) Show that

$$z_+(t) = e^{j2\pi f_1 t} v(t)$$

and

$$H_{rf+}(f) = 2H_1(f - f_1) \qquad H_{if+}(f) = 2H_2(f - f_{if})$$

(b) Show that

$$U(f) = H_1(f)V(f), \qquad W(f) = H_2(f)U(f) = H_1(f)H_2(f)V(f)$$

and that $p(t)$ is the result of passing the signal Re $\{e^{j2\pi f_{if} t} v(t)\}$ through a filter with transfer function

$$H_{if}(f)[H_1^*(-f - f_{if}) + H_1(f - f_{if})]$$

The effect of the process described in Problem 5-1 is thus simply to shift the band-pass signal $z(t)$ from the original frequency f_1 to the intermediate frequency $f_{if} = f_1 - f_0$ and replace the filters H_{rf} and H_{if} with a single equivalent filter centered at f_{if}. Note the practical application of this. In communication receivers extensive filtering is required to separate a desired signal from undesired signals at different frequencies and to eliminate noise. Such filtering requires a cascade of filter stages *all* turned to the same frequency. For practical reasons it is much easier if all of these stages can be tuned to a *fixed* frequency. By employing the above procedure, we can tune to signals at different frequencies (different values of f_1) by varying f_0 and keeping the frequency difference $f_1 - f_0$ equal to the intermediate frequency f_{if}. High selectivity is then achieved by making the fixed filter H_{if} sharply tuned (note that the center frequency of the filter H_{rf} must be variable).

One difficulty with such a mixing or intermediate frequency tuning procedure is interference from signals at *image frequencies*. This point is discussed in Problem 5-2.

Problem 5-2. Let the input to the receiver of Fig. 5-6 be the two signals

$$\text{Re } \{v_1(t)e^{j2\pi f_1 t}\} \qquad \text{and} \qquad \text{Re } \{v_2(t)e^{j2\pi f_2 t}\}$$

Assume that the oscillator frequency f_0, is $f_1 - f_{if}$ and that the center frequency of the second signal is given by

$$f_2 = f_1 - 2f_{if}, \qquad f_2 > 2f_{if}$$

Let both $v_1(t)$ and $v_2(t)$ have Fourier transforms which are zero for $|f| \geq f_v$, $f_v < f_{if}$; and let $H_1(f)$ and $H_2(f)$ be as shown in Fig. 5-7. Find the response of the receiver [the signal $p(t) = \text{Re } \{e^{j2\pi f_{if} t} w(t)\}$] to these two inputs.

The filter assumed in Fig. 5-7 for H_{rf} is overidealized (with a flat skirt instead of one which monotonically decreases) to make the solution of Problem 5-2 simple. However, in practice the problem of image signals

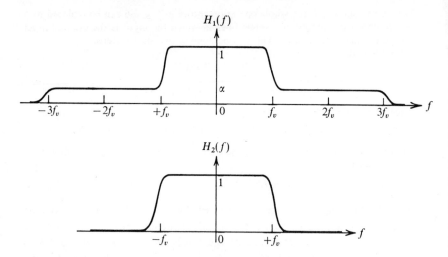

Figure 5-7   Filter characteristic for Problem 5-2.

(as the second signal in Problem 5-2 is referred to) is serious whenever the second signal at $f = f_1 - 2f_{if}$ is not greatly attenuated; i.e., whenever the ratio of incoming carrier frequency to i-f frequency is comparable to or greater than the Q of the r-f filter (Q = ratio filter center frequency/filter bandwidth).   Since the Q of the filter is limited by problems in circuit design, this sets a lower limit on the i-f frequency that may be used.

Representation of Band-Pass Random Processes

Up to this point we have confined our remarks to the relationship between a deterministic band-pass signal and its quadrature components. We now focus our attention on the case in which these signals are random processes.   In particular, consider the following two problems:

1. Expressing the correlation function of a modulated band-pass signal in terms of the correlation function of the modulating signal.
2. Finding the statistical properties of the quadrature components of a band-pass noise process such as the noise at the output of a band-pass filter caused by thermal noise in the resistors in the filter.

Let us consider the first problem.   In generating a modulated signal, we recognize that our oscillator is not tied to an absolute time reference, so that the phase of the modulated signal would be random from one experiment to the next. Thus we will incorporate into our modulated signal a random phase angle Θ, which is uniformly distributed from 0 to 2π

$$f_\Theta(\theta) = \begin{cases} \dfrac{1}{2\pi} & 0 \le \theta < 2\pi \\ 0 & \text{elsewhere} \end{cases} \tag{5-34}$$

and which we assume to be independent of the modulating signal. The modulated signal is then given by

$$Z(t) = \text{Re}\,\{V(t)e^{j\Theta}\,e^{j2\pi f_0 t}\} \tag{5-35}$$

in which f_0 is the carrier frequency and the process $V(t)$ may be complex valued (this will be useful in Chapter 6 where we consider angle modulation). We now wish to show that if $V(t)$ is wide-sense stationary, $Z(t)$ is also, and then to find $R_z(\tau)$ in terms of $R_v(\tau)$.

In dealing with complex-valued random processes, it is convenient to define the correlation function with the second term conjugated

$$R_v(\tau) = E\{V_{t+\tau}V_t^*\} \tag{5-36}$$

The quantity $E\{V_{t+\tau}V_t\}$ is used so seldom that we do not adopt any special notation for it.

Now, for $Z(t)$ as defined by Eq. 5-35, we see by comparison with Eqs. 5-14 and 5-13' that

$$Z_+(t) = Z(t) + j\hat{Z}(t) = V(t)e^{j\Theta}\,e^{j2\pi f_0 t} \tag{5-37}$$

Thus, using the statistical independence of $V(t)$ and Θ, we have from Eq. 5-37:

$$\begin{aligned} E\{Z_{+,t+\tau}Z_{+,t}\} &= E\{Z_{t+\tau}Z_t - \hat{Z}_{t+\tau}\hat{Z}_t\} + jE\{\hat{Z}_{t+\tau}Z_t + Z_{t+\tau}\hat{Z}_t\} \\ &= E\{V_{t+\tau}e^{j\Theta}e^{j2\pi f_0(t+\tau)}V_t e^{j\Theta}e^{j2\pi f_0 t}\} \\ &= E\{V_{t+\tau}V_t\}E\{e^{j2\Theta}\}e^{j2\pi f_0(2t+\tau)} = 0 \end{aligned} \tag{5-38}$$

since

$$\begin{aligned} E\{e^{j2\Theta}\} &= E\{\cos 2\Theta + j\sin 2\Theta\} \\ &= \frac{1}{2\pi}\int_0^{2\pi} [\cos 2\theta + j\sin 2\theta]\,d\theta = 0 \end{aligned} \tag{5-39}$$

Equating the real part in Eq. 5-38 to zero, we have

$$E\{Z_{t+\tau}Z_t\} = E\{\hat{Z}_{t+\tau}\hat{Z}_t\} \tag{5-40}$$

From Eq. 5-37 we also have

$$\begin{aligned} E\{Z_{+,t+\tau}Z_{+,t}^*\} &= E\{Z_{t+\tau}Z_t + \hat{Z}_{t+\tau}\hat{Z}_t\} + jE\{\hat{Z}_{t+\tau}Z_t - Z_{t+\tau}\hat{Z}_t\} \\ &= E\{V_{t+\tau}e^{j\Theta}e^{j2\pi f_0(t+\tau)}\,V_t^*e^{-j\Theta}e^{-j2\pi f_0 t}\} \\ &= e^{j2\pi f_0\tau}R_v(\tau) \end{aligned} \tag{5-41}$$

Equating real parts of Eq. 5-41 and using Eq. 5-40, we have

$$2E\{Z_{t+\tau}Z_t\} = \text{Re}\,\{e^{j2\pi f_0\tau}R_v(\tau)\}$$

Since the right-hand side of this equation is a function only of τ, $Z(t)$ is wide-sense stationary and has the correlation function

$$R_z(\tau) = \tfrac{1}{2}\,\text{Re}\,\{e^{j2\pi f_0\tau}R_v(\tau)\} \qquad (5\text{-}42)$$

We will make future use of this equation in this chapter and also in Chapter 6.

Now consider the second problem, determining the statistical description of the quadrature components of a band-pass stationary random process. Such a process might result from broad-band thermal noise generated in a resistor and then passed through the band-pass filter in the front end of a receiver. In this case the process $Z(t)$ would be a zero-mean gaussian process whose spectral density would be

$$S_z(f) = N_0|H_F(f)|^2 \qquad (5\text{-}43)$$

in which $H_F(f)$ denotes the transfer function of the filter. Note that this equation assumes the noise generated in the resistor has a spectrum that is flat with magnitude N_0 over all frequencies passed by the filter. This is a good assumption: the "white" thermal noise generated in a resistor is flat to frequencies almost out to the infrared region [2].

Our interest is in the two processes $X(t)$ and $Y(t)$ that result from synchronous demodulation of such a process $Z(t)$. Combining Eqs. 5-6, 5-15, and 5-16 we have that

$$X(t) = \text{Re}\,[e^{-j2\pi f_0 t}Z_+(t)] = Z(t)\cos 2\pi f_0 t + \hat{Z}(t)\sin 2\pi f_0 t \quad (5\text{-}44)$$

$$Y(t) = \text{Im}\,[e^{-j2\pi f_0 t}Z_+(t)] = \hat{Z}(t)\cos 2\pi f_0 t - Z(t)\sin 2\pi f_0 t \quad (5\text{-}45)$$

in which $\hat{Z}(t)$ is the random process resulting from passing the random process $Z(t)$ through a filter with transfer function $-j\,\text{sgn}\,f$. If $Z(t)$ is a stationary gaussian process, $\hat{Z}(t)$ is thus a stationary gaussian process and $Z(t)$ and $\hat{Z}(t)$ are *jointly* gaussian. The processes $X(t)$ and $Y(t)$ are then jointly gaussian processes since they are weighted sums of jointly gaussian processes. However, since these weighting functions ($\cos 2\pi f_0 t$ and $\sin 2\pi f_0 t$) vary with time, we cannot directly assert that $X(t)$ and $Y(t)$ are stationary. To show this we have to express their correlation functions in terms of those of $Z(t)$; we now proceed to do this.

Now note that since $X(t)$ and $Y(t)$ are linear combinations of $Z(t)$ and $\hat{Z}(t)$, the correlation functions R_x and R_y will be combinations of the correlation functions R_z and $R_{\hat{z}}$, and the cross-correlation functions $R_{z\hat{z}}$ and $R_{\hat{z}z}$. We thus must first express all of these correlation functions

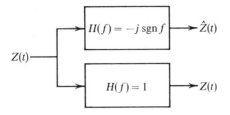

Figure 5-8   Situation used in finding the correlation functions of $Z(t)$ and $\hat{Z}(t)$.

solely in terms of R_z.   Toward this end, consider the situation shown in Fig. 5-8.   Comparing this situation with the one considered in Problem 4-7, we see that

$$S_{z\hat{z}}(f) = (-j\,\text{sgn}\,f)^*S_{zz}(f) = (+j\,\text{sgn}\,f)S_z(f) \qquad (5\text{-}46)$$

$$S_{\hat{z}z}(f) = (-j\,\text{sgn}\,f)S_{zz}(f) = (-j\,\text{sgn}\,f)S_z(f) \qquad (5\text{-}47)$$

And from Eq. 4-59 we have

$$S_{\hat{z}}(f) = |-j\,\text{sgn}\,f|^2 S_z(f) = \begin{cases} S_z(f) & f \neq 0 \\ 0 & f = 0 \end{cases} \qquad (5\text{-}48)$$

Let us now express these relations in the time domain.   Noting that multiplication by $(-j\,\text{sgn}\,f)$ in the frequency domain corresponds to taking the Hilbert transform in the time domain, Eqs. 5-46 to 5-48 imply

$$R_{z\hat{z}}(\tau) = -\hat{R}_z(\tau) \qquad (5\text{-}49)$$

$$R_{\hat{z}z}(\tau) = +\hat{R}_z(\tau) \qquad (5\text{-}50)$$

$$R_{\hat{z}}(\tau) = R_z(\tau) - E^2\{Z_t\} \qquad (5\text{-}51)$$

The presence of the term $E^2\{Z_t\}$ arises because $S_{\hat{z}}(0) = 0$, so that if $S_z(f)$ contains an impulse at $f = 0$ it must be subtracted from $S_{\hat{z}}(f)$.   The area of this impulse would be $E^2\{Z_t\}$, the mean-square value of the d-c term in $Z(t)$.   Now consider the quadrature components of $Z(t)$; that is, the real and imaginary parts of

$$V(t) = X(t) + jY(t) = e^{-j2\pi f_0 t}Z_+(t)$$
$$= e^{-j2\pi f_0 t}[Z(t) + j\hat{Z}(t)] \qquad (5\text{-}52)$$

Problem 5-3.   Starting with Eq. 5-52 and making use of Eqs. 5-49 to 5-51, show that if $E\{Z_t\} = 0$ then

$$E\{V_{t+\tau}V_t\} = E\{X_{t+\tau}X_t - Y_{t+\tau}Y_t\} + jE\{Y_{t+\tau}X_t + X_{t+\tau}Y_t\}$$
$$= 0 \qquad (5\text{-}53)$$

and

$$R_v(\tau) = E\{V_{t+\tau}V_t^*\} = E\{X_{t+\tau}X_t + Y_{t+\tau}Y_t\} + jE\{Y_{t+\tau}X_t - X_{t+\tau}Y_t\}$$

$$= 2e^{-j2\pi f_0\tau}[R_z(\tau) + j\hat{R}_z(\tau)] \qquad (5\text{-}54)$$

and then combine these two equations to obtain

$$R_x(\tau) = R_y(\tau) = E\{X_{t+\tau}X_t\} = E\{Y_{t+\tau}Y_t\}$$

$$= \mathrm{Re}\,\{e^{-j2\pi f_0\tau}[R_z(\tau) + j\hat{R}_z(\tau)]\}$$

$$= R_z(\tau)\cos 2\pi f_0\tau + \hat{R}_z(\tau)\sin 2\pi f_0\tau \qquad (5\text{-}55)$$

and

$$R_{xy}(\tau) = -R_{yx}(\tau) = E\{X_{t+\tau}Y_t\} = -E\{Y_{t+\tau}X_t\}$$

$$= -\mathrm{Im}\,\{e^{-j2\pi f_0\tau}[R_z(\tau) + j\hat{R}_z(\tau)]\}$$

$$= R_z(\tau)\sin 2\pi f_0\tau - \hat{R}_z(\tau)\cos 2\pi f_0\tau \qquad (5\text{-}56)$$

From Eqs. 5-55 and 5-56 we see that R_x, R_y, and R_{xy} depend only on the time shift τ. Furthermore, since $\hat{Z}(t)$ is obtained by passing $Z(t)$ through a linear filter, $\hat{Z}(t)$ will have zero mean if $E\{Z_t\} = 0$. From Eqs. 5-44 and 5-45 the processes $X(t)$ and $Y(t)$ are thus zero mean if $Z(t)$ is zero mean. Combining these remarks, we see that *if $Z(t)$ is a zero-mean wide-sense stationary random process, the processes $X(t)$ and $Y(t)$ will both be zero mean and jointly wide-sense stationary.* As we have already observed, if $Z(t)$ is gaussian, $X(t)$ and $Y(t)$ are jointly gaussian. Thus *if $Z(t)$ is a zero-mean stationary gaussian process, the processes $X(t)$ and $Y(t)$ are both zero-mean and jointly stationary and gaussian.*

To obtain information concerning the frequency band occupied by the processes $X(t)$ and $Y(t)$, it is useful to convert Eqs. 5-55 and 5-56 into the frequency domain.

Problem 5-4. Starting with Eqs. 5-55 and 5-56 and using appropriate transform properties, show that

$$S_x(f) = S_y(f) = \tfrac{1}{2}\{S_z(f + f_0) + S_z(f - f_0)$$

$$+ [\mathrm{sgn}\,f S_z(f)]*[\delta(f + f_0) - \delta(f - f_0)]\} \quad (5\text{-}57)$$

and

$$S_{xy}(f) = S_{yx}^*(f) = \frac{j}{2}\{S_z(f + f_0) - S_z(f - f_0)$$

$$+ [\mathrm{sgn}\,f S_z(f)]*[\delta(f + f_0) + \delta(f - f_0)]\} \quad (5\text{-}58)$$

These relationships are illustrated in Fig. 5-9 in which it is assumed that the pass-band of $Z(t)$ is centered near the frequency f_0 so that $X(t)$ and $Y(t)$ are low-pass processes. Note from this figure that if $S_z(f)$ *is symmetric about the frequency f_0* then the quadrature processes $X(t)$ and $Y(t)$ derived by synchronous demodulation of $Z(t)$ are such that

$$S_{xy}(f) \equiv 0 \qquad (5\text{-}59)$$

so that

$$R_{xy}(t - s) \equiv E\{X_t Y_s\} \equiv 0 \qquad (5\text{-}60)$$

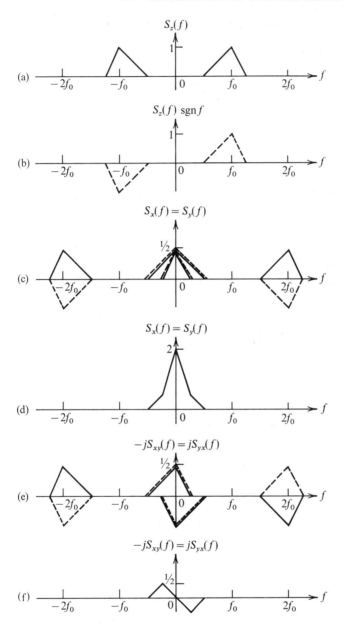

Figure 5-9   Spectra involved in finding $S_x(f)$ and $S_{xy}(f)$:

(a) $S_z(f)$ (d) resultant $S_x(f)$

(b) $S_z(f)$ sgn f (e) components of $S_{xy}(f)$

(c) components of $S_x(f)$ (f) resultant $S_{xy}(f)$

If $Z(t)$ is a zero mean gaussian process so that $X(t)$ and $Y(t)$ are zero mean and jointly gaussian, then Eq. 5-60 implies that $X(t)$ and $Y(t)$ are statistically independent processes in the sense that any set of observations taken from the process $X(t)$ will be statistically independent of any set of observations taken from the process $Y(t)$. This case is of physical interest because for either thermal or shot noise $S_z(f)$ will be as given by Eq. 5-43:

$$S_z(f) = N_0|H_F(f)|^2 \qquad (5\text{-}43)$$

In most cases of interest the center frequency of the filter $H_F(f)$ will be much, much greater than the bandwidth; in such cases $H_F(f)$ will be symmetric about the center frequency to a good approximation.

5-2   Amplitude Modulation

Let $M(t)$ denote the random process which is the output of some message source (such as a microphone or vidicon tube). We will assume that $M(t)$ is a stationary random process. Almost invariably the power spectral density of such a message source will be a low-pass function with the bulk of the power concentrated in some band $\pm W$ about $f = 0$. Before transmission, $M(t)$ is usually used to modulate some carrier signal so that the resulting signal, $S(t)$, is a band-pass process centered about the carrier frequency f_0. This modulation is performed for the reasons discussed at the beginning of this chapter. If the modulated signal is given by

$$S(t) = A[k + M(t)] \cos (2\pi f_0 t + \Theta) \qquad (5\text{-}61)$$

we say that $S(t)$ is the result of amplitude modulating $\cos (2\pi f_0 t + \Theta)$ by $M(t)$. Note that amplitude modulation is a *linear operation* on $M(t)$ *if* we ignore the bias term $Ak \cos (2\pi f_0 t + \Theta)$. For consider modulating $\cos (2\pi f_0 t + \Theta)$ by $M_1(t)$ and $M_2(t)$:

$$S_1(t) = AM_1(t) \cos (2\pi f_0 t + \Theta) + Ak \cos (2\pi f_0 t + \Theta)$$
$$S_2(t) = AM_2(t) \cos (2\pi f_0 t + \Theta) + Ak \cos (2\pi f_0 t + \Theta)$$

The result of modulating $\cos (2\pi f_0 t + \Theta)$ by the linear combination $aM_1(t) + bM_2(t)$ is

$$S(t) = aAM_1(t) \cos (2\pi f_0 t + \Theta) + bAM_2(t) \cos (2\pi f_0 t + \Theta)$$
$$+ Ak \cos (2\pi f_0 t + \Theta)$$

The purpose of the bias term $Ak \cos (2\pi f_0 t + \Theta)$ is to allow easy demodulation. We shall explore this point in detail in a later subsection.

Now let us consider the spectrum associated with $S(t)$. If we make the associations

$$V(t) = A[k + M(t)] \tag{5-62}$$
$$Z(t) = S(t)$$

we can make direct use of Eq. 5-42

$$R_s(\tau) = \tfrac{1}{2} \operatorname{Re} \{e^{j2\pi f_0 \tau} R_v(\tau)\} \tag{5-42'}$$

Now for $V(t)$ given by Eq. 5-62:

$$R_v(\tau) = A^2 E\{(k + M_{t+\tau})(k + M_t)\}$$
$$= A^2[k^2 + 2kE\{M_t\} + R_m(\tau)]$$

If we assume that $M(t)$ has zero mean; then, since $M(t)$ is real valued, combining the above two equations yields

$$R_s(\tau) = \frac{A^2}{2} [k^2 + R_m(\tau)] \cos 2\pi f_0 \tau \tag{5-63}$$

The corresponding power spectral density is

$$S_s(f) = \frac{A^2}{4} \{k^2[\delta(f + f_0) + \delta(f - f_0)] + S_m(f + f_0) + S_m(f - f_0)\}$$
$$\tag{5-64}$$

Note from Eq. 5-64 that if the power of the message signal is concentrated in a band of $\pm W$ about $f = 0$, the power in the modulated signal

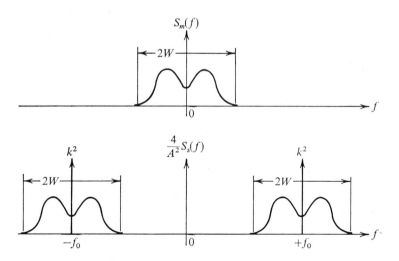

Figure 5-10 Power density spectra of the message process and the amplitude modulated process.

$S(t)$ is concentrated in bands $\pm W$ about the frequencies $\pm f_0$. This relationship is illustrated in Fig. 5-10. The impulses in $S_s(f)$ represent discrete components (the presence of periodic sinusoidal waves) at the frequencies $\pm f_0$).

Reception of Double Sideband AM

The front end of an AM receiver, consisting of an r-f filter, a mixer, and an i-f filter, is shown in Fig. 5-11a. By virtue of Problem 5-1, the receiver in Fig. 5-11b which has only an r-f filter is equivalent in the sense that the quadrature components of both $Z_{rf}(t)$ and $Z_{if}(t)$ will be the same. As the discussion following Problem 5-1 indicated, the receiver employing i-f conversion would be used for practical reasons. However, for ease of manipulation, we analyze the performance of the receiver of Fig. 5-11b. We will drop the subscript rf on the output of this receiver and denote the output simply by

$$Z(t) = \text{Re}\,\{V(t)e^{j2\pi f_0 t}\} = X(t)\cos 2\pi f_0 t - Y(t)\sin 2\pi f_0 t \qquad (5\text{-}65)$$

We denote the noise present at the receiver input (due to thermal noise in the antenna and resistors in the receiver first stage and shot noise in the first stage of the receiver) by $N'(t)$. We assume that $N'(t)$ is a stationary zero-mean random process with spectral density

$$S_{n'}(f) = N_0 \qquad (5\text{-}66)$$

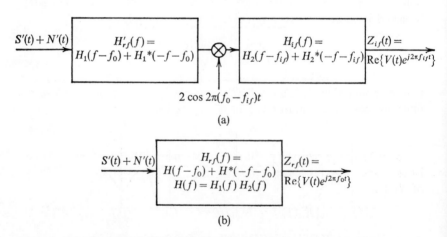

(a)

(b)

Figure 5-11 (a) Front end of an AM receiver with if conversion.
(b) Front end of an equivalent receiver without conversion.

For the physical noise sources listed above, $N'(t)$ would be gaussian. However, we will not need this property in the present discussion. We denote the modulated message signal appearing at the receiver input by

$$S'(t) = A[k + M(t)] \cos 2\pi f_0 t \tag{5-67}$$

In the present discussion we do not include a random phase in the transmitted carrier for the following reason. We assume for the time being that the transmitted phase is measured and known at the receiver. The appearance of a known phase in Eq. 5-67 would not change anything in the discussion to follow, and we have thus set this phase equal to zero for convenience.

Let us now consider the response of the receiver to the two processes $S'(t)$ and $N'(t)$. Since the filter $H_{rf}(f)$ is linear, the output $Z(t)$ may be split up into two parts: the first, $S(t)$, due to the input $S'(t)$; and the second, $N(t)$, due to the input $N'(t)$.

$$Z(t) = S(t) + N(t) \tag{5-68}$$

Let us express both of these in terms of their quadrature components:

$$S(t) = \text{Re}\{V_m(t)e^{j2\pi f_0 t}\} = X_m(t) \cos 2\pi f_0 t - Y_m(t) \sin 2\pi f_0 t \tag{5-69}$$

$$N(t) = \text{Re}\{V_n(t)e^{j2\pi f_0 t}\} = X_n(t) \cos 2\pi f_0 t - Y_n(t) \sin 2\pi f_0 t \tag{5-70}$$

Now we have assumed that $S_m(f)$, the power spectral density of the message, is concentrated in a band $\pm W$ about zero; let us further assume that f_0 (or f_{if} in the i-f case) is larger than W. If $H(f)$ is flat in the band $-W \leq f \leq W$ and zero outside this band as shown in Fig. 5-12, then $S'(t)$ is passed without distortion by H_{rf} and $S(t) = CS'(t)$, thus:

$$X_m(t) = AC[M(t) + k] \tag{5-71}$$

$$Y_m(t) = 0 \tag{5-72}$$

If in demodulating $Z(t)$, a d-c blocking capacitor is used in the low-pass filter, the constant term in Eq. 5-71 is removed and we have

$$X_m(t) = ACM(t) \tag{5-73}$$

To evaluate the receiver performance, we need only find the characteristics of the noise processes $X_n(t)$ and $Y_n(t)$. The power spectral density of $N(t)$ is

$$S_n(f) = N_0|H_{rf}(f)|^2 = N_0[|H(-f - f_0)|^2 + |H(f - f_0)|^2] \tag{5-74}$$

Assuming that $|H(f)|$ is symmetric about $f = 0$ (this will be true to a very good approximation for an i-f or r-f filter whose bandwidth is much

$$H_{rf}(f) = H^*(-f - f_0) + H(f - f_0)$$

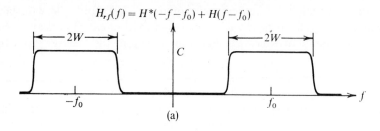

(a)

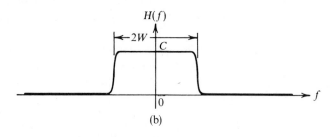

(b)

Figure 5-12   Ideal filter assumed in derivation of performance of AM:
(a) $H_{rf}(f)$,   (b) $H(f)$.

narrower than its center frequency), we have from Eqs. 5-57 and 5-58 and
the discussion following that

$$S_{x_n}(f) = S_{y_n}(f) = 2N_0|H(f)|^2 \qquad (5\text{-}75)$$

and

$$S_{x_n y_n}(f) = 0 \qquad (5\text{-}76)$$

Synchronous Demodulation

By synchronous demodulation of $Z(t)$ by $\cos 2\pi f_0 t$ (multiplication by
$2 \cos 2\pi f_0 t$ and low-pass filtering) we can obtain the signal

$$X(t) = X_m(t) + X_n(t) = ACM(t) + X_n(t) \qquad (5\text{-}77)$$

which is a faithful reproduction of the message signal (except for the change
of scale AC) plus interferring noise.   A common and useful measure of
the fidelity of the received signal is the *output signal-to-noise ratio*

$$\left(\frac{S}{N}\right)_o = \frac{\text{average power of received message process}}{\text{average power of received noise process}} \qquad (5\text{-}78)$$

For AM with synchronous demodulation, we have from above

$$\left(\frac{S}{N}\right)_o = \frac{C^2 A^2 E\{M_t^2\}}{E\{X_{n,t}^2\}} = \frac{C^2 A^2 R_m(0)}{R_{x_n}(0)} \qquad (5\text{-}79)$$

But, from Eq. 5-75,

$$R_{x_n}(0) = \int_{-\infty}^{\infty} S_{x_n}(f)\, df = 2N_0 \int_{-\infty}^{\infty} |H(f)|^2\, df \qquad (5\text{-}80)$$

For $H(f)$ the ideal low-pass filter and $H_{rf}(f)$ the ideal band-pass filter assumed in Fig. 5-12, we have

$$H(f) = \begin{cases} C & |f| \le W \\ 0 & |f| > W \end{cases}$$

so that

$$R_{x_n}(0) = 4C^2 N_0 W \qquad (5\text{-}81)$$

and the output signal-to-noise ratio is

$$\left(\frac{S}{N}\right)_{o,\text{AM}} = \frac{A^2 R_m(0)}{4 N_0 W} \qquad (5\text{-}82)$$

In the future we will wish to compare the signal-to-noise ratio performance of different modultion methods.   In comparing them we wish to do so on the basis that each modulation method produces the same modulated message power at the receiver and has to cope with the same noise spectral density at the receiver input.   For this reason let us define the *channel signal-to-noise ratio* as

$$\left(\frac{S}{N}\right)_c = \frac{\text{average power of modulated message signal at receiver input}}{\text{average power of input noise in the bandwidth of the } message}$$
$$= \frac{R_{s'}(0)}{2 W N_0} \qquad (5\text{-}83)$$

We can normalize our performance for comparison purposes by dividing the output signal-to-noise ratio by this channel signal-to-noise ratio.
For AM, we have from Eq. 4-64 (assuming $E\{M\} = 0$),

$$R_{s'}(0) = \tfrac{1}{2}A^2[k^2 + R_m(0)] \qquad (5\text{-}84)$$

so that

$$\left(\frac{S}{N}\right)_{c,\text{AM}} = \frac{\tfrac{1}{2}A^2[k^2 + R_m(0)]}{2 W N_0} \qquad (5\text{-}85)$$

and

$$\frac{(S/N)_o}{(S/N)_c}\bigg|_{\text{AM}} = \frac{R_m(0)}{k^2 + R_m(0)} \qquad (5\text{-}86)$$

When synchronous detection is employed, the purpose of the $Ak \cos 2\pi f_0 t$ term in the modulated signal

$$S'(t) = AM(t)\cos 2\pi f_0 t + Ak \cos 2\pi f_0 t$$

is to provide a signal to which a local oscillator in the receiver can lock onto. This local oscillator provides the $2 \cos 2\pi f_0 t$ signal which multiplies $Z(t)$, thus accomplishing the synchronous demodulation. We shall discuss in Chapter 10 the phase-lock loop, a device for providing a local carrier signal in phase with the transmitted carrier. For the purpose of providing a carrier to lock onto, the power required in the signal $Ak \cos 2\pi f_0 t$ is very small, so that

$$k^2 \ll R_m(0)$$

and, for synchronous demodulation,

$$\left.\frac{(S/N)_o}{(S/N)_c}\right|_{\text{AM sync. demod.}} = \frac{R_m(0)}{k^2 + R_m(0)} \approx 1 \qquad (5\text{-}87)$$

Envelope Demodulation

The complexity of "tracking" the $Ak \cos 2\pi f_0 t$ term and generating a signal of the same frequency and phase to synchronously demodulate $Z(t)$ greatly adds to the complexity and cost of a receiver. For a point-to-point communication system (such as a satellite relay system) in which only a few receivers are involved, this is not a great drawback. In entertainment broadcasting where literally millions of receivers may be tuned in on the same transmitter, it is desirable to keep the receiver as simple and in-expensive as possible (at the possible expense of having to increase the power of the *single* transmitter). Here envelope demodulation is employed. The signal $Z(t)$ of Eq. 5-65 (in actual practice, the signal $Z_{\text{if}}(t)$ of Fig. 5-11a) is rectified and the resulting signal low-pass filtered. This operation is shown in Fig. 5-13, together with the resulting waveforms. The waveforms for $Z(t)$ and $|Z(t)|$ are sketched in Fig. 5-13b, assuming that the noise is small. The output of the rectifier is

$$|Z(t)| = A(t)|\cos [2\pi f_0 t + \theta(t)]| \qquad (5\text{-}88)$$

We postpone briefly the problem of finding analytically the output of the receiver (the result of low-pass filtering $|Z(t)|$). In the case of greatest practical interest, an easy intuitive argument suffices to deduce the demodulator output. Consider those situations in which the carrier frequency f_0 (or in actuality, the i-f frequency f_{if}) is much, much greater than the bandwidth of the signals $X(t)$ and $Y(t)$ [whose bandwidth is determined by the bandwidth of $H_{\text{rf}}(f)$]. Thus $A(t)$ changes only very slowly compared to one r-f cycle. Picture the action on $|Z(t)|$ of an R-C filter whose time constant is short compared to $1/W$ but long compared to $1/f_0$. The voltage across the capacitor remains almost constant from the peak of one r-f cycle to the next, but decays fast enough to follow

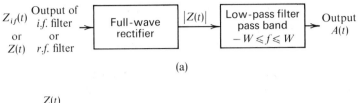

(a)

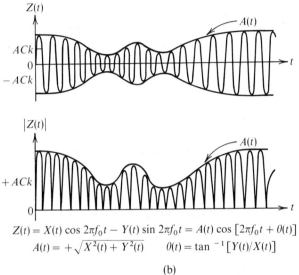

$$Z(t) = X(t) \cos 2\pi f_0 t - Y(t) \sin 2\pi f_0 t = A(t) \cos \left[2\pi f_0 t + 0(t) \right]$$
$$A(t) = +\sqrt{X^2(t) + Y^2(t)} \qquad 0(t) = \tan^{-1}\left[Y(t)/X(t) \right]$$

(b)

Figure 5-13   Envelope modulation:
(a) Block diagram of envelope detector receiver.
(b) Signals involved in envelope demodulation, assuming very low noise.

accurately the variations in the heights of the peaks caused by changes in $A(t)$. Thus, for $f_0 \gg W$, we have approximately for the receiver output

$$A(t) = +\sqrt{X^2(t) + Y^2(t)}$$

$$= +\sqrt{\{AC[k + M(t)] + X_n(t)\}^2 + Y_n^2(t)} \qquad (5\text{-}89)$$

Problem 5-5. Let $|m(t)| \le k$ so that $k + m(t) \ge 0$ for all t and assume that the Fourier transform of $m(t)$ is zero for $|f| \ge W$. Let

$$Z(t) = [k + m(t)] \cos 2\pi f_0 t, \qquad f_0 > W$$

Show that if $|Z(t)|$ is passed through an ideal low-pass filter

$$H(f) = \begin{cases} 1 & |f| \le W \\ 0 & |f| > W \end{cases}$$

then the output is $(2/\pi)[k + m(t)]$. *Hint:* Note that $|\cos 2\pi f_0 t|$ is periodic in t with period $1/2f_0$ and can be expanded in a Fourier series

$$|\cos 2\pi f_0 t| = \sum_{k=-\infty}^{\infty} c_k e^{jk 4\pi f_0 t}$$

Let us consider $A(t)$ as given by Eq. 5-89. We would like to represent $A(t)$ as the sum of a message term plus a term due to noise and distortion. For arbitrary signal-to-noise ratios this is quite difficult. However, the case of greatest practical interest is when the receiver is operating satisfactorily; that is, when the noise is small with respect to the signal. Thus let us assume that

$$P\{|Y_{n,t}| > \epsilon AC|k + M(t)|\} \le \delta_1 \tag{5-90}$$

with

$$\epsilon \ll 1, \qquad \delta_1 \ll 1$$

Then, with probability greater than $1 - \delta_1$,

$$A(t) \approx +\sqrt{\{AC[k + M(t)] + X_n(t)\}^2} \tag{5-91}$$

Now note that if

$$M(t) < -k$$

then

$$+\sqrt{[M(t) + k]^2} \ne k + M(t)$$

so that even in the absence of noise the output is badly distorted if $M(t) < -k$. Thus we shall assume that k is adjusted relative to the message source such that

$$P\{AC(k + M_t) + X_{n,t} < 0\} \le \delta_2 \tag{5-92}$$

with

$$\delta_2 \ll 1$$

Combining Eqs. 5-90–92, we have that with probability greater than $(1 - \delta_1)(1 - \delta_2)$

$$A(t) \approx AC[k + M(t)] + X_n(t) = X_m(t) + X_n(t) \tag{5-93}$$

This is the output of a synchronous demodulator; thus the *expression for* $(S/N)_o$ *derived for synchronous demodulation applies to envelope demodulation with two qualifications.   The expression applies to envelope demodulation only if:*

1. *The noise is small with respect to the signal.*
2. *$ACM_t + X_{n,t}$ is greater than $-k$ with probability close to one.*

Moreover, the expression for $(S/N)_c$ remains unchanged; the only difference is in the relative magnitude of k^2 and $R_m(0)$. To satisfy inequality 5-92 we must have at least

$$k^2 > R_m(0) + \frac{R_{x_n}(0)}{A^2 C^2}$$

and more usually

$$k^2 = \text{two to six times } R_m(0) + \frac{R_{x_n}(0)}{A^2 C^2}$$

If condition (1) above is satisfied, the second term on the right-hand side of this expression is negligible compared to the first, and we shall ignore it. The ratio between k^2 and $R_m(0)$ depends on the statistics of M_t. For voice k^2 might need to be only three times $R_m(0)$, while for classical music with its greater dynamic range k^2 might need to be four to seven times $R_m(0)$. Thus we have

$$\left.\frac{(S/N)_o}{(S/N)_c}\right|_{\text{AM env. demod.}} = \frac{R_m(0)}{R_m(0) + k^2} < \frac{1}{2}$$

$$\text{and} \approx \tfrac{1}{3} \text{ to } \tfrac{1}{8} \tag{5-94}$$

For a discussion of envelope demodulation in the low signal-to-noise ratio case (referred to as operation below threshold), consult reference [3] or [4].

Single-Sideband Amplitude Modulation (SSB-AM)

We saw in the beginning of this section that if the power spectral density of the message signal occupied a band of width $2W$ about $f = 0$ then the power density spectrum of the resulting AM signal occupied a band of $2W$ about both $+f_0$ and $-f_0$; a total bandwidth occupancy of $4W$. We saw in Sec. 5-1 that the AM signal could have its lower (or upper) sidebands removed and the original message signal could still be recovered from this single-sideband AM signal. Furthermore, since SSB-AM results by passing a conventional AM signal through the filter

$$H_F(f) = \begin{cases} 1 & f_0 \leq |f| \leq f_0 + W \\ 0 & \text{elsewhere} \end{cases} \tag{5-28}$$

the power spectral density of SSB-AM occupies only a total bandwidth of $2W$; this relationship was shown in Fig. 5-5. In this section we denote the SSB-AM signal by $S''(t)$ [the signal whose transform is labeled $Z(f)$ in Fig. 5-5]. Inasmuch as SSB-AM occupies only one-half the bandwidth of conventional AM (thus allowing twice as many stations to operate in the same portion of the spectrum), it has an advantage over conventional AM.

We now explore the performance of SSB-AM. If we consider conventional AM without the presence of a carrier term (double-sideband suppressed carrier, DSB-SC)

$$S'(t) = AM(t) \cos 2\pi f_0 t \tag{5-95}$$

we saw in Sec. 5-1 that the signal resulting from SSB-AM would be

$$S''(t) = A[M(t) \cos 2\pi f_0 t - \hat{M}(t) \sin 2\pi f_0 t]$$

In practice the transmitted signal would be

$$S''(t) = A[M(t) \cos 2\pi f_0 t - \hat{M}(t) \sin 2\pi f_0 t + k \cos 2\pi f_0 t] \quad (5\text{-}96)$$

The inclusion of the $Ak \cos 2\pi f_0 t$ term is to provide a "pilot tone" to which a local oscillator at the receiver can "lock onto." This local oscillator is used to synchronously demodulate the received signal. In general, high-quality SSB-AM reception requires synchronous demodulation to separate the $M(t)$ term from the $\hat{M}(t)$ term appearing in Eq. 5-96. Since the ear is relatively insensitive to phase and $M(t)$ differs from $\hat{M}(t)$ only by a phase shift of $-90°$ for $f > 0$ and $+90°$ for $f < 0$, the envelope demodulated signal $\sqrt{M^2(t) + \hat{M}^2(t) + k^2}$ is somewhat intelligible for voice signals. Under certain restricted conditions, high quality SSB demodulation appears possible without synchronous demodulation; the interested reader should refer to the articles by Powers [5] and Voelcker [6].

Consider now the signals obtained at the output of the r-f filter (or in actual practice out of the i-f filter) of the SSB receiver. This situation is shown in Fig. 5-14. We assume that $H_{rf}(f)$ has a pass-band such that

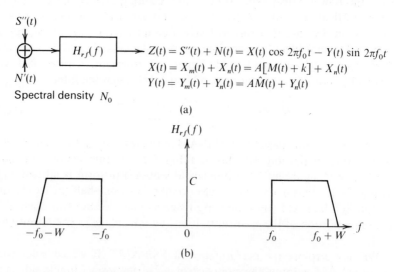

(a)

(b)

Figure 5-14 Configuration pertinent to calculation of SSB performance:
(a) signals involved,
(b) filter characteristic.

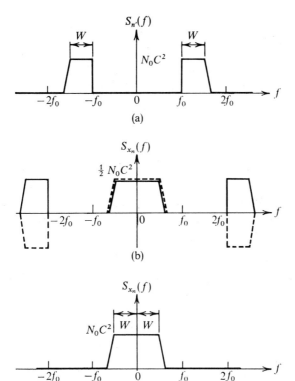

Figure 5-15   Spectra involved in finding $S_x(f)$:
(a) $S_{n'}(f)$,
(b) components of $S_{x_n}(f)$,
(c) resultant $S_{x_n}(f)$.

$S''(t)$ is passed without distortion.   Thus the output of the filter is

$$Z(t) = \{CA[M(t) + k] + X_n(t)\} \cos 2\pi f_0 t$$
$$- [CA\hat{M}(t) + Y_n(t)] \sin 2\pi f_0 t \quad (5\text{-}97)$$

and the output of a synchronous demodulator is (assuming the d-c term is blocked)

$$X(t) = ACM(t) + X_n(t) \quad (5\text{-}98)$$

To calculate $(S/N)_o$ we need only the mean-square value of $X_n(t)$. Now the spectrum of $N(t)$ is $N_0|H_{rf}(f)|^2$. From this the power spectral density of $X_n(t)$ can be found from Eq. 5-57. The computations involved are illustrated in Fig. 5-15.   From this we see that

$$S_{x_n}(f) \approx \begin{cases} N_0 C^2 & |f| \le W \\ 0 & |f| > W \end{cases}$$

and

$$E\{X_{n,t}^2\} = R_{x_n}(0) = \int_{-\infty}^{\infty} S_{x_n}(f)\,df = 2WN_0C^2 \qquad (5\text{-}99)$$

for the ideal bandpass filter shown in Fig. 5-14.

The output signal-to-noise ratio is obtained from Eq. 5-99

$$\left(\frac{S}{N}\right)_{o,\text{SSB}} = \frac{A^2 C^2 R_m(0)}{2WN_0 C^2} = \frac{A^2 R_m(0)}{2WN_0} \qquad (5\text{-}100)$$

Next, let us calculate the channel signal-to-noise ratio:

$$\left(\frac{S}{N}\right)_c = \frac{E\{S_t''^2\}}{2WN_0} \qquad (5\text{-}101)$$

From Eq. 5-96 we have

$$E\{S_t''^2\} = A^2 E\{[M_t \cos 2\pi f_0 t - \hat{M}_t \sin 2\pi f_0 t + k \cos 2\pi f_0 t]^2\}$$
$$= A^2 [R_m(0)(\cos^2 2\pi f_0 t + \sin^2 2\pi f_0 t)$$
$$- 2R_{m\hat{m}}(0) \cos 2\pi f_0 t \sin 2\pi f_0 t + k^2 \cos^2 2\pi f_0 t] \qquad (5\text{-}102)$$

in which we have assumed that the mean of M_t is zero and used the fact that

$$R_{\hat{m}}(\tau) = R_m(\tau)$$

Now,

$$R_{m\hat{m}}(0) = \int_{-\infty}^{\infty} S_{m\hat{m}}(f)\,df = (-j) \int_{-\infty}^{\infty} S_m(f)\,\text{sgn}\,f\,df = 0 \qquad (5\text{-}103)$$

since $S_m(f)$ is symmetric in f.   Using Eqs. 5-102 and 5-103 and averaging the $\cos^2 2\pi f_0 t$ term over one cycle (or taking a statistical average over the random phase of the carrier), we have

$$E\{S_t''^2\} = A^2 [R_m(0) + \tfrac{1}{2}k^2] \qquad (5\text{-}104)$$

so that

$$\left(\frac{S}{N}\right)_{c,\text{SSB-AM}} = \frac{A^2 [R_m(0) + \tfrac{1}{2}k^2]}{2WN_0} \qquad (5\text{-}105)$$

and

$$\frac{(S/N)_o}{(S/N)_c}\bigg|_{\text{SSB-AM}} = \frac{R_m(0)}{R_m(0) + \tfrac{1}{2}k^2} \qquad (5\text{-}106)$$

Again, the power in the pilot tone used to synchronize the receiver local oscillator can be small compared to the message power in the side-bands, so that

$$\frac{(S/N)_o}{(S/N)_c}\bigg|_{\text{SSB-AM}} \approx 1 \qquad (5\text{-}107)$$

Thus SSB-AM yields the same performance as conventional AM with synchronous demodulation and occupies only one-half the bandwidth. The disadvantage is that (like synchronously detected conventional AM) it requires tracking the pilot tone and generating a local carrier of the same

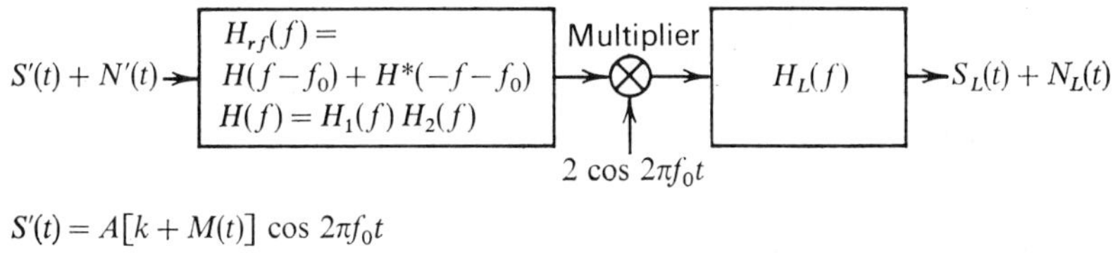

$$S'(t) = A[k + M(t)] \cos 2\pi f_0 t$$

Figure 5-16 AM receiver with synchronous detection and low-pass filtering.

frequency and phase. Moreover, the design of the filters required to reject the unwanted sidebands can be a complicated task.

The performance and relative merits of the different methods of AM are summarized in the table on page 162.

Problem 5-6. Consider the situation originally shown in Fig. 5-11; this same situation is repeated in Fig. 5-16 with the addition of a synchronous demodulator. The signal $S'(t)$ is again given by

$$S'(t) = A[k + M(t)] \cos 2\pi f_0 t$$

and the noise $N'(t)$ has a flat spectrum

$$S_{n'}(f) = N_0$$

Instead of letting the filter $H(f)$ be the ideal filter of Fig. 5-12, we leave this filter arbitrary and denote the transfer function of the cascade by

$$H_c(f) = H_L(f)H(f) = H_L(f)H_1(f)H_2(f)$$

and denote the impulse response of the cascade by

$$h_c(t) = \mathcal{F}^{-1}[H_c(f)]$$

Let us denote the component of the output of H_L due to $S'(t)$ by $S_L(t)$ and the component of the output due to $N'(t)$ by $N(t)$. If $H_c(0) = 0$, then from Problem 5-1 and the discussion in this section it follows that $S_L(t)$ is the response of $H_c(f)$ to $AM(t)$. Further, from the discussion in this section it follows that the spectral density of $N(t)$ is given by

$$S_n(f) = 2N_0|H_c(f)|^2$$

(a) The total error in the output due to both noise and distortion caused by the filter is

$$E(t) = [S_L(t) - M(t)] + N(t)$$

Show that the mean-square error in the output is given by

$$\mathcal{E} = E\{E_t^2\} = \int_{-\infty}^{\infty} |1 - AH_c(f)|^2 S_m(f) \, df + 2N_0 \int_{-\infty}^{\infty} |H_c(f)|^2 \, df$$

$$= \int_{-\infty}^{\infty} |1 - AH_c(f)|^2 S_m(f) \, df + \frac{2N_0}{A^2} \int_{-\infty}^{\infty} |AH_c(f)|^2 \, df \quad (5\text{-}108)$$

(b) The problem of how to select $H_c(f)$ in such a manner as to minimize $\mathcal{E}$ is a topic which is considered in detail in Chapter 7. Here we consider this only briefly. Let $A = 1$ and

$$S_m(f) = \frac{M_0}{f^2 + W^2}$$

and

$$H_c(f) = \begin{cases} 1 & |f| \le f_c \\ 0 & |f| > f_c \end{cases}$$

Find the value of f_c that minimizes $\mathscr{E}$.

SUMMARY OF AM PERFORMANCE

(Assuming a message spectrum limited to $|f| \le W$ and ideal filtering)

CONVENTIONAL

(Double Sideband) AM   SSB-AM

	Envel. Demod.	Synch. Demod.	Synchronous Demodulation
Bandwidth Occupancy	$4W$	$4W$	$2W$
Transmitted Signal	$S'(t) = A[M(t) + k]\cos 2\pi f_0 t$ $k^2 > R_m(0)$	$k^2 \ll R_m(0)$	$S''(t) = A[-\hat{M}(t)\sin 2\pi f_0 t + (M(t) + k)\cos 2\pi f_0 t]$ $k^2 \ll R_m(0)$
$(S/N)_o$	$\dfrac{A^2 R_m(0)}{4WN_0}$		$\dfrac{A^2 R_m(0)}{2WN_0}$
$(S/N)_c$	$\dfrac{\frac{1}{2}A^2[R_m(0) + k^2]}{2WN_0}$		$\dfrac{A^2[R_m(0) + \frac{1}{2}k^2]}{2WN_0}$
$\dfrac{(S/N)_o}{(S/N)_c}$ Approximate Operating Value	$\dfrac{R_m(0)}{R_m(0) + k^2}$ $\frac{1}{8}$ to $\frac{1}{3}$	1	$\dfrac{R_m(0)}{R_m(0) + \frac{1}{2}k^2}$ 1
Comments:	Requires more transmitter power for equal performance than synch. demod. suitable for use when receiver simplicity outweighs transmitter power	Requires tracking and generating local carrier. Suitable when transmitter power conservation is more important than receiver complexity	Requires tracking and generating local carrier and intricate filtering. Suitable for use when conservation of transmitter power and bandwidth occupancy outweighs receiver complexity

We have not yet commented as to the optimality of the form of receivers considered in this section (in particular the receivers of Figs. 5-11 and 5-16). At this point we only wish to comment that if the bandwidth of $H_{rf}(f)$ is sufficiently broad that it passes $S'(t)$ without distortion, then the synchronous demodulation has not done anything that cannot be undone (i.e., $S'(t) + N'(t)$ could be recovered from the output of the synchronous demodulator). Thus the problem of designing an optimum receiver resolves to designing an optimum filter to follow the multiplier in Fig. 5-16. This problem is discussed further in Chapter 7, where it is pointed out that if $M(t)$ and $N(t)$ are jointly gaussian, then the optimum filter is linear. The problem of how to design the optimum linear filter and calculate its performance is discussed in that chapter.

REFERENCES

[1] Rowe, Harrison, *Signals and Noise in Communication Systems*, D. Van Nostrand, Princeton, N.J., 1965.

[2] Van der Ziel, A., *Noise*, Prentice-Hall, Englewood Cliffs, N.J., 1954.

[3] Grumet, A., "Demodulation effect of an envelope detector at low signal-to-noise ratios," *Proc. IRE*, **50**, 2135–36, Oct. 1962.

[4] Middleton, D., *An Introduction to Statistical Communication Theory*, McGraw-Hill Book Co., New York, 1960; Chap. 13.

[5] Powers, K. H., "The compatibility problem in single-sideband transmission," *Proc. IRE*, **48**, 1431–35, Aug. 1960.

[6] Voelcker, H., "Demodulation of single-sideband signals via envelope detection," *IEEE Trans. on Comm. Tech.*, **COM 14**, 23–30, Feb. 1966.

Chapter 6

Frequency Modulation

In the preceding chapter, we saw that single-sideband amplitude modulation (SSB-AM) had a bandwidth occupancy equal to that of the original message signal. Also, the normalized signal-to-noise ratio of the output of a synchronous detector was only slightly less than unity

$$\left. \frac{(S/N)_o}{(S/N)_c} \right|_{\text{SSB-AM}} \approx 1$$

This would be the same performance that would be obtained by simply transmitting the message signal itself in the presence of the same noise. The only effect of amplitude modulation is thus to shift the message signal to a different frequency band. As we stated earlier, this function of frequency translation is useful both for providing a signal that will propagate more readily over a certain transmission medium and for translating a number of low-pass message signals to different adjacent frequency bands for simultaneous transmission over a single transmission medium (frequency multiplexing).

This behavior is the best that can be achieved by a linear operation (such as AM) on the message process. However, by using a nonlinear modulation process, it is possible to change both the bandwidth occupancy of the modulated signal and the normalized output signal-to-noise ratio. In this chapter we discuss the most widely used nonlinear modulation method, frequency modulation (FM), and show that by causing the modulated signal to occupy a greater bandwidth than the original message signal, the normalized signal-to-noise ratio can be made greater than unity. The practical significance of this fact is that, at the expense of greater bandwidth occupancy, we can reduce the transmitter power (over SSB-AM or DSB-AM) and still achieve the same output signal-to-noise ratio $[(S/N)_o]$ at the receiver.

We will mention only briefly the physical means of implementing demodulation of FM signals and the distortion or errors introduced by practical demodulation circuits. Our attention will be focused on analyzing the bandwidth occupancy of FM signals and the performance of an ideal demodulator. This focus of attention is consistent with the two overall objectives of this book: presenting the methods and concepts which are useful in analyzing communication systems and imparting a familiarity with the capabilities of different methods of information transmission.

6-1   Angle Modulation

In *angle modulation* the angle of a sinusoidal carrier is varied in accordance with a message signal, as contrasted to amplitude modulation in which the amplitude of the signal was varied. We denote the modulated signal by

$$Z(t) = A \cos [2\pi f_0 t + \Theta + \mu(t)]$$
$$= A \operatorname{Re} [e^{j\Psi(t)}] \tag{6-1}$$

in which the angle of the sinusoid, $\Psi(t)$, is given by

$$\Psi(t) = 2\pi f_0 t + \Theta + \mu(t) \tag{6-2}$$

The carrier frequency is f_0, Θ represents the (random but constant with time) phase of the carrier, and $\mu(t)$ is a varying angle which is changed by the message. As before, we denote the message process by $M(t)$; here we take $M(t)$ to be a dimensionless quantity. If the original (dimensioned) message signal is $M_0(t)$, we might thus take $M(t)$ to be

$$M(t) = M_0(t)/k_m \tag{6-3}$$

in which k_m has the same units as $M_0(t)$.

If the angle $\mu(t)$ is made to vary in direct proportion to the message

$$\mu(t) = \phi_d M(t) \tag{6-4}$$

we say that the signal $Z(t)$ is the result of *phase modulation* of the carrier by $M(t)$. We assume that the constant k_m in Eq. 6-3 is adjusted such that

$$P\{|M_t| \leq 1\} = 1 - \delta; \qquad \delta \ll 1 \tag{6-5}$$

The quantity ϕ_d in Eq. 6-4 then is termed the *modulation index*; it is the *peak phase deviation* in the sense that, except for a negligible fraction of the time, δ, the phase deviation remains less than ϕ_d.

The rate of change of the angle of the sinusoidal carrier is

$$\Psi'(t) = \frac{d}{dt} \Psi(t) = 2\pi f_0 + \mu'(t) \tag{6-6}$$

If $\mu'(t)$ is varied in direction proportion to the message

$$\mu'(t) = \omega_d M(t) = (2\pi f_d)M(t) \tag{6-7}$$

we say that $Z(t)$ is the result of *frequency modulation* of the sinusoidal carrier by $M(t)$, for in this case the rate of change of the angle of the sinusoid or instantaneous frequency[1] of the sinusoid is varied in direct relation to the message $M(t)$. If k_m is again adjusted such that Eq. 6-5 is true, we refer to the quantity f_d as the *peak "frequency" deviation.* Except for a negligible fraction of the time, δ, the "frequency" deviation of the carrier in c.p.s. is less than f_d.

To gain some familiarity with the process of angle modulation, let us consider modulation by a sinusoidal message signal. Specifically, we will take the carrier phase, Θ, to be zero and let

$$\mu(t) = \phi_d \sin \omega_m t = \phi_d \sin (2\pi f_m t) \tag{6-8}$$

so that

$$\mu'(t) = \omega_m \phi_d \cos \omega_m t = (2\pi f_m \phi_d) \cos (2\pi f_m t) \tag{6-9}$$

This thus represents phase modulation of the carrier with modulation index ϕ_d and message $M(t) = \sin \omega_m t$ or frequency modulation with peak frequency deviation

$$f_d = f_m \phi_d \tag{6-10}$$

and message $M(t) = \cos \omega_m t$. The modulated signal is

$$z(t) = \text{Re } [e^{j\Psi(t)}] = \text{Re } \{e^{j2\pi f_0 t} e^{j\mu(t)}\} = \cos [2\pi f_0 t + \phi_d \sin 2\pi f_m t] \tag{6-11}$$

It is easily shown that $z(t)$ is periodic and may be expressed in a Fourier cosine series as

$$z(t) = \sum_{k=-\infty}^{\infty} J_k(\phi_d) \cos [(2\pi f_0 + k2\pi f_m)t] \tag{6-12}$$

in which

$$J_k(a) = \frac{1}{2\pi} \int_0^{2\pi} e^{-j[kt - a \sin t]} dt \tag{6-13}$$

The sequence of functions $J_k(\ )$, $k = 0, \pm 1, \pm 2, \ldots$, appears many places in applied mathematics. The function $J_k(\ )$ is known as the kth Bessel function of the first kind. A tabulation of these Bessel functions is given in Jahnke and Emde [1].

---

[1] The reader should note the distinction between instantaneous "frequency" which is taken to be the rate of change of an angle of a sinusoid and frequency used in the Fourier sense; that is, in representing a signal as a combination of sinusoids of different *constant* frequencies.

Note that the modulated signal contains components not only at the carrier frequency and sideband frequencies $f_0 \pm f_m$ (as would be the case with AM) but at all frequencies $f_0 \pm kf_m$ differing by integral multiples of the modulation frequency from the carrier frequency. Although the modulated signal contains theoretically an infinite number of frequency components, the coefficients $J_k(\phi_d)$ die off rapidly to zero for sufficiently large k. The value of k for which this attenuation occurs depends in an involved manner upon ϕ_d. Thus even in the simple case of sinusoidal modulation there is no straightforward relation between the bandwidths of the modulated and modulating signals.

Problem 6-1. Derive Eqs. 6-12 and 6-13. *Hint:* Note that

$$e^{j\mu(t)} = e^{j\phi_d \sin 2\pi f_m t}$$

is a periodic function with period $T = 1/f_m$ and hence may be expanded in a Fourier series.

Problem 6-2. Plot or tabulate the first 11 coefficients $J_k(\phi_d)$, $k = 0, 1, 2, \ldots, 10$ for $\phi_d = 1, 2,$ and 10. Note that

$$J_{-k}(a) = (-1)^k J_k(a)$$

For a discussion of how angle modulation signals are generated, see references [2] and [3].

6-2 Demodulation of FM Signals

In this section we briefly discuss demodulation of FM signals. We focus our attention on FM because it is in more common usage than phase modulation (PM). All of the methods that we use to analyze FM would also be useful in analyzing PM. In fact, PM can be considered approximately as FM with a particular choice of pre-emphasis, a discussion of which is given in Sec. 6-5. Phase demodulation by means of the phase-lock loop is discussed in some detail in Chapter 10.

The Discriminator

We now consider how to recover the signal $\mu'(t)$ from the modulated signal

$$z(t) = \mathrm{Re}\,[e^{j2\pi f_0 t}\, e^{j\mu(t)}] = \mathrm{Re}\,[e^{j2\pi f_0 t}\, v(t)] \qquad (6\text{-}1')$$

in which we have denoted

$$v(t) = e^{j\mu(t)} \qquad (6\text{-}14)$$

To study the effect of different operations on $z(t)$, it is convenient to represent the signals involved in the frequency domain and to make note of the bandwidth occupancy of the different signals. Let $V(f) = \mathscr{F}[v(t)]$. We assume that $v(t)$ is bandlimited to some band W, $W < f_0$.

$$V(f) = 0 \quad \text{for} \quad |f| \geq W \tag{6-15}$$

Although $V(f)$ is not strictly bandlimited, the above assumption will be a good approximation to practice as long as f_0, the carrier frequency, is very much greater than the width of the band of frequencies over which $V(f)$ is appreciable.

Now consider a filter

$$H_d(f) = H^*(-f - f_0) + H(f - f_0) \tag{6-16}$$

with

$$H(f) = \begin{cases} j2\pi f & |f| \leq W \\ \text{arbitrary} & |f| > W \end{cases} \tag{6-17}$$

The transfer function for $|f| > W$ can be picked in any manner such that $\mathscr{F}^{-1}[H_d(f)]$ is real valued. Consider passing $z(t)$ through this filter and denote the output of this filter by $q(t)$ and the pre-envelope of $q(t)$ by $u(t)$:

$$q(t) = \text{Re}\left\{ e^{j2\pi f_0 t} u(t) \right\} \tag{6-18}$$

In Problem 5-1 we saw that

$$\mathscr{F}[u(t)] = U(f) = V(f)H(f) \tag{6-19}$$

For the particular filter transfer function chosen, we have

$$U(f) = j2\pi f V(f) \tag{6-20}$$

or, denoting differentiation by a prime,

$$u(t) = v'(t) = je^{j\mu(t)}\mu'(t) \tag{6-21}$$

The output of the filter is thus

$$\begin{aligned} q(t) &= \text{Re}\left\{ j\mu'(t)e^{j[2\pi f_0 t + \mu(t)]} \right\} \\ &= \mu'(t)\cos\left(2\pi f_0 t + \mu(t) + \pi/2\right) \end{aligned} \tag{6-22}$$

The signal $\mu'(t)$ can then be recovered from $q(t)$ by the type of detector used for AM demodulation.

One way of obtaining the desired frequency characteristic of Eq. 6-17 and simultaneously performing the amplitude demodulation is shown in Fig. 6-1. Two resonant circuits tuned to different frequencies, one above f_0 and the other below f_0, could yield the s-shaped characteristic shown in Fig. 6-1a if their responses are subtracted one from the other. By

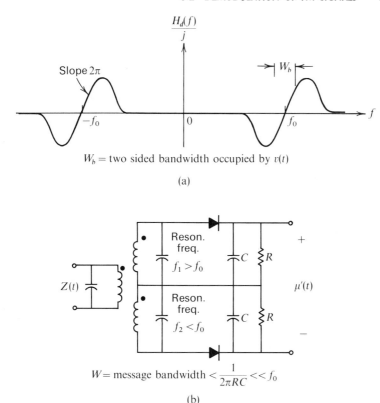

W_b = two sided bandwidth occupied by $v(t)$

(a)

W = message bandwidth $< \dfrac{1}{2\pi RC} << f_0$

(b)

Figure 6-1   FM discriminator:
(a) S-shaped discriminator characteristic.
(b) Circuit diagram of idealized discriminator.

subtracting the *envelopes* of these two responses, rather than subtracting the responses and then envelope detecting, the signal $\mu'(t)$ rather than $|\mu'(t)|$ is obtained.   An idealized circuit for achieving this is shown in Fig. 6-1b.   The purpose of using two such resonant circuits rather than a single resonant circuit is to achieve greater linearity in the response characteristic. In practice one would not use the circuit of Fig. 6-1b with two separate tuned circuits tuned to different frequencies because the two secondary coils cannot be isolated from one another and a different arrangement of tuned circuits would be used.   For a discussion of this point refer to Arguimbau [4] or Pederson [5].

An ideal instantaneous "frequency" detector is called a *discriminator*. In a practical realization of a discriminator, such as the one briefly described above, there will be error or distortion in the output due to:

1. $V(f)$ is not exactly zero for $|f| > $ W as assumed.
2. $\mu'(t)$ will not be strictly bandlimited, thus some distortion is introduced by the low-pass filter following the rectifier in the envelope detector.
3. The filter characteristic will not be linear over the whole frequency band of $v(t)$.

For a further discussion of these errors, see Secs. IV-6 and IV-7 of Rowe [6].

The Limiter

We have seen that the configuration of the filter $H_d(f)$ followed by an AM demodulator could recover the message $\mu'(t)$ from the signal:

$$z(t) = \text{Re } [e^{j2\pi f_o t} v(t)] = \text{Re } [e^{j2\pi f_o t} e^{j\mu(t)}] \qquad (6\text{-}1')$$

Now let us suppose that the received signal is not given by this equation but contains some extraneous amplitude modulation of positive amplitude $a(t)$:

$$z(t) = a(t) \text{ Re } [e^{j2\pi f_o t} v(t)] = \text{Re } [e^{j2\pi f_o t} a(t) v(t)] \qquad (6\text{-}23)$$

This unwanted modulation could result from random fluctuations in the "path strength" of the transmission channel or from the effects of filtering the incoming signal in the r-f or i-f filter with a filter having too narrow a pass-band.

Let us now consider the effects of this unwanted modulation upon the output of the discriminator. If we assume that the signal $a(t)v(t)$ is still restricted to a band of width $\pm W$ c.p.s., then the response of $H_d(f)$ to $z(t)$ as given by Eq. 6-23 would be

$$q(t) = \text{Re } \{e^{j2\pi f_o t} u(t)\} \qquad (6\text{-}18)$$

with $u(t)$ now given by

$$u(t) = \frac{d}{dt} [a(t)v(t)]$$

$$= \frac{d}{dt} [a(t)e^{j\mu(t)}]$$

$$= a(t)e^{j\mu(t)}[j\mu'(t) + a'(t)/a(t)] \qquad (6\text{-}24)$$

Let us assume that the amplitude modulation is slowly varying compared to $\mu(t)$ so that

$$|\mu'(t)| \gg |a'(t)/a(t)|$$

Then $u(t)$ is approximately given by

$$u(t) = a(t)e^{j\mu(t)}j\mu'(t)$$

and the output of $H_d(f)$ by

$$q(t) = \text{Re } \{j\mu'(t)a(t)e^{j[2\pi f_0 t + \mu(t)]}\} \tag{6-25}$$
$$= \mu'(t)a(t) \cos [2\pi f_0 t + \mu(t) + \pi/2] \tag{6-26}$$

The output of the AM demodulator following $H_d(f)$ would thus be

$$r(t) = a(t)\mu'(t) \tag{6-27}$$

The output of the discriminator has thus become distorted by the presence of the unwanted amplitude modulation. To eliminate this, a *limiter* consisting of a clipper and band-pass filter is used preceding the discriminator. If $z(t)$ denotes the input to a clipper, the behavior of an ideal clipper is given by

$$z_c(t) = \text{clipper output} = \text{sgn } [z(t)]$$
$$= \begin{cases} +1 & z(t) > 0 \\ -1 & z(t) < 0 \end{cases} \tag{6-28}$$

Let us now consider the output of this clipper. From Eq. 6-23 we have, noting that $a(t)$ is positive,

$$z_c(t) = \text{sgn } \{a(t) \cos [2\pi f_0 t + \mu(t)]\}$$
$$= \text{sgn } \{\cos [2\pi f_0 t + \mu(t)]\} \tag{6-29}$$

Now consider $\Psi(t) = 2\pi f_0 t + \mu(t)$ as the variable. The function sgn $\{\cos (\Psi)\}$ viewed as a function of Ψ is a square wave of peak value ± 1 and period 2π as shown in Fig. 6-2.

Problem 6-3. Expand $f(\Psi) = \text{sgn } [\cos (\Psi)]$ as given above in a cosine or exponential Fourier series and show that

$$f(\Psi) = \text{sgn } [\cos (\Psi)] = \frac{2}{\pi} \sum_{k=0}^{\infty} (-1)^k \frac{e^{j(2k+1)\Psi} + e^{-j(2k+1)\Psi}}{2k + 1} \tag{6-30}$$

From Eq. 6-30 we thus see that the output of the clipper is given by

$$z_c(t) = \frac{2}{\pi} \sum_{k=0}^{\infty} \frac{(-1)^k}{2k + 1} [e^{j(2k+1)[2\pi f_0 t + \mu(t)]} + e^{-j(2k+1)[2\pi f_0 t + \mu(t)]}] \tag{6-31}$$

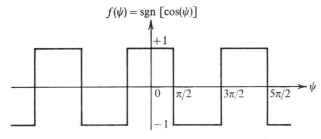

$f(\psi) = \text{sgn } [\cos(\psi)]$

Figure 6-2 Limiter characteristic.

Now consider the frequency content of the term

$$e^{j(2k+1)[2\pi f_0 t + \mu(t)]} = e^{j(2k+1)2\pi f_0 t}e^{j(2k+1)\mu(t)}$$

$$= e^{j(2k+1)2\pi f_0 t}[v(t)]^{2k+1} \qquad (6\text{-}32)$$

The signal $v(t)$ is low-pass, so the signal of Eq. 6-32 is band-pass centered about $f = (2k+1)f_0$. Furthermore, the transform of $v^{2k+1}(t)$ is $V(f)$ convolved with itself $2k$ times; thus the bandwidth of $[v(t)]^{2k+1}$ is $\pm(2k+1)W$. If f_0 is greater than W, then none of the terms corresponding to values of k greater than zero will overlap (in spectrum) the k equals zero term. A bandpass filter of bandwidth $\pm W$ and center frequency $\pm f_0$ would thus filter out from $z_c(t)$ all terms except the $k=0$ term, and the overall limiter output (the output of the filter) would be

$$z_l(t) = \frac{2}{\pi}\left[e^{2j\pi f_0 t}e^{j\mu(t)} + e^{-j2\pi f_0 t}e^{-j\mu(t)}\right]$$

$$= \frac{4}{\pi}\,\mathrm{Re}\,\left[e^{j2\pi f_0 t}e^{j\mu(t)}\right] \qquad (6\text{-}33)$$

This output (except for a multiplicative constant) is thus the original angle modulated signal with the undesired amplitude modulation removed.

A high-quality receiver will usually include such a limiter to remove any undesired amplitude modulation and to partially eliminate the effects of

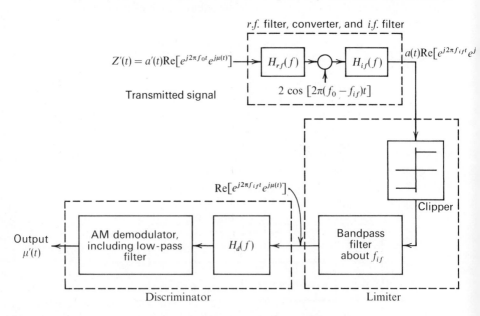

Figure 6-3   Block diagram of an FM receiver.

noise. The output of the limiter is then demodulated by a discriminator to recover $\mu'(t)$. The overall block diagram of an FM receiver is shown in Fig. 6-3, including the r-f filtering, i-f conversion, and i-f filtering stages. The signals shown at various stages are based on the assumption that the bandwidth of these filters is sufficiently broad to pass the modulated signal without distortion.

6-3 Spectrum of a Sinusoidal Carrier Angle Modulated by a Gaussian Process[1]

In the design of a modulation system, it is necessary to be able to evaluate the power spectrum of the modulated signal, in order to calculate bandwidth occupancy and the bandwidth required in the r-f and i-f filters of the receiver. In this section we consider calculation of the spectral density of an angle modulated process.

The spectrum of the modulated process

$$Z(t) = A \cos \left[2\pi f_0 t + \Theta + \mu(t)\right] \qquad (6\text{-}1)$$

is not determined simply by the spectrum of $\mu(t)$ as was the case in AM. This is because $Z(t)$ is a nonlinear function of $\mu(t)$. To be able to find the spectrum of $Z(t)$, or requivalently $R_z(\tau)$, we require a knowledge of the statistics of μ_t sufficient to be able to calculate

$$E\{\cos \left[2\pi f_0 t + \Theta + \mu_t\right] \cos \left[2\pi f_0 t + \Theta + 2\pi f_0 \tau + \mu_{t+\tau}\right]\}$$

We will thus not be able to calculate $R_z(\tau)$ in general, but must restrict ourselves to special cases. We have already considered the case

$$\mu(t) = \phi_d \sin \omega_m t$$

but this signal is of interest only for test purposes (since it conveys no information, except perhaps the value of ω_m). Our interest is in the case in which the modulating signal $M(t)$ is a random process. Since we cannot calculate $R_z(\tau)$ for a general message distribution, we assume throughout the balance of this chapter that $\mu(t)$ is a zero-mean, gaussian random process. This would be the case for either phase or frequency modulation by a zero-mean gaussian message process $M(t)$. (Why?)

Let us then proceed to calculate $R_z(\tau)$ upon the assumption that $\mu(t)$ is a zero-mean gaussian process and that the carrier phase Θ is uniformly distributed and statistically independent of $\mu(t)$.

---

[1] The methods of this section are based on the work of Abramson [7].

Problem 6-4.   (a) Assume that Θ is uniformly distributed from 0 to 2π and is statistically independent of $\mu(t)$ and that $e^{j\mu(t)}$ has a spectrum that is nonzero only for $|f| < f_0$. Show that

$$E\{Z_{t+\tau}Z_t\} = \frac{A^2}{2} \operatorname{Re} [e^{j2\pi f_0\tau} E\{e^{jQ_{t,\tau}}\}] \qquad (6\text{-}34)$$

in which

$$Q_{t,\tau} = \mu_{t+\tau} - \mu_t \qquad (6\text{-}35)$$

Hint: Note that $Z(t)$ may be expressed in the form

$$Z(t) = A \operatorname{Re} [e^{j\mu(t)}e^{j\Theta}e^{j2\pi f_0 t}]$$

and make use of the derivation of Eq. 5-42.

   (b) Now assume that $\mu(t)$ is a *zero-mean gaussian* process. Show that under this added assumption Eq. 6-34 reduces to

$$E\{Z_{t+\tau}Z_t\} = \frac{A^2}{2} \cos 2\pi f_0\tau \exp \{-\tfrac{1}{2}\sigma_Q^2(t + \tau, t)\} \qquad (6\text{-}36)$$

in which

$$\sigma_Q^2(t + \tau, t) = \operatorname{var} \{\mu_{t+\tau} - \mu_t\} = E\{(\mu_{t+\tau} - \mu_t)^2\} \qquad (6\text{-}37)$$

Hint: Make use of the known properties of gaussian random variables and the form of the characteristic function of a gaussian random variable.

At two points in our discussion of angle modulation, we will have occasion to assume that $\mu(t)$ is stationary and consider the Fourier transform of the term

$$g(\tau) \triangleq E\{e^{jQ_{t,\tau}}\} = E\{e^{j(\mu_{t+\tau}-\mu_t)}\} \qquad (6\text{-}38)$$

which appears in Eq. 6-34. It will be useful to consider some properties of this function $g(\tau)$ before further considering the spectrum of $Z(t)$.

Note that by means of Euler's formula, $g(\tau)$ can be expressed as

$$g(\tau) = E\{\cos (\mu_{t+\tau} - \mu_t)\} + jE\{\sin (\mu_{t+\tau} - \mu_t)\} \qquad (6\text{-}38')$$

In many situations we would expect the probability distribution of the process μ_t to be invariant to the direction in which time runs; such a process might be termed *reversible*. An example of a reversible process is the signal generated by scanning a picture; we would expect the statistical properties of this signal to be independent of whether the picture is scanned from left to right or vice-versa. Note that if $\mu(t)$ is reversible and stationary, then

$$E\{\sin (\mu_{t+\tau} - \mu_t)\} = E\{\sin (\mu_t - \mu_{t+\tau})\}$$
$$= -E\{\sin (\mu_{t+\tau} - \mu_t)\}$$

and hence

$$E\{\sin (\mu_{t+\tau} - \mu_t)\} \equiv 0$$

Thus if $\mu(t)$ is a reversible process, $g(\tau)$ is real:

$$g(\tau) = E\{\cos(\mu_{t+\tau} - \mu_t)\} \qquad (6\text{-}38'')$$

If $\mu(t)$ is a gaussian process, then from the derivation of Eq. 6-36 it follows that

$$g(\tau) = \exp\{-\tfrac{1}{2}\sigma_Q{}^2(t + \tau, t)\} \qquad (6\text{-}39)$$

and hence $g(\tau)$ is again real.

Let us now examine the consequence of $g(\tau)$ being purely real. We do this by expanding $g(\tau)$ in the form

$$
\begin{aligned}
g(\tau) &= E\{e^{j\mu_{t+\tau}}e^{-j\mu_t}\} \\
&= E\{\cos\mu_{t+\tau}\cos\mu_t\} + E\{\sin\mu_{t+\tau}\sin\mu_t\} \\
&\quad + jE\{\sin\mu_{t+\tau}\cos\mu_t - \cos\mu_{t+\tau}\sin\mu_t\}
\end{aligned}
$$

If $g(\tau)$ is purely real, it is thus the sum of two correlation functions:

$$g(\tau) = E\{\cos\mu_{t+\tau}\cos\mu_t\} + E\{\sin\mu_{t+\tau}\sin\mu_t\} \qquad (6\text{-}38''')$$

In this case $G(f)$, the Fourier transform of $g(\tau)$, consists of the sum of two spectral density functions and $G(f)$ must be non-negative.

Let us now return to finding the spectrum of $Z(t)$. We first relate the term $\sigma_Q{}^2(t + \tau, t)$ appearing in Eq. 6-36 to the message correlation function. For phase modulation

$$Q_{t,\tau} = \mu_{t+\tau} - \mu_t = \phi_d[M_{t+\tau} - M_t] \qquad (6\text{-}40)$$

We have already assumed that $M(t)$ is a zero-mean gaussian process; let us now also assume that $M(t)$ is also stationary. The variance of $Q_{t,\tau}$ is then

$$\sigma_Q{}^2(t + \tau, t) = 2\phi_d{}^2[R_m(0) - R_m(\tau)] \qquad (6\text{-}41)$$

Our main concern is with FM. In this case,

$$Q_{t,\tau} = \mu_{t+\tau} - \mu_t = \omega_d \int_t^{t+\tau} M(\zeta)\,d\zeta \qquad (6\text{-}42)$$

Again assuming $M(t)$ is a zero-mean stationary gaussian process, we have

$$
\begin{aligned}
\sigma_Q{}^2(t + \tau, t) &= E\left\{\left[\omega_d \int_t^{t+\tau} M(\zeta)\,d\zeta\right]^2\right\} \\
&= \omega_d{}^2 E\left\{\int_t^{t+\tau} d\zeta_1 \int_t^{t+\tau} d\zeta_2 M(\zeta_1)M(\zeta_2)\right\}
\end{aligned}
$$

Interchanging the order of integration and expectation, this equation becomes

$$\sigma_Q{}^2(t + \tau, t) = \omega_d{}^2 \int_t^{t+\tau} d\zeta_1 \int_t^{t+\tau} d\zeta_2 R_m(\zeta_1 - \zeta_2)$$

$$= \omega_d{}^2 \int_0^\tau d\zeta_1 \int_0^\tau d\zeta_2 R_m(\zeta_1 - \zeta_2)$$

$$= 2\omega_d{}^2 \int_0^\tau d\zeta_1 \int_0^{\zeta_1} d\zeta_2 R_m(\zeta_1 - \zeta_2) \qquad (6\text{-}43)$$

in which the second equality follows by a change of variable of integration, and the third equality follows from the symmetry of $R_m(\tau)$.

Note that for either phase modulation (Eq. 6-41) or FM (Eq. 6-43) $\sigma_Q{}^2(t + \tau, t)$ is a function only of τ; in the future we will thus denote this quantity by $\sigma_Q{}^2(\tau)$. Note then from Eq. 6-36 that $E\{Z_{t+\tau}Z_t\}$ is only a function of τ; we now rewrite this equation as

$$E\{Z_{t+\tau}Z_t\} = R_z(\tau) = \frac{A^2}{2} \cos 2\pi f_0 \tau \exp\{-\tfrac{1}{2}\sigma_Q{}^2(\tau)\} \qquad (6\text{-}44)$$

with

$$\sigma_Q{}^2(\tau) = 2\phi_d{}^2[R_m(0) - R_m(\tau)] \qquad (6\text{-}45)$$

for phase modulation and

$$\sigma_Q{}^2(\tau) = \omega_d{}^2 \int_0^\tau d\zeta_1 \int_0^\tau d\zeta_2 R_m(\zeta_1 - \zeta_2)$$

$$= 2\omega_d{}^2 \int_0^\tau d\zeta_1 \int_0^{\zeta_1} d\zeta_2 R_m(\zeta_1 - \zeta_2) \qquad (6\text{-}46)$$

for FM.

These equations give explicit expressions for $R_z(\tau)$; the correlation function of the modulated signal, in terms of $R_m(\tau)$, the correlation function of the modulating message. Unfortunately, this is not usually adequate for practical purposes. The design of filters to handle the modulated signal is usually done in the frequency domain, requiring knowledge of the spectral density $S_z(f) = \mathscr{F}[R_z(\tau)]$. Furthermore, questions of frequency allocation and calculation of "cross talk" or interchannel interference are done directly in the frequency domain, again requiring $S_z(f)$. The difficulty lies in finding the transform of the term

$$g(\tau) = \exp\{-\tfrac{1}{2}\sigma_Q{}^2(\tau)\} \qquad (6\text{-}39')$$

Let us denote the transform of this function by $G(f)$:

$$G(f) = \mathscr{F}[g(\tau)] \qquad (6\text{-}47)$$

In terms of $G(f)$, the power density spectrum of the modulated signal can be expressed simply by means of the frequency translation property as

$$S_z(f) = \frac{A^2}{4} [G(f + f_0) + G(f - f_0)] \qquad (6\text{-}48)$$

Although $-\frac{1}{2}\sigma_Q^2(\tau)$, the argument of the exponential in Eq. 6-46, can usually be evaluated by straightforward methods for $\sigma_Q^2(\tau)$ given by either Eq. 6-45 or 6-46, it is usually impossible to obtain analytic expressions for the transform integral giving $G(f)$. For a thorough discussion of approximate methods of computing this transform integral, refer to Secs. IV-3 through IV-5 of Rowe [6] and Abramson [7]. Here we will only mention the idea behind Abramson's method.

Abramson expands the exponential function of Eq. 6-39 in a series expansion

$$g(\tau) = \exp\{-\tfrac{1}{2}\sigma_Q^2(\tau)\} = 1 + \sum_{k=1}^{\infty} [-\tfrac{1}{2}\sigma_Q^2(\tau)]^k/k! \qquad (6\text{-}49)$$

He then approximates $g(\tau)$ by a finite number of terms in this series and takes as a corresponding approximation of $G(f)$ the finite sum of the transforms of these terms. The transforms of $[\sigma_Q^2(\tau)]^k$ for $f = 2, 3, \ldots$ are calculated by appropriate repeated convolutions of the spectrum of $\sigma_Q^2(\tau)$. For a complete discussion of this method and examples giving computations, the reader is referred to the original article by Abramson. We now turn to a way of obtaining a rough measure of the bandwidth occupancy of $G(f)$.

R.M.S. Bandwidth of the Modulated Signal

We now discuss a way of estimating the bandwidth occupancy $S_z(f)$. Our treatment follows basically the work of Abramson [7]. From Eq. 6-48 we see that the spectrum of $S_z(f)$ consists (except for a multiplicative constant) of $G(f)$ translated to $\pm f_0$. Thus the bandwidth occupancy of $S_z(f)$ about $\pm f_0$ is the same as the bandwidth occupancy of $G(f)$ about $f = 0$. We therefore turn to determining the range of frequencies over which $G(f)$ is non-negligible.

We first note, from Eq. 6-38″ and the remarks following this equation, that $G(f)$ is a non-negative even function of f. Now in our discussion of probability theory we have seen that a useful measure of the dispersion of a (positive-valued) probability density function of a random variable X is the variance of that random variable

$$E\{(X - m_x)^2\} = \int_{-\infty}^{\infty} f_X(x)(x - m_x)^2 \, dx \qquad (6\text{-}50)$$

Similarly, the dispersion of the spectrum $G(f)$ about its mean at $f = 0$ [$G(f)$ is symmetric about zero] could be measured by an integral similar to that of Eq. 6-50. We need only to normalize $G(f)$ to a function whose integral is one, so we consider

$$\frac{G(f)}{\int_{-\infty}^{\infty} G(f)\, df}$$

The mean square dispersion of $G(f)$ about $f = 0$ would then be given by

$$\overline{f_G^2} = \frac{\int_{-\infty}^{\infty} f^2 G(f)\, df}{\int_{-\infty}^{\infty} G(f)\, df} \qquad (6\text{-}51)$$

We refer to this quantity as the *mean-square bandwidth* and its positive square root as the *r.m.s. bandwidth*. We now turn to finding an explicit relation giving $\overline{f_G^2}$ in terms of the message correlation function. Using the transform properties

$$j2\pi f G(f) \leftrightarrow \frac{d}{d\tau} g(\tau); \qquad g(0) = \int_{-\infty}^{\infty} G(f)\, df$$

Eq. 6-51 becomes

$$\overline{f_G^2} = -\frac{\left[\frac{d^2}{d\tau^2} g(\tau)\right]_{\tau=0}}{(2\pi)^2 g(0)} \qquad (6\text{-}52)$$

Starting from Eq. 6-39' and twice differentiating gives

$$\frac{d^2 g(\tau)}{d\tau^2} = \left\{ -\frac{1}{2}\left[\frac{d^2}{d\tau^2} \sigma_Q^2(\tau)\right] + \left[\frac{1}{2}\frac{d}{d\tau} \sigma_Q^2(\tau)\right]^2 \right\} \exp\left\{-\tfrac{1}{2}\sigma_Q^2(\tau)\right\} \quad (6\text{-}53)$$

It is now trivial to combine Eqs. 6-45, 6-39', 6-52, and 6-53 to obtain the mean-square bandwidth for phase modulation. We leave it to the reader to show that if we denote the mean-square message bandwidth by $\overline{f_M^2}$, then

$$\overline{f_G^2} = -\left(\frac{\phi_d}{2\pi}\right)^2 R_m''(0) = \left(\frac{\phi_d}{2\pi}\right)^2 R_M(0)\overline{f_M^2} \qquad (6\text{-}54)$$

for phase modulation. In evaluating this equation, the reader should note that if $R_m''(0)$ is finite, it is negative and $R_m'(0) = 0$.

Let us now consider FM. We must consider differentiation of $\sigma_Q^2(\tau)$ as given by Eq. 6-46. Leibnitz's rule [8] for differentiation of an integral states

$$\frac{d}{d\tau} \int_{a(\tau)}^{b(\tau)} h(\tau, x)\, dx = b'(\tau)h[\tau, b(\tau)] - a'(\tau)h[\tau, a(\tau)]$$
$$+ \int_{a(\tau)}^{b(\tau)} \left[\frac{d}{d\tau} h(\tau, x)\right] dx \qquad (6\text{-}55)$$

Applying this rule twice in succession to

$$\frac{1}{\omega_d{}^2} \sigma_Q{}^2(\tau) = \int_0^\tau d\zeta_1 \left[\int_0^\tau d\zeta_2 R_m(\zeta_1 - \zeta_2) \right] \tag{6-46'}$$

yields

$$\frac{1}{\omega_d{}^2} \frac{d}{d\tau} \sigma_Q{}^2(\tau) = \int_0^\tau d\zeta_2 R_m(\tau - \zeta_2) + \int_0^\tau d\zeta_1 R_m(\zeta_1 - \tau)$$

$$= 2 \int_0^\tau R_m(\tau - \zeta) \, d\zeta \tag{6-56}$$

and

$$\frac{1}{\omega_d{}^2} \frac{d^2}{d\tau^2} \sigma_Q{}^2(\tau) = 2R_m(0) + 2 \int_0^\tau R_m'(\tau - \zeta) \, d\zeta \tag{6-57}$$

Combining Eqs. 6-53, 6-56, and 6-57 yields

$$g''(0) = +\omega_d{}^2 R_m(0) \tag{6-58}$$

And, from Eqs. 6-46 and 6-39',

$$g(0) = 1$$

Thus, substituting into Eq. 6-52, the mean-square bandwidth of $G(f)$ for FM is given by

$$\overline{f_G{}^2} = (f_d)^2 R_m(0) \qquad (f_d = \omega_d/2\pi) \tag{6-59}$$

The r.m.s. bandwidth is thus

$$+\sqrt{\overline{f_G{}^2}} = \text{r.m.s. bandwidth} = +f_d R_m^{1/2}(0)$$
$$= \text{peak frequency deviation} \times \text{r.m.s. power of message signal} \tag{6-60}$$

Note that the r.m.s. bandwidth of the modulated signal depends only on the average power of the message and not at all on the shape of the message spectrum.

The r.m.s. bandwidth provides an estimate of the bandwidth required of the filters in the r-f and i-f stages of an FM receiver and of the bandwidth that must be allocated for transmission of the signal $Z(t)$. Note that we assumed $M(t)$ was scaled so that its magnitude exceeds one only occasionally and thus referred to f_d as the peak frequency deviation. This implies that

$$R_m(0) \leq 1$$

so that

$$\sqrt{\overline{f_G{}^2}} = f_d R_m^{1/2}(0) \leq f_d$$

that is, the r.m.s. bandwidth is less than the peak frequency deviation.

The reader should note that the r.m.s. bandwidth is only an estimate of the bandwidth occupancy of the signal, for it is easy to envisage spectra with radically different power distributions having the same r.m.s. bandwidth. To demonstrate this, calculate the r.m.s. bandwidth of an ideal flat low-pass spectrum and various low-pass spectra with rational density functions. The advantage of the r.m.s. bandwidth is that it can be quickly computed. Carson's rule-of-thumb (attributed to J. R. Carson; see Sec. IV-2 of Rowe [6]) takes $f_d + W$ as an approximate value of the bandwidth of the modulated signal in which W represents the bandwidth of the modulation. From the r.m.s. bandwidth we could use the Chebyshev inequality to bound the power lying outside a band of arbitrary width $\pm f_1$

$$\text{fraction of power in freqs. } |f| > f_1 = \frac{\int_{|f|>f_1} G(f)\, df}{\int_{-\infty}^{\infty} G(f)\, df} \leq \frac{\overline{f_G^2}}{f_1^2} \quad (6\text{-}61)$$

Final system design would require more accurate estimates of the spectrum $G(f)$ than those mentioned above. Either of the approximation methods of Rowe [6] or Abramson [7] could be used in this regard.

Now let us consider the average power in the modulated signal. From Eq. 6-38 we see that

$$g(0) = E\{e^{j(\mu_t - \mu_t)}\} = 1$$

so that, from Eq. 6-34, the average power in an angle-modulated signal is given by

$$R_z(0) = \frac{A^2}{2} \quad (6\text{-}62)$$

The average power is thus independent of the modulating message.

6-4   FM Performance—Output Signal-to-Noise Ratio[1]

We now turn to calculating the performance that may be achieved with frequency modulation when the bandwidth of the modulated signal is large compared to the message bandwidth (wide-band FM). The model that we consider is shown in Fig. 6-4. The transmitted FM signal is here denoted by

$$Z'(t) = A \operatorname{Re} [e^{j2\pi f_0 t} e^{j\mu(t)}] \quad (6\text{-}63)$$

The noise in the input is denoted by $N'(t)$. We assume that this noise has a flat spectral density over all frequencies passed by the filter in the first stage of the receiver.

$$S_{n'}(f) \equiv N_0 \quad (6\text{-}64)$$

---

[1] The method of representing the noise component of the phase used in this section was suggested to the author by the work of Csibi [9].

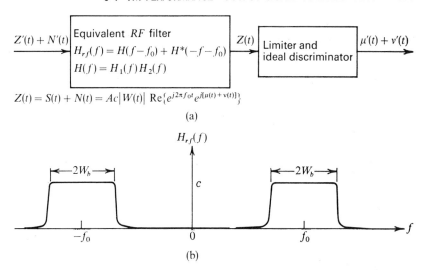

$$Z(t) = S(t) + N(t) = Ac|W(t)| \operatorname{Re}\{e^{j2\pi f_0 t} e^{j[\mu(t) + v(t)]}\}$$

(a)

(b)

Figure 6-4 Situation assumed to calculate FM performance:
(a) Equivalent rf receiver block diagram.
(b) Ideal characteristic assumed for rf filter.

Let W_b denote a frequency sufficiently large that only a negligible amount of the power in the *modulated* signal lies outside a band of width $\pm W_b$ about $\pm f_0$. We assume then that the filter $H_{rf}(f)$ passes $Z'(t)$ without distortion, so that

$$S(t) = cZ'(t) = cA \operatorname{Re} \{e^{j2\pi f_0 t} e^{ju(t)}\} \qquad (6\text{-}65)$$

As in examining the performance of AM, we deal for convenience with an equivalent r-f receiver in which the filter $H_{rf}(f)$ represents the cascade effect of the r-f and i-f stages of the receiver. In Problem 5-1 we have shown that the effect of $H_{rf}(f)$ would be equivalent to the cascade combination of the r-f filter

$$H'_{rf}(f) = H_1(f - f_0) + H_1^*(-f - f_0)$$

and the i-f filter

$$H_{if}(f) = H_2(f - f_{if}) + H_2^*(-f - f_{if})$$

that is,

$$H_{rf}(f) = H(f - f_0) + H^*(-f - f_0)$$

in which

$$H(f) = H_1(f)H_2(f)$$

We assume that $H(f)$ is conjugate symmetric about zero

$$H(-f) = H^*(f) \qquad (6\text{-}66)$$

This will be true if the filter $H_{rf}(f)$ is properly tuned and has a bandwidth small compared to its center frequency. The power spectral density of the noise process $N(t)$ at the output of the filter is thus

$$S_n(f) = N_0|H_{rf}(f)|^2 \tag{6-67}$$

In Chapter 5 we saw that if we represent the noise in the form

$$N(t) = \text{Re}\,\{V_n(t)e^{j2\pi f_0 t}\}$$
$$= X_n(t)\cos 2\pi f_0 t - Y_n(t)\sin 2\pi f_0 t \tag{6-68}$$

$$V_n(t) = X_n(t) + jY_n(t) \tag{6-69}$$

then the spectral densities of $X_n(t)$ and $Y_n(t)$ are given by

$$S_{x_n}(f) = S_{y_n}(f) = 2N_0|H(f)|^2 \tag{6-70}$$

and, in light of Eq. 6-66,

$$S_{x_n y_n}(f) = S_{y_n x_n}(f) = 0 \tag{6-71}$$

so that

$$R_{v_n}(\tau) = E\{V_{t+\tau}V_t^*\} = 2R_{x_n}(\tau) \tag{6-72}$$

Our motivation is to find the error in the instantaneous frequency caused by the presence of the noise $N(t)$; toward this end, let us express the output of the filter in the form

$$Z(t) = S(t) + N(t)$$
$$= Ac\,\text{Re}\,\{e^{j2\pi f_0 t}e^{j\mu(t)}\} + \text{Re}\,\{e^{j2\pi f_0 t}V_n(t)\}$$
$$= Ac\,\text{Re}\,\{e^{j2\pi f_0 t}e^{j\mu(t)}[1 + e^{-j\mu(t)}V_n(t)/Ac]\}$$
$$= Ac\,\text{Re}\,\{e^{j2\pi f_0 t}e^{j\mu(t)}W(t)\} \tag{6-73}$$

in which we have taken $W(t)$ to be

$$W(t) = 1 + e^{-j\mu(t)}V_n(t)/Ac \tag{6-74}$$

If we express $W(t)$ in the form

$$W(t) = |W(t)|e^{jv(t)} \tag{6-75}$$

then the expression for the filter output becomes

$$Z(t) = Ac|W(t)|\,\text{Re}\,\{e^{j2\pi f_0 t}e^{j[\mu(t) + v(t)]}\} \tag{6-76}$$

The output of the discriminator, which we have assumed is an ideal discriminator, is then

$$U(t) = \mu'(t) + v'(t)$$

Any d-c term in the ideal discriminator output is assumed removed by a blocking capacitor.

We now need to examine the noise term $v'(t)$ appearing in the output. The angle $v(t)$ is defined by Eqs. 6-74 and 6-75 as

$$v(t) = \angle W(t) \tag{6-77}$$

in which

$$W(t) = 1 + e^{-j\mu(t)} V_n(t)/Ac \tag{6-74}$$

To obtain the statistical characteristics of $v(t)$, we must at this point make an approximation. Our interest will be in the high signal-to-noise ratio case in which the receiver is functioning properly. We assume that the real and imaginary components of $V_n(t)$ satisfy the condition

$$P\{|X_{n,t}/Ac| \leq \epsilon\} = P\{|Y_{n,t}/Ac| \leq \epsilon\} = 1 - \delta \qquad \epsilon \ll 1, \delta \ll 1 \tag{6-78}$$

so that, except for a small fraction, δ, of the time, the normalized noise components are much less than one in magnitude.

Under this assumption, the real part of $W(t)$ is approximately one and the imaginary part of $W(t)$ is much less than one so that

$$v(t) = \angle W(t) \approx \frac{\text{Im } W(t)}{\text{Re } W(t)} \approx \text{Im } \{e^{-j\mu(t)} V_n(t)/Ac\}$$

$$= \frac{1}{Ac} \text{Im } \{e^{-j\mu(t)} V_n(t)\} \tag{6-79}$$

The noise signal appearing at the output of the discriminator is $v'(t)$. To find the power spectral density of $v'(t)$, we start by finding the power density spectrum of $v(t)$.

Problem 6-5. Let us define $Q(t)$ to be

$$Q(t) = e^{-j\mu(t)} V_n(t)$$

and

$$X_q(t) = \text{Re } \{Q(t)\}; \qquad Y_q(t) = \text{Im } \{Q(t)\}$$

thus

$$v(t) = \frac{1}{Ac} Y_q(t)$$

Note that Eqs. 5-53 and 5-54 apply to $V_n(t)$. Making use of Eq. 5-53, show that

$$E\{X_{q,t+\tau} X_{q,t}\} = E\{Y_{q,t+\tau} Y_{q,t}\} \tag{6-80}$$

Then, making use of Eqs. 5-54, 6-38″, 6-72, and 6-80, show that

$$R_v(\tau) = E\{v_{t+\tau} v_t\} = \left(\frac{1}{Ac}\right)^2 E\{Y_{q,t+\tau} Y_{q,t}\}$$

$$= \left(\frac{1}{Ac}\right)^2 \text{Re } [R_{x_n}(\tau) E\{e^{-j[\mu_{t+\tau} - \mu_t]}\}]$$

$$= \left(\frac{1}{Ac}\right)^2 R_{x_n}(\tau) E\{\cos [\mu_{t+\tau} - \mu_t]\}$$

$$= \left(\frac{1}{Ac}\right)^2 R_{x_n}(\tau) g(\tau) \tag{6-81}$$

and thus

$$S_v(f) = \mathscr{F}[R_v(\tau)] = \left(\frac{1}{Ac}\right)^2 [S_{x_n}(f) * G(f)]$$

$$= \frac{2N_0}{(Ac)^2} [|H(f)|^2 * G(f)] \qquad (6\text{-}82)$$

Now the output of the discriminator will be

$$U(t) = \mu'(t) + v'(t) = \omega_d M(t) + v'(t)$$
$$= 2\pi f_d M(t) + v'(t) \qquad (6\text{-}83)$$

The power spectral density of the noise process $v'(t)$ can easily be expressed in terms of $S_v(f)$ since an ideal differentiator has transfer function $j2\pi f$:

$$S_{v'}(f) = |j2\pi f|^2 S_v(f) = (2\pi f)^2 S_v(f) \qquad (6\text{-}84)$$

In order that the effect of the noise $v'(t)$ be kept to a minimum, the output of the discriminator will be filtered by a low-pass filter, $H_L(f)$, whose (one-sided) bandwidth, W, is just sufficient to pass the message signal $M(t)$ with no appreciable distortion.   This situation is shown in Fig. 6-5 in which $P(t)$ denotes the response of the filter to the noise $v'(t)$.

The spectra of the various signals involved in the input of this filter are shown in Fig. 6-6 assuming near ideal filters for both $H(f)$ and $H_L(f)$. These figures have been drawn under the assumption that f_d is considerably greater than W, so that W_b, the bandwidth of $G(f)$ (the bandwidth of the modulated signal about $\pm f_0$), is appreciably greater than W, the bandwidth of the message.   The reason for our interest in the large index case, $f_d \gg W$, will become apparent when we obtain an expression for the signal-to-noise ratio.   The spectrum $S_v(f)$ is sketched from graphical convolution of S_{x_n} and G.   Note that since our interest is in

$$S_p(f) = |H_L(f)|^2 (2\pi f)^2 S_v(f) \qquad (6\text{-}85)$$

we need be concerned with $S_v(f)$ only for $|f| \leq W$.   Assuming that $H(f)$ is an ideal filter as shown in Fig. 6-4,

$$H(f) = \begin{cases} c & |f| \leq W_b \\ 0 & |f| > W_b \end{cases} \qquad (6\text{-}86)$$

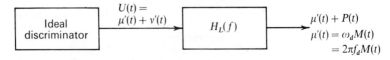

Figure 6-5   Discriminator followed by low-pass filter.

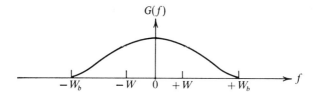

$$G(f)$$

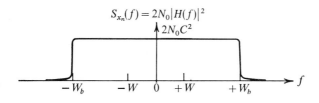

$$S_{x_n}(f) = 2N_0|H(f)|^2$$
$$2N_0C^2$$

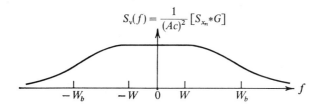

$$S_v(f) = \frac{1}{(Ac)^2}[S_{x_n}*G]$$

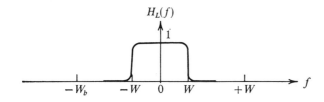

$$H_L(f)$$

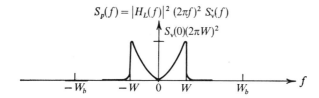

$$S_p(f) = |H_L(f)|^2 (2\pi f)^2 S_v(f)$$
$$S_v(0)(2\pi W)^2$$

Figure 6-6   Spectra involved in FM demodulation.

the equation expressing $S_v(f)$ as the convolution of $G(f)$ and $S_{xn}(f) = 2N_0|H(f)|^2$ is

$$S_v(f) = \frac{2N_0 c^2}{(Ac)^2} \int_{f-W_b}^{f+W_b} G(\zeta)\, d\zeta \tag{6-87}$$

Now W_b, the pass-band of $H(f)$, has been picked sufficiently large that from frequencies $W_b - W(W \ll W_b)$ and beyond $G(f)$ is down to a negligible value. Thus for any value of f in the interval $|f| \le W \ll W_b$ the area of $G(\zeta)$ in the tails $\zeta > f + W_b$ and $\zeta < f - W_b$ is negligible compared to the total area of $G(\zeta)$ and

$$\int_{f-W_b}^{f+W_b} G(\zeta)\, d\zeta \approx \int_{-\infty}^{\infty} G(\zeta)\, d\zeta = g(0), \qquad |f| \le W$$

Thus

$$S_v(f) \approx \frac{2N_0}{A^2} g(0) \qquad |f| \le W \tag{6-88}$$

This relation can also be seen by visualizing the convolution graphically. Our definition of $g(\tau)$ in the preceding section was

$$g(\tau) = E\{e^{j(\mu_{t+\tau} - \mu_t)}\} \tag{6-38}$$

so that

$$g(0) = 1$$

and

$$S_v(f) \approx \frac{2N_0}{A^2} \qquad |f| \le W \tag{6-89}$$

Assuming the low-pass filter following the discriminator is ideal then gives

$$S_p(f) = \begin{cases} \dfrac{2N_0(2\pi f)^2}{A^2} & |f| \le W \\[2mm] 0 & |f| > W \end{cases} \tag{6-90}$$

From this expression for the spectral density of the noise in the output we can finally obtain an expression for the noise power in the output:

$$R_p(0) = E\{P_t^2\} = \int_{-\infty}^{\infty} S_p(f)\, df$$
$$= \frac{2N_0}{A^2} \int_{-W}^{W} (2\pi f)^2\, df = \frac{4N_0(2\pi)^2 W^3}{3A^2} \tag{6-91}$$

The message component in the output is $2\pi f_d M(t)$; thus the output signal-to-noise ratio is

$$\left(\frac{S}{N}\right)_{o,\text{FM}} = \frac{(2\pi f_d)^2 R_m(0) 3A^2}{4N_0(2\pi)^2 W^3} = \frac{3A^2 R_m(0) f_d^2}{4N_0 W^3} \tag{6-92}$$

Recalling our expression for the r.m.s. bandwidth of the modulated signal, this ratio can be expressed as

$$\left(\frac{S}{N}\right)_{o,\text{FM}} = \frac{3A^2}{2N_0 2W} \frac{\overline{f_G^2}}{W^2} \tag{6-93}$$

In the preceding section we saw that the average power in the modulated signal was $\frac{1}{2}A^2$. Thus the channel signal-to-noise ratio (modulated signal power/noise power in the band occupied by the message signal) is

$$\left(\frac{S}{N}\right)_c = \frac{A^2}{2N_0 2W} \tag{6-94}$$

so that the normalized signal-to-noise ratio for FM is

$$\left.\frac{(S/N)_o}{(S/N)_c}\right|_{\text{FM}} = 3 \frac{\overline{f_G^2}}{W^2} \tag{6-95}$$

The normalized signal-to-noise ratio for FM is *thus proportional to the square of the ratio of the r.m.s. bandwidth of the modulated signal to the bandwidth of the message (modulating) signal.* This is the feature of FM that distinguishes it from AM: by increasing the bandwidth occupancy of the transmitted signal we have increased the normalized signal-to-noise ratio, thus allowing the same output performance with decreased transmitter power.

It should be noted that the signal-to-noise ratio cannot be indefinitely increased by increasing f_d (and hence $\overline{f_G^2}$). Our derivation for $v(t)$ assumed that the magnitudes of the noise components $X_n(t)$ and $Y_n(t)$ were much less than Ac with probability close to one. As f_d is increased, the bandwidth of $H(f)$ and hence the noise power $R_{x_n}(0)$ is correspondingly increased until a point is reached where this assumption on the magnitude of the noise components is no longer valid. In this chapter we do not pursue the problem of finding for what values of f_d and channel signal-to-noise ratios this approximation is valid. This topic is discussed extensively for the phase-lock loop demodulator in Chapter 10.

6-5 Pre-Emphasis

In the preceding section, we saw that the noise in the output, $P(t)$, had a parabolic power density spectrum,

$$S_p(f) = \begin{cases} \dfrac{2N_0}{A^2} (2\pi f)^2 & |f| \le W \\[2mm] 0 & |f| > W \end{cases} \tag{6-96}$$

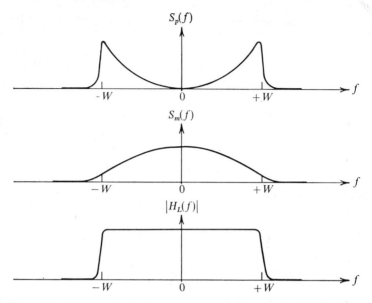

$S_p(f)$

$-W$ 0 $+W$ f

$S_m(f)$

$-W$ 0 $+W$ f

$|H_L(f)|$

$-W$ 0 $+W$ f

Figure 6-7   Spectra of message and noise in the output of an FM receiver.

This spectrum is plotted in Fig. 6-7 together with the power density spectrum of a typical message source and the transfer function of the low-pass filter following the discriminator. The message density spectrum shown in the figure falls off appreciably for higher frequencies; this is characteristic of the outputs generated by most information sources. Audio and video signals typically have spectra of this form. The relative value of the message spectrum at $f = \pm W$ is quite low while the relative value of the noise spectrum is quite high at the same frequency. One can then see that the message makes very inefficient use of the pass-band allowed to it, for if we were to decrease the width of the filter slightly, we would eliminate a large amount of noise while losing only a small amount of message power.

However, simply reducing the bandwidth of the filter is not a satisfactory answer. Although this would considerably reduce the noise power in the output while only slightly distorting the message component, this small amount of distortion might not be tolerable. In music, for example, the high notes contribute only a very small fraction of the power yet contribute a great deal from an aesthetic standpoint.

A more satisfactory solution is through the use of pre-emphasis. This method is based on the observation that the message would make better use of the alloted bandwidth if it contained appreciable power throughout this whole bandwidth.   The frequency content of the message is thus shaped prior to transmission by a pre-emphasis circuit and the original message restored by a de-emphasis circuit in the receiver.   These operations are depicted functionally in Fig. 6-8.

We will select the pre-emphasis circuit so that the average power of the emphasized message $M_1(t)$ has the same power as the original message

$$R_{m_1}(0) = \int_{-\infty}^{\infty} |B(f)|^2 S_m(f)\, df = \int_{-\infty}^{\infty} S_m(f)\, df = R_m(0) \quad (6\text{-}97)$$

The r.m.s. bandwidth will thus be the same with or without pre-emphasis.

Either with or without pre-emphasis the output is $\omega_d M(t) = 2\pi f_d M(t)$ and the output signal power is thus $(2\pi f_d)^2 R_m(0)$.   In the absence of pre-emphasis, we saw in the preceding section that the noise power in the output was

$$E\{P_t^2\} = R_p(0) = \frac{2N_0}{A^2} \int_{-W}^{W} (2\pi f)^2\, df = \frac{4 N_0 W^3 (2\pi)^2}{3 A^2} \quad (6\text{-}91)$$

When pre-emphasis is used, the noise $P(t)$ is passed through the de-emphasis circuit; thus the power density spectrum of the output noise, $P_b(t)$, is

$$S_{p_b}(f) = |B^{-1}(f)|^2 S_p(f) = |B^{-1}(f)|^2 \frac{2 N_0 (2\pi f)^2}{A^2} \qquad |f| \le W \quad (6\text{-}98)$$

The average noise power in the output is thus

$$E\{P_{b,t}^2\} = R_{p_b}(0) = \frac{2N_0}{A^2} \int_{-W}^{W} (2\pi f)^2 |B^{-1}(f)|^2\, df \quad (6\text{-}99)$$

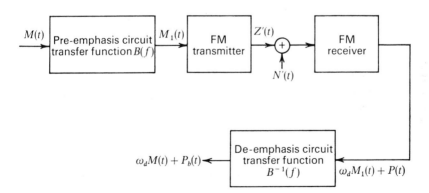

Figure 6-8   Use of pre-emphasis in FM transmission.

Recall from Sec. 6-3 that the power in the modulated signal was $\frac{1}{2}A^2$, independent of the modulation.   Thus the channel signal-to-noise ratio remains unaffected by pre-emphasis (under the constraint of Eq. 6-97) as does the r.m.s. bandwidth and the output message power.   Any improvement brought about by the use of pre-emphasis is thus measured directly by the change in output noise power; that is, comparing $E\{P_{b,t}^2\}$ of Eq. 6-99 with the original noise output power $E\{P_t^2\}$ of Eq. 6-91.   Let us take the improvement ratio to be the ratio of the output signal-to-noise ratios with and without pre-emphasis.   This ratio is thus

$$R_{\substack{\text{pre-emp.}\\ \text{improv.}}} = \frac{(S/N)_{o\ \text{pre-emp.}}}{(S/N)_{o\ \text{no pre-emp.}}} = \frac{E\{P_t^2\}}{E\{P_{b,t}^2\}}$$

$$= \frac{\int_{-W}^{W} (2\pi f)^2\, df}{\int_{-W}^{W} (2\pi f)^2 |B^{-1}(f)|^2\, df} \tag{6-100}$$

The improvement that can be obtained is best studied by means of an example.

Problem 6-6.   Assume the message power density spectrum is

$$S_m(f) = \begin{cases} S_0 \dfrac{(\alpha W)^2}{f^2 + (\alpha W)^2} & |f| \le W \\ 0 & |f| > W \end{cases} \tag{6-101}$$

and that the pre-emphasis and de-emphasis circuits are given by

$$B(f) = \begin{cases} k\dfrac{jf + \alpha W}{\alpha W} & |f| \le W \\ 0 & |f| > W \end{cases} \tag{6-102}$$

$$B^{-1}(f) = \begin{cases} \dfrac{1}{k}\dfrac{\alpha W}{jf + \alpha W} & |f| \le W \\ 0 & |f| > W \end{cases} \tag{6-103}$$

(a)   Derive an expression for the value of k such that Eq. 6-97 is satisfied.
(b)   Making use of (a), show that the improvement ratio is given by

$$R_{\substack{\text{improv.}\\ \text{pre-emp.}}} = \frac{1}{3\alpha^2}\frac{\alpha \tan^{-1}(1/\alpha)}{1 - \alpha \tan^{-1}(1/\alpha)} \tag{6-104}$$

If α is substantially less than one so that most of the message power is concentrated at low frequencies, then R will be considerably greater than one.   For very small α

$$1 - \alpha \tan^{-1}(1/\alpha) \approx 1$$

and

$$\tan^{-1}(1/\alpha) \approx \pi/2$$

and the improvement ratio in the Problem 6-6 is approximately

$$R \approx \frac{\pi}{6\alpha}, \quad \alpha \ll 1 \tag{6-105}$$

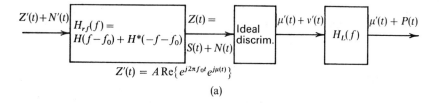

$$Z'(t) = A\,\mathrm{Re}\{e^{j2\pi f_0 t}e^{j\mu(t)}\}$$

(a)

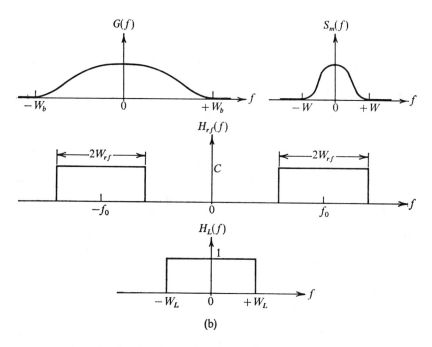

(b)

Figure 6-9   FM receiver discussed in Problem 6-7:
(a) Block diagram.
(b) Spectra and filter transform functions.

In commercial FM, the pre-emphasis network is of the form given by Eq. 6-103 with $\alpha W = 2.1$ kc. The frequency band of the message signal is limited to 15 kc. Thus here α is $1/7.5$; if the message spectrum had the form of Eq. 6-101, the improvement ratio would thus be 4.7.

Problem 6-7. In this problem we consider the effect of changing the bandwidth of the different filters in the FM receiver. The signals and filters that we wish to refer to are shown in Fig. 6-9a. The receiver shown is an equivalent r-f receiver; the reader should be aware that the statements made about the equivalent r-f filter $H_{rf}(f)$ apply in practice to the cascade of the i-f and r-f filters. The signals

$Z'(t)$, $N'(t)$, $Z(t)$, $S(t)$, $N(t)$, $\mu'(t)$, $\nu'(t)$, and $P(t)$ have the same meaning as in Sec. 6-4.   The noise $N'(t)$ again is assumed to have a white power density spectrum

$$S_{n'}(f) = N_0$$

The modulated signal $Z'(t)$ has the power spectral density

$$S_{Z'}(f) = \frac{A^2}{4} [G(f - f_0) + G(f + f_0)]$$

The spectra $S_m(f)$ and $G(f)$ and the filter transfer functions $H_{rf}(f)$ and $H_L(f)$ are shown in Fig. 6-9b.   The signal $P(t)$ denotes the response of $H_L(f)$ to $\nu'(t)$.

In answering the questions below, make any references to equations or statements in the text that are useful in explaining the answer.

(a) Assume $W_L = W$.

    (i) Sketch the spectra $S_\nu(f)$ and $S_p(f)$ for $W_{rf} = W_b$ and $W_{rf} = 3W_b$. Note $W_b \gg W$.

    (ii) How does increasing W_{rf} from W_b to $3W_b$ change the output signal-to-noise ratio? Explain briefly.

    (iii) What effect might enter in changing W_{rf} from W_b to $3W_b$ other than revealed by your answers to (i) and (ii)? Make reference to any useful equations.

(b) Assume $W_{rf} = W_b$.

    (i) Sketch $S_p(f)$ for $W_L = W$ and $W_L = 2W$.

    (ii) How does changing W_L from W to $2W$ affect the output signal-to-noise ratio? Explain briefly.

(c) What are the optimum choices for W_{rf} and W_L? Explain briefly.

REFERENCES

[1] Jahnke, E., and F. Emde, *Tables of Functions*, 4th ed., Dover, New York, 1945.

[2] Schwartz, M., *Information Transmission, Modulation and Noise*, McGraw-Hill Book Co., New York, 1959; pp. 132–141.

[3] Terman, F. E., *Electronic and Radio Engineering*, McGraw-Hill Book Co., New York, 1955; pp. 600–605.

[4] Arguimbau, L. B., and R. B. Adler, *Vacuum Tube Circuits and Transistors*, John Wiley and Sons, New York, 1956; Section XII-7.

[5] Pederson, D. O., *Electronic Circuits*, McGraw-Hill Book Co., New York, 1967; Section 13.5.

[6] Rowe, H. E., *Signals and Noise in Communication Systems*, D. Van Nostrand, Princeton, N.J., 1965.

[7] Abramson, N., "Bandwidth and spectra of phase- and frequency-modulated waves," *IEEE Trans. on Comm. Systems*, **CS-11**, No. 4, 407–414, 1963.

[8] Kaplan, W., *Advanced Calculus*, Addison-Wesley, Reading, Mass., 1953; pp. 219–221.

[9] Csibi, Sandor, "On angle-modulated processes," *Studia Scientiarum Mathematicarum Hungarica*, **2**, 153–157, 1967.

Chapter 7

Optimum Linear Filtering

In this chapter we consider the following problem. Given some observed random process $X(t)$, try to find the linear filter which operates on $X(t)$ to yield the best possible estimate, $\hat{S}(t)$, of some random process $S(t)$ associated with the observable process $X(t)$.[1] The situation is shown in Fig. 7-1.

The process $S(t)$ may represent an information-bearing message process and $X(t)$ a corrupted or noisy version of this process; the objective of the filter in this case is to restore the corrupted signal or remove the noise. Alternately $S(t)$ might be $X(t + t_0)$, in which case the objective of the filter is to predict the value of $X(t)$ t_0 seconds ahead.

The filter problem as described above might occur in the design of an AM or FM receiver where one wishes to design an i-f or audio filter to pass the signal with as little distortion as possible and eliminate as much of the noise as possible. In Chapter 5 we noted that optimum demodulation of an amplitude modulated signal reduced to the problem of finding

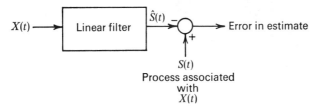

Figure 7-1   Filter problem.

---

[1] The reader should not confuse the use of a circumflex or "hat" over a random variable used to denote an estimate or "guess" with the use of the circumflex to denote a Hilbert transform in Chapters 5 and 6. This dual use is unfortunate; we use it because in both cases the convention is strongly established. In all cases, it will be clear from the context whether the circumflex is to indicate an estimate of a random variable or the Hilbert transform of a time signal.

the optimum filter to separate the message process from additive broadband noise.   In such communication systems, a filter with very close to optimum performance can usually be designed from an intuitive knowledge of the spectra of the signal and noise.   Even in this circumstance, optimum filter theory is quite useful in that it tells one exactly what performance can be achieved by an optimum filter and thus provides a basis of comparison for judging the performance of filters designed on an intuitive basis.   Further, in certain applications such as seismic signal processing, the signal is corrupted in a rather complicated manner and intuitive methods do not indicate how to design a proper filter.   In situations such as this, optimum filter theory is extremely useful.

We shall take the *optimum filter* (or best filter) to be that filter of all possible linear filters which yields the minimum possible mean-square error

$$\mathscr{E}_{sq}(t) = E\{(S_t - \hat{S}_t)^2\} \qquad (7\text{-}1)$$

Such a filter is sometimes referred to as a *Wiener filter* or *Wiener-Kolmogorov filter* after the two men who laid the foundations of minimum mean-square error filtering.

Our approach is as follows.   In Sec. 7-1 we study a simple example of minimum mean-square estimation to allow us to deduce the defining property of an optimum filter.   In Sec. 7-2 we use this to derive the equations determining the optimum filter, and in Sec. 7-3 and 7-4 we study the solution of these equations.   In Sec. 7-5 we consider the computation of the mean-square error and evaluate the performance of AM for various message spectra.

7-1   Estimation Theory and Projection

Let us consider the following situation.   There are two random variables X and Y which we are able to observe.   We wish to use these to estimate the value of a third unobservable random variable Z.   We constrain our estimate of Z to be a linear combination of X and Y:

$$\hat{Z} = aX + bY \qquad (7\text{-}2)$$

and wish to pick the values of a and b to minimize the mean-square estimation error

$$\mathscr{E}_{sq} = E\{(Z - \hat{Z})^2\} \qquad (7\text{-}3)$$

We approach this problem in what seems to be quite an artificial way.   We associate with the random variables X, Y, and Z, the respective three-dimensional vectors $\mathbf{x}$, $\mathbf{y}$, and $\mathbf{z}$.   Although X, Y, and Z take on different values from experiment to experiment, the vectors **x**, **y**, and **z** will be fixed. The lengths and orientations of these vectors are determined by their lengths and inner (or dot) products as follows:

$$\|\mathbf{x}\|^2 = E\{X^2\}; \qquad \|\mathbf{y}\|^2 = E\{Y^2\}; \qquad \|\mathbf{z}\|^2 = E\{Z^2\}$$
$$(\mathbf{x}, \mathbf{y}) = E\{XY\}; \qquad (\mathbf{x}, \mathbf{z}) = E\{XZ\}; \qquad (\mathbf{y}, \mathbf{z}) = E\{YZ\} \qquad (7\text{-}4)$$

The lengths and inner products of these three vectors thus specify all the second moments of the three random variables. Note also that specifying the above six quantities does not specify the absolute orientation of the three vectors **x**, **y**, and **z**, but only their orientation relative to one another; this is sufficient for our purposes. We also associate with random variables such as $V = aX + bY + cZ$ and $U = a'X + b'Y + c'Z$ the vectors $\mathbf{v} = a\mathbf{x} + b\mathbf{y} + c\mathbf{z}$ and $\mathbf{u} = a'\mathbf{x} + b'\mathbf{y} + c'\mathbf{z}$, and take the inner product of **u** and **v** to be

$$(\mathbf{u}, \mathbf{v}) = E\{UV\} \qquad (7\text{-}5)$$

To be sure that it is possible to find vectors whose orientation can be defined in the above manner, it is necessary that the inner product defined in terms of the moments of the random variables satisfy all the properties of an inner product.[1] It is easy to check that this is so:

1. $(\mathbf{u}, \mathbf{v}) = E\{UV\} = E\{VU\} = (\mathbf{v}, \mathbf{u})$
2. $(c\mathbf{u}, \mathbf{v}) = E\{cUV\} = cE\{UV\} = c(\mathbf{u}, \mathbf{v})$
3. $(\mathbf{u} + \mathbf{v}, \mathbf{w}) = E\{(U + V)W\} = E\{UW\} + E\{VW\} = (\mathbf{u}, \mathbf{w}) + (\mathbf{v}, \mathbf{w})$
4. $\|\mathbf{u}\|^2 = (\mathbf{u}, \mathbf{u}) = E\{U^2\} > 0$ unless **u** is the zero vector corresponding to a random variable of 0 mean-square value.

Now let us note why this vector association is pertinent to the estimation problem. Associated with our estimate $\hat{Z} = aX + bY$ we have the vector $\hat{\mathbf{z}} = a\mathbf{x} + b\mathbf{y}$. The estimation error is expressible as

$$\mathscr{E}_{sq} = E\{(Z - \hat{Z})^2\} = \|\mathbf{z} - \hat{\mathbf{z}}\|^2 = \|\mathbf{z} - (a\mathbf{x} + b\mathbf{y})\|^2 \qquad (7\text{-}6)$$

The optimum estimate is thus the one corresponding to the vector $\hat{\mathbf{z}}$ *lying closest to* **z**. Note that $\hat{\mathbf{z}}$ must be a linear combination of **x** and **y**, and hence must lie in the plane spanned or determined by **x** and **y** (note that **x** and **y** are not necessarily orthogonal). The vector **z**, however, does not in general lie in this plane. This situation is depicted in Fig. 7-2. From this figure we can quickly recognize that the optimum vector $\hat{\mathbf{z}}$, which we will denote by $\hat{\mathbf{z}}_o$, is the orthogonal or perpendicular projection of **z** onto

[1] Note that all these properties apply to the familiar inner or dot product in three-dimensional space with coordinates x, y, and z where $(\mathbf{u}, \mathbf{v}) = u_x v_x + u_y v_y + u_z v_z$. For a brief discussion of inner products on a general linear vector space, see Sec. 8-2.

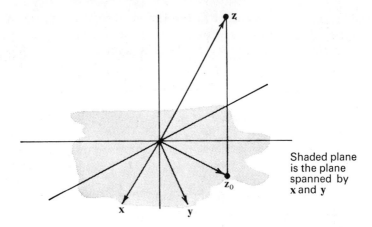

Figure 7-2   Geometry of minimum mean-square-error estimation.

the plane spanned by $\mathbf{x}$ and $\mathbf{y}$, for the distance between $\mathbf{z}$ and this projection is the minimum distance between $\mathbf{z}$ and this plane. Thus *the optimum estimate vector is characterized* by the following property:

$\mathbf{z} - \hat{\mathbf{z}}_o$ *must be orthogonal (or perpendicular) to the plane spanned by* $\mathbf{x}$ *and* $\mathbf{y}$; in particular

$$(\mathbf{z} - \hat{\mathbf{z}}_o, \mathbf{x}) = (\mathbf{z} - \hat{\mathbf{z}}_o, \mathbf{y}) = 0 \qquad (7\text{-}7)$$

In terms of the random variables, *this means that* $Z - \hat{Z}_o$, *the error in the optimum estimate, must be uncorrelated with* X *and* Y

$$E\{(Z - \hat{Z}_o)X\} = E\{(Z - \hat{Z}_o)Y\} = 0 \qquad (7\text{-}8)$$

If we express the optimum estimate in the form

$$\hat{Z}_o = a_o X + b_o Y \qquad (7\text{-}9)$$

then substitution of this expression into the Eqs. 7-8 yields the set of simultaneous equations

$$a_o E\{X^2\} + b_o E\{XY\} = E\{XZ\}$$
$$a_o E\{XY\} + b_o E\{Y^2\} = E\{YZ\}$$

These may be solved by the usual means to find a_o and b_o.

Now let us note that the discussion leading up to Eq. 7-8 did not depend on the dimensionality of the vector space. If we observe n random variables, $X_1, X_2, \ldots, X_n$, then, $\hat{Z}_o$, the *best estimate of all estimates which are linear combinations of these observable random variables*

$$\hat{Z} = \sum_{k=1}^{n} a_k X_k$$

is the one for which the error $Z - \hat{Z}_o$ is uncorrelated with all the observable random variables, $X_1, X_2, \ldots, X_n$.

In what follows, we use the insight gained in deducing the above property to obtain the equations defining the optimum estimate. However, we use independent means in each case to prove that these equations are the right ones.

7-2   The Optimum Filter

Let us now turn back to the problem of original interest: designing a linear filter to operate on $X(t)$ to yield an output which is the best estimate of $S(t)$. We start out by assuming that this linear filter is causal but may be time varying, and not assuming that $S(t)$ and $X(t)$ are stationary. The estimate $\hat{S}(t)$ is then of the form

$$\hat{S}(t) = \int_0^\infty h(t, t - \tau)X(t - \tau)\, d\tau \qquad (7\text{-}10)$$

in which $h(t, t - \tau)$ denotes the response at time t to an impulse applied at time $t - \tau$.

Let $\hat{S}_o(t)$ denote the response to $X(t)$ of a filter with impulse response $h_o(t, t - \tau)$

$$\hat{S}_o(t) = \int_0^\infty h_o(t, t - \sigma)X(t - \sigma)\, d\sigma \qquad (7\text{-}11)$$

and let $h_o(t, t - \sigma)$ be determined such that

$$E\{(S_t - \hat{S}_{o,t})X_{t-\tau}\} = 0 \qquad \text{all } \tau \geq 0 \qquad (7\text{-}12)$$

Since the estimates $\hat{S}(t)$ under consideration are linear combinations of $X(t - \tau)$, $\tau \geq 0$, we would expect from Sec. 7-1 that Eq. 7-12 defines the optimum filter.

We now show that this expectation is borne out; that is, that the filter defined by Eqs. 7-11 and 7-12 is indeed optimum. Let $\hat{S}(t)$ be any arbitrary estimate as given by Eq. 7-10 and $\hat{S}_o(t)$ be the estimate defined by Eqs. 7-11 and 7-12. Then the error using the estimate $\hat{S}(t)$ is given by

$$\begin{aligned}
\mathscr{E}_{sq}(t) &= E\{(S_t - \hat{S}_t)^2\} = E\{[(S_t - \hat{S}_{o,t}) + (\hat{S}_{o,t} - \hat{S}_t)]^2\} \\
&= E\{(S_t - \hat{S}_{o,t})^2\} + E\{(\hat{S}_{o,t} - \hat{S}_t)^2\} \\
&\quad + 2E\{(S_t - \hat{S}_{o,t})(\hat{S}_{o,t} - \hat{S}_t)\} \qquad (7\text{-}13)
\end{aligned}$$

But combining Eq. 7-11 with Eq. 7-12 yields

$$E\{(S_t - \hat{S}_{o,t})\hat{S}_{o,t}\} = 0$$

and combining Eq. 7-10 with Eq. 7-12 yields

$$E\{(S_t - \hat{S}_{o,t})\hat{S}_t\} = 0$$

so that Eq. 7-13 becomes

$$\mathscr{E}_{sq}(t) = E\{(S_t - \hat{S}_t)^2\} = E\{(S_t - \hat{S}_{o,t})^2\}$$
$$+ E\{(\hat{S}_{o,t} - \hat{S}_t)^2\} \geq E\{(S_t - \hat{S}_{o,t})^2\} \quad (7\text{-}14)$$

which states that the error using any arbitrary linear filter is at least as great as the error obtained using the filter specified by Eqs. 7-11 and 7-12. The filter defined by these two equations must then be the optimum filter. If we combine Eqs. 7-11 and 7-12, we obtain

$$E\left\{\left[S_t - \int_0^\infty h_o(t, t - \sigma)X(t - \sigma)\, d\sigma\right]X_{t-\tau}\right\} = 0 \quad \text{all } \tau \geq 0$$

After interchanging the order of expectation and integration, this equation becomes

$$\int_0^\infty h_o(t, t - \sigma)R_x(t - \sigma, t - \tau)\, d\sigma = R_{sx}(t, t - \tau) \quad \text{all } \tau \geq 0 \quad (7\text{-}15)$$

This equation specifying the impulse response of the optimum filter is known as the *Wiener-Hopf equation.*

Let us now assume that the processes $X(t)$ and $S(t)$ are jointly wide-sense stationary so that

$$R_x(t - \sigma, t - \tau) = R_x(\tau - \sigma)$$
$$R_{sx}(t, t - \tau) = R_{sx}(\tau)$$

In this case none of the known quantities appearing in Eq. 7-15 depend on the observation time t, so that the time-varying filter $h_o(t, t - \sigma)$ may be replaced with a time invariant filter $h_o(\sigma)$. In the stationary case Eq. 7-15 thus becomes

$$\int_0^\infty h_o(\sigma)R_x(\tau - \sigma)\, d\sigma = R_{sx}(\tau) \quad \text{all } \tau \geq 0 \quad (7\text{-}16)$$

We consider how to solve this equation in the next two sections. In the remainder of this section we focus our attention on two other signal estimation problems.

Suppose that, during the time interval 0 to T, we observe a random process $X(t)$ given by

$$X(t) = A\phi(t) + N(t) \quad 0 \leq t \leq T \quad (7\text{-}17)$$

in which $\phi(t)$ is a known pulse, $N(t)$ is stationary noise, and A is a random variable we wish to estimate. We assume that A is statistically independent

of the noise.   For simplicity of implementation, we consider estimates
which are linear operations on $X(t)$:

$$\hat{A} = \int_0^T f(t)X(t)\,dt \qquad (7\text{-}18)$$

different possible estimates corresponding to different choices of the
function $f(t)$.   We denote by $\hat{A}_o$ the optimum estimate (the one that
minimizes $E\{(A - \hat{A})^2\}$)

$$\hat{A}_o = \int_0^T f_0(t)X(t)\,dt \qquad (7\text{-}19)$$

We would again venture that $\hat{A}_o$ is determined by the equation

$$E\{(A - \hat{A}_o)X_t\} = 0 \qquad 0 \le t \le T \qquad (7\text{-}20)$$

Problem 7-1.   Prove that the estimate given by Eqs. 7-19 and 7-20 is indeed optimum.
Do this by considering an arbitrary estimate given by Eq. 7-18 and showing that
the error for this estimate must be at least as large as the error using the estimate of
Eqs. 7-19 and 7-20.

In order to determine $f_0(t)$ more explicitly, we combine Eqs. 7-17, 7-19,
and 7-20 and write

$$E\left\{\left[A - \int_0^T f_0(\sigma)[A\phi(\sigma) + N(\sigma)]\,d\sigma\right](A\phi(t) + N_t)\right\} = 0 \qquad 0 \le t \le T$$

If we interchange the order of integration and expectation and assume
that $N(t)$ is zero mean, this equation becomes

$$\int_0^T f_0(\sigma)R_n(t - \sigma)\,d\sigma = \phi(t)\overline{A^2}\left[1 - \int_0^T f_0(\sigma)\phi(\sigma)\,d\sigma\right] \qquad 0 \le t \le T$$
$$(7\text{-}21)$$

in which $R_n(\tau)$ is the correlation function of the noise

$$R_n(\tau) = E\{N_{t+\tau}N_t\} \qquad (7\text{-}22)$$

Note that the quantity $\int_0^T f(t)X(t)\,dt$ could be physically obtained by
observing at time T the output of a filter with impulse response $h(\tau) = f(T - \tau)$.

Problem 7-2.   Let us use the shorthand notation introduced in Chapter 2:

$$(f, \phi) = \int_0^T f(t)\phi(t)\,dt$$
$$(f, N) = \int_0^T f(t)N(t)\,dt$$

(It is not necessary to conjugate $\phi(t)$ since it is real.)   The signal-to-noise ratio at the output of the filter $f(t)$ of Eq. 7-18 is defined to be the square of the signal component of the output divided by the mean-square value of the noise component of the output,

$$\left(\frac{S}{N}\right)_o = \frac{E\{A^2\}(f, \phi)^2}{E\{(f, N)^2\}} \qquad (7\text{-}23)$$

or simply

$$\left(\frac{S}{N}\right)_o = \frac{A^2(f, \phi)^2}{E\{(f, N)^2\}} \qquad (7\text{-}24)$$

if A is a constant instead of a random variable.

Show that the filter which minimizes $\mathscr{E}_{sq}$ maximizes $(S/N)_o$.   *Hint:* Use the independence of A and $N(t)$ to show that

$$\mathscr{E}_{sq} = E\{A^2\}[1 - (f, \phi)]^2 + E\{(f, N)^2\}$$

Next let $f_0(t)$ denote the filter that minimizes $\mathscr{E}_{sq}$, and note that among all filters satisfying the constraint

$$(f, \phi) = (f_0, \phi) \qquad \text{(a fixed real number)}$$

f_0 is the filter that minimizes $E\{(f, N)^2\}$.

The filter which maximizes the output signal-to-noise ratio is termed the *matched filter*.   This terminology arises from the fact that when the noise $N(t)$ is white, $f(t)$ is proportional to the signal $\phi(t)$ or is "matched" to $\phi(t)$. This is considered in Problem 7-4.

Problem 7-3.   Assume that we can find a function $g_0(t)$ satisfying the equation

$$\int_0^T g_0(\sigma) R_n(t - \sigma) \, d\sigma = \phi(t) \qquad 0 \le t \le T \qquad (7\text{-}25)$$

Show that the function $f_0(\sigma)$ satisfying Eq. 7-21 is given by

$$f_0(\sigma) = g_0(\sigma) \frac{E\{A^2\}}{1 + E\{A^2\} \int_0^T \phi(t) g_0(t) \, dt} \qquad 0 \le \sigma \le T \qquad (7\text{-}26)$$

Problem 7-4.   Assume that the noise has a white spectrum, $S_n(f) = N_0$, or

$$R_n(\tau) = N_0 \delta(\tau) \qquad (7\text{-}27)$$

Show that the function determining the optimum estimate is given by

$$f_0(t) = \frac{1}{N_0} \phi(t) \frac{E\{A^2\}}{1 + (E\{A^2\}/N_0) \int_0^T \phi^2(t) \, dt}$$

$$= \phi(t) \frac{E\{A^2\}}{N_0 + E\{A^2\} \int_0^T \phi^2(t) \, dt} \qquad (7\text{-}28)$$

so that the optimum filter in this case is a filter with impulse response proportional to $\phi[T - t]$.

Problem 7-5.   Consider the discrete-time stationary processes S_k and X_k, $k = 0$, $\pm 1, \pm 2, \dots$.   These may represent samples taken from continuous-time processes

$S(t)$ and $X(t)$ (with the time scale chosen for convenience so that the time between samples is one unit). Suppose we wish to find an estimate of S_k of the form

$$\hat{S}_k = \sum_{j=0}^{n} a_j X_{k-j} \qquad (7\text{-}29)$$

Show by an argument similar to that leading to Eq. 7-16 that $a_{o,j}$, the coefficients of the *optimum* estimate, are the solutions of the equations

$$\sum_{j=0}^{n} a_{o,j} E\{X_{k-m} X_{k-j}\} = E\{S_k X_{k-m}\} \qquad m = 0, 1, \ldots, n$$

or

$$\sum_{j=0}^{n} a_{o,j} R_x(m - j) = R_{sx}(m) \qquad m = 0, 1, \ldots, n \qquad (7\text{-}30)$$

If this estimate can be a function of all the past values of X_k,

$$\hat{S}_k = \sum_{j=0}^{\infty} a_j X_{k-j} \qquad (7\text{-}31)$$

then Eq. 7-30 becomes

$$\sum_{j=0}^{\infty} a_{o,j} R_x(m - j) = R_{sx}(m) \qquad m = 0, 1, 2, \ldots \qquad (7\text{-}32)$$

This equation is the discrete-time analog of the Wiener-Hopf equation.

Throughout this chapter, we consider only linear estimates. One may ask why we do not consider estimates of a more general form. Outside of the fact that linear filters or estimates are easy to describe analytically, there are two practical reasons for focusing attention on linear filters. First, linear filters or estimates are easy to build or implement on a computer. Second, as we have seen above, the design of a linear filter to minimize mean-square error requires *only* a knowledge of the *correlation functions* of the random processes involved and not a more detailed description of the distributions of the random processes. These two considerations would usually deter us from investigating the design of a nonlinear filter unless there were good reason to believe that its performance would be substantially better than that of a linear filter.

There is another consideration. In Problem 3-8 it was shown that the best (minimum mean-square error) estimate of the random variable S given that the random variable X took on the value x was

$$\hat{S} = E\{S \mid X = x\} \qquad (7\text{-}33)$$

This can be extended as follows. The best estimate of S observing that $X_{t_k} = x_k$, $k = 1, \ldots, n$, is

$$\hat{S} = E\{S \mid X_{t_k} = x_k, k = 1, \ldots, n\} \qquad (7\text{-}34)$$

Extending this point further, if we wish to estimate the value of the process $S(t)$ at time t having observed that $X(\tau) = x(\tau)$, $\tau \leq t$, the best estimate is

$$\hat{S}_t = E\{S_t \mid X_\tau = x(\tau), \tau \leq t\} \tag{7-35}$$

In Problems 3-20 and 3-22, we observed that if S and X are jointly gaussian, then $E\{S \mid X = x\}$ is of the form

$$E\{S \mid X = x\} = ax + b \tag{7-36}$$

in which $b = 0$ if $E\{S\} = 0$. Coupled with Eq. 7-33, this equation shows that if $E\{S\} = 0$, the best (minimum mean-square error) estimate of S observing X is a linear one. This property also extends. If S and $X_{t_1}, X_{t_2}, \ldots, X_{t_n}$ are jointly gaussian and $E\{S\} = 0$, then

$$E\{S \mid X_{t_k} = x_k, k = 1, \ldots, n\} = \sum_{k=1}^{n} a_k x_k \tag{7-37}$$

and if $S(t)$ and $X(t)$ are jointly gaussian random processes with $m_s(t) = 0$, then

$$E\{S_t \mid X_\tau = x(\tau), \tau \leq t\} = \int_0^\infty h(t, t - \sigma) x(t - \sigma) \, d\sigma \tag{7-38}$$

Equations 7-34 and 7-37 can be proved simply by extending the methods used to prove Eqs. 7-33 and 7-36 to the multivariable case. Equations 7-35 and 7-38 must be shown by limiting arguments. The important consequence of these remarks is that *if the random variable we are trying to estimate and our observable quantities have a joint gaussian distribution and the random variable we wish to estimate is zero mean, then the optimum estimate is a linear operation on the observables*, and no more complicated form of estimate need even be considered.

7-3   Solution of the Wiener-Hopf Equation: Noncausal Filter

Equation 7-16 specifies the impulse response of the optimum filter, but only in an indirect way. To complete the job of specifying the filter, we need to find an *explicit* rule for calculating $h_o(t)$. It is this problem that we consider in this section and the next.

First let us note that in the formulation that led up to Eq. 7-16 the filter $h_o(t)$ was assumed to be causal; that is, to operate only on the past of the input $X(t)$:

$$\hat{S}_o(t) = \int_0^\infty h_o(\tau) X(t - \tau) \, d\tau \tag{7-10'}$$

For reasons that will soon be discussed, let us relax this restriction and allow $h_o(t)$ to operate on the past and future of $X(t)$:

$$\hat{S}_o(t) = \int_{-\infty}^{\infty} h_o(\tau)X(t - \tau)\,d\tau \qquad (7\text{-}39)$$

By following the derivation of Eq. 7-16, one can easily deduce that in the present case, the equation must hold for all τ and not just positive values of τ:

$$\int_{-\infty}^{\infty} h_o(\sigma)R_x(\tau - \sigma)\,d\sigma = R_{sx}(\tau) \qquad -\infty < \tau < \infty \qquad (7\text{-}40)$$

We can easily find an explicit equation for the transfer function of the impulse response $h_o(\sigma)$ appearing in this equation by taking the Fourier transform of both sides of the equation. This yields

$$H_o(f)S_x(f) = S_{sx}(f)$$

or

$$H_o(f) = \frac{S_{sx}(f)}{S_x(f)} \qquad (7\text{-}41)$$

Thus, in the case in which the filter can operate on both the past and future of the input, it is easy to find an explicit expression for the optimum filter. We now inquire when such a situation would be of interest. First, in certain data processing operations such as seismic signal processing, the observed signal is stored on tape and the processing is done on a digital computer. In this case, operation is not in real time and to obtain an estimate of $S(t)$ the computer is free to operate on any of the values of $X(t + \tau)$, $-\infty < \tau < \infty$. The filter thus need not be causal in this situation. Second, the noncausal filter has implications to the design of causal filters. Let the inverse transform of $H_o(f)$, given by Eq. 7-41, be as shown in Fig. 7-3a. A good approximation to this filter can be obtained by truncating it at some negative time shift T_d, as shown in Fig. 7-3b. This impulse response can then be shifted to the right by T_d seconds, as shown in Fig. 7-3c, to yield a causal filter whose output is a good approximation to $\hat{S}_o(t)$ with T_d seconds delay

$$\int_0^{\infty} h_{T_d}(\tau)X(t - \tau)\,d\tau \approx \hat{S}_o(t - T_d) \qquad (7\text{-}42)$$

Thus in situations in which a delay is acceptable, Eq. 7-41 coupled with the procedure shown in Fig. 7-3 yields an explicit rule for finding an approximation to the optimum filter.

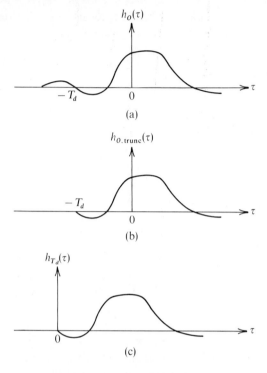

Figure 7-3   Design of a near optimum filter with T_d seconds delay:
(a) $h_o(\tau)$.
(b) Truncated approximation to $h_o(\tau)$.
(c) Causal approximate version of $h_o(\tau)$ incorporating T_d seconds delay.

7-4   Solution of the Wiener-Hopf Equation: Causal Filter[1]

Let us consider the solution of Eq. 7-16, the Wiener-Hopf equation specifying the optimum causal linear filter. We start by observing that Eq. 7-16 depends only on the correlation functions $R_x(\tau)$ and $R_{sx}(\tau)$. Thus, if there is a second pair of processes, $X'(t)$ and $S'(t)$, which have the same pair of auto- and cross-correlation functions, the filter for estimating $S'(t)$ from $X'(t)$ is the same as the filter for estimating $S(t)$ from $X(t)$. Our strategy is to find a pair of processes for which the optimum filter can be determined by inspection. Before we can proceed directly,

[1] The reader unfamiliar with the Laplace transform should omit this section on first reading and proceed to Sec. 7-5.

we find it convenient to introduce a number of quantities. Let us start by factoring the spectral density of $X(t)$ into two parts.

First, we assume that $R_x(\tau)$ is Fourier transformable with spectral density $S_x(f)$. Thus $R_x(\tau)$ is Laplace transformable with a region of convergence that includes the imaginary axis, $s = j\omega$. We denote this Laplace transform by

$$\tilde{S}_x(s) = \mathscr{L}[R_x(\tau)] = \int_{-\infty}^{\infty} R_x(\tau)e^{-s\tau}\, d\tau \qquad (7\text{-}43)$$

It is easily verified that since $R_x(\tau)$ is an even function of τ,

$$R_x(-\tau) = R_x(\tau)$$

then $\tilde{S}_x(s)$ is an even function of s

$$\tilde{S}_x(-s) = \tilde{S}_x(s)$$

Let us consider the case in which $\tilde{S}_x(s)$ is rational; since $\tilde{S}_x(s)$ is even, if it has a zero at $s = s_1$ it also has one at $s = -s_1$, and if it has a pole at $s = s_1'$ it also has one at $s = -s_1'$. Thus $\tilde{S}_x(s)$ may be written in the form

$$\tilde{S}_x(s) = k \frac{(s_1 + s)(s_1 - s)\cdots(s_m + s)(s_m - s)}{(s_1' + s)(s_1' - s)\cdots(s_n' + s)(s_n' - s)}$$

in which

$$\text{Re}\,\{s_k\} \geq 0 \quad k = 1, 2, \ldots, m \qquad \text{Re}\,\{s_k'\} > 0 \quad k = 1, 2, \ldots, n$$

The real part of all the s_k' must be *strictly* greater than zero since the region of definition of $\tilde{S}_x(s)$ includes the $s = j\omega$ axis. It is easily verified that since $\tilde{S}_x(j2\pi f) = S_x(f) \geq 0$, then the constant k must be positive. We now factor $\tilde{S}_x(s)$ into two terms

$$\tilde{S}_x(s) = \tilde{S}_x{}^+(s)\tilde{S}_x{}^-(s) \qquad (7\text{-}44)$$

in which

$\tilde{S}_x{}^+(s)$ has all poles and zeros in the left-half plane
$\tilde{S}_x{}^-(s)$ has all poles and zeros in the right-half plane

$$\tilde{S}_x{}^+(s) = +\sqrt{k}\, \frac{(s_1 + s)\cdots(s_m + s)}{(s_1' + s)\cdots(s_n' + s)}$$

and

$$\tilde{S}_x{}^-(s) = +\sqrt{k}\, \frac{(s_1 - s)\cdots(s_m - s)}{(s_1' - s)\cdots(s_n' - s)}$$

Note from the choice of factorization that

$$\tilde{S}_x{}^-(-s) = \tilde{S}_x{}^+(s) \qquad (7\text{-}45)$$

Let us use the following explicit notation for the three functions:

$$p_x(t) = \mathscr{L}^{-1}[\tilde{S}_x{}^+(s)] \tag{7-46}$$

$$p_x^{\text{in}}(t) = \mathscr{L}^{-1}[1/\tilde{S}_x{}^+(s)] \tag{7-47}$$

and

$$p_s(t) = \mathscr{L}^{-1}[\tilde{S}_{sx}(s)/\tilde{S}_x{}^-(s)] \tag{7-48}$$

in which

$$\tilde{S}_{sx}(s) = \mathscr{L}[R_{sx}(\tau)]$$

We note from Eq. 2-115 that because $\tilde{S}_x{}^+(s)$ has all its zeros and poles in the left-half plane, *both* $p_x(t)$ and $p_x^{\text{in}}(t)$ *are zero for* $t < 0$ {a pole at $s = 0$ in $[1/\tilde{S}_x{}^+(s)]$ corresponds to a positive going step}.   Note that, in general, $p_s(t)$ is *not* zero for $t < 0$.   We denote the "positive part" of $p_s(t)$ by

$$[p_s]_+(t) = \begin{cases} 0 & t < 0 \\ p_s(t) & t \geq 0 \end{cases} \tag{7-49}$$

Since $p_s(t)$ is specified in terms of $\tilde{S}_{sx}(s)/\tilde{S}_x{}^-(s)$, it will also be convenient to denote the Laplace transform of the positive part of $p_s(t)$ by

$$\left[\frac{\tilde{S}_{sx}(s)}{\tilde{S}_x{}^-(s)}\right]_+ = \mathscr{L}[[p_s]_+(t)] = \mathscr{L}[u(t - 0_-)p_s(t)] \tag{7-50}$$

in which 0_- denotes any time instant just prior to $t = 0$.

With the above terms defined, we can now proceed to find the optimum causal filter (the solution of Eq. 7-16) by inspection.   As we have already observed, the optimum filter $h_0(t)$ depends only on the correlation functions $R_x(\tau)$ and $R_{sx}(\tau)$, and if the processes $X'(t)$ and $S'(t)$ have the same pair of correlation functions as $X(t)$ and $S(t)$,

$$R_{x'}(\tau) = R_x(\tau) \tag{7-51}$$

$$R_{s'x'}(\tau) = R_{sx}(\tau) \tag{7-52}$$

then the optimum filter for estimating $S(t)$ *from* $X(t)$ *is the same as the optimum filter for estimating* $S'(t)$ *from* $X'(t)$.   We now proceed to consider a pair of processes, $X'(t)$ and $S'(t)$, which have the same correlation functions as the given processes and for which it is particularly simple to determine the optimum causal linear filter.

Let $D(t)$ denote a process which consists of impulses of unit area occurring at event points which are Poisson distributed with an expected number of 1 event points occurring per second.   From Problem 4-8 we have that

$$R_d(\tau) = \delta(\tau) \tag{7-53}$$

Let us generate the processes $X'(t)$ and $S'(t)$ by passing $D(t)$ through filters with impulse responses $p_x(t)$ and $p_s(t)$, respectively. This method of generating $X'(t)$ and $S'(t)$ is shown in Fig. 7-4a; Fig. 7-4b shows typical sample functions.

Problem 7-6. Show that for the process $X'(t)$ and $S'(t)$ defined as shown in Fig. 7-4a that Eqs. 7-51 and 7-52 are satisfied. *Hint:* It is sufficient to show that

$$S_x(f) = \tilde{S}_x(j2\pi f) = \tilde{S}_{x'}(j2\pi f) = S_{x'}(f)$$

and

$$S_{sx}(f) = \tilde{S}_{sx}(j2\pi f) = \tilde{S}_{s'x'}(j2\pi f) = S_{s'x'}(f)$$

Make use of Eq. 7-45 to show that

$$S^-(f) = \tilde{S}^-(j2\pi f) = \tilde{S}^+(-j2\pi f) = S^+(-f) = [S^+(f)]^* \qquad (7\text{-}54)$$

Now let us consider the optimum causal linear filter for estimating $S'(t)$ from $X'(t)$. We separate this filter into the cascade of two separate filters as shown in Fig. 7-4a. The first filter in this cascade is $[1/\tilde{S}_x{}^+(s)]$ and its output is again the sequence of impulses $D(t)$. Note that we lose nothing by such a cascade, since the second filter can contain a term $\tilde{S}_x{}^+(s)$ (which represents a causal filter) and undo the effect of the first filter should this be desirable. We now ask what is the optimum choice of causal impulse response for the second filter; that is, what *causal* filter operates on the sequence of impulses, $D(t)$, to yield the best estimate of $S'(t)$, the sequence of pulses $p_s(t)$? Consider a single impulse $\delta(t - t_k)$ in the sequence $D(t)$ and the corresponding pulse $p_s(t - t_k)$ in the sequence $S'(t)$. The corresponding pulse in the filter output will be $h_2(t - t_k)$, where $h_2(t)$ is the impulse response of the second portion of the filter. First, we observe that the best that can be done is for $h_2(t - t_k)$ to approximate $p_s(t - t_k)$, for succeeding pulses, $p_s(t - t_m)$, $m > k$, occur at random times which are independent of t_k. Second, since $h_2(t)$ *must be causal*, the choice of $h_2(t)$ that minimizes the error between $h_2(t - t_k)$ and $p_s(t - t_k)$ is

$$h_2(t) = \begin{cases} 0 & t < 0 \\ p_s(t) & t \geq 0 \end{cases}$$

or

$$h_2(t) = [p_s]_+(t) \qquad (7\text{-}55)$$

This means that the transfer function of the second filter in the cascade is

$$\left[\frac{\tilde{S}_{sx}(s)}{\tilde{S}_x{}^-(s)} \right]_+$$

The *transfer function of the optimum filter* (the transfer function of the cascade) is thus

$$\tilde{H}_0(s) = \frac{1}{\tilde{S}_x{}^+(s)} \left[\frac{\tilde{S}_{sx}(s)}{\tilde{S}_x{}^-(s)} \right]_+ \qquad (7\text{-}56)$$

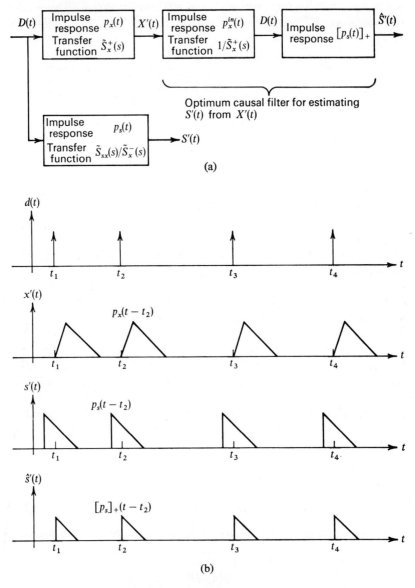

Figure 7-4   Processes used in deducing optimum casual filter:
(a) System configuration.
(b) Typical sample functions.

We again emphasize that although we derived the optimum filter for the processes $X'(t)$ and $S'(t)$, Eq. 7-56 is the optimum linear filter for any pair of processes $X(t)$ and $S(t)$ having the same correlation function $R_x(\tau)$ and cross-correlation function $R_{sx}(\tau)$.

EXAMPLE 1. Let $X(t) = S(t) + N(t)$, in which the message process $S(t)$ and noise process $N(t)$ are both zero mean and uncorrelated. We assume that the noise is white

$$\tilde{S}_n(s) = N_0 \qquad (7\text{-}57)$$

and that the signal process has the spectrum

$$\tilde{S}_s(s) = \frac{D}{-s^2 + 1} = \frac{D}{(s + 1)(1 - s)} \qquad (7\text{-}58)$$

This signal spectrum is the spectrum that would result by passing white noise through an R-C filter with unity time constant.

Under the assumption that the signal and noise are uncorrelated, the spectra $\tilde{S}_x(s)$ and $\tilde{S}_{sx}(s)$ are given by

$$\tilde{S}_{sx}(s) = \tilde{S}_s(s) = \frac{D}{(s + 1)(1 - s)} \qquad (7\text{-}59)$$

and

$$\tilde{S}_x(s) = \tilde{S}_n(s) + \tilde{S}_s(s) =$$
$$N_0 + \frac{D}{(s + 1)(1 - s)} = N_0 \frac{(s + q)(q - s)}{(s + 1)(1 - s)} \qquad (7\text{-}60)$$

in which

$$q = +\sqrt{\frac{N_0 + D}{N_0}} = +\sqrt{1 + \frac{D}{N_0}} \qquad (7\text{-}61)$$

The desired factorization of $\tilde{S}_x(s)$ is now

$$\tilde{S}_x{}^+(s) = \sqrt{N_0}\,\frac{s + q}{s + 1}; \qquad \tilde{S}_x{}^-(s) = \sqrt{N_0}\,\frac{(q - s)}{(1 - s)} \qquad (7\text{-}62)$$

Thus

$$\frac{\tilde{S}_{sx}(s)}{\tilde{S}_x{}^-(s)} = \frac{D}{(s + 1)(1 - s)}\,\frac{1}{\sqrt{N_0}}\,\frac{(1 - s)}{(q - s)} = \frac{D}{\sqrt{N_0}}\,\frac{1}{(s + 1)(q - s)} \qquad (7\text{-}63)$$

Expanding this into a partial fraction expansion, we obtain

$$\frac{\tilde{S}_{sx}(s)}{\tilde{S}_x{}^-(s)} = \frac{D}{\sqrt{N_0}}\left[\frac{1}{q + 1}\frac{1}{s + 1} + \frac{1}{q + 1}\frac{1}{q - s}\right] \qquad (7\text{-}64)$$

The pole at $s = +q$ corresponds to a time function nonzero for $t < 0$ and the pole at $s = -1$ to a time function nonzero for $t > 0$. Thus the quantity we wish is

$$\left[\frac{\tilde{S}_{sx}(s)}{\tilde{S}_x{}^-(s)}\right]_+ = \frac{D}{\sqrt{N_0}} \frac{1}{q+1} \frac{1}{s+1} \tag{7-65}$$

Combining Eqs. 7-56, 7-62, and 7-65 then yields the transfer function of the optimum filter:

$$\tilde{H}_o(s) = \frac{1}{\sqrt{N_0}} \frac{s+1}{s+q} \frac{D}{\sqrt{N_0}} \frac{1}{1+q} \frac{1}{s+1} = \frac{D}{N_0} \frac{1}{1+q} \frac{1}{s+q} \tag{7-66}$$

This is simply a low-pass filter; note that q, the cutoff frequency of the filter, depends on the signal-to-noise ratio D/N_0, as can be seen from Eq. 7-61.

EXAMPLE 2. Let us now consider the same input process and message process considered in Example 1; now, however, we allow either some lag in filtering or require prediction as well as filtering. This can be formulated in the following manner. Let $Y(t)$ and $N(t)$ be zero-mean uncorrelated processes. The process $N(t)$ is again white noise with spectral density N_0 and $Y(t)$ has the spectrum of Eq. 7-58. The observed signal $X(t)$ and signal we wish to obtain, $S(t)$, are given by

$$X(t) = Y(t) + N(t); \qquad S(t) = Y(t + T) \tag{7-67}$$

If T is positive, this means we wish to both remove the noise and predict the value of $Y(t)$ T seconds ahead of the observed noisy value. If T is negative, we are allowed a lag in our attempts to filter out the noise. The correlation functions of interest now become

$$R_x(\tau) = E\{(Y_{t+\tau} + N_{t+\tau})(Y_t + N_t)\} = R_y(\tau) + R_n(\tau) \tag{7-68}$$

$$R_{sx}(\tau) = E\{Y_{t+T+\tau}(Y_t + N_t)\} = R_y(\tau + T) \tag{7-69}$$

The spectrum $\tilde{S}_x(s)$ and its factorization remain the same as in the previous example. The quantity $\tilde{S}_{sx}(s)/\tilde{S}_x{}^-(s)$ now becomes e^{sT} times the value used in Example 1:

$$\tilde{S}_{sx}(s)/\tilde{S}_x{}^-(s) = e^{sT} \frac{D}{\sqrt{N_0}} \frac{1}{(q+1)} \left[\frac{1}{s+1} + \frac{1}{q-s}\right] \tag{7-70}$$

Let us assume that we are interested in prediction so that T is positive. Noting that

$$\operatorname*{Res}_{s=-1}\left[\frac{e^{st}}{s+1}\right] = e^{-t}$$

$$-\operatorname*{Res}_{s=+q}\left[\frac{e^{st}}{q-s}\right] = e^{qt}$$

and using Eq. 2-115 would allow us immediately to write the inverse transform of $[1/(s + 1) + 1/(q - s)]$. The expression for $p_s(t)$ then follows directly from the shifting theorem:

$$p_s(t) = \begin{cases} \dfrac{D}{\sqrt{N_0}} \dfrac{1}{q + 1} e^{-(t+T)} & t > -T \\[3ex] \dfrac{D}{\sqrt{N_0}} \dfrac{1}{q + 1} e^{q(t+T)} & t < -T \end{cases} \qquad (7\text{-}71)$$

For t greater than zero, $p_s(t)$ is thus given by

$$p_s(t) = \frac{D}{\sqrt{N_0}} \frac{1}{(q + 1)} e^{-(t+T)} = \frac{De^{-T}}{\sqrt{N_0}(q + 1)} e^{-t} \qquad t > 0 \quad (7\text{-}72)$$

The transform of the positive part of this function is

$$\left[\frac{\tilde{S}_{sx}(s)}{\tilde{S}_x^-(s)} \right]_+ = \int_0^\infty p_s(t) e^{-st}\, dt = \frac{De^{-T}}{\sqrt{N_0}(q + 1)} \frac{1}{s + 1} \qquad (7\text{-}73)$$

Combining this equation with Eqs. 7-56 and 7-62 finally yields the transfer function for the optimum filter that predicts T seconds ahead of the observed value

$$\tilde{H}_o(s) = \frac{1}{\sqrt{N_0}} \frac{(s + 1)}{(s + q)} \frac{De^{-T}}{\sqrt{N_0}(q + 1)} \frac{1}{s + 1} = \frac{De^{-T}}{N_0(q + 1)} \frac{1}{s + q} \qquad (7\text{-}74)$$

Problem 7-7.   Find the optimum filter for the above example when we allow a delay so that T has a negative value.   Plot the impulse responses of the optimum filters for $T = +\dfrac{1}{q}$, 0, and $-\dfrac{1}{q}$.

Numerical Methods

We now consider what should be done if $R_x(\tau)$ is known only numerically, perhaps from measurements.   We can (numerically) transform $R_x(\tau)$ to obtain a numerical tabulation of $S_x(f)$.[1]   To evaluate the filter we could approximate $S_x(f)$ by a rational function of finite order and then proceed as above.   However, this approximation process can be very cumbersome and time consuming.   An alternate method is available.   It can be shown by using only fundamental concepts from

---

[1] It should be pointed out that there are some inherent dangers in estimating $S_x(f)$ from measurements.   Small errors in the estimation of $R_x(\tau)$ accumulate and transform into large errors in the value of $S_x(f)$; it is thus possible only to estimate a smoothed version of $S_x(f)$.   We do not discuss this problem here.   The interested reader is referred to Blackman and Tukey [1].

Fourier transform theory and complex variable theory, that there is a unique relation between the spectral density, which is the squared magnitude of its factors

$$S_x(f) = |S_x{}^+(f)|^2 = |S_x{}^-(f)|^2$$

and the phase of the factor $S_x{}^+(f)$. If we denote the angle of $S_x{}^+(f)$ by

$$\theta(f) = \tan^{-1}\{I_m[S_x{}^+(f)]/\mathrm{Re}\,[S_x{}^+(f)]\} \tag{7-75}$$

then it can be shown (see for example pp. 195–212 of Papoulis [2]) that

$$\theta(f) = \frac{f}{\pi}\int_{-\infty}^{\infty} \frac{\tfrac{1}{2}\ln\,[S_x(\beta)]}{\beta^2 - f^2}\,d\beta \tag{7-76}$$

This phase can thus be evaluated by numerical means from a numerical tabulation of $S_x(f)$. From this we can solve for $S_x{}^+(f)$ and $S_x{}^-(f)$:

$$S_x{}^+(f) = +\sqrt{S_x(f)}\,e^{j\theta(f)}; \qquad S_x{}^-(f) = +\sqrt{S_x(f)}\,e^{-j\theta(f)} \tag{7-77}$$

The function $p_s(\tau)$ can then be calculated by numerically evaluating $\mathscr{F}^{-1}[S_{sx}(f)/S_x{}^-(f)]$. The transfer function $H_o(j2\pi f)$ can then be found by numerical evaluation of Eq. 7-56 for $s = j2\pi f$.

Minimum Mean-Square Error

It is often of interest to be able to evaluate the mean-square error obtained by using the optimum filter. This allows a comparison with the performance of other filters which might be easier to synthesize. We should point out that the error cannot be determined from the equivalent processes $X'(t)$ and $S'(t)$ used to derive the optimum filter; although the functions $R_x(\tau)$ and $R_{x'}(\tau)$ are equal as are $R_{sx}(\tau)$ and $R_{s'x'}(\tau)$, the correlation functions $R_s(\tau)$ and $R_{s'}(\tau)$ are not in general equal. We cannot therefore make a straightforward interpretation of the error from Fig. 7-4b.

The mean-square error using the optimum filter is

$$\mathscr{E}_{sq} = E\{(S_t - \hat{S}_{o,t})^2\} = E\{(S_t - \hat{S}_{o,t})(S_t - \hat{S}_{o,t})\}$$

But, as we have seen, $S_t - \hat{S}_{o,t}$ must be uncorrelated with the output of any filter, in particular with $\hat{S}_{o,t}$, thus

$$\mathscr{E}_{sq} = E\{S_t^2\} - E\{S_t\hat{S}_{o,t}\} = R_s(0) - R_{s\hat{s}_o}(0) \tag{7-78}$$

But $\hat{S}_o(t)$ is the response of $h_o(\tau)$ to $X(t)$, thus

$$R_{s\hat{s}_o}(0) = \int_{-\infty}^{\infty} h_o(\tau)R_{sx}(\tau)\,d\tau \tag{7-79}$$

(Note that $h_o(\tau)$ is zero for $\tau < 0$.)   Using Eqs. 7-50 and 7-56, we have for $h_o(\tau)$:

$$h_o(\tau) = \int_{-\infty}^{\infty} df \frac{e^{j2\pi f \tau}}{S_x{}^+(f)} \int_0^{\infty} d\sigma \, p_s(\sigma) e^{-j2\pi f \sigma} \qquad (7\text{-}80)$$

Substituting from Eq. 7-80 into Eq. 7-79 and interchanging the order of integration yields

$$R_{s\hat{s}_o}(0) = \int_0^{\infty} d\sigma \, p_s(\sigma) \int_{-\infty}^{\infty} df \frac{e^{-j2\pi f \sigma}}{S_x{}^+(f)} \int_{-\infty}^{\infty} d\tau R_{sx}(\tau) e^{j2\pi f \tau}$$

We next note the last integral in this equation is $S_{sx}(-f)$, and from Eq. 7-45 we note that $S_x{}^+(f) = S_x{}^-(-f)$; the expression for $R_{s\hat{s}_o}(0)$ then becomes

$$R_{s\hat{s}_o}(0) = \int_0^{\infty} d\sigma \, p_s(\sigma) \int_{-\infty}^{\infty} df \, e^{-j2\pi f \sigma} \frac{S_{sx}(-f)}{S_x{}^-(-f)}$$

But the last integral in this equation is $p_s(\sigma)$; therefore,

$$R_{s\hat{s}_o}(0) = \int_0^{\infty} p_s{}^2(\sigma) \, d\sigma \qquad (7\text{-}81)$$

The expression for the mean-square error is then

$$\mathscr{E}_{sq} = R_s(0) - \int_0^{\infty} p_s{}^2(\sigma) \, d\sigma \qquad (7\text{-}82)$$

in which $p_s(\sigma)$ must be evaluated from Eq. 7-48.

Problem 7-8.   Show that the minimum mean-square error associated with using the unrealizable filter of Eq. 7-41 is

$$\mathscr{E}_{sq} = R_s(0) - \int_{-\infty}^{\infty} \frac{|S_{sx}(f)|^2}{S_x(f)} \, df = R_s(0) - \int_{-\infty}^{\infty} p_s{}^2(t) \, dt \qquad (7\text{-}83)$$

Problem 7-9.   Consider the problem discussed in Example 2 and Problem 7-7. Calculate the mean-square error as a function of T for $T < 0$, $T = 0$, and $T > 0$.

7-5 Filtering a Message from Additive Noise: Mean-Square Error

In many situations it is useful to be able to evaluate the error that can be obtained with the optimum filter without going through the tedium of finding the transfer function of the filter.   One such situation arises in calculating the optimum performance of various modulation methods; this is explored in some detail in Chapter 10.   Another such situation arises when we wish to compare the performance of a simple filter to the performance that could be obtained using the optimum filter. In this section, we consider several expressions for the mean-square error for the case of additive signal and noise.

In the design of optimum filters for receivers, the model most frequently considered is additive signal and noise:

$$X(t) = S(t) + N(t) \tag{7-84}$$

in which the signal $S(t)$ and noise $N(t)$ are both zero mean and uncorrelated. Furthermore, the most common case is when the noise $N(t)$ has a white spectrum

$$S_n(f) = N_0 \tag{7-85}$$

so that

$$S_x(f) = S_s(f) + N_0; \qquad S_{sx}(f) = S_s(f) \tag{7-86}$$

We now expand in some detail on this case of particular interest in receiver design.

Following the reasoning used in part (a) of Problem 5-6, it is quite easy to show that

$$\mathscr{E}_{sq} = \int_{-\infty}^{\infty} |1 - H_o(f)|^2 S_s(f)\, df + N_0 \int_{-\infty}^{\infty} |H_o(f)|^2\, df \tag{7-87}$$

This expression is valid for either the optimum (causal or noncausal) filter or for $H_o(f)$ the transfer function of an arbitrary filter; the only restriction is that the equation applies for additive signal and white, zero-mean, noise. For the noncausal filter of Eq. 7-41 and the spectra of Eq. 7-86, Eq. 7-87 reduces after some simple algebra to

$$\mathscr{E}_{sq} = N_0 \int_{-\infty}^{\infty} \frac{S_s(f)}{N_0 + S_s(f)}\, df \tag{7-88}$$

In the additive signal and white noise case, if $S_s(f)$ is a rational function of f, it is possible to show that the optimum causal filter is given by

$$\tilde{H}_o(s) = 1 - \frac{(N_0)^{1/2}}{[N_0 + \tilde{S}_s(s)]^+} \tag{7-89}$$

in which $[N_0 + \tilde{S}_s(s)]^+$ denotes the product of all the zeros and poles of $[N_0 + \tilde{S}_s(s)]$ lying in the left-hand plane. Further, the error using this filter can be expressed in the form

$$\mathscr{E}_{sq} = N_0 \int_{-\infty}^{\infty} \ln\left[1 + \frac{S_s(f)}{N_0}\right] df \tag{7-90}$$

We do not prove Eqs. 7-89 and 7-90 here: the reader interested in their derivation may consult the original paper by Yovits and Jackson [3] or

Sec. 5.7 of Viterbi [4].   Note that the mean-square error can be evaluated from either Eq. 7-88 (noncausal filter) or Eq. 7-90 (causal filter) *without going through the tedious procedure of spectral factorization.*

An interesting class of message-signal spectra is the set of Butterworth spectra:

$$S_s(f, k) = \beta^2 \frac{(k/\pi f_0) \sin (\pi/2k)}{1 + (f/f_0)^{2k}} \qquad k = 1, 2, 3, \ldots \qquad (7\text{-}91)$$

These spectra would result from passing white noise through a maximally flat filter of order k, $k = 1, 2, \ldots$.   The constant $(k/\pi f_0) \sin (\pi/2k)$ is included to normalize the power to

$$R_s(0) = \beta^2 \qquad (7\text{-}92)$$

For $k = 1$, the spectrum is the response of white noise to a first order *R-C* filter with cut-off frequency f_0

$$S_s(f, 1) = \beta^2 \frac{1}{\pi f_0} \frac{1}{1 + (f/f_0)^2} \qquad (7\text{-}93)$$

while for $k = \infty$, the spectrum is the ideal low-pass spectrum:

$$S_s(f, \infty) = \begin{cases} \dfrac{\beta^2}{2f_0} & |f| \le f_0 \\ 0 & |f| > f_0 \end{cases} \qquad (7\text{-}94)$$

As k increases, the "corners" of the spectrum at $f = \pm f_0$ become progressively sharper.

Problem 7-10.   Using Eq. 7-90, show that for the optimum causal filter the error for the signal spectrum $S_s(f, k)$ is given by

$$\mathscr{E}_{\text{causal}}(k) = \frac{2\pi f_0 N_0}{\sin (\pi/2k)} \left[\left(1 + k \frac{\beta^2 \sin (\pi/2k)}{\pi N_0 f_0} \right)^{1/2k} - 1 \right] \qquad (7\text{-}95)$$

and

$$\mathscr{E}_{\text{causal}}(\infty) = 2f_0 N_0 \ln (1 + \beta^2/2N_0 f_0) \qquad (7\text{-}96)$$

Hint: Note that $\ln \left[1 + \dfrac{c}{1 + x^{2k}} \right] = \displaystyle\int_0^c \frac{dz}{z + 1 + x^{2k}}$

Problem 7-11.   Using Eq. 7-88, show that for the optimum noncausal filter the error for the signal spectrum $S_s(f, k)$ is given by

$$\mathscr{E}_{\text{noncausal}}(k) = \beta^2 \left[1 + \frac{\beta^2}{2f_0 N_0} \frac{\sin (\pi/2k)}{(\pi/2k)} \right]^{(1/2k) - 1} \qquad (7\text{-}97)$$

Note that the results of Problems 7-10 and 7-11 may be easily modified to give the performance of AM.   As discussed in Problem 5-6, the receiver output with an optimum filter would consist of the response of $H_o(f)$ to

$AM(t)$ and a noise term with spectral density $2N_0|H_o(f)|^2$. Thus the above results apply directly to the AM case if we substitute $2N_0/A^2$ for N_0 in Eqs. 7-96 and 7-97.

In some situations it may be impossible to evaluate the integral of Eq. 7-88 or Eq. 7-90 from available tables. In this eventuality, it is useful to be aware of an alternate method of evaluating the integral of Eq. 7-87 or 7-88. This method requires that the integrand be factored into its left- and right-hand plane components.

In either Eq. 7-87 or 7-88 it is easy to show that the integrand is *even* in *f*. Furthermore, if $S_s(f)$ is rational, the transfer function of the optimum filter (causal or noncausal) is rational and hence the integrand of either Eq. 7-87 or 7-88 is rational. Let the integrand of the equation in question be denoted by $I(f)$. Setting $s = \sigma + j2\pi f$ and $\tilde{I}(0 + j2\pi f) = I(f)$, $\tilde{I}(s)$ is even and rational and hence may be factored into the form

$$\tilde{I}(s) = F(s)F(-s)$$

in which $F(s)$ has all its poles and zeros in the left half of the complex s-plane. The integral to be evaluated is thus of the form

$$\mathscr{E} = \frac{1}{2\pi j} \int_{\substack{0-j\infty \\ s=0+j2\pi f}}^{0+j\infty} F(s)F(-s) \, ds \qquad (7\text{-}98)$$

in which $F(s)$ is a rational function. Tables of this integral are available in Appendix E of Newton, Gould, and Kaiser [5]; these tables express the value of $\mathscr{E}$ in terms of the coefficients of F.

As an example of using this method, let us consider Example 1 of Sec. 7-4. We have

$$\tilde{S}_n(s) = N_0, \qquad \tilde{S}_s(s) = \frac{D}{(s+1)(1-s)}$$

and

$$\tilde{H}_o(s) = \frac{D}{N_0} \frac{1}{1+q} \frac{1}{s+q} \qquad (7\text{-}66)$$

in which

$$q = +\sqrt{1 + D/N_0} \qquad (7\text{-}61)$$

Note first from Eqs. 7-66 and 7-61 that

$$H_o(f) = \frac{D}{N_0} \frac{1}{1+q} \frac{1}{j2\pi f + q} = \frac{D(q-1)}{N_0(q-1)(q+1)} \frac{1}{j2\pi f + q}$$

$$= \frac{D(q-1)}{N_0(q^2-1)(j2\pi f + q)} = \frac{q-1}{j2\pi f + q} \qquad (7\text{-}99)$$

Substituting into Eq. 7-87 then yields

$$\mathscr{E}_{sq} = \int_{-\infty}^{\infty} \left| 1 - \frac{(q-1)}{(j2\pi f + q)} \right|^2 \frac{D}{(j2\pi f + 1)(1 - j2\pi f)} + N_0 \left| \frac{(q-1)}{(j2\pi f + q)} \right|^2 df$$

$$= \int_{-\infty}^{\infty} \frac{D[(2\pi f)^2 + q^2 - 2q(q-1) + (q-1)^2]}{[(2\pi f)^2 + q^2][(2\pi f)^2 + 1]} + \frac{N_0(q-1)^2}{(2\pi f)^2 + q^2} df$$

$$= [D + N_0(q-1)^2] \int_{-\infty}^{\infty} \frac{1}{(2\pi f)^2 + q^2} df$$

Or, setting $s = 0 + j2\pi f$,

$$= [D + N_0(q-1)^2] \frac{1}{2\pi j} \int_{\substack{0-j\infty \\ s=0+j2\pi f}}^{0+j\infty} \frac{1}{s+q} \frac{1}{q-s} ds \qquad (7\text{-}100)$$

In this example, $F(s) = 1/(s+q)$. From the tables in reference [5]

$$\frac{1}{2\pi j} \int_{0-j\infty}^{0+j\infty} \frac{1}{s+q} \frac{1}{q-s} ds = \frac{1}{2q}$$

and

$$\mathscr{E} = \frac{D + N_0(q-1)^2}{2q} \qquad (7\text{-}101)$$

In closing this chapter, we should like to point out that the discrete time Wiener-Hopf equation (Eq. 7-32) can be solved by transform methods in a manner exactly analogous to the methods considered in Secs. 7-3 and 7-4. This requires a knowledge of z-transform methods, and for this reason we do not discuss this point here.

For a thorough discussion of optimum filter theory, the reader may wish to consult the original book by Wiener [6] or the more readable book by Lee [7]. For an alternate abbreviated treatment, refer to Chapter 11 of Davenport and Root [8].

REFERENCES

[1] Blackman, R. B., and J. W. Tukey, *The Measurement of Power Spectra*, Dover, New York, 1958.

[2] Papoulis, A., *The Fourier Integral and Its Applications*, McGraw-Hill Book Co., New York, 1962.

[3] Yovits, M. C., and J. L. Jackson, "Linear Filter Optimization with Game Theory Considerations," *IRE International Convention Record*, Part 4, 193–199, March 1955.

[4] Viterbi, A. J., *Principles of Coherent Communications*, McGraw-Hill
     Book Co., New York, 1966.
[5] Newton, G., L. Gould, and J. Kaiser, *Analytic Design of Linear
     Feedback Systems*, John Wiley and Sons, New York, 1958; see
     Appendix E.
[6] Wiener, N., *The Extrapolation, Interpolation, and Smoothing of
     Stationary Time Series*, John Wiley and Sons, New York, 1949.
[7] Lee, Y. W., *Statistical Theory of Communication*, John Wiley and
     Sons, New York, 1960.
[8] Davenport, W., and W. Root, *Random Signals and Noise*, McGraw-
     Hill Book Co., New York, 1958.

Chapter 8

Communication of Digital Data in the Presence of Additive Noise

In this chapter we make a distinct break with the situation considered in the preceding chapters. Instead of a continuous-time, continuous-valued waveform message $M(t)$, we now consider the case of a discrete-valued or digital information source. We assume as before that communication is to take place by the transmission of signals that are received in the presence of additive noise. Our discussion will follow the geometric interpretation first developed by Kotelnikov [1] and recently brought to fuller fruition by Wozencraft and Jacobs [2].

The information source emits one letter every T seconds, the letters belonging to an alphabet of q letters or symbols which we denote by $m_1, m_2, \ldots, m_q$. An example of such an information source is stock market prices or English text placed in suitable format for teletype transmission. In either case the alphabet consists of the 26 Roman letters, 10 numerals, and frequently used punctuation symbols. A second example is the remote connection of one or more digital computers. Here one computer acts as an information source calculating outputs from observations and inputs fed into it. The computer output is expressed as a sequence of zeros and ones which are transmitted to a second computer. In this case our alphabet consists simply of the two symbols 0 and 1.

Physical transmission must take place via signals. Thus, corresponding to each letter m_i, $i = 1, 2, \ldots, q$, there will be a signal $s_i(t)$ of T seconds duration which will be transmitted to indicate the present output letter of the source. This transmitted signal $s_i(t)$ is observed in the presence of additive noise $N(t)$. The receiver observes the signal $Z(t) = N(t) + s_i(t)$ ($i = $?) for the T-second duration of $s_i(t)$ and must make a guess as to which of the q signals is being transmitted (and hence which of the q letters the source generated). This whole procedure is repeated every T-seconds. The situation is depicted in Fig. 8-1.

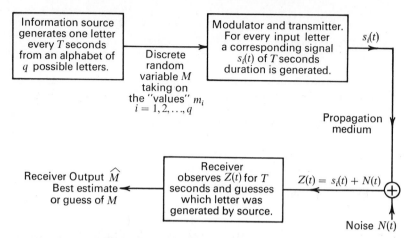

Figure 8-1   Digital communication system.

Our interest is in making this digital communication system as reliable as possible; that is, in minimizing the probability of an error between the receiver output and letter generated by the source.   In particular, we study how the receiver should operate to minimize this error probability and how the choice of signals used affects the error probability.

We progress by stages, first considering a situation in which vectors or n-tuples of real numbers (or voltages) are transmitted instead of signals to indicate which message letter was generated by the source.   This vector is received in the presence of an additive noise vector, that is, an n-tuple whose components are random variables.   The signal and noise vectors can be thought of respectively as incomplete characterizations of the signal and noise waveforms physically occurring in an actual transmission system.   We next consider in some detail the representation of signals or waveforms as vectors.   We then analyze the physical system in which transmission takes place via signals or waveforms.   In building up this analysis, we assume that the interfering noise, $N(t)$, is white gaussian noise. Although this is a restrictive assumption, it is a valid model for the classes of physical transmission systems of greatest current importance, line of sight propagation via satellite or microwave link.   In Sec. 8-4 we generalize on our transmission model to include a random phase disturbance that occurs in many types of physical propagation.   The chapter then concludes in Sec. 8-5 with a brief discussion of the important phenomenon of channel capacity and the achievement of reliable transmission by appropriately encoding long sequences of letters into an appropriately chosen set of signals.

8-1 Transmission via Vector Channels

We will denote an n-dimensional vector with components $s_1, s_2, \ldots, s_n$ by

$$\mathbf{s} = (s_1, s_2, \ldots, s_n) \qquad (8\text{-}1)$$

Instead of the digital communication system in which a physical signal $s_i(t)$ is transmitted, we now consider a system in which every T seconds we transmit a vector $\mathbf{s}_i$ given by

$$\mathbf{s}_i = (s_1{}^i, s_2{}^i, \ldots, s_n{}^i) \qquad i = 1, 2, \ldots, q \qquad (8\text{-}2)$$

to indicate that the source output was the letter m_i. Although it is not possible to physically transmit a vector, consideration of such a vector transmission system is a useful prelude to our discussion of transmission via physical signals. We further assume that in transmission a noise vector $\mathbf{N}$,

$$\mathbf{N} = (N_1, N_2, \ldots, N_n)$$

whose components are random variables, is added to $\mathbf{s}_i$. The receiver thus observes the vector

$$\mathbf{Z} = \mathbf{s}_i + \mathbf{N} \qquad i = ? \qquad (8\text{-}3)$$

and must try to guess which of the q source letters was generated. As before, this process is repeated every T seconds. We assume that the noise vector $\mathbf{N}$ is statistically independent of the message source.

We now consider how to find the rule for making a guess, based on an observation of $\mathbf{Z}$, as to the source letter; also, we would like to guess in such a manner as to have a minimum probability of error. Let $f_{\mathbf{Z}}(\mathbf{z})$ denote the probability density of the received vector and $P(C)$ the probability of a correct decision. The conditional probability of making a correct decision when we observe the vector $\mathbf{Z} = \mathbf{z}$ at the receiver is denoted by $P(C \mid \mathbf{z})$. We can thus write

$$P(C) = \int_{-\infty}^{\infty} \cdots \int_{-\infty}^{\infty} P(C \mid \mathbf{z}) f(\mathbf{z}) \, d\mathbf{z} \qquad (8\text{-}4)$$

in which $d\mathbf{z}$ denotes $dz_1 \, dz_2 \cdots dz_n$. Since $f(z)$ is non-negative, we note that we maximize $P(C)$ if for each possible value of the received vector $\mathbf{z}$ we maximize $P(C \mid \mathbf{z})$.

Let us consider how to maximize $P(C \mid \mathbf{z})$. For each value of the received vector we will decide upon a particular letter as our guess for the source letter; this guess or *estimate* we denote by $\hat{M}(\mathbf{z})$.[1] Now, since

---

[1] The reader should not confuse the use of a circumflex or "hat" over a random variable used to denote an estimate or "guess" with the use of the circumflex to denote a Hilbert transform in Chapters 5 and 6. This dual use is unfortunate; we use it because in both cases the convention is strongly established. In all cases, it will be clear from the context whether the circumflex is to indicate an estimate of a random variable or the Hilbert transform of a time signal.

$\hat{M}(\mathbf{z})$ is one of the possible letters of the source alphabet, we can write

$$\hat{M}(\mathbf{z}) = m_{j(\mathbf{z})} \qquad (8\text{-}5)$$

in which the index $j(\mathbf{z})$ takes on one of the values from 1 to q. The quantity $m_{j(\mathbf{z})}$ represents a decision based on an observation of $\mathbf{z}$; this decision may be in error.   We have denoted the source output letter by M, so the conditional probability of a correct decision or guess is

$$\begin{aligned} P(C \mid \mathbf{z}) &= P(M = \hat{M}(\mathbf{z}) \mid \mathbf{z}) \\ &= P(M = m_{j(\mathbf{z})} \mid \mathbf{z}) \qquad (8\text{-}6) \end{aligned}$$

To maximize this conditional probability of a correct decision, note that $j(\mathbf{z})$ can have any one of the q possible values: we should clearly pick $j(\mathbf{z})$ to be that value of the index which maximizes the right-hand side of Eq. 8-6.   Thus the decision rule for the receiver which maximizes the probability of a correct decision is to pick

$$\hat{M}(\mathbf{z}) = m_{j(\mathbf{z})}$$

where j is the value of the index for which the probability

$$P(M = m_j \mid \mathbf{z}) \qquad j = 1, 2, \ldots, q$$

is the largest.   It will be more convenient to denote the conditional probability that the source output was m_j having observed that the received vector $\mathbf{Z}$ took the value $\mathbf{z}$ by $P(m_j \mid \mathbf{z})$ rather than $P(M = m_j \mid \mathbf{z})$. In this notation, the optimum (minimum probability of error) decision rule is thus

set $\hat{M}(z) = m_j$ where j is the index such that $P(m_j \mid \mathbf{z}) \geq P(m_i \mid \mathbf{z})$
$$i = 1, 2, \ldots, q \qquad i \neq j \quad (8\text{-}7)$$

If there is more than one value of j satisfying this inequality, we may arbitrarily pick $\hat{M}(z)$ to be any one of these m_j.   (Why?)

To be able to carry out this decision rule, we must be able to calculate the probabilities $P(m_i \mid \mathbf{z})$ for all i and all values of $\mathbf{z}$.   For our vector channel with noise that is additive and independent of the message source

$$f_{\mathbf{Z}\mid M}(\mathbf{z} \mid m_i) = f_{\mathbf{Z}\mid \mathbf{S}_i}(\mathbf{z} \mid \mathbf{s}_i) = f_{\mathbf{N}}(\mathbf{z} - \mathbf{s}_i) \qquad (8\text{-}8)$$

in which $f_{\mathbf{N}}(\mathbf{n})$ is the probability density function for the noise vector $\mathbf{N}$.

For $d\mathbf{z}$ an infinitesimal change in $\mathbf{z}$, we have

$$\begin{aligned} P(m_i \mid \mathbf{z}) f(\mathbf{z}) \, d\mathbf{z} &= P\{m_i \text{ sent and } z_k - dz_k < Z_k \leq z_k, k = 1, 2, \ldots, n\} \\ &= f(\mathbf{z} \mid m_i) P(m_i) \, d\mathbf{z} \end{aligned}$$

This result can also be expressed in the form

$$P(m_i \mid \mathbf{z}) = \frac{f(\mathbf{z} \mid m_i)}{f(\mathbf{z})} P(m_i) \qquad (8\text{-}9)$$

This equation, in various forms, is often referred to as *Bayes' rule*. If we combine this equation with inequality 8-7 and cancel out the $f(\mathbf{z})$ term on both sides, we can then express the optimum decision rule in the following form:

having observed that $\mathbf{Z} = \mathbf{z}$, *pick the receiver output to be* $\hat{M}(\mathbf{z}) = m_{j(\mathbf{z})}$, *where* $j(\mathbf{z})$ *is the index such that*

$$f(\mathbf{z} \mid m_j)P(m_j) \geq f(\mathbf{z} \mid m_i)P(m_i) \qquad i = 1, 2, \ldots, q \qquad i \neq j \quad \text{(8-10)}$$

For the additive independent noise case we can substitute from Eq. 8-8, and inequality 8-10 becomes

$$f_{\mathbf{N}}(\mathbf{z} - \mathbf{s}_j)P(m_j) \geq f_{\mathbf{N}}(\mathbf{z} - \mathbf{s}_i)P(m_i) \qquad i = 1, 2, \ldots, q \qquad i \neq j \quad \text{(8-11)}$$

Decision Regions

It is helpful to visualize the optimum decision rule geometrically. Given any value for the received vector $\mathbf{z}$, the receiver output is one of the q letters

$$\hat{M}(\mathbf{z}) = m_{j(\mathbf{z})}$$

where the index $j(\mathbf{z})$ is decided by the rule expressed by Eq. 8-10 or Eq. 8-11 in the independent, additive noise case. In the event that there is more than one index i for which the quantity

$$f_{\mathbf{N}}(\mathbf{z} - s_i)P(m_i)$$

is a maximum for a given vector $\mathbf{z}$, we may arbitrarily pick one of these indices [without affecting $P(C)$], say, $i = p$, and set $\hat{M}(\mathbf{z})$ equal to m_p for that value of $\mathbf{z}$. Thus with each value of $\mathbf{z}$ we have associated *one* of the q indices. Let I_i denote the set of all the vectors $\mathbf{z}$ for which the receiver guesses m_i. We refer to I_i as the ith *decision region*, since if $\mathbf{z}$ falls in I_i we decide in favor of m_i.

Now let us consider the probability of a correct decision. We can write

$$P(C) = \sum_{i=1}^{q} P(m_i)P(C \mid m_i) \qquad \text{(8-12)}$$

Let us consider $P(C \mid m_i)$. Given that m_i was the source output and s_i the transmitted vector, a correct decision will be made if and only if the received vector $\mathbf{Z}$ falls in the ith decision region I_i. Thus the probability of a correct decision is given by

$$P(C) = \sum_{i=1}^{q} P(m_i)P\{\mathbf{Z} \text{ falls in } I_i \text{ given that } s_i \text{ was transmitted}\}$$

$$= \sum_{i=1}^{q} P(m_i) \int \cdots \int_{I_i} f(\mathbf{z} \mid m_i) \, d\mathbf{z} \qquad \text{(8-13)}$$

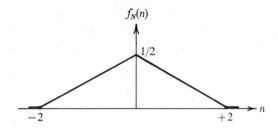

Figure 8-2 Noise probability density function for Problem 8-1.

In the independent additive noise case which we are considering, $f(\mathbf{z} \mid m_i)$ is given by

$$f(\mathbf{z} \mid m_i) = f_{\mathbf{N}}(\mathbf{z} - \mathbf{s}_i)$$

and Eq. 8-13 becomes

$$P(C) = \sum_{i=1}^{q} P(m_i) \int \cdots \int_{I_i} f_{\mathbf{N}}(\mathbf{z} - \mathbf{s}_i) \, d\mathbf{z} \qquad (8\text{-}14)$$

Problem 8-1. Consider the case in which the vectors **N**, **Z**, and **s** are all one-dimensional. Let $f_N(n)$ have the density shown in Fig. 8-2 and assume that N is independent of the message source. There are two letters in the source alphabet: $m_1 = 0$ and $m_2 = 1$. To transmit m_1 we send $s_1 = -1$, and to transmit m_2 we send $s_2 = +1$. Assume $P(M_1) = P(M_2) = \frac{1}{2}$.

  (a) Sketch the decision regions I_1 and I_2 along an axis representing the value of the single component of the vector z.

  (b) Calculate the probability of an error.

Sufficient Statistics

Suppose there is a vector-valued function of **z**, $\tilde{\mathbf{M}}(\mathbf{z})$, such that the conditional density $f(\mathbf{z} \mid m_i)$ can be expressed in the form

$$f(\mathbf{z} \mid m_i) = g[m_i; \tilde{\mathbf{M}}(\mathbf{z})]w(\mathbf{z}) \qquad i = 1, 2, \ldots, q \qquad (8\text{-}15)$$
$$w(\mathbf{z}) \geq 0$$

We then say that $\tilde{\mathbf{M}}(\mathbf{z})$ is a *sufficient statistic for M.*

The significance of this concept lies in the fact that an optimum guess as to the source symbol M may be made on the basis of the function $\tilde{\mathbf{M}}(\mathbf{z})$ and need not involve the value of **z** itself. To show this, note that the optimum (minimum probability of error) decision rule of inequality 8-10 becomes, upon substitution from Eq. 8-15,

set $\hat{M}(\mathbf{z}) = m_{j(\mathbf{z})}$ where $j(\mathbf{z})$ is the index such that

$$g[m_j; \tilde{\mathbf{M}}(\mathbf{z})]w(\mathbf{z})P(m_j) \geq g[m_i; \tilde{\mathbf{M}}(\mathbf{z})]w(\mathbf{z})P(m_i) \qquad \begin{matrix} i = 1, 2, \ldots, q \\ i \neq j \end{matrix}$$

Since $w(\mathbf{z})$ is non-negative, it factors out of this inequality and the decision rule is stated in a form in which the index j satisfying this rule depends only on the value of $\tilde{\mathbf{M}}(\mathbf{z})$ and not on the value of $\mathbf{z}$ itself.

The practical significance of this result is that $\tilde{\mathbf{M}}(\mathbf{z})$ may be a less complicated quantity to deal with than $\mathbf{z}$ itself, so that the problem of implementing the decision rule is simplified. We now give an example of this that will be of direct use later.

Let the transmission vectors $\mathbf{s}_i$, $i = 1, 2, \ldots, q$, all have their last n-p components zero

$$\mathbf{s}_k = (s_1{}^k, s_2{}^k, \ldots, s_p{}^k, \underbrace{0, \ldots, 0}_{}) \qquad k = 1, 2, \ldots, q \qquad (8\text{-}16)$$
$$\underbrace{}_{\substack{p \text{ nonzero} \\ \text{components}}} \quad \underbrace{}_{\substack{n\text{-}p \text{ components} \\ \text{all zero}}}$$

Now let the noise vector $\mathbf{N}$ be written in the form

$$\mathbf{N} = (N_1, N_2, \ldots, N_p, N_{p+1}, \ldots, N_n)$$
$$= \mathbf{N}_1 + \mathbf{N}_2 \qquad (8\text{-}17)$$

in which

$$\mathbf{N}_1 = (N_1, N_2, \ldots, N_p, 0, \ldots, 0) \qquad (8\text{-}18)$$

and

$$\mathbf{N}_2 = (0, \ldots, 0, N_{p+1}, \ldots, N_n) \qquad (8\text{-}19)$$

The received vector may be written in terms of $\mathbf{s}$, $\mathbf{N}_1$, and $\mathbf{N}_2$, as

$$\mathbf{Z} = \mathbf{Z}_1 + \mathbf{Z}_2 \qquad (8\text{-}20)$$

in which

$$\mathbf{Z}_1 = \mathbf{s}_k + \mathbf{N}_1; \qquad \mathbf{Z}_2 = \mathbf{N}_2 \qquad (8\text{-}21)$$

Note that the last n-p components of $\mathbf{Z}_1$ are zero, as are the first p components of $\mathbf{Z}_2$.

We now assume that the first p components of the noise vector $\mathbf{N}$ are statistically independent of the last n-p components:

$$f_{\mathbf{N}}(\mathbf{n}) = f_{\mathbf{N}_1, \mathbf{N}_2}(\mathbf{n}_1, \mathbf{n}_2) = f_{\mathbf{N}_1}(\mathbf{n}_1) f_{\mathbf{N}_2}(\mathbf{n}_2) \qquad (8\text{-}22)$$

Under this assumption, the vector $\mathbf{Z}_1$ constitutes a sufficient statistic for M. To show this, combine Eqs. 8-8 and 8-22 to obtain

$$f(\mathbf{z} \mid m_i) = f_{\mathbf{N}}(\mathbf{z} - \mathbf{s}_i) = f_{\mathbf{N}_1}(\mathbf{z}_1 - \mathbf{s}_i) f_{\mathbf{N}_2}(\mathbf{z}_2) \qquad (8\text{-}23)$$

Thus, identifying $\tilde{\mathbf{M}}(\mathbf{z})$ with $\mathbf{z}_1$, $g[m_i; \tilde{\mathbf{M}}(\mathbf{z})]$ with $f_{\mathbf{N}_1}(\mathbf{z}_1 - \mathbf{s}_i)$, and $w(\mathbf{z})$ with $f_{\mathbf{N}_2}(\mathbf{z}_2)$, the desired result follows.

The significance of this is as follows. If all the signal vectors have only their first p components nonzero, *and* if the remainder of the components of the noise vector are independent of the first p components, then an optimum decision can be based solely upon the first p components of the received vector $\mathbf{Z}$, that is, on the p-dimensional vector

$$\mathbf{Z}' = (Z_1, \ldots, Z_p)$$

8-2   Representation of Signals as Vectors

Consider vectors in three-dimensional space. We say that three vectors $\mathbf{v}_1$, $\mathbf{v}_2$, and $\mathbf{v}_3$ are *linearly independent* if there does not exist any set of constants c_1, c_2, c_3, such that

$$\sum_{i=1}^{3} c_i \mathbf{v}_i = 0$$

except the set $c_1 = c_2 = c_3 = 0$. Put another way, the vectors $\mathbf{v}_1$, $\mathbf{v}_2$, and $\mathbf{v}_3$ are linearly independent if no one of them can be expressed as a linear combination of the remaining ones. If the three vectors $\mathbf{v}_1$, $\mathbf{v}_2$, $\mathbf{v}_3$ are linearly independent, they *span* three-dimensional space in the sense that *any* three-dimensional vector $\mathbf{v}$ may be expressed as a linear combination of $\mathbf{v}_1$, $\mathbf{v}_2$, and $\mathbf{v}_3$:

$$\mathbf{v} = \alpha \mathbf{v}_1 + \beta \mathbf{v}_2 + \gamma \mathbf{v}_3$$

Any set of linearly independent vectors which spans three dimensional space is said to be a *basis* for that space. For many reasons it is usually convenient to pick a set of three perpendicular vectors of unit length as a basis. Such a set is termed *orthonormal*. A familiar example is the set of three unit vectors $\mathbf{i}_x$, $\mathbf{i}_y$, and $\mathbf{i}_z$ in the x-, y-, and z-directions. In terms of these $\mathbf{v}$ is expressed

$$\mathbf{v} = v_x \mathbf{i}_x + v_y \mathbf{i}_y + v_z \mathbf{i}_z$$

Figure 8-3 illustrates the manner in which a two-dimensional vector $\mathbf{v}$ may be represented either in terms of the orthogonal unit vectors $\mathbf{i}_x$ and $\mathbf{i}_y$ or two nonorthogonal vectors $\mathbf{v}_1$ and $\mathbf{v}_2$.

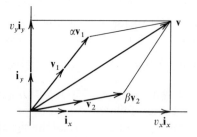

Figure 8-3   Representation of a vector in terms of an orthogonal ($\mathbf{i}_x$, $\mathbf{i}_y$) and non-orthogonal ($\mathbf{v}_1$, $\mathbf{v}_2$) basis.

The two geometrical concepts that we associate with vectors are:

1. The norm or length of a vector $\mathbf{v}$, $\|\mathbf{v}\|$.

2. The angle between two vectors $\mathbf{v}$ and $\mathbf{u}$, $\angle^{\mathbf{v}}_{\mathbf{u}}$.

Note that *both* of these concepts are described by *the inner product* (or dot product) of any two vectors $\mathbf{v}$ and $\mathbf{u}$

$$(\mathbf{v}, \mathbf{u}) = \mathbf{v} \cdot \mathbf{u} = v_x u_x + v_y u_y + v_z u_z$$

for the square of the norm or length of a vector can be expressed as

$$\|\mathbf{v}\|^2 = (\mathbf{v}, \mathbf{v}) \tag{8-24}$$

and the angle between two vectors as

$$\cos \left[\angle^{\mathbf{v}}_{\mathbf{u}} \right] = \frac{(\mathbf{v}, \mathbf{u})}{\|\mathbf{v}\| \, \|\mathbf{u}\|} = \frac{(\mathbf{v}, \mathbf{u})}{+\sqrt{(\mathbf{v}, \mathbf{v})(\mathbf{u}, \mathbf{u})}} \tag{8-25}$$

Two vectors are thus *orthogonal* or *perpendicular* if their inner product is zero.

We now wish to think of a more general vector space, one in which the vectors are not points in three-dimensional space but functions of time on some interval $0 \le t \le T$. In Chapter 2 we stated that any time function of finite energy could be expressed in the form

$$g(t) = \sum_{k=1}^{\infty} g_k \psi_k(t)$$

in which the $\psi_k(t)$ are a complete orthonormal set of functions. We could thus associate with $g(t)$ the infinite dimensional vector $(g_1, g_2, \ldots)$. However, this does not tell us how to set up a geometrical structure on this space. To do this, we need to consider the fundamental aspects of a vector space from a slightly more abstract point of view. The essential attributes of an abstract linear vector space are as follows.

DEFINITION.   We say that a collection of vectors, V, is a *linear vector space* if the addition of two vectors and multiplication of a vector by a scalar is defined, and:

(1) for any two vectors $\mathbf{u}$ and $\mathbf{v}$ in the space, the vector $a\mathbf{u} + b\mathbf{v}$ is in the space for any two scalars a and b.

(2) $a(\mathbf{u} + \mathbf{v}) = a\mathbf{u} + a\mathbf{v}$ for any two vectors $\mathbf{u}$ and $\mathbf{v}$ and any scalar a; also $(a + b)\mathbf{v} = a\mathbf{v} + b\mathbf{v}$ for any vector $\mathbf{v}$ and any two scalars a and b.

(3) $a(b\mathbf{v}) = (ab)\mathbf{v}$ for any vector $\mathbf{v}$ and any two scalars a and b. Also $1 \cdot \mathbf{v} = \mathbf{v}$ for any vector $\mathbf{v}$.

Let us note that under the above definition, the set of all functions $g(t)$, $0 \leq t \leq T$, of bounded energy

$$\int_0^T g^2(t)\, dt < \infty$$

forms a linear vector space. This is the vector space we wish to consider.

Recall that in a three-dimensional vector space the geometrical structure of the space (length of a vector and angle between two vectors) is determined by the inner product between two vectors. We thus wish to extend this concept of an inner product to our vector space of functions.

DEFINITION. In a general vector space, a scalar-valued function of two vectors, denoted $(\mathbf{u}, \mathbf{v})$, is said to be an *inner product* if it has the following properties:

(1) $(\mathbf{u}, \mathbf{v}) = (\mathbf{v}, \mathbf{u})$.
(2) $(a\mathbf{u}, \mathbf{v}) = a(\mathbf{u}, \mathbf{v})$.
(3) $(\mathbf{u} + \mathbf{v}, \mathbf{w}) = (\mathbf{u}, \mathbf{w}) + (\mathbf{v}, \mathbf{w})$.
(4) $(\mathbf{u}, \mathbf{u}) > 0$ unless $\mathbf{u} = \mathbf{0}$, in which case $(\mathbf{u}, \mathbf{u}) = 0$.

Note that the familiar three-dimensional inner (dot) product

$$(\mathbf{u}, \mathbf{v}) = u_x v_x + u_y v_y + u_z v_z$$

satisfies all these properties. As in the familiar three-dimensional case, we again take the *norm* or *length* of a vector to be given by

$$\|\mathbf{v}\| = (\mathbf{v}, \mathbf{v})^{\frac{1}{2}}$$

and say that two vectors $\mathbf{v}$ and $\mathbf{u}$ are *orthogonal* if their inner product is zero:

$$(\mathbf{u}, \mathbf{v}) = 0$$

Let us note how these definitions of inner product, length, and orthogonality extend our intuitive notions. Using the above definitions, the square of the length of the vector $\mathbf{u} + \mathbf{v}$ can be expressed as

$$\|\mathbf{u} + \mathbf{v}\|^2 = (\mathbf{u} + \mathbf{v}, \mathbf{u} + \mathbf{v}) = (\mathbf{u}, \mathbf{u} + \mathbf{v}) + (\mathbf{v}, \mathbf{u} + \mathbf{v})$$
$$= \|\mathbf{u}\|^2 + 2(\mathbf{u}, \mathbf{v}) + \|\mathbf{v}\|^2 \qquad (8\text{-}26)$$

Thus the length squared of the sum of two vectors adds as the sum of the squares of the lengths,

$$\|\mathbf{u} + \mathbf{v}\|^2 = \|\mathbf{u}\|^2 + \|\mathbf{v}\|^2$$

if and only if the vectors $\mathbf{u}$ and $\mathbf{v}$ are orthogonal,

$$(\mathbf{u}, \mathbf{v}) = 0$$

The question now is as follows. There are many ways of selecting inner products that will satisfy the above definition; how shall we select an inner product for our vector space of functions of finite energy that is physically meaningful? One particularly useful measure of the size of a time function $g(t)$ is its energy:

$$\int_0^T g^2(t)\, dt$$

From the second property of an inner product above we see that we must have

$$\|\alpha \mathbf{v}\|^2 = \alpha^2 \|\mathbf{v}\|^2$$

Thus if we take energy as our measure of the size of the function, we will have to take energy to be the square of the length of a function

$$\|g\|^2 = \int_0^T g^2(t)\, dt \tag{8-27}$$

or the length to be the square root of the energy

$$\|g\| = +\left[\int_0^T g^2(t)\, dt\right]^{\frac{1}{2}} \tag{8-28}$$

To see what is the corresponding inner product of two functions x and y, we may then use Eq. 8-26 and note that

$$\|x\|^2 + 2(x, y) + \|y\|^2 = \|x + y\|^2$$
$$= \int_0^T [x(t) + y(t)]^2\, dt$$
$$= \int_0^T x^2(t)\, dt + 2\int_0^T x(t)y(t)\, dt + \int_0^T y^2(t)\, dt$$

Identifying terms on both sides of this equation, we have the following expression for the *inner product between two vectors in our vector space of finite energy functions,*

$$(x, y) = \int_0^T x(t)y(t)\, dt \tag{8-29}$$

Problem 8-2. Show that this definition satisfies all the properties of an inner product listed in the definition on page 228.

Problem 8-3. Prove the Schwartz inequality for two vectors in an arbitrary (real scalar) vector space

$$|(x, y)| \le \|x\| \, \|y\|$$

Hint: Consider the inequality $\|x \pm cy\|^2 \ge 0$ and make an appropriate choice of the scalar c.

Note that the choice of inner product defined by Eq. 8-29 is consistent with our terminology of Chapter 2 in which we referred to a set of real-valued functions $\psi_k(t)$, $k = 1, 2, \ldots$, as *orthonormal* if

$$(\psi_j, \psi_k) = \int_0^T \psi_j(t)\psi_k(t)\, dt = \delta_{jk} = \begin{cases} 1 & j = k \\ 0 & j \neq k \end{cases} \qquad (8\text{-}30)$$

Then we further said that a set of such orthonormal functions was *complete* if any function $g(t)$ of finite energy could be written in the form

$$g(t) = \sum_{k=1}^{\infty} g_k \psi_k(t) \qquad (8\text{-}31)$$

Recall that the coefficients g_k in this equation were given by

$$g_k = \int_0^T g(t)\psi_k(t)\, dt = (g, \psi_k) \qquad (8\text{-}32)$$

and that equality in Eq. 8-31 was in the sense that

$$\lim_{m \to \infty} \left\| g - \sum_{k=1}^{m} g_k \psi_k \right\|^2 = \lim_{m \to \infty} \int_0^T \left[g(t) - \sum_{k=1}^{m} g_k \psi_k(t) \right]^2 dt = 0$$

A complete set of functions ψ_k thus forms a *basis* for our vector space of finite energy functions in the sense that any such function may be expressed as a linear combination of these ψ_k. Note also that if we express any two functions of finite energy $x(t)$ and $y(t)$ in the form of Eq. 8-31, then *Parseval's theorem* gives the inner product of $x(t)$ and $y(t)$ as

$$(x, y) = \int_0^T x(t)y(t)\, dt = \sum_{k=1}^{\infty} x_k y_k \qquad (8\text{-}33)$$

which is a direct extension of the expression in the familiar three-dimensional case.

The Gram-Schmidt Procedure

Let us now consider a situation in which there is a given set of functions $s_i(t)$, $i = 1, 2, \ldots, q$, defined for $0 \leq t \leq T$; our interest is in all functions that may be written as linear combinations of these functions

$$g(t) = \sum_{k=1}^{q} g_k' s_k(t) \qquad 0 \leq t \leq T \qquad (8\text{-}34)$$

Note that the set of all such functions forms a vector space. If all the $s_i(t)$ are *linearly independent,* that is no one of the $s_i(t)$ may be written as a linear combination of the remaining $s_i(t)$, then this vector space is of dimension q because we require q scalar coefficients (the g_k' in Eq. 8-34) to specify a function in the space. If the $s_k(t)$ are not linearly independent, any function of the form of Eq. 8-34 may be expressed as a linear combination of fewer than q of the $s_i(t)$ (Why?) and the space is of dimension less than q.

For some purposes it is convenient to have an orthonormal basis for the above vector space *spanned* by the $s_i(t)$, $i = 1, 2, \ldots, q$. We now give a procedure, known as the *Gram-Schmidt orthogonalization procedure*, for forming an orthonormal basis for this space.

1. Set $v_1(t) = s_1(t)$ and $\psi_1(t) = v_1(t)/\|v_1\|$; then $\|\psi_1\| = 1$
2. Set $v_2(t) = s_2(t) - (s_2, \psi_1)\psi_1(t)$; note that

$$(v_2, \psi_1) = (s_2, \psi_1) - (s_2, \psi_1)(\psi_1, \psi_1) = 0$$

   so that v_2 and ψ_1 are orthogonal. Then set

$$\psi_2(t) = v_2(t)/\|v_2\|$$

3. Set $v_3(t) = s_3(t) - (s_3, \psi_2)\psi_2(t) - (s_3, \psi_1)\psi_1(t)$. Note that

$$(v_3, \psi_2) = (v_3, \psi_1) = 0$$

   so that v_3 is orthogonal to both ψ_2 and ψ_1. Then set

$$\psi_3(t) = v_3(t)/\|v_3\|$$

4. Continue in this fashion until all of the $s_i(t)$ have been used. If the $s_i(t)$ are not linearly independent, then one or more steps in the procedure will yield $v(t)$'s for which $\|v\| = 0$. Omit these functions whenever they occur so that one finally ends up with n orthonormal functions $\psi_i(t)$; $i = 1, 2, \ldots, n$; $n \leq q$.

The set of $\psi(t)$'s generated by this procedure is the desired orthonormal basis for, by the method of construction,

$$(\psi_j, \psi_k) = \delta_{jk} \qquad j, k = 1, 2, \ldots, n$$

Also, note that by the method of construction

$$s_k(t) = \|v_k\| \psi_k(t) + \sum_{j=1}^{k-1} (s_k, \psi_j)\psi_j(t)$$

This equation assumes that the first k $s_j(t)$ are linearly independent; if this is not the case, this equation is slightly modified, $s_k(t)$ being expressed in terms of the first q_k $\psi_i(t)$, for some number q_k, $q_k < k$. Any function in the space spanned by the $s_k(t)$ (any function of the form of Eq. 8-34) can then be expressed as a linear combination of the n $\psi_i(t)$ determined in steps 1 through 4:

$$g(t) = \sum_{i=1}^{n} g_i\psi_i(t) \qquad 0 \leq t \leq T \qquad (8\text{-}35)$$

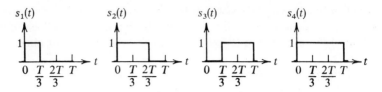

Figure 8-4   Set of functions to be orthogonalized.

Let us now consider an example.   We will use the Gram-Schmidt procedure to find an orthonormal basis for the functions $s_1(t)$, $s_2(t)$, $s_3(t)$, and $s_4(t)$ shown in Fig. 8-4.   We note immediately that this set of functions is not linearly independent since $s_4(t) = s_1(t) + s_3(t)$.   Therefore, the space spanned by this set of functions is only three-dimensional and our Gram-Schmidt procedure will terminate after finding three $\psi_i(t)$.

The first step in the Gram-Schmidt procedure is to note that

$$\|s_1\|^2 = \int_0^{T/3} (1)^2 \, dt = \frac{T}{3}$$

Thus

$$\psi_1(t) = \sqrt{3/T}\, s_1(t) = \begin{cases} \sqrt{3/T} & 0 \le t \le T/3 \\ 0 & \text{elsewhere} \end{cases}$$

Next

$$(s_2, \psi_1) = \int_0^T s_2(t)\psi_1(t) = \int_0^{T/3} 1 \cdot \sqrt{3/T} \, dt$$

$$= \sqrt{3T}/3$$

and

$$v_2(t) = s_2(t) - (s_2, \psi_1)\psi_1(t) = \begin{cases} 1 & T/3 \le t \le 2T/3 \\ 0 & \text{elsewhere} \end{cases}$$

so that

$$\|v_2\|^2 = \int_{T/3}^{2T/3} 1^2 \, dt = \frac{T}{3}$$

and

$$\psi_2(t) = v_2/\|v_2\| = \begin{cases} \sqrt{3/T} & T/3 \le t \le 2T/3 \\ 0 & \text{elsewhere} \end{cases}$$

Finally,

$$v_3(t) = s_3(t) - (s_3, \psi_2)\psi_2(t) - (s_3, \psi_1)\psi_1(t)$$

Carrying out the integrals

$$(s_3, \psi_1) = 0$$

and

$$(s_3, \psi_2) = \int_{T/3}^{2T/3} \sqrt{3/T} \, dt = \sqrt{3T}/3$$

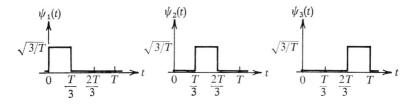

Figure 8-5. The resulting orthonormal functions.

so that

$$v_3(t) = s_3(t) - \sqrt{3T}/3\,\psi_2(t) = \begin{cases} 1 & 2T/3 \le t \le T \\ 0 & \text{elsewhere} \end{cases}$$

and

$$\|v_3\|^2 = \frac{T}{3}$$

Thus $\psi_3(t)$ is given by

$$\psi_3(t) = v_3(t)/\|v_3\| = \begin{cases} \sqrt{3/T} & 2T/3 \le t \le T \\ 0 & \text{elsewhere} \end{cases}$$

The resulting $\psi_i(t)$, $i = 1, 2, 3$, are shown in Fig. 8-5. It is obvious that they are orthonormal and that any of the original $s_k(t)$, $k = 1, 2, 3, 4$ can be expressed as linear combinations of these $\psi_i(t)$.

Problem 8-4. Consider the set of signals

$$s_i(t) = \begin{cases} \sqrt{2}\,A\cos(2\pi f_0 t + i\pi/4) & 0 \le t \le N/f_0 \\ 0 & \text{elsewhere} \end{cases}$$
$$N \text{ an integer} \qquad i = 1, 2, 3, 4$$

What is the dimensionality, n, of the space spanned by this set of signals? Find an orthonormal basis, $\psi_1(t), \ldots, \psi_n(t)$ for the space spanned by these signals. Any signal in this space can then be expressed as

$$g(t) = \sum_{k=1}^{n} g_k\psi_k(t)$$

Draw a set of coordinate axes whose coordinates are $g_1, g_2, \ldots, g_n$ and plot the locations of $s_i(t)$, $i = 1, 2, 3, 4$.

Representation of "White" Noise

Let us conclude this section by considering how to represent broad-band or "white" noise in an orthonormal expansion. By white noise we mean any noise process whose spectral density function is flat out to frequencies

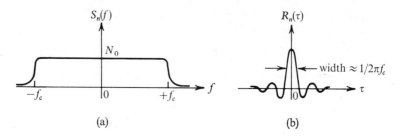

Figure 8-6   Spectral density and correlation function of a wide-band or "white" noise process.

well beyond those occupied by any message-bearing signals under consideration. Expressed in the time domain, this would mean that white noise is any process whose correlation function is nonzero only over an interval of time much smaller than the timing tolerances associated with any message-bearing signals which we may wish to generate. Such a spectral density function and its corresponding correlation function are shown in Fig. 8-6. If this represented the spectral density of thermal noise generated in a resistor, then the cut-off frequency f_c would fall somewhere in the infrared region.

Note that the average power in any *physical* noise process

$$R_n(0) = \int_{-\infty}^{\infty} S_n(f) \, df$$

(which is approximately $2N_0 f_c$ for the spectrum shown in Fig. 8-6) must be finite. This means that if we consider sample functions of T seconds duration from such a process, the average energy in these sample functions is finite. In fact, for a physical noise process, *all* the sample functions of a physical noise process have finite energy (except perhaps a set of probability zero; that is, a set no member of which ever occurs in repeated observations). Thus *any sample function* can be represented in an orthonormal expansion and the random noise process may be represented on the interval $0 \le t \le T$ as

$$N(t) = \sum_{k=1}^{\infty} N_k \psi_k(t) \qquad 0 \le t \le T \qquad (8\text{-}36)$$

in which the functions $\psi_k(t)$ are a complete orthonormal set. The coefficients N_k depend on which sample function occurs (which point s in the sample space is drawn) and hence are random variables. We shortly consider the distribution of these random variables.

Although the spectral density and correlation function of a physical process are well-behaved functions as shown in Fig. 8-6, these functions are inconvenient from a computational point of view. Specifically, if the cut-off frequency, f_c, is somewhere in the infrared region, we know that any computations we make should depend only negligibly on the value of f_c [for example, in calculating the power spectral density of the output of a practical filter when its input is $N(t)$]. Thus, for *computational convenience*, we *approximate* the power spectral density of *white noise* by

$$S_n(f) \equiv N_0 \qquad (8\text{-}37)$$

and the corresponding correlation function by

$$R_n(\tau) = N_0 \delta(\tau) \qquad (8\text{-}38)$$

Note that these *approximations*, which we adopt for *computational convenience*, correspond to a process with infinite power, and hence do not correspond to any physical process.

Let us now consider the distribution of the random variables N_k appearing in Eq. 8-36 under the assumption that $N(t)$ is a zero-mean gaussian process whose correlation function can be approximated for all practical purposes by the expression of Eq. 8-38.

Problem 8-5.   Assume that the $\psi_k(t)$ in Eq. 8-36 are a complete orthonormal set so that the random variables N_k are given by

$$N_k = \int_0^T N(t)\psi_k(t)\, dt \qquad (8\text{-}39)$$

Assume that $N(t)$ is a zero-mean gaussian white noise process; that is, its correlation function is given approximately by Eq. 8-38 and

$$E\{N_t\} = 0 \qquad (8\text{-}40)$$

(a) Find the joint distribution of $N_1, N_2, \ldots, N_k$.   *Hint:* Think of approximating the integral of Eq. 8-39 by a sum.

(b) Consider the random process $Z(t)$ given by

$$Z(t) = s(t) + N(t)$$

in which $N(t)$ is the noise process of (a) and $s(t)$ is a known function with the expansion

$$s(t) = \sum_{k=1}^{\infty} s_k \psi_k(t) \qquad 0 \le t \le T$$

consider representing $Z(t)$ by the expansion

$$Z(t) = \sum_{k=1}^{\infty} Z_k \psi_k(t) \qquad 0 \le t \le T$$

Find the joint distribution of $Z_1, Z_2, \ldots, Z_k$.

8-3   Digital Communication in the Presence of Additive White Gaussian Noise

We now return to the original situation of interest which is depicted in Fig. 8-1. Every T seconds we wish to transmit *one* of q source letters m_i, $i = 1, 2, \ldots$, or q, by transmitting a corresponding signal $s_i(t)$ of T seconds duration. We assume that at the receiver the signal $Z(t) = s_i(t) + N(t)$ is observed, in which $N(t)$ is a stationary zero-mean white gaussian noise process. The receiver must observe the sample function $z(t)$, of T seconds duration, and make a best estimate of the corresponding transmitted signal $s_i(t)$ (or equivalently of the corresponding letter m_i).

Our first step in analyzing this problem is to recast this situation in such a form that it falls into the finite-dimensional vector framework of Sec. 8-1 in which transmission took place via vectors. This allows us to accomplish two things.

First, we can use our previous expression determining the optimum decision rule for the receiver. Second, we can *visualize the transmission geometrically* and use our previous expression for the probability of a correct decision, $P(C)$, allowing us to study the effects of different choices of signal sets on $P(C)$.

We start by representing the received random process, $Z(t), 0 \le t \le T$, in a complete orthonormal expansion

$$Z(t) = \sum_{k=1}^{\infty} Z_k \psi_k(t) \qquad 0 \le t \le T \tag{8-41}$$

in which the coefficients Z_k are given by

$$Z_k = \int_0^T Z(t)\psi_k(t) \, dt \tag{8-42}$$

We wish to pick the set of complete orthonormal functions $\psi_k(t)$, $k = 1, 2, \ldots$, in a particularly convenient way. Let $\varphi_j(t), j = 1, 2, \ldots$, be any set of complete orthonormal functions, $0 \le t \le T$, such as the sines and cosines with fundamental period T. Then arrange the transmitted signals and these orthonormal functions in the following sequence:

$$s_1(t), s_2(t), \ldots, s_q(t), \varphi_1(t), \varphi_2(t), \ldots$$

We will then form a new set of orthonormal functions $\psi_k(t)$, $k = 1, 2, \ldots$ by using the Gram-Schmidt procedure on the above sequence of functions. Let us note the following properties of this resulting set of functions:

1. Since the set of functions $\varphi_j(t)$, $j = 1, 2, \ldots$, was assumed complete, the set of functions $\psi_k(t)$, $k = 1, 2, \ldots$, is complete;

2. Suppose that among the set of signals $s_i(t)$, $i = 1, 2, \ldots, q$, there are n linearly independent signals; then any of the q $s_i(t)$ are expressible as linear combinations of only the first n $\psi_k(t)$:

$$s_i(t) = \sum_{k=1}^{n} s_k{}^i \psi_k(t) \qquad 0 \le t \le T \tag{8-43}$$

$$i = 1, 2, \ldots, q$$

The received process can be represented in terms of the $\psi_k(t)$ as

$$Z(t) = s_i(t) + N(t) = \sum_{k=1}^{\infty} Z_k \psi_k(t)$$

$$= \sum_{k=1}^{n} s_k{}^i \psi_k(t) + \sum_{k=1}^{\infty} N_k \psi_k(t) \qquad 0 \le t \le T \tag{8-44}$$

in which the coefficients, given by Eq. 8-42, can be expressed as

$$Z_k = s_k{}^i + N_k \tag{8-45}$$

with

$$s_k{}^i = \begin{cases} \int_0^T s_i(t) \psi_k(t)\, dt & k = 1, 2, \ldots, n \\ 0 & k > n \\ & i = 1, 2, \ldots, q \end{cases} \tag{8-46}$$

and

$$N_k = \int_0^T N(t) \psi_k(t)\, dt \qquad k = 1, 2, \ldots \tag{8-47}$$

Let us now comment on the distribution of the random variables N_k. In working Problem 8-5, the reader should have come to the following conclusions:

1. The N_k all have zero mean, $E\{N_k\} = 0$, $k = 1, 2, \ldots$.
2. The N_k are all uncorrelated with variance N_0:

$$E\{N_k N_j\} = N_0 \delta_{jk} \qquad j, k = 1, 2, \ldots$$

3. The N_k have a joint gaussian distribution; the fact that the N_k are uncorrelated then implies that all the N_k are statistically independent.

This is the situation of the example of Sec. 8-1. If we consider the first m coefficients of the expansion of $Z(t)$, for $m \ge n$ we have

$$Z_k = \begin{cases} s_k{}^i + N_k & 1 \le k \le n \\ N_k & k > n \end{cases} \tag{8-48}$$

in which the N_k are all statistically independent. *The first n coefficients, $Z_1, \ldots, Z_n$, thus constitute a sufficient statistic for detecting which of the q*

letters was transmitted.   We may therefore denote these first n-coefficients by the n-dimensional vector $\mathbf{Z}$:

$$\mathbf{Z} = \mathbf{s}_i + \mathbf{N} \qquad i = ?\, 1, 2, \ldots, q$$

$$\mathbf{Z} = (Z_1, \ldots, Z_n); \qquad \mathbf{N} = (N_1, \ldots, N_n); \qquad \mathbf{s}_i = (s_1{}^i, \ldots, s_n{}^i) \quad (8\text{-}49)$$

and treat the signal transmission problem exactly as we treated the vector transmission problem of Sec. 8-1.

From the distribution of the components of $\mathbf{N}$, it follows that if the ith signal is transmitted, then the components of $\mathbf{Z}$ are statistically independent gaussian random variables, each of variance N_0, and the mean of $\mathbf{Z}$ is

$$E\{\mathbf{Z} \mid M = m_i\} = E\{\mathbf{Z} \mid m_i\} = \mathbf{s}_i; \qquad \mathbf{s}_i = (s_1{}^i, s_2{}^i, \ldots, s_n{}^i) \quad (8\text{-}50)$$

Thus the conditional probability density for Z, assuming the ith source symbol is transmitted, is

$$f_{\mathbf{Z}\mid M}(\mathbf{z} \mid m_i) = f_{\mathbf{N}}(\mathbf{z} - \mathbf{s}_i)$$

$$= (1/\sqrt{2\pi N_0})^n \exp\left\{ -\sum_{k=1}^{n} (z_k - s_k{}^i)^2/2N_0 \right\}$$

$$= (1/\sqrt{2\pi N_0})^n \exp\left\{ -\|\mathbf{z} - \mathbf{s}_i\|^2/2N_0 \right\} \quad (8\text{-}51)$$

The decision rule of Eq. 8-10 thus becomes: Having observed $\mathbf{Z} = \mathbf{z}$, pick the message symbol having the index $j = j(\mathbf{z})$ such that

$$(1/\sqrt{2\pi N_0})^n \exp\left\{ -\|\mathbf{z} - \mathbf{s}_j\|^2/2N_0 \right\} P(m_j)$$

$$\geq (1/\sqrt{2\pi N_0})^n \exp\left\{ -\|\mathbf{z} - \mathbf{s}_i\|^2/2N_0 \right\} P(m_i) \qquad \text{all } i \neq j$$

The factors $(1/\sqrt{2\pi N_0})^n$ cancel out of this inequality.   Moreover, since $\ln(x)$ is a monotone function of x, we can take ln of both sides of this inequality, yielding the rule: *pick the index j for which*

$$-\|\mathbf{z} - \mathbf{s}_j\|^2 + 2N_0 \ln P(m_j) \geq -\|\mathbf{z} - \mathbf{s}_i\|^2 + 2N_0 \ln P(m_i) \quad \text{all } i \neq j$$

Reversing the sign on the inequality, we can finally rephrase our decision rule as:

having received $\mathbf{Z} = \mathbf{z}$, *pick the index of the message symbol for which the quantity*

$$Q_j(\mathbf{z}) = \|\mathbf{z} - \mathbf{s}_j\|^2 - 2N_0 \ln P(m_j) \quad (8\text{-}52)$$

is a minimum, $j = 1, 2, \ldots, q$.

There now remain two points to consider regarding digital communication via transmission of signals in the presence of additive white gaussian noise.   First, we need to consider how this decision rule can be physically implemented. Second, it will be useful to consider some examples of signal transmission in order that we can see how this vector formulation allows us to visualize the transmission geometrically and to calculate the probability of an error in transmission.

Physical Implementation of the Receiver

Let us turn to the physical implementation of the decision rule expressed by Eq. 8-52.

Problem 8-6. Show that the quantity $Q_j(\mathbf{z})$ may be written as

$$Q_j(\mathbf{z}) = \|\mathbf{z}\|^2 - 2 \int_0^T s_j(t)z(t)\, dt + E_j - 2N_0 \ln P(m_j) \tag{8-53}$$

in which the quantity E_j is the energy of the jth signal

$$E_j = \int_0^T [s_j(t)]^2\, dt \tag{8-54}$$

Let us now note that the decision rule may be slightly reformulated. Since the quantity

$$\|\mathbf{z}\|^2 = \sum_{k=1}^n z_k{}^2; \qquad z_k = \int_0^T z(t)\psi_k(t)\, dt$$

does not depend on the index j, we can compare the quantities

$$R_j(\mathbf{z}) = -\tfrac{1}{2}[Q_j(\mathbf{z}) - \|\mathbf{z}\|^2]$$
$$= \int_0^T s_j(t)z(t)\, dt + [N_0 \ln P(m_j) - \tfrac{1}{2}E_j] \tag{8-55}$$

for the value of the index j that yields a maximum. Note that of the terms appearing in the right-hand side of Eq. 8-55, only the term

$$T_j(\mathbf{z}) = \int_0^T s_j(t)z(t)\, dt \tag{8-56}$$

depends on the received signal, while the bias term

$$B_j = N_0 \ln P(m_j) - \tfrac{1}{2}E_j \tag{8-57}$$

is a fixed quantity, dependent only on the index j, and can be calculated and stored in the receiver. If we had the quantities $T_j(\mathbf{z})$ available, the receiver would then function as shown in the block diagram of Fig. 8-7.

We now need to examine how the quantities $T_j(\mathbf{z})$ can be formed from the received signal $z(t)$. The way directly indicated by the expression

$$T_j(\mathbf{z}) = \int_0^T s_j(t)z(t)\, dt \qquad j = 1, 2, \dots, q \tag{8-56}$$

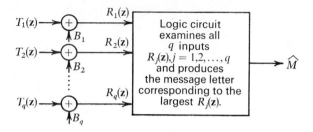

Figure 8-7   Block diagram of the optimum receiver.

was first suggested by J. M. Wozencraft and is referred to as an "integrate and dump filter." The received signal $z(t)$ is multiplied by the stored signal $s_j(t)$ and then integrated for T seconds. Physically this integration can be performed by passing a current proportional to $s_j(t)z(t)$ into an R-C circuit whose time constant is very long compared to T. At the end of the T-second interval the voltage across the capacitor is sampled and then the capacitor is short circuited to dump its charge, preparing the circuit for use during the succeeding T-second interval. This operation is shown functionally in Fig. 8-8. A receiver forming $T_j(\mathbf{z})$ in this manner is usually referred to as a *correlation receiver*.

An alternate form of receiver is the so called *matched filter receiver* in which the quantities T_j are formed by applying the signal $z(t)$ as inputs to q filters with the impulse responses

$$h_j(\tau) = \begin{cases} s_j(T - \tau) & 0 \le \tau \le T \quad j = 1, 2, \ldots, q \\ 0 & \text{elsewhere} \end{cases} \tag{8-58}$$

Such a filter $h_j(\tau)$ is said to be *matched*[1] to the signal $s_j(t)$. The output

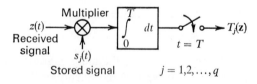

Figure 8-8   Formation of the quantities $T_j(\mathbf{z})$ by an integrate and dump filter.

---

[1] Note that the matched filter derived here as part of the optimum receiver for the detection of signals in gaussian noise is the same as the matched filter derived in Sec. 7-2 on the basis of maximizing the signal to noise ratio.

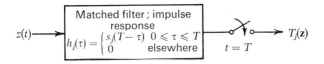

Figure 8-9   Formation of the quantities $T_j(\mathbf{z})$ by a matched filter.

of the jth filter *at time* $t = T$ is the desired quantity T_j. This operation is shown functionally in Fig. 8-9.

Problem 8-7. Consider a filter with impulse response given by Eq. 8-58. Show that if its input is $z(t)$, the output *at time* $t = T$ is given by the right-hand side of Eq. 8-56.

Problem 8-8. Consider a source with binary output symbols 0 and 1: $q = 2$, $m_1 = 0$, $m_2 = 1$. Let the corresponding signals be

$$s_1(t) = \begin{cases} \cos 2\pi f_0 t & 0 \le t \le T \\ 0 & \text{elsewhere} \end{cases} \qquad s_2(t) = \begin{cases} \sin 2\pi f_0 t & 0 \le t \le T \\ 0 & \text{elsewhere} \end{cases}$$

with T an integer times $1/f_0$. Assume $P(0) = P(1) = \frac{1}{2}$ and the transmission takes place in the presence of zero-mean white gaussian noise of spectral density N_0.

(a) Show that the receiver implementation simplifies to that shown in the block diagram in Fig. 8-10.

(b) Pick a pair of orthonormal functions $\psi_1(t)$ and $\psi_2(t)$ which span the space spanned by $s_1(t)$ and $s_2(t)$. Consider the two-dimensional space whose components are $z_k = \int_0^T \psi_k(t) z(t) \, dt$, $k = 1, 2$, and indicate the decision regions I_1 and I_2 in this space.

Geometrical Properties of the Signal Sets and Decision Regions: Probability of Error

We have shown that digital communication in which transmission takes place via signals in the presence of additive white gaussian noise could be analyzed as if transmission were taking place via finite dimensional vectors. So far, this analysis has allowed us to deduce the optimum (minimum

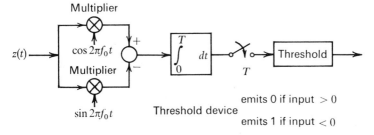

Figure 8-10   Receiver block diagram for the signal set of Problem 8-7.

probability of error) receiver. We now show how this vector model for physical signaling allows us to calculate the probability of error for a given signal set and deduce general properties of the performance of certain signal sets. Before turning to deducing these properties or calculating error probabilities, let us consider a specific signal set and focus our attention on the geometric or vector-channel model for transmission via this set of signals.

Consider a situation in which there are four equiprobable source letters, $m_1, \ldots, m_4$. We will indicate which letter is the current source output by transmitting one of the four corresponding signals:

$$s_j(t) = \begin{cases} \sqrt{2E/T} \sin \left[2\pi f_0 t + (j-1)\dfrac{\pi}{2} \right] & 0 \le t \le T \\ \\ 0 & \text{elsewhere} \end{cases} \tag{8-59}$$

$$j = 1, 2, 3, 4 \qquad\qquad T = \text{integer times } 1/f_0$$

The quantity E denotes the energy of each of the transmission signals. Such a mode of transmission is referred to as *phase-shift keying*[1] because the phase shift of the carrier indicates the message letter. Note that these four functions can be expressed as

$$s_1(t) = -s_3(t) = \sqrt{2E/T} \sin 2\pi f_0 t \qquad 0 \le t \le T$$

and

$$s_2(t) = -s_4(t) = \sqrt{2E/T} \cos 2\pi f_0 t \qquad 0 \le t \le T$$

Since $f_0 T$ is an integer number of cycles, the functions

$$\psi_1(t) = \sqrt{2/T} \sin 2\pi f_0 t \qquad 0 \le t \le T$$

$$\psi_2(t) = \sqrt{2/T} \cos 2\pi f_0 t \qquad 0 \le t \le T$$

are orthonormal. They span the space spanned by the transmitted signals since we can express the transmitted signals as

$$s_1(t) = -s_3(t) = \sqrt{E}\, \psi_1(t) \tag{8-60}$$

$$s_2(t) = -s_4(t) = \sqrt{E}\, \psi_2(t) \tag{8-61}$$

[1] Note that the phase-shift keying system described above requires an absolute phase reference and hence cannot tolerate phase fluctuations in the transmission channel. In practice, a system known as *differential phase-shift keying* would be used. In such a system, a signal of T seconds duration and arbitrary phase is transmitted to start communication. From that point on, the nth letter in the sequence to be transmitted is indicated by the *difference* of the phase between the nth and $(n+1)$th signals. This system maintains a phase reference only between successive symbols and is insensitive to phase fluctuations in the transmission channel as long as these fluctuations are negligible during the duration of a symbol interval T. Such a system is said to be *differentially coherent*.

It is easily verified that these functions $\psi_1(t)$ and $\psi_2(t)$ would be the first functions obtained by carrying out the Gram-Schmidt procedure on the list of functions

yielding the resulting list of orthogonal functions

$$\underbrace{s_1(t),\ s_2(t),\ s_3(t),\ s_4(t),\ \varphi_1(t),}\ \ldots$$

$$\underbrace{\psi_1(t),\psi_2(t),}\ \text{------},\ \text{------},\ \psi_3(t),\ \ldots$$

as discussed previously. As we have already pointed out, an optimum decision need not be based on observation of the received signal

$$z(t) = \sum_{k=1}^{\infty} z_k \psi_k(t)$$

but can be based on the *n*-dimensional vector (in this example $n = 2$) **z** which is a sufficient statistic

$$\mathbf{z} = (z_1, z_2)$$

$$z_k = \int_0^T z(t)\psi_k(t)\,dt \qquad k = 1, 2, \ldots$$

Recall that this vector **z** is the sum of the signal vector

$$\mathbf{s}_i = (s_1{}^i, s_2{}^i)$$

and a noise vector

$$\mathbf{N} = (N_1, N_2)$$

whose components are statistically independent zero-mean gaussian random variables of variance N_0. From Eqs. 8-60 and 8-61 we see that the signal vectors are

$$\mathbf{s}_1 = (\sqrt{E}, 0); \qquad \mathbf{s}_2 = (0, \sqrt{E})$$
$$\mathbf{s}_3 = (-\sqrt{E}, 0); \qquad \mathbf{s}_4 = (0, -\sqrt{E})$$

in which $\sqrt{E}$ is the square root of the energy of each of the signals. Since $P(m_i) = \frac{1}{4}$, $i = 1, 2, 3, 4$, the decision rule associated with Eq. 8-52 reduces to: Having observed $\mathbf{Z} = \mathbf{z}$, pick as the index of the transmitted symbol the index i for which $\|\mathbf{z} - \mathbf{s}_i\|^2$ is a minimum.

We can now depict this geometrically in a plane whose coordinates are z_1 and z_2. The signal vectors and decision regions are as shown in Fig. 8-11. A typical noise vector and received vector are shown under the assumption that $\mathbf{s}_1$ is transmitted. Note that the probability that an error is committed is the probability that the noise vector causes the received vector **z** to leave the decision region associated with the transmitted

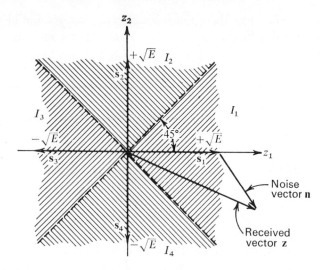

Figure 8-11   Vectors and decision regions for the phase-shift keying example.

vector.   From the geometrical structure, we can see that for any of the transmitted vectors the conditional probability of a correct decision, $P(C \mid s_i)$, will be the probability that the gaussian noise vector N lies inside the region shown in Fig. 8-12.   We will actually calculate this probability of error later.   Before doing so, it will be useful to consider two general properties of signal sets.

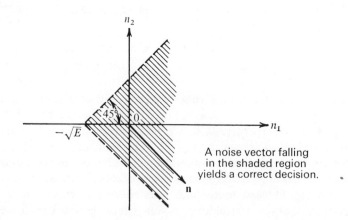

Figure 8-12   The region used for calculating $P(C \mid s_1)$.

Let us recall Eq. 8-14 giving the probability of a correct decision for the vector representation

$$P(C) = \sum_{i=1}^{q} P(m_i) \int \cdots \int_{I_i} f_N(\mathbf{z} - \mathbf{s}_i)\, d\mathbf{z} \qquad (8\text{-}14)$$

and the decision rule associated with Eq. 8-52: having received $\mathbf{Z} = \mathbf{z}$, pick the index of the message symbol to be the index for which the quantity

$$Q_j(\mathbf{z}) = \|\mathbf{z} - \mathbf{s}_j\|^2 - 2N_0 \ln P(m_j) \qquad (8\text{-}52)$$

is a minimum, $j = 1, 2, \ldots, q$.

Now consider a set of q signals

$$s_j(t) = \sum_{k=1}^{n} s_k{}^j \psi_k(t) \qquad j = 1, 2, \ldots, q \qquad (8\text{-}62)$$

which are represented by the q vectors

$$\mathbf{s}_j = (s_1{}^j, \ldots, s_n{}^j) \qquad j = 1, 2, \ldots, q \qquad (8\text{-}63)$$

Note that the probability distribution of the noise vector $\mathbf{N} = (N_1, \ldots\ N_n)$

$$N_k = \int_0^T N(t)\psi_k(t)\, dt \qquad k = 1, 2, \ldots, n$$

as discussed earlier depends only on the fact that the ψ_k are orthonormal and not on the $\psi_k(t)$ themselves. Moreover, the decision rule associated with Eq. 8-52 depends only on the vectors $\mathbf{s}_j$ and not upon the functions $\psi_k(t)$. Thus we have:

Property I. The probability of a correct decision, $P(C)$, is independent of the particular choice of the $\psi_k(t)$ appearing in Eq. 8-62 (as long as they are orthonormal) and depends only on the vectors $\mathbf{s}_j, j = 1, 2, \ldots, q$.

Next, let us consider a rigid motion of the set of signal vectors. By such a rigid motion, we mean a motion in which *all* of the points representing the signals (the *points* at the "tips" of the vectors) undergo exactly the same motion. This can be visualized as follows. Consider a sheet of paper with a set of coordinate axes drawn upon it. Over this lay a clear sheet of rigid plastic. Now put a set of points on the plastic indicating the location of the signals. By a rigid motion of the set of signal vectors, we mean any motion that this set of points undergoes as the sheet of plastic is moved around. Note that the "*geometrical vectors*" consisting of the *lines* from the coordinate origin to the points do *not* themselves undergo a rigid motion. In speaking of a vector, we really mean the *n*-tuple of coordinates or the corresponding *point* in the space and *not* the *line* joining the origin and this point.

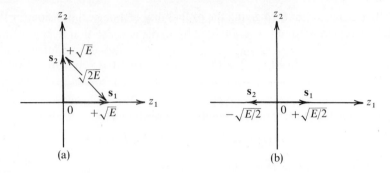

Figure 8-13   Rigid motion transformation of a set of signal vectors by a counterclockwise rotation of $45°$ and downward translation of $\sqrt{E/2}$:
(a) Original set of vectors.
(b) Transformed set of vectors.

Any rigid motion can be decomposed into a rotation and a translation. As an example, consider the two vectors s_1 and s_2 shown in Fig. 8-13a. They can be changed into the new set of vectors s_1' and s_2' of Fig. 8-13b by rotating the two signal points counterclockwise by $45°$ and translating the resulting points downward a distance of $\sqrt{E/2}$.

Now let us note several properties of a rigid transformation of points. Let z denote an arbitrary point and consider the point coincident with it on the sheet of plastic.   Now suppose the sheet of plastic is moved carrying the old signal set s_i into the new signal set s_i'; let the point on the plastic that was coincident with z be termed z'.   Note that since the plastic is rigid, $\|z' - s_i'\|$ is unchanged from the original value $\|z - s_i\|$.   Now suppose that the point z was in the i_0th decision region; that is, the quantity

$$Q_i(z) = \|z - s_i\|^2 - 2N_0 \ln P(m_i)$$

is a minimum for $i = i_0$.   Then the quantity

$$Q_i'(z') = \|z' - s_i'\|^2 - 2N_0 \ln P(m_i)$$

is also a minimum for $i = i_0$, so that z', the point resulting from a rigid motion of z, is in the same decision region as z. *Thus the decision regions undergo the same rigid motion as the set of signal vectors.*   Next, consider the effect of the rigid motion transformation of the set of signal vectors on the value of the integral

$$P(C \mid m_i) = \int \cdots \int_{I_i} f_N(z - s_i)\, dz \tag{8-64}$$

For every dummy point in the original region of integration (the decision region I_i) there is a corresponding point in the new decision region I_i', and since $f_N(\mathbf{z} - \mathbf{s}_i)$ depends only on $\|\mathbf{z} - \mathbf{s}_i\|$, the value of the integrand at this corresponding point is equal to the value of the integrand at the original point if $\mathbf{s}_i$ is replaced by $\mathbf{s}_i'$. Furthermore, a rigid motion transformation leaves the volume of a set of points unchanged. Thus the integral of Eq. 8-64 has the same value as the integral

$$\int \cdots \int_{I_i'} f_N(\mathbf{z} - \mathbf{s}_i') \, d\mathbf{z}$$

and we have:

Property II. Consider an arbitrary set of signal vectors. The probability of a correct decision, $P(C)$, is equal to that of any other set of signal vectors obtained from the first by a rigid motion transformation (i.e., a rigid motion of the *points* representing the coordinates of the signals).

Properties I and II point out that the performance of a signal set does not depend on the specific set of signals used but only on its geometric representation, and that any two sets related to one another by a rigid motion transformation have the same performance. To explore this in more detail, let us now return to our phase-shift keying example. First, note by Property I that our calculation of $P(C)$ will be pertinent not only to the phase shift keying signals, but to any set of signals of the form given by Eqs. 8-60 and 8-61, provided only that $\psi_1(t)$ and $\psi_2(t)$ are orthonormal. For example, instead of phase-shift keying

$$\psi_1(t) = \sqrt{2/T} \sin 2\pi f_0 t \qquad 0 \le t \le T$$
$$\psi_2(t) = \sqrt{2/T} \cos 2\pi f_0 t \qquad 0 \le t \le T$$

we might have picked

$$\psi_1(t) = \sqrt{2/T} \sin 2\pi f_0 t \qquad\qquad 0 \le t \le T$$
$$\psi_2(t) = \sqrt{2/T} \sin 2\pi (f_0 + f_m)t \qquad 0 \le t \le T \qquad \text{Frequency-shift keying}$$
$$f_0/T, f_m/T \text{ integers}$$

or

$$\psi_1(t) = \begin{cases} (2/\sqrt{T}) \sin 2\pi f_0 t & 0 \le t \le T/2 \\ 0 & T/2 \le t \le T \end{cases} \qquad \text{Pulse-delay keying}$$
$$\psi_2(t) = \begin{cases} 0 & 0 \le t \le T/2 \\ (2/\sqrt{T}) \sin 2\pi f_0 t & T/2 \le t \le T \end{cases}$$

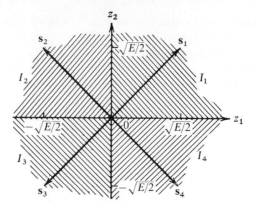

Figure 8-14 Signal vectors of Figure 8-11 transformed by a counterclockwise rotation of 45°.

Next, let us use Property II to facilitate computation of $P(C)$. We consider the set of signals to be rotated 45° counterclockwise. If this is done, the signal set and decision regions of Fig. 8-11 are transformed into the set shown in Fig. 8-14, and the region used for calculating $P(C \mid s_1)$ shown in Fig. 8-12 is transformed into the region shown in Fig. 8-15.

From Fig. 8-15 we can quickly calculate $P(C \mid s_1)$

$$P(C \mid s_1) = \int_{-\sqrt{E/2}}^{\infty} dn_1 \int_{-\sqrt{E/2}}^{\infty} dn_2 \, f_N(n) \qquad (8\text{-}65)$$

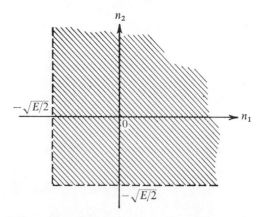

Figure 8-15 Transformed region for calculating $P(C \mid s_1)$.

However, referring back to Eq. 8-51 and the discussion preceding it, we have

$$f_{\mathbf{N}}(\mathbf{n}) = \left(\frac{1}{2\pi N_0}\right)^{n/2} \exp\{-\|\mathbf{n}\|^2/2N_0\}$$

$$= \left(\frac{1}{2\pi N_0}\right)^{n/2} \prod_{k=1}^{n} \exp\{-n_k{}^2/2N_0\} \tag{8-66}$$

For our two-dimensional case, Eq. 8-65 thus becomes

$$P(C \mid \mathbf{s}_1) = \left[\frac{1}{\sqrt{2\pi N_0}} \int_{-\sqrt{E/2}}^{\infty} \exp\{-n^2/2N_0\}\, dn\right]^2$$

$$= \left[\frac{1}{\sqrt{2\pi}} \int_{-\sqrt{E/2N_0}}^{\infty} \exp\{-\theta^2/2\}\, d\theta\right]^2 \tag{8-67}$$

The quantity appearing in the brackets represents the probability associated with the tail of a gaussian distribution; it occurs so frequently that we shall denote it simply by

$$Q(x) = \frac{1}{\sqrt{2\pi}} \int_{x}^{\infty} \exp\{-\theta^2/2\}\, d\theta \tag{8-68}$$

In using Q to denote this function, we follow the notation of the National Bureau of Standards tables which contain an extensive numerical tabulation of this function [4]. This function is not to be confused with the Q-function of Marcus which also appears in detection theory and, unfortunately, uses the same notation. The reader should verify for himself that

$$Q(-x) = 1 - Q(x) \tag{8-69}$$

The probability $P(C \mid \mathbf{s}_1)$ may thus be expressed

$$P(C \mid \mathbf{s}_1) = [1 - Q(\sqrt{E/2N_0})]^2 \tag{8-70}$$

As we remarked earlier, by the symmetry of the decision regions the quantities $P(C \mid \mathbf{s}_i)$ are all equal, $i = 1, 2, 3, 4$. Thus,

$$P(C) = \sum_{i=1}^{4} P(m_i) P(C \mid \mathbf{s}_i) = P(C \mid \mathbf{s}_1) = [1 - Q(\sqrt{E/2N_0})]^2 \tag{8-71}$$

The set of signals that we have been discussing is the two-dimensional case ($n = 2$) of what is referred to as a *biorthogonal signal set*. For a general n, the set of $q = 2n$ biorthogonal signals is formed by starting with any set of n orthonormal signals and taking

$$\begin{aligned} s_{2k-1}(t) &= +\sqrt{E}\,\psi_k(t) \\ s_{2k}(t) &= -\sqrt{E}\,\psi_k(t) \end{aligned} \qquad k = 1, 2, \ldots, n \tag{8-72}$$

Another signal set of interest is simply an *orthogonal set* in which the q transmission signals are formed directly from q orthonormal signals

$$s_k(t) = \sqrt{E}\,\psi_k(t) \qquad k = 1, 2, \ldots, q \qquad (8\text{-}73)$$

One reason for the interest in these signals is the ease with which they can be generated, since the transmission signals are all direct multiples of orthonormal signals. A set of orthonormal signals may be easily physically generated in many ways, for example, frequency-shift keying

$$\psi_k(t) = \begin{cases} \sqrt{2/T}\,\sin\{2\pi[f_0 + (k-1)f_m]t + \theta\} & 0 \le t \le T \\ 0 & \text{elsewhere} \end{cases}$$

$$k = 1, 2, \ldots, q \qquad f_0/T \quad \text{and} \quad f_m/T \text{ integers}$$

or pulse-delay keying

$$\psi_k(t) = \begin{cases} \sqrt{2qT}\,\sin(2\pi f_0 t + \theta) & \dfrac{(k-1)T}{q} \le t \le \dfrac{kT}{q} \\ 0 & \text{elsewhere} \end{cases}$$

$$k = 1, 2, \ldots, q$$

Let us now consider the probability of error for an orthogonal set. We will start for convenience of visualization with the $q = n = 2$ case pictured in Fig. 8-16. The decision regions are shown for the case $P(m_1) = P(m_2) = \frac{1}{2}$. From the symmetry of the decision regions and the form of $f_N(\mathbf{n})$ it follows that

$$P(C \mid \mathbf{s}_1) = P(C \mid \mathbf{s}_2)$$

and hence,

$$P(C) = P(C \mid \mathbf{s}_1) \qquad (8\text{-}74)$$

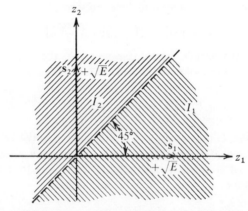

Figure 8-16 Signal vectors and decision regions for equiprobable binary orthogonal signals.

Let us thus concentrate on finding $P(C \mid s_1)$. Instead of using property II to find an equivalent signal set for which $P(C \mid s_1)$ can be easily evaluated, we set up a direct expression for $P(C \mid s_1)$, since this method of evaluation generalizes to the case $n > 2$. We have

$$P(C \mid s_1) = \int\int_{I_1} f_N(z - s_1)\, dz$$

$$= \frac{1}{2\pi N_0} \int_{-\infty}^{\infty} dz_1 \exp\{-(z_1 - \sqrt{E})^2/2N_0\} \int_{-\infty}^{z_1} dz_2 \exp\{-z_2{}^2/2N_0\}$$

$$= \frac{1}{2\pi N_0} \int_{-\infty}^{\infty} dn_1 \exp\{-n_1{}^2/2N_0\} \int_{-\infty}^{\sqrt{E}+n_1} dn_2 \exp\{-n_2{}^2/2N_0\}$$

$$= \frac{1}{\sqrt{2\pi}} \int_{-\infty}^{\infty} d\theta_1 \exp\{-\theta_1{}^2/2\} \frac{1}{\sqrt{2\pi}} \int_{-\infty}^{\sqrt{E/N_0}+\theta_1} d\theta_2 \exp\{-\theta_2{}^2/2\}$$

$$= \frac{1}{\sqrt{2\pi}} \int_{-\infty}^{\infty} \exp\{-\theta^2/2\}[1 - Q(\sqrt{E/N_0} + \theta)]\, d\theta \qquad (8\text{-}75)$$

in which several appropriate changes of integration variables have been used to reduce this expression to the final form.

Problem 8-9. Show that for q equiprobable message symbols and q orthogonal signals

$$s_k(t) = \sqrt{E}\,\psi_k(t) \qquad k = 1, 2, \ldots, q$$

the probability of a correct decision is given by

$$P(C) = P(C \mid s_1) = \frac{1}{\sqrt{2\pi}} \int_{-\infty}^{\infty} \exp\{-\theta^2/2\}[1 - Q(\sqrt{E/N_0} + \theta)]^{q-1}\, d\theta$$

$$(8\text{-}76)$$

Your line of reasoning should follow a direct extension of the case for $q = 2$.

We should remark at this point that the probability of a correct decision as given by Eq. 8-76 cannot be further evaluated analytically but must be done numerically by a digital computer. A plot of the probability of an error, $P(\mathscr{E}) = 1 - P(C)$, is shown in Fig. 8-17 as a function of the signal to noise ratio, E/N_0, for a number of values of q. Note that a symbol from an alphabet of q symbols is determined by $\log_2 q$ binary digits. The horizontal scale in Fig. 8-17 is in terms of the energy per binary digit, $E/\log_2 q$, divided by the noise level N_0.

Problem 8-10. Show that for $q = 2$, the expression for the probability of a correct decision for equiprobable orthogonal signals can be alternately expressed as

$$P(C) = Q(-\sqrt{E/2N_0}) = 1 - Q(\sqrt{E/2N_0}) \qquad (8\text{-}77)$$

Hint: The easiest way to derive this expression is to use a starting point completely different from that taken above.   Try making an appropriate rigid transformation of the signal set.

Translation of Signal Sets and Simplex Signals

Given a set of signals

$$s_j(t) = \sum_{k=1}^{n} s_k{}^j \psi_k(t) \qquad \mathbf{s}_j = (s_1{}^j, \ldots, s_n{}^j) \qquad j = 1, 2, \ldots, q$$

we have seen that $P(C)$ [or $P(\mathscr{E}) = 1 - P(C)$] is independent of a rotation or translation of the signal set.   Another quantity of interest is the average transmitted power (the average energy divided by the time per letter, T),

$$P = \sum_{j=1}^{q} P(m_j) \frac{1}{T} \int_0^T s_j{}^2(t)\, dt$$

$$= \frac{1}{T} \sum_{j=1}^{q} P(m_j) \|\mathbf{s}_j\|^2 = \frac{1}{T} \sum_{j=1}^{q} P(m_j) \sum_{k=1}^{n} (s_k{}^j)^2 \qquad (8\text{-}78)$$

The average power of a signal set is invariant to a rotation since the vector lengths $\|\mathbf{s}_j\|$ are unchanged by a rotation.   However, P does vary with translation.   Inasmuch as $P(C)$ is invariant to translation, it is worthwhile to ask if the average power of a given set of transmission signals can be reduced by an appropriate translation, and, if so, what is the translation that minimizes P.   Let $\mathbf{\Delta} = (\Delta_1, \Delta_2, \ldots, \Delta_n)$ denote this minimizing translation, so that the new set of signal vectors is given by

$$\mathbf{s}_j{}' = \mathbf{s}_j + \mathbf{\Delta} = (s_1{}^j + \Delta_1, s_2{}^j + \Delta_2, \ldots, s_n{}^j + \Delta_n) \qquad j = 1, 2, \ldots, q$$

Problem 8-11. Show that the translation of a given set of signal vectors that minimizes the average power, P, is given by

$$\mathbf{\Delta} = - \sum_{j=1}^{q} P(m_j)\mathbf{s}_j \qquad (8\text{-}79)$$

Note that the result expressed by Eq. 8-79 is what we might expect.   If we regard probability as mass, this equation simply says that the moment of inertia (the average power) of the set of masses $P(m_j)$ located at the positions $\mathbf{s}_j$ is minimized by subtracting off the center of mass of the set; i.e., locating the center of mass at the origin.

As an example of this procedure, we will consider q equiprobable orthogonal signals and the minimum power-signal set obtained from them, termed the *simplex signal set*.   The set of signal vectors $\mathbf{s}_j$ corresponding to the orthogonal signal set of Eq. 8-73 is given by

$$\mathbf{s}_j = (0, \ldots, 0, \sqrt{E}, 0, \ldots, 0) \qquad (8\text{-}80)$$
$$\uparrow j\text{th component}$$

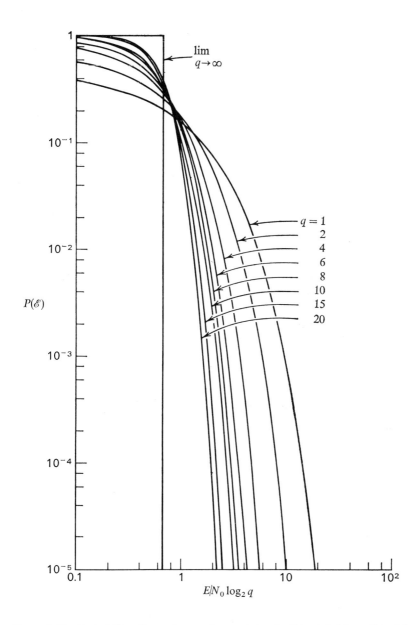

Figure 8-17   Probability of error for q orthogonal signals. (Reprinted from *Principles of Coherent Communication* through the courtesy of A. J. Viterbi [5] and the McGraw-Hill Book Company.)

The resulting set of minimum power signals is given by [noting that we have assumed that $P(m_j) = 1/q$ all j]

$$\mathbf{s}_j' = \mathbf{s}_j - \sum_{k=1}^{q} (1/q)\mathbf{s}_k \qquad j = 1, 2, \ldots, q \qquad (8\text{-}81)$$

These translated signal vectors are thus given by

$$\mathbf{s}_j' = \sqrt{E}\left(-\frac{1}{q}, \ldots, -\frac{1}{q}, \frac{q-1}{q}, -\frac{1}{q}, \ldots, -\frac{1}{q}\right) \qquad (8\text{-}82)$$

$\uparrow$ jth component

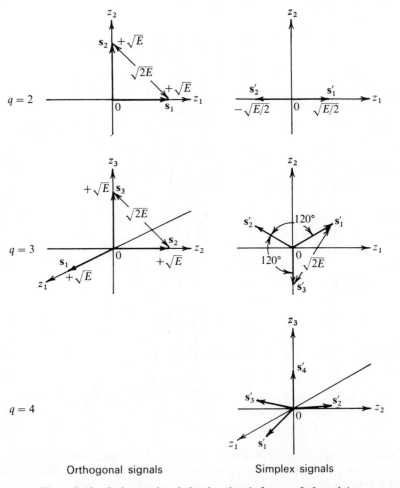

Orthogonal signals   Simplex signals

Figure 8-18   Orthogonal and simplex signals for $q = 2$, 3, and 4.

Figure 8-18 shows the original and resulting signal vector sets for $q = 2, 3$, and 4. The resulting simplex signal vector sets have been rotated in each case.

Note that as evidenced by Fig. 8-18 a set of q simplex signals occupies $q - 1$ dimensions.

Problem 8-12. Show that for the simplex set the distance between any pair of vectors is the same; i.e., that

$$\|s_j' - s_k'\|^2 = C \text{ for all } j \text{ and } k = 1, 2, \ldots, q \quad j \neq k$$

Problem 8-13. Show that the average power of the set of orthogonal signals discussed above is E/T while that of the corresponding set of simplex signals is $(E/T)(q - 1)/q$.

From Problem 8-13 we see that the fractional savings in power of the simplex signal set over the orthogonal signal set is $1/q$ which is of little practical importance for large q. For this reason and because orthogonal signals are easier to generate, they would almost always be used in practice for q greater than, say, 4 or 5.

Slepian and Landau [6] have recently proved a long conjectured fact: namely, that the simplex set of signals yields the smallest probability of error among all sets of signals for which the energy of each signal is less than or equal to a prescribed (but arbitrary) value E. Although the simplex set is optimal in this regard, it is quite costly in terms of band-width. The minimum bandwidth that it is possible for q orthogonal signals of duration T seconds to occupy is given approximately by $W \approx q/2T$. Thus, for the simplex set, the bandwidth occupancy is proportional to q.

Another set of signals which makes much more efficient use of band-width occupancy is the set referred to as the *vertices of a hypercube*. This set generates q signals from $n = \log_2 q$ orthonormal signals by using all signals of the form

$$s_j(t) = \sqrt{E/n} \sum_{k=1}^{n} \alpha_{jk}\psi_k(t) \quad j = 1, 2, \ldots, q; \quad q = 2^n \quad (8\text{-}83)$$

in which all the coefficients α_{jk} are either plus or minus one. This set is shown in Fig. 8-19 for $q = 8, n = 3$.

Problem 8-14. Show that for the signal set of Eq. 8-83 the probability of a correct decision assuming equiprobable source letters is given by

$$P(C) = P(C \mid m_1) = [1 - Q(\sqrt{E/nN_0})]^n$$

This set of signals occupies bandwidth efficiently since, for a fixed bandwidth W, the number of signals that can be transmitted grows exponentially with T:

$$q = 2^n = 2^{2WT}$$

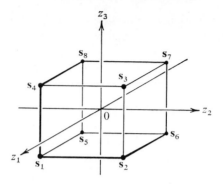

Figure 8-19   Vertices of a hypercube signal set.

This is just the manner in which q would have to grow if we were to collect letters from a source which emits binary letters at a uniform rate, and then assign a block of binary letters collected in T seconds to the q transmission signals (since the number of possible binary sequences would grow exponentially with T, the time for which they were collected). However, if we were to do this, keeping the average power $P = E/T$ constant so that $E = PT = Pn/2W$, we see from the result of Problem 8-14 that the probability of an error would approach one since

$$\lim_{n \to \infty} [1 - Q(\sqrt{P/2WN_0})]^n = 0$$

This procedure of collecting a sequence of source symbols and using different signals in a set to represent the different possible sequences of symbols is explored further in Sec. 8-5.

Problem 8-15.   Let us consider two possible transmission systems for transmitting binary data and two possible signal sets for each system.

SYSTEM A: Frequency-shift keying:

SIGNAL SET 1

$$s_1(t) = \sqrt{2} \cos 2\pi f_0 t \qquad\qquad 0 \leq t \leq T$$
$$s_2(t) = \sqrt{2} \cos [2\pi (f_0 + \Delta f_1)t] \qquad 0 \leq t \leq T$$
$$f_0 T = 10^5 \qquad \Delta f_1 T = 1$$

SIGNAL SET 2

$$s_1(t) = \sqrt{2} \cos 2\pi f_0 t \qquad\qquad 0 \leq t \leq T$$
$$s_2(t) = \sqrt{2} \cos [2\pi (f_0 + \Delta f_2)t] \qquad 0 \leq t \leq T$$
$$f_0 T = 10^5 \qquad \Delta f_2 T = 100$$

SYSTEM B: Pulse-delay keying:

Let

$$p(t) = \begin{cases} 2 & 0 \leq t \leq T/4 \\ 0 & T/4 \leq t \leq T \end{cases}$$

SIGNAL SET 1

$$s_1(t) = p(t)$$

$$s_2(t) = p\left(t - \frac{T}{4}\right)$$

SIGNAL SET 2

$$s_1(t) = p(t)$$

$$s_2(t) = p\left(t - \frac{T}{2}\right)$$

Since all four signal sets have the same geometric representation, the results of this section indicate that their performance should be identical. Intuitively, however, we would believe that for either system A or B, signal set two would be superior to signal set 1. Discuss the implementation of the receiver for both systems A and B, and point out practical considerations that would give substance to this intuitive notion.

8-4 Digital Communication over the Incoherent Gaussian Channel

In the previous section we considered transmission over a channel whose only effect was to add white gaussian noise to the transmitted signal. In practice, the signals that we wish to transmit will be band-pass signals. To make this point explicit, let us write the ith transmitted signal as

$$s_{i,tr}(t) = s_{i,c}(t) \cos 2\pi f_0 t - s_{i,s}(t) \sin 2\pi f_0 t \quad i = 1, 2, \ldots, q$$

in which the signals $s_{i,s}(t)$ and $s_{i,c}(t)$ are low-pass signals of duration T seconds. Alternately, we could express this real-valued transmitted signal as

$$s_{i,tr}(t) = \text{Re}\,\{s_i(t)e^{j2\pi f_0 t}\} \quad i = 1, 2, \ldots, q \qquad (8\text{-}84)$$

in which

$$s_i(t) = s_{i,c}(t) + js_{i,s}(t)$$

Now let us observe that for a channel with additive white gaussian noise, the optimum receiver formed the quantities

$$T_i(\mathbf{z}) = \int_0^T s_{i,tr}(t)z(t)\,dt \quad i = 1, 2, \ldots, q \qquad (8\text{-}56)$$

Note that in order to form these quantities for the band-pass signals of Eq. 8-84 *we must know the phase associated with the transmitted signals.* In many cases of interest, this might not be practical or possible. We might be unwilling to go to the trouble of synchronously demodulating the received signal. Even if we were, errors in the phase of the receiver local oscillator or fluctuations in the phase of the received signal due to slow variations in the channel might make recovery of the two quadrature components $s_{i,s}(t)$ and $s_{i,c}(t)$ impossible.

In this section we consider a channel which, in addition to additive white gaussian noise, corrupts the received signal by adding a random phase. Thus the received signal corresponding to the transmitted signal of Eq. 8-84 is

$$Z(t) = \text{Re} \{s_i(t)e^{j(2\pi f_0 t - \Theta)}\} + N(t) \qquad (8\text{-}85)$$

The quantity Θ being a random variable and $N(t)$ a white gaussian noise process. We assume that the channel variations cause the phase shift Θ to be completely random; i.e., uniformly distributed

$$f_\Theta(\theta) = \begin{cases} \dfrac{1}{2\pi} & 0 \le \theta \le 2\pi \\ 0 & \text{elsewhere} \end{cases} \qquad (8\text{-}86)$$

Our objective will be to deduce the structure of the optimum (minimum probability of error) receiver.

First, let us note that the random fluctuations of phase make it impossible to separate the two quadrature components $s_{i,c}(t)$ and $s_{i,s}(t)$. The result of cosine demodulating $Z(t)$ would be $(\cos \Theta)s_{i,c}(t) + (\sin \Theta)s_{i,s}(t)$ and the result of sine demodulating $Z(t)$ would be $(\cos \Theta)s_{i,s}(t) - (\sin \Theta)s_{i,c}(t)$. Since Θ is a random variable whose value is unknown, these two demodulator outputs cannot be resolved into $s_{i,c}(t)$ and $s_{i,s}(t)$. For this reason there is nothing to be gained by using two distinct quadrature modulation components and one of the quadrature components may as well be set to zero. For this reason we consider $s_{i,c}(t) = \sqrt{2}\,s_i(t)$, $s_{i,s}(t) = 0$, with $s_i(t)$ real, so that the transmitted signals are

$$s_{i,tr}(t) = \sqrt{2}\,s_i(t) \cos 2\pi f_0 t \qquad i = 1, 2, \ldots, q \qquad (8\text{-}87)$$

in which the q signals $s_i(t)$ are low-pass signals of duration T seconds. As in the preceding section, we take n to be the number of linearly independent $s_i(t)$ and let $\psi_k(t)$, $k = 1, \ldots, n$ denote a set of orthonormal functions spanning the space spanned by these $s_i(t)$. Thus all of the $s_i(t)$ can be represented in the form

$$s_i(t) = \sum_{k=1}^{n} s_k^i \psi_k(t) \qquad 0 \le t \le T \qquad (8\text{-}88)$$
$$i = 1, 2, \ldots, q$$

The signals $\psi_k(t)$, being linear combinations of the $s_i(t)$'s, are also low-pass functions. Note from Eqs. 8-85 and 8-87 that the received signal can be expressed in the form

$$Z(t) = (\cos \Theta)\sqrt{2}\,s_i(t) \cos 2\pi f_0 t$$
$$+ (\sin \Theta)\sqrt{2}\,s_i(t) \sin 2\pi f_0 t + N(t) \qquad (8\text{-}89)$$

Problem 8-16. Assume that the transforms of the functions $\psi_k(t)$ are nonzero only in a band $|f| \le W < f_0$.[1] Show that the $2n$ functions

$$\sqrt{2}\,\psi_k(t)\cos 2\pi f_0 t, \quad \sqrt{2}\,\psi_k(t)\sin 2\pi f_0 t \quad k = 1, 2, \ldots, n$$

are a set of $2n$ orthonormal functions. *Hint:* Use Parseval's theorem.

Now let us find a suitable set of coordinates such that we can reduce our signal transmission situation to a vector representation. Let us pick a complete orthonormal set of functions on the interval $0 \le t \le T$ by starting with the $2n$ orthonormal functions listed in Problem 8-15. We can then proceed to make this set complete by taking any complete set of functions and using the Gram-Schmidt procedure to make them orthonormal to these first $2n$ functions. We thus have a complete orthonormal set, the first $2n$ functions in this set being

$$\sqrt{2}\,\psi_k(t)\cos 2\pi f_0 t \quad k = 1, 2, \ldots, n$$

and

$$\sqrt{2}\,\psi_k(t)\sin 2\pi f_0 t \quad k = 1, 2, \ldots, n$$

If we expand $Z(t)$ in terms of this set, then by using Eqs. 8-42 and 8-89 we see that the first $2n$ expansion coefficients will be given by

$$Z_k = (\cos \Theta)s_k{}^i + N_k \qquad k = 1, 2, \ldots, n \qquad (8\text{-}90)$$

$$Z_{k+n} = (\sin \Theta)s_k{}^i + N_{k+n} \qquad k = 1, 2, \ldots, n \qquad (8\text{-}91)$$

and the remainder of the coefficients will be given by

$$Z_k = N_k \qquad k = 2n+1, 2n+2, \ldots \qquad (8\text{-}92)$$

The random variables $N_k, k = 1, 2, \ldots$, appearing in these three equations are again zero-mean statistically independent gaussian random variables. Thus we see that the n coefficients of Eq. 8-90, together with the n coefficients of Eq. 8-91, constitute a sufficient statistic for deciding which one of the q signals $s_{i,tr}(t)$ was transmitted. Let us take these two sets of n coefficients as the components of the two n-dimensional vector random variables

$$\mathbf{Z}_c = (Z_1, \ldots, Z_n) = (\cos \Theta)\mathbf{s}_i + \mathbf{N}_c \qquad (8\text{-}93)$$

$$\mathbf{Z}_s = (Z_{n+1}, \ldots, Z_{2n}) = (\sin \Theta)\mathbf{s}_i + \mathbf{N}_s \qquad (8\text{-}94)$$

$$i = ?; 1, 2, \ldots, \text{or } q$$

in which the vectors $\mathbf{N}_c$ and $\mathbf{N}_s$ are given by

$$\mathbf{N}_c = (N_1, \ldots, N_n)$$

$$\mathbf{N}_s = (N_{n+1}, \ldots, N_{2n})$$

[1] Strictly speaking it is not possible for $\psi_k(t)$ to be nonzero only over the interval $0 \le t \le T$ and have a Fourier transform which is zero outside some interval of frequency. However, if $f_0 \gg 1/T$, then the Fourier transform of $\psi_k(t)$ can be negligible for $|f| > f_0$, and the above assumption is true to a good approximation.

Note from the above discussion that all the components of both the noise vectors $\mathbf{N}_c$ and $\mathbf{N}_s$ are statistically independent zero-mean gaussian random variables. As in the previous section, they all have variance N_0.

We now concern ourselves with deriving a useful form of the optimum decision rule based on observation of these two vectors, $\mathbf{Z}_c$ and $\mathbf{Z}_s$; that is, the rule which decides upon m_j where j is the index for which the quantity

$$P_{M|\mathbf{Z}_c,\mathbf{Z}_s}(m_i \mid \mathbf{z}_c, \mathbf{z}_s) \qquad i = 1, 2, \ldots, q$$

takes on its maximum. Following the same line of reasoning that led to Eq. 8-9, we have

$$P(m_i \mid \mathbf{z}_c, \mathbf{z}_s) = \frac{f(\mathbf{z}_c, \mathbf{z}_s \mid \mathbf{s}_i)}{f(\mathbf{z}_c, \mathbf{z}_s)} P(m_i) \qquad (8\text{-}95)$$

Since the denominator of this expression is independent of the index i, we can examine the quantities

$$Q_i(\mathbf{z}_c, \mathbf{z}_s) = f(\mathbf{z}_c, \mathbf{z}_s \mid \mathbf{s}_i)P(m_i) \qquad i = 1, 2, \ldots, q \qquad (8\text{-}96)$$

for a maximum over the index i. Now the density function $f(\mathbf{z}_c, \mathbf{z}_s \mid \mathbf{s}_i)$ can be written

$$f(\mathbf{z}_c, \mathbf{z}_s \mid \mathbf{s}_i) = \int_0^{2\pi} f(\mathbf{z}_c, \mathbf{z}_s \mid \mathbf{s}_i, \theta)f_\Theta(\theta) \, d\theta = \frac{1}{2\pi} \int_0^{2\pi} f(\mathbf{z}_c, \mathbf{z}_s \mid \mathbf{s}_i, \theta) \, d\theta \quad (8\text{-}97)$$

But from Eqs. 8-93 and 8-94 and the fact that the components of $\mathbf{N}_c$ and $\mathbf{N}_s$ are independent gaussian random variables of variance N_0, we have

$$f(\mathbf{z}_c, \mathbf{z}_s \mid \mathbf{s}_i, \theta) = f_{\mathbf{N}_c}(\mathbf{z}_c - \mathbf{s}_i \cos \theta)f_{\mathbf{N}_s}(\mathbf{z}_s - \mathbf{s}_i \sin \theta)$$

$$= \left(\frac{1}{2\pi N_0}\right)^n \exp\left\{ -\frac{[\|\mathbf{z}_c - \mathbf{s}_i \cos \theta\|^2 + \|\mathbf{z}_s - \mathbf{s}_i \sin \theta\|^2]}{2N_0} \right\}$$

$$(8\text{-}98)$$

Expanding out the norms appearing in the exponent and collecting terms yields

$$f(\mathbf{z}_c, \mathbf{z}_s \mid \mathbf{s}_i, \theta) = \left\{ \left(\frac{1}{2\pi N_0}\right)^n \exp\left[-(\|\mathbf{z}_c\|^2 + \|\mathbf{z}_s\|^2)/2N_0 \right] \right\}$$

$$\times \exp\left[-\|\mathbf{s}_i\|^2/2N_0 \right] \exp\left[\frac{(\mathbf{z}_c, \mathbf{s}_i) \cos \theta + (\mathbf{z}_s, \mathbf{s}_i) \sin \theta}{N_0} \right]$$

$$(8\text{-}99)$$

Recognizing that $\|\mathbf{s}_i\|^2$ is E_i, the energy in the ith signal, and noting that the term in braces in Eq. 8-99 does not depend on i, we see from Eqs. 8-96 and 8-97 that we can examine the quantities

$$G_i(\mathbf{z}_c, \mathbf{z}_s) = P(m_i) \exp \left\{ -E_i/2N_0 \right\}$$

$$\times \frac{1}{2\pi} \int_0^{2\pi} \exp \left\{ \frac{(\mathbf{z}_c, \mathbf{s}_i) \cos \theta + (\mathbf{z}_s, \mathbf{s}_i) \sin \theta}{N_0} \right\} d\theta$$

$$i = 1, 2, \ldots, q \quad (8\text{-}100)$$

and decide upon the value of the index for which this quantity is a maximum. Now, if we define the quantities ρ_i, $\sin \phi_i$, and $\cos \phi_i$ by the equations

$$\rho_i = +\sqrt{(\mathbf{z}_c, \mathbf{s}_i)^2 + (\mathbf{z}_s, \mathbf{s}_i)^2} \quad (8\text{-}101)$$

$$\cos \phi_i = (\mathbf{z}_c, \mathbf{s}_i)/\rho_i; \qquad \sin \phi_i = (\mathbf{z}_s, \mathbf{s}_i)/\rho_i \quad (8\text{-}102)$$

Then Eq. 8-100 becomes

$$G_i(\mathbf{z}_c, \mathbf{z}_s) = P(m_i) \exp \left\{ -E_i/2N_0 \right\} \frac{1}{2\pi} \int_0^{2\pi} \exp \left\{ \rho_i \cos (\phi_i - \theta)/N_0 \right\} d\theta$$

Since the integrand appearing above is periodic in θ with period 2π, the integral is independent of ϕ_i and depends only on ρ_i/N_0. The function of ρ_i/N_0 defined by taking $(1/2\pi)$ times the value of the integral is denoted by $I_0(\rho_i/N_0)$. This function is directly related to the Bessel function of the first kind and *zero*-th order which we encountered in Chapter 6. In fact, $I_0(\rho_i/N_0) = J_0(-j\rho_i/N_0)$. Thus our decision rule resolves to: *Pick the index of the message symbol to be that value of the index i, $i = 1, 2, \ldots, q$, for which the quantity*

$$G_i(\mathbf{z}_c, \mathbf{z}_s) = G_i(\rho_i) = P(m_i) \exp \left\{ -E_i/2N_0 \right\} I_0(\rho_i/N_0) \quad (8\text{-}103)$$

is a maximum.

Note that in this expression for $G_i(\mathbf{z}_c, \mathbf{z}_s)$, the only quantity that depends upon the received signal is ρ_i. We now consider how to implement the receiver, and in particular how to form ρ_i from $z(t)$. Note that

$$(\mathbf{z}_c, \mathbf{s}_i) = \sum_{k=1}^{n} z_k s_k{}^i$$

$$(\mathbf{z}_s, \mathbf{s}_i) = \sum_{k=1}^{n} z_{k+n} s_k{}^i$$

$$s_i(t) = \sum_{k=1}^{n} s_k{}^i \psi_k(t)$$

$$z_k = \int_0^T z(t) \sqrt{2}\, \psi_k(t) \cos 2\pi f_0 t \, dt \qquad k = 1, 2, \ldots, n$$

$$z_{k+n} = \int_0^T z(t) \sqrt{2}\, \psi_k(t) \sin 2\pi f_0 t \, dt \qquad k = 1, 2, \ldots, n$$

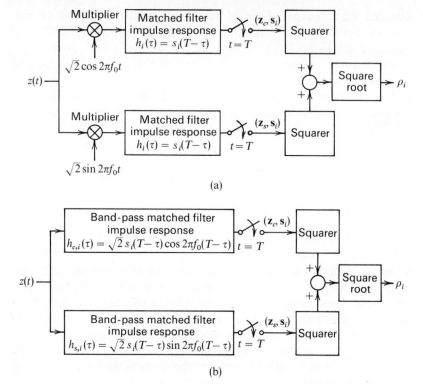

Figure 8-20 (a) Method of obtaining ρ_1 by synchronous demodulation.
(b) Method of obtaining ρ_1 by band-pass matched filters.

Thus, if we let

$$z_c(t) = \sqrt{2}\, z(t) \cos 2\pi f_0 t$$
$$z_s(t) = \sqrt{2}\, z(t) \sin 2\pi f_0 t$$

then by direct evaluation it follows that

$$(\mathbf{z}_c, \mathbf{s}_i) = (z_c(t), s_i(t)) = \int_0^T s_i(t)\sqrt{2}\, z(t) \cos 2\pi f_0 t \qquad (8\text{-}104)$$

and

$$(\mathbf{z}_s, \mathbf{s}_i) = (z_s(t), s_i(t)) = \int_0^T s_i(t)\sqrt{2}\, z(t) \sin 2\pi f_0 t \qquad (8\text{-}105)$$

The quantities $(\mathbf{z}_c, \mathbf{s}_i)$, $(\mathbf{z}_s, \mathbf{s}_i)$, and ρ_i can thus be derived from the signal $z(t)$ as indicated in either Fig. 8-20a or 8-20b. It should be noted that since $s_i(t)$ is a low-pass signal, the matched filters in Fig. 8-20a could be preceded by a low-pass filter of bandwidth greater than that of $s_i(t)$; equivalently, the demodulator could be preceded by a band-pass filter of the same bandwidth. This would be the case in actual practice. A similar remark applies to the matched filter of Fig. 8-20b. We now wish to show that ρ_i can be realized by the much simpler scheme shown in Fig. 8-21.

Problem 8-17. A simple implementation of ρ_i can be found. Note that the quantity given by Eq. 8-104 is the output at time $t = T$ to a filter with impulse response

$$h_{c,i}(\tau) = \sqrt{2}\, s_i(T - \tau)\cos 2\pi f_0(T - \tau)$$

and whose input is the signal $z(t)$. Show that ρ_i is the *envelope* of the output of this filter at time $t = T$. *Hint:* Assume that the bandwidth of $s_i(t)$ is much less than f_0.

Having discussed the implementation required to obtain ρ_i, we return to the decision rule of Eq. 8-103 and its implementation. Note that if $P(m_i) = 1/q$ and $E_i = E$ for all i that we only need to examine the quantities $I_0(\rho_i/N_0)$. However, it can be shown that the function $I_0(x)$ increases monotonically with x. Thus in the equiprobable equi-energy case we need examine only the quantities ρ_i, which are the envelopes of the filters $h_{c,i}(\tau)$ at time $t = T$, and build a comparator to output the index corresponding to the largest ρ_i.

Since there is an additional source of disturbance in the incoherent channel, its transmission performance must always be poorer than that of the coherent channel. It is interesting to compare this difference in performance numerically. Let us consider the case of equiprobable orthogonal waveforms of energy E.

$$s_i(t) = \sqrt{2E}\, \psi_i(t)\cos 2\pi f_0 t, \qquad 0 \le t \le T \qquad i = 1, 2, \ldots, q$$
$$P(m_i) = 1/q \qquad i = 1, 2, \ldots, q$$

The method of calculating $P(C)$ for transmission over the incoherent channel using q equiprobable orthogonal signals of energy E is conceptually simple but analytically involved. For this reason we will only outline the steps required.

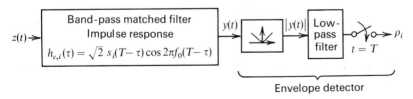

Figure 8-21   Method of obtaining ρ_1 by envelope demodulation.

First, by symmetry we note that we will have

$$P(C) = P(C \mid m_i) \qquad i = 1, 2, \ldots, q.$$

Thus we need calculate only $P(C \mid m_1)$. Now in the equiprobable equi-energy case the receiver decides on m_1 if

$$\rho_1 > \rho_j \qquad j = 2, 3, \ldots, q$$

Thus, noting that the ρ's must always be positive and that the ρ's are statistically independent, the probability of a correct decision is given by

$$P(C) = P(C \mid m_1) = \int_0^\infty f_{\rho_1 \mid M_1}(r_1 \mid m_1) P(\rho_2 < r_1 \mid m_1)^{q-1} \, dr_1 \quad (8\text{-}106)$$

in which we have noted that by symmetry

$$P(\rho_j < r_1 \mid m_1) = P(\rho_2 < r_1 \mid m_1) \qquad j = 3, 4, \ldots, q$$

Problem 8-18. Let X_k and Y_k be defined as

$$X_k = (Z_c(t), \psi_k(t)); \qquad Y_k = (Z_s(t), \psi_k(t))$$

so that X_k and Y_k are the kth components respectively of the vector $\mathbf{Z}_c$ defined by Eq. 8-93 and the vector $\mathbf{Z}_s$ defined by Eq. 8-94. Note that X_k and Y_k are uncorrelated gaussian random variables each of variance N_0 and that, if the transmitted letter is m_1, then

$$E\{X_k\} = E\{Y_k\} = 0, \qquad k = 2, 3, \ldots, q$$

while if $\Theta = \theta$, and $k = 1$, then

$$E\{X_1 \mid \theta\} = \sqrt{E} \cos \theta; \qquad E\{Y_1 \mid \theta\} = \sqrt{E} \sin \theta$$

Also note that

$$\rho_k^2 = X_k^2 + Y_k^2$$

Show that if the transmitted letter is m_1 then

$$f_1(r) \triangleq f_{\rho_1 \mid M}(r \mid m_1) = \begin{cases} \dfrac{r}{2\pi N_0} \exp\left\{-(r^2 + E)/2N_0\right\} I_0(r\sqrt{E}/N_0) & r > 0 \\[2mm] 0 & r < 0 \end{cases} \quad (8\text{-}107)$$

and

$$f_0(r) \triangleq f_{\rho_k \mid M}(r \mid m_1) = \begin{cases} \dfrac{r}{2\pi N_0} \exp\left\{-r^2/2N_0\right\} & r > 0 \\[2mm] 0 & r < 0 \end{cases} \quad k > 1 \quad (8\text{-}108)$$

Integrating $f_0(r)$ to obtain the corresponding distribution function then yields from Eq. 8-106

$$P(C) = \int_0^\infty f_1(r)[1 - \exp(-r^2/2N_0)]^{q-1} \, dr$$

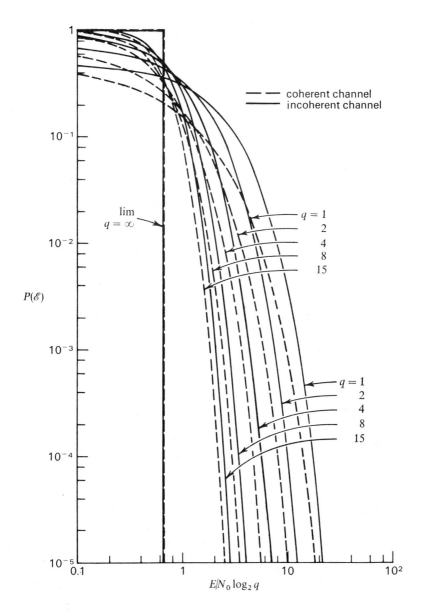

Figure 8-22   Probability of error for orthogonal signals on coherent and incoherent channels. (Reprinted from *Principles of Coherent Communication* through the courtesy of W. C. Lindsey [8], A. J. Viterbi [5], and the McGraw-Hill Book Company.)

This expression can be evaluated analytically by using the binomial expansion for the term $[1 - \exp(-r^2/2N_0)]^{q-1}$ and making use of the Weber-Sonine formula [7]

$$\int_0^\infty I_0(at)e^{-p^2 t^2} t \, dt = \frac{1}{2p^2} \exp(a^2/2p^2)$$

The end result can be expressed as

$$P(\mathscr{E}) = [\exp\{-E/2N_0\}/q] \sum_{k=2}^{q} \binom{q}{k}(-1)^k \exp\{E(2 - k)/4N_0 k\} \quad \text{(8-109)}$$

This result was first obtained by Turin in 1953 in a classified report.

This performance has been calculated for a number of values of q; it is plotted in Fig. 8-22. The plot shows the probability of error $P(\mathscr{E})$ versus $10 \log_{10}(E/N_0 \log_2 q)$, the signal-to-noise ratio per binary digit expressed in decibels. For comparison, the performance of the coherent channel is also plotted. Since the incoherent channel contains an additional source of disturbance, we know that its performance must be inferior. We see from Fig. 8-22 that for $q = 2$ the incoherent channel is about 3 db inferior for low signal-to-noise ratios, while for larger values of q and larger signal-to-noise ratios the difference is rather small.

8-5   Capacity of the Band-Limited Gaussian Channel

In this section we briefly investigate the ultimate reliability that can be obtained in transmitting digital information over a coherent channel with additive white gaussian noise. Our discussion is patterned on the geometric derivation of channel capacity due to Shannon [9]. Our discussion only sketches the framework of the argument; the reader interested in more detail can consult the original article by Shannon [9], or, for a detailed and thorough discussion, Chapter 5 of Wozencraft and Jacobs [2].

Our discussion hinges around the effects that can be obtained by varying the time duration, T, of our transmitted signals. Let us consider the situation shown in Fig. 8-23. A digital source emits equiprobable binary letters, 0 or 1. We assume that successive letters are statistically independent and that R binary letters are emitted by the source per second. The output of this digital source is collected for T seconds into a *block* of RT binary digits. For this reason we will refer to T as the *block time*. The transmitter then transmits one of $q = 2^{RT}$ signals, $s_i(t)$, to indicate which one of the 2^{RT} equiprobable sequences of RT binary digits was emitted by the source. The signals s_i, $i = 1, 2, \ldots, q$, are all assumed to be of duration T seconds or less, and limited essentially to a (one-sided)

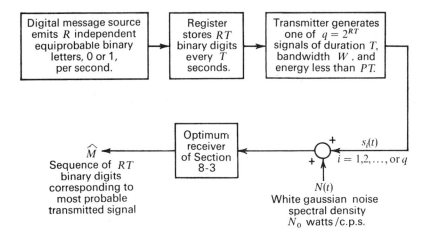

Figure 8-23 Sequential transmission of binary letters over a channel with additive white gaussian noise.

bandwidth of W c.p.s. We further assume that the transmitter is limited to a time-average power of P watts; we thus restrict all of the q signals to have an energy of less than or equal to $E = PT$ joules.

Note that inasmuch as we store binary letters for T seconds and then transmit a corresponding signal of T seconds duration, our system involves a *transmission delay of* $2T$ *seconds*. We wish to see what can be gained by the introduction of such a delay.

There are two effects that come into play as T becomes large. The first is the following. For large values of WT the space of signals that are of duration T and are essentially limited to a (one-sided) bandwidth of W c.p.s. is spanned by a set of $n = 2WT$ orthogonal signals. For a brief discussion of this point, refer to Appendix 5A of Wozencraft and Jacobs [2]; for a complete discussion of this subject, consult the series of articles by Slepian, Landau, and Pollack [10 to 13]. The result of this fact is that the message signals that can be transmitted can be expressed in the form

$$s_i(t) = \sum_{k=1}^{n} s_k{}^i \psi_k(t) \qquad n = 2WT \qquad (8\text{-}110)$$

in which the $\psi_k(t)$ are a set of orthonormal functions. The transmitted signals are thus described by n-dimensional vectors

$$\mathbf{s}_i = (s_1{}^i, \ldots, s_n{}^i) \qquad n = 2WT \qquad (8\text{-}111)$$

As in Sec. 8-3, our transmission and reception process is then characterized by the n-dimensional vector

$$Z = s_i + N \tag{8-112}$$

in which

$$Z_k = s_k{}^i + N_k = \int_0^T Z(t)\psi_k(t)\,dt \tag{8-113}$$

and the N_k are independent zero-mean gaussian random variables of variance N_0.

Since we wish to vary T and constrain the time-average *power* of the transmitted signals, it is convenient in this section to renormalize our vectors so that their lengths represent power instead of energy

$$\|s_i\|^2 = \frac{1}{T}\sum_{k=1}^{n}(s_k{}^i)^2; \qquad \|N\|^2 = \frac{1}{T}\sum_{k=1}^{n}(N_k)^2 \qquad n = 2WT \tag{8-114}$$

With this normalization, we see that the $q = 2^{RT}$ *transmission vectors can lie anywhere in an $n = 2WT$ dimensional sphere of radius $\sqrt{P}$.*

The second effect we wish to consider is the effect on the random noise vector N of making the dimension n large.

Problem 8-19. Let N be an n-dimensional random vector whose components are independent zero-mean gaussian random variables of variance N_0. Let the norm of N be as defined by Eq. 8-114 and $n = 2WT$. Show that

$$E\{\|N\|^2\} = 2WN_0 \tag{8-115}$$

and

$$\operatorname{var}\{\|N\|^2\} = 4WN_0{}^2/T \tag{8-116}$$

From Eqs. 8-115 and 8-116 and the Chebyshev inequality, it follows that

$$P\{|\;\|N\|^2 - 2WN_0| > \epsilon\} \le \frac{4WN_0{}^2}{\epsilon^2 T}$$

Letting $\epsilon = 1/T^{\frac{1}{3}}$, this inequality becomes

$$P\{|\;\|N\|^2 - 2WN_0| > 1/T^{\frac{1}{3}}\} \le \frac{4WN_0{}^2}{T^{\frac{1}{3}}} \tag{8-117}$$

This inequality has the following implication: by making T *sufficiently large, the probability that the noise vector has a length that departs more than an arbitrarily small amount from $\sqrt{2WN_0}$ can be made arbitrarily small.* Moreover, the distribution of the vector N is spherically symmetric since its components are independent, equal variance gaussian random variables. Thus, *as T becomes large, the noise vector almost always lies on the surface of an n-dimensional sphere ($n = 2WT$) of radius $\sqrt{2WN_0}$.*

As a consequence of this second fact, we see that *we could obtain reliable (error-free) communication in the presence of noise if:* (1) *we make T sufficiently large,* and (2) *all of the signals can be positioned such that the decision region around each signal vector contains an n-dimensional sphere of radius* $\sqrt{2WN_0}$ *centered on the signal vector.*

The question is then how many signal vectors can we place inside the signal sphere of dimension n ($n = 2WT$) and radius $\sqrt{P}$ such that the second requirement on the decision regions is satisfied. As Shannon has shown, the logarithm of the number of signals that can be so placed is equal to the logarithm of the ratio of the volume of a $2WT$-dimensional sphere of radius $\sqrt{2WN_0 + P}$ to the volume of a $2WT$-dimensional sphere of radius $\sqrt{2WN_0}$. The logarithm of the ratio of these two volumes turns out to be proportional to T; let us denote this logarithm by CT. Since the logarithm of the number of signals generated in time T is RT, we can thus meet the second requirement for a nonzero rate R, provided that $R < C$. Shannon's result may thus be expressed as follows.

We define the *capacity*, C, of a channel of (one-sided) bandwidth W, average power P, and interfering additive white gaussian noise of spectral density N_0, to be

$$C = W \log_2 (1 + P/2WN_0) \qquad (8\text{-}118)$$

Then:

(a) *For a source rate $R < C$, it is possible, by making T sufficiently large and properly choosing the set of $q = 2^{RT}$ signals, to make the probability of an error in transmission as small as desired.*

(b) *For a rate $R > C$, it is not possible to make the probability of an error arbitrarily small with any choice of T or any choice of signal set.*

These two statements give substance to the choice of the term channel *capacity* for the quantity C, since C sets a sharply defined limit on the number of independent equiprobable binary digits per second that can be transmitted reliably over the specified channel.

Again, we have only sketched the reasons why this phenomenon of reliable communication can be achieved and have slurred over many (important) details. The reader interested in these details should consult either the original paper by Shannon [9], or the thorough treatment in Chapter 5 of Wozencraft and Jacobs [2].

In closing, it should again be pointed out that this phenomenon of reliable communication, which occurs for large T, can be obtained only at the expense of introducing a delay of $2T$ seconds into the transmission system. Moreover, the reader should note that the receiver must examine

$q = 2^{RT}$ quantities in deciding which of the sequences of RT digits was generated by the source. Thus, the complexity of the receiver grows *geometrically* with T. This fact is the stumbling block in practically realizing the reliable communication guaranteed by Shannon's theorem.

Problem 8-20. The channel capacity given by Eq. 8-118 depends on the average transmitter power P, the noise spectral density N_0, and the allowed bandwidth W.

$$C = C(P, N_0, W) = W \log_2 (1 + P/2WN_0) \qquad (8\text{-}118)$$

Show, by taking an appropriate limit of this expression, that if the bandwidth restriction is removed the capacity of the infinite bandwidth channel is

$$C_\infty(P, N_0) = \frac{P}{2N_0} \log_2 e \qquad \text{binary digits/second} \qquad (8\text{-}119)$$

Problem 8-21. Consider transmission over a channel with additive white gaussian noise of spectral density N_0. We assume that there is no bandwidth constraint, but a constraint that the average transmitted power be less than P. If we use q orthogonal signals each of energy E, we showed in Sec. 8-3 that the probability of a correct decision was given by

$$P(C) = \frac{1}{\sqrt{2\pi}} \int_{-\infty}^{\infty} \exp \{-\theta^2/2\}[1 - Q(\sqrt{E/N_0} + \theta)]^{q-1} \, d\theta \qquad (8\text{-}76)$$

in which

$$Q(x) = \frac{1}{\sqrt{2\pi}} \int_{x}^{\infty} e^{-\theta^2/2} \, d\theta \qquad (8\text{-}68)$$

Let us now consider transmitting q signals in time T where

$$q = 2^{RT} \qquad \text{or} \qquad RT = \log_2 q \qquad (8\text{-}120)$$

and the energy of each signal is given by

$$E = PT \qquad (8\text{-}121)$$

Note by the dominated convergence theorem (see page 59) that if

$$|h(q, \theta)| \le g(\theta) \quad \text{for all } g \quad \text{and} \quad \int_{-\infty}^{\infty} g(\theta) \, d\theta < \infty$$

then

$$\lim_{q \to \infty} \int_{-\infty}^{\infty} h(q, \theta) \, d\theta = \int_{-\infty}^{\infty} \lim_{q \to \infty} h(q, \theta) \, d\theta \qquad (8\text{-}122)$$

Show, using Eq. 8-122 and certain suitable approximations for $Q(\sqrt{PT/N_0} + \theta)$, that

$$\lim_{T \to \infty} P(C) = \begin{cases} 1 \text{ if } R < \dfrac{P}{2N_0} \log_2 e \\[2mm] 0 \text{ if } R > \dfrac{P}{2N_0} \log_2 e \end{cases} \qquad (8\text{-}123)$$

What does that imply about using orthogonal signals as a "code" or signal set for the infinite bandwidth channel?

REFERENCES

[1] Kotelnikov, V. A., *The Theory of Optimum Noise Immunity*, McGraw-Hill Book Co., New York, 1959, R. A. Silverman translator; see especially Part II.

[2] Wozencraft, J. M., and I. M. Jacobs, *Principles of Communication Engineering*, John Wiley and Sons, New York, 1965; see especially Chapter 4.

[3] Hildebrand, F. B., *Methods of Applied Mathematics*, Prentice-Hall, Englewood Cliffs, N.J., 1952; Section 1.12.

[4] Abramowitz, M., and I. A. Stegun, Eds., *Handbook of Mathematical Functions*, National Bureau of Standards, Washington, D.C., 1964; Section 26.

[5] Viterbi, A. J., *Principles of Coherent Communication*, McGraw-Hill Book Co., New York, 1966; Chapter 8.

[6] Landau, H. J., and D. Slepian, "On the Optimality of the Regular Simplex Code," *The Bell System Tech. Journal*, XLV, No. 8, 1247–1272, October 1966.

[7] Magnus, W. and F. Oberhetinger, *Formulas and Theorems for the Functions of Mathematical Physics*, Chelsea, New York, 1943; p. 35.

[8] Lindsey, W. C., "Coded Noncoherent Communications," *IEEE Trans. Space Electron. Telemetry*, SET-11, No. 3, 6–13, March, 1965.

[9] Shannon, C. E., "Communication in the presence of noise," *Proc. IRE*, 37, No. 1, 10–21, January 1949.

[10] Slepian D., H. O. Pollack, and H. J. Landau, "Prolate spheroidal wave functions. Fourier analysis and uncertainty, Parts I and II," *The Bell System Technical Journal*, 40, 43–84, January, 1961.

[11] Landau, H. J. and H. O. Pollack, "Prolate spheroidal functions, Fourier analysis and Uncertainty, Part III,—The dimension of the space of essentially time and band limited signals," *The Bell System Technical Journal*, 41, 1295–1336, July 1962.

[12] Pollack, H. O., "Energy distribution of bandlimited functions whose samples on the half line vanish," *Journal of Mathematical Analysis and Applications*, 2, 299–322, April 1961.

[13] Slepian, D., "Some Asymptotic Expansions for Prolate Spheroidal Wave Functions," Unpublished Bell Laboratories Memorandum; see particularly Eqs. 1.40 and 1.41.

Chapter 9

Pulse Modulation

In this chapter, we study a method of modulation or information transmission which is based on the sampling theorem. Instead of trying to transmit a waveform message process as a continuous function of time, we consider transmitting samples of the message process and using these at the receiver to reconstruct an approximation to the original process. Such a procedure allows the flexibility of *time-division multiplexing* several message sources onto the same channel by interleaving samples from different sources onto the channel. Moreover, if we use a larger bandwidth for transmission of the samples than that occupied by the message process, we are again able to trade bandwidth for improved signal-to-noise ratio as was the case with FM.

We start by considering reconstruction of stationary message processes from their samples. We next consider a particular pulse modulation method, pulse amplitude modulation (PAM). From this, we pass on to the general aspects of transmitting a sample value and study a geometric model which places in clear perspective why a nonlinear modulation system has the ability to trade bandwidth for signal-to-noise ratio and why a threshold effect is a necessary consequence of such a system. Lastly, we give a detailed treatment of pulse-position modulation (PPM) and pulse-code modulation (PCM).

9-1   Reconstruction of Message Processes from Samples

We start our discussion by reconsidering the sampling theorem discussed in Chapter 2. We make such extensive use of this theorem in this chapter that it is worthwhile adopting special notation for the sin x/x function. We use the notation in Chapter 2 of Woodward [1]; namely,

$$\text{sinc}\,(t) \triangleq \frac{\sin \pi t}{\pi t} \qquad (9\text{-}1)$$

It is also convenient to use Woodward's notation for the transform of this function; we define

$$\text{rect}(f) = \begin{cases} 1 & |f| < 1/2 \\ 0 & |f| > 1/2 \end{cases} \tag{9-2}$$

In terms of this notation, we have the transform pair

$$\text{sinc}(2Wt) \leftrightarrow (1/2W)\,\text{rect}(f/2W) = T\,\text{rect}(f/2W) \tag{9-3}$$

in which

$$T = 1/2W$$

is the sampling interval for a function whose transform is zero for $|f| > W$.

In this notation, the sampling theorem becomes

Theorem. If $g(t)$ and $G(f)$ are transform pairs and

$$G(f) \equiv 0 \qquad |f| > W$$

then

$$g(t) = \sum_{k=-\infty}^{\infty} g(kT)\,\text{sinc}\,[2W(t - kT)] \tag{9-4}$$

Let us note an immediate corollary of the sampling theorem.   Since $g(t - \theta) \leftrightarrow e^{-j2\pi f\theta}G(f)$, $g(t - \theta)$ is also band-limited, and hence, applying the sampling theorem to $h(t) = g(t - \theta)$, we have the following:

Corollary. If $g(t)$ is band-limited to $|f| \leq W$, then

$$g(t - \theta) = \sum_{k=-\infty}^{\infty} g(kT - \theta)\,\text{sinc}\,[2W(t - kT)] \tag{9-5}$$

for any value of θ.   Note that by a change of variable, Eq. 9-5 becomes

$$g(t) = \sum_{k=-\infty}^{\infty} g(kT - \theta)\,\text{sinc}\,[2W(t - kT + \theta)] \tag{9-5'}$$

Now let us use this corollary to establish the following form of the sampling theorem for stationary random processes.

Theorem. Let $S(t)$ denote a wide-sense stationary random process with power spectral density $S_s(f)$ and correlation function $R_s(\tau)$.   If

$$S_s(f) \equiv 0 \qquad \text{for } |f| > W$$

then the approximation to $S(t)$ formed from uniformly spaced samples

$$\hat{S}(t) = \sum_{k=-\infty}^{\infty} S_{kT}\,\text{sinc}\,[2W(t - kT)] \tag{9-6}$$

has zero mean-square error:

$$E\{(\hat{S}_t - S_t)^2\} = 0$$

Proof. The proof of this statement was assigned as Problem 4-8. We give the proof now because of its pertinence to our present purposes. Let us evaluate the error, substituting from Eq. 9-6 for $\hat{S}(t)$

$$\mathscr{E} = E\{(S_t - \hat{S}_t)^2\} = E\left\{\left[S_t - \sum_{k=-\infty}^{\infty} S_{kT} \operatorname{sinc}\left[2W(t - kT)\right]\right] \right.$$
$$\left. \times \left[S_t - \sum_{j=-\infty}^{\infty} S_{jT} \operatorname{sinc}\left[2W(t - jT)\right]\right]\right\}$$

Expanding and interchanging the order of expectation and summation yields[1]

$$\mathscr{E} = R_s(0) - \sum_{k=-\infty}^{\infty} R_s(kT - t) \operatorname{sinc}\left[2W(t - kT)\right]$$

$$- \sum_{j=-\infty}^{\infty} R_s(jT - t) \operatorname{sinc}\left[2W(t - jT)\right]$$

$$+ \sum_{j=-\infty}^{\infty} \operatorname{sinc}\left[2W(t - jT)\right]$$

$$\times \sum_{k=-\infty}^{\infty} R_s(kT - jT) \operatorname{sinc}\left[2W(t - kT)\right] \quad (9\text{-}7)$$

The transform of $R_s(\tau)$ is nonzero only for $|f| \leq W$; thus Eq. 9-5 applies with g replaced by R_s. Using this relation on the summations appearing in Eq. 9-7 and noting that R_s is even yields

$$\mathscr{E} = R_s(0) - R_s(t - t) - R_s(t - t) + \sum_{j=-\infty}^{\infty} \operatorname{sinc}\left[2W(t - jT)\right]R_s(t - jT)$$

$$= R_s(0) - 2R_s(0) + \sum_{j=-\infty}^{\infty} R_s(jT - t) \operatorname{sinc}\left[2W(t - jT)\right] \quad (9\text{-}8)$$

Applying Eq. 9-5 once more finally yields

$$\mathscr{E} = -R_s(0) + R_s(t - t) = 0$$

as originally stated.

Let us note that, since the process $S(t)$ was stationary, the sampling need not be at $t = kT$, $k = 0, \pm 1, \pm 2, \ldots$, but could have occurred at any set of uniformly spaced sample times:

$$t = kT + \theta, \quad k = 0, \pm 1, \pm 2, \ldots; \quad \theta \text{ arbitrary}$$

---

[1] To be rigorous, we should start with the mean-square error, using samples from $k = -N$ to $k = +N$. The limit of this value as $N \to \infty$ is equal to the value of Eq. 9-7 if $|R_s(kT)| \leq Ck^{-(1+\epsilon)}$; $\epsilon, k > 0$. This follows from straightforward manipulations and the dominated convergence theorem mentioned on page 59.

in which case $S(t)$ could be represented without error by the form of Eq. 9-5':

$$\hat{S}(t) = \sum_{k=-\infty}^{\infty} S_{kT-\theta} \operatorname{sinc} [2W(t - kT + \theta)]; \quad \theta \text{ arbitrary} \quad (9\text{-}9)$$

Now let us consider what happens when we try to reconstruct a message process from samples when the message process $S(t)$ is not strictly band-limited to band W; i.e.,

$$S_s(f) \neq 0 \qquad |f| \geq W$$

For this purpose we will study the situation shown in Fig. 9-1; the filter $H_W(f)$ is an ideal low-pass filter with impulse response $2W \operatorname{sinc} (2W\tau)$

$$H_W(f) = \operatorname{rect} (f/2W) = \begin{cases} 1 & |f| < W \\ 0 & |f| > W \end{cases} \quad (9\text{-}10)$$

Problem 9-1. Consider the two random processes $S_u(t)$ and $S_l(t)$ defined in Fig. 9-1. Since

$$1 = [1 - H_W(f)] + H_W(f)$$

it follows that

$$S(t) = S_l(t) + S_u(t) \quad (9\text{-}11)$$

Show that

$$S_{s_l}(f) = \begin{cases} S_s(f) & |f| \leq W \\ 0 & |f| > W \end{cases} \quad (9\text{-}12)$$

$$S_{s_u}(f) = \begin{cases} 0 & |f| \leq W \\ S_s(f) & |f| > W \end{cases} \quad (9\text{-}13)$$

and

$$R_{s_u s_l}(\tau) \equiv 0 \quad (9\text{-}14)$$

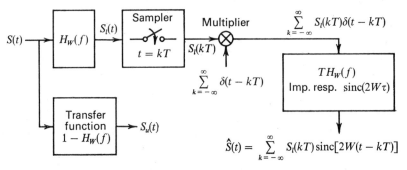

Figure 9-1 Approximate reconstruction of $S(t)$ from its samples.

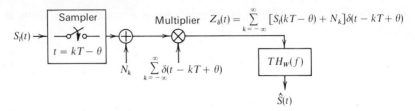

Figure 9-2   Sample transmission system with additive errors.

Now let us note that since $S_{s_i}(f)$ is band-limited, $S_i(t)$ can be constructed exactly from its samples. One physical method of achieving this is to modulate the sequence $S_i(kT)$ by a sequence of uniformly spaced impulses, the resulting sequence then being the input to an ideal low-pass filter with impulse response $\mathrm{sinc}(2W\tau)$. This method is shown in Fig. 9-1. The resulting output $\hat{S}(t)$ is then equal (in the sense of zero mean-square difference) to $S_i(t)$, and from Eq. 9-11, we have

$$\hat{S}(t) = S(t) - S_u(t) \tag{9-15}$$

Thus the mean-square error is

$$\mathscr{E} = E\{(\hat{S}_t - S_t)^2\} = E\{S_{u,t}^2\} = R_{S_u}(0) = \int_{|f| > W} S_s(f)\, df \tag{9-16}$$

The situation shown in Fig. 9-1 may be referred to as *sample transmission of S(t) with ideal low-pass pre-filtering*; Eq. 9-16 gives the error for such transmission.

Next let us consider such transmission when additive errors occur in the samples. This situation is shown in Fig. 9-2. We assume that the "phase," Θ, associated with the sampling is uniformly distributed over a sample interval

$$f_\Theta(\theta) = \begin{cases} 1/T & 0 \le \theta \le T \\ 0 & \text{elsewhere} \end{cases} \tag{9-17}$$

Thus the resulting sampled process will also be stationary.

If the sequence of errors, N_k, is zero-mean and uncorrelated with the process $S_i(t)$ being sampled, then the mean-square error in the output is just the mean-square value of the output that would result from the errors acting alone. Thus let us consider the correlation function of the sampled noise process,

$$N_\delta(t) = \sum_{k=-\infty}^{\infty} N_k \delta(t - kT + \Theta) \tag{9-18}$$

Letting

$$\rho(k - j) = E\{N_k N_j\} \tag{9-19}$$

denote the correlation function of the different error samples, we have, since Θ and the noise samples are independent,

$$R_{n_\delta}(\tau) = E\{N_{\delta,t}N_{\delta,t+\tau}\}$$

$$= E\left\{\sum_{j=-\infty}^{\infty} N_j\delta(t - jT + \Theta) \sum_{k=-\infty}^{\infty} N_k\delta(t + \tau - kT + \Theta)\right\}$$

$$= \sum_{k=-\infty}^{\infty} \sum_{j=-\infty}^{\infty} \rho(k - j)\frac{1}{T}\int_0^T \delta(t - jT + \theta)\delta(t + \tau - kT + \theta)\, d\theta$$

Now let t be written in the form

$$t = mT - \Delta t \qquad \text{with } 0 \leq \Delta t < T \text{ and } m \text{ an integer}$$

Then the only term in the summation over j for which the term

$$\delta(t - jT + \theta) = \delta[(m - j)T + \theta - \Delta t]$$

is nonzero for $0 \leq \theta < T$ is the $j = m$ term. Thus

$$R_{n_\delta}(\tau) = \sum_{k=-\infty}^{\infty} \rho(k - m)\frac{1}{T}\int_0^T \delta(\theta - \Delta t)\delta[(m - k)T + \tau + \theta - \Delta t]\, d\theta$$

$$= \sum_{k=-\infty}^{\infty} \rho(k - m)\frac{1}{T}\delta[\tau - (k - m)T]$$

If the index of summation is changed to $n = k - m$, this equation becomes

$$R_{n_\delta}(\tau) = \frac{1}{T}\sum_{n=-\infty}^{\infty} \rho(n)\delta(\tau - nT) \qquad (9\text{-}20)$$

The spectrum of $N_\delta(t)$ is thus

$$S_{N_\delta}(f) = \frac{1}{T}\sum_{n=-\infty}^{\infty} \rho(n)e^{-jnT2\pi f} \qquad (9\text{-}21)$$

We can now easily find the spectrum of the error term in the output. If we denote by $N(t)$ the response of $TH_W(f)$ to $N_\delta(t)$, then

$$S_n(f) = |TH_W(f)|^2 S_{n_\delta}(f) = T^2 H_W(f)S_{n_\delta}(f)$$

$$= TH_W(f)\sum_{n=-\infty}^{\infty} \rho(n)e^{-jnT2\pi f} \qquad (9\text{-}22)$$

in which we have used the fact that

$$H_W(f) = |H_W(f)|^2$$

It will also be useful to have an expression for $R_n(\tau)$. Since

$$2W \text{ sinc } (2W\tau) \leftrightarrow H_W(f)$$

we have from Eqs. 9-20 and 9-22 and the frequency domain multiplication property that

$$R_n(\tau) = TR_{n_\delta}(\tau) * \text{sinc}\,(2W\tau)$$

$$= \sum_{n=-\infty}^{\infty} \rho(n)\,\text{sinc}\,[2W(\tau - nT)] \qquad (9\text{-}23)$$

In particular, the mean-square error is

$$R_n(0) = \sum_{n=-\infty}^{\infty} \rho(n)\,\text{sinc}\,(-2WnT) = \rho(0) = E\{N_k^2\} \qquad (9\text{-}24)$$

In writing this equation, we have used the fact that

$$\text{sinc}\,(2WNT) = \frac{\sin 2\pi WNT}{2\pi WNT} = \frac{\sin (2\pi WN/2W)}{(2\pi WN/2W)}$$

$$= \frac{\sin N\pi}{N\pi} = 0 \qquad \text{all } N \neq 0$$

Note that Eq. 9-24 shows that the mean-square error in the output *depends only on the mean-square value of the error samples and not on the correlation between different error samples.* This property results from the fact that the functions sinc $[2W(t - nT)]$ used to reconstruct the signal are orthogonal. Thus, if we are content to find the mean-square error in the output of a sample transmission system, we need only to be able to evaluate the mean-square value of the error samples. *The total mean-square error resulting from the transmission system of Fig. 9-2 is thus the error due to noise, $E\{N_k^2\}$, plus the sampling error whose value is given by the integral of Eq. 9-16.*

Problem 9-2. Consider the sampling transmission system shown in Fig. 9-3. Since the message process is sampled directly, we can refer to this system as sample transmission *without prefiltering.* By writing $S(t) = S_u(t) + S_l(t)$ and noting that $S_u(t)$ and $S_l(t)$ are uncorrelated, show that the mean-square error in this system

$$E\{(S_t - \hat{S}_t)^2\}$$

is just twice that given by Eq. 9-16.

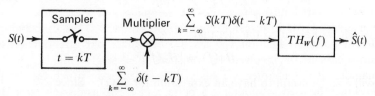

Figure 9-3   Sample transmission without prefiltering.

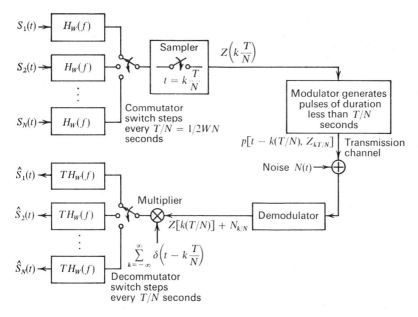

Figure 9-4   Time division multiplexing accomplished by a pulse modulation system.

In practice, the values of the samples $S(kT)$ or $S_i(kT)$ in a sample transmission system are usually represented physically by pulses transmitted at the rate of $2W$ pulses per second.   Some attribute of each single pulse (such as its amplitude or position) is modulated by the value of a corresponding single sample.   Such transmission systems are therefore referred to as *pulse modulation systems.*   Note that these modulation systems allow *time division multiplexing* of several sources onto a single pulse transmission channel.   If we have N message signals each of approximate (one-sided) bandwidth W c.p.s., then we can represent each of the N message processes by $2W$ samples per second.   If we can transmit $2NW$ pulses per second, then each source can be assigned every Nth pulse in the transmission sequence as shown in Fig. 9-4.

As we have shown, the mean-square error in a pulse modulation system can be separated into a term due to sampling and a term due to the mean-square error in transmitting a single sample.   Thus in examining different pulse modulation systems, we can focus our attention on the mean-square error involved in transmitting a single sample.   In the remainder of this chapter, we study different ways in which the sample values may be used to modulate a pulse, and the transmission error that occurs when these pulses are received in the presence of additive noise.

9-2   Pulse-Amplitude Modulation

In *pulse-amplitude modulation* (PAM), the value of a sample S is transmitted by transmitting a pulse of duration T_d whose amplitude is proportional to S

$$p(t, S) = kS\phi(t) \qquad 0 \le t \le T_d \qquad (9\text{-}25)$$

The transmitted signal corresponding to a sequence of samples S_{mT}, $m = 0, \pm 1, \pm 2, \ldots$, is thus

$$X(t) = k \sum_{m=-\infty}^{\infty} S_{mT}\phi(t - mT)$$

Before turning to some of the considerations determining the form and duration of the pulse $\phi(t)$, let us find the best way of estimating the value of the random variable S.

Estimation of a Sample Value

Consider the signal $kS\phi(t)$ which we assume is transmitted over a physical channel and is observed in the presence of white gaussian noise, $N(t)$ (by "white" gaussian noise, we mean the process discussed in Sec. 8-2). We thus have to try to estimate the value of S from the observation

$$Z(t) = kS\phi(t) + N(t) \qquad 0 \le t \le T_d \qquad (9\text{-}26)$$

To start with, let us describe the process $Z(t)$ in terms of an orthonormal set of functions, $\psi_k(t)$, $k = 1, 2, 3, \ldots$, which are complete on the interval $0 \le t \le T_d$ and for which the first function in the set is the function $\phi(t)$ appearing in the transmitted signal

$$\psi_1(t) = \phi(t)$$

This assumes that $\phi(t)$ is normalized. Since the transmitted signal includes a multiplier k, we lose nothing by restricting $\phi(t)$ to be normalized to unit energy. Then

$$Z(t) = \sum_{k=1}^{\infty} Z_k\psi_k(t) \qquad 0 \le t \le T_d \qquad (9\text{-}27)$$

in which the random variables Z_k are given by

$$Z_k = \int_0^{T_d} Z(t)\psi_k(t) \, dt \qquad (9\text{-}28)$$

Noting Eqs. 9-26 and 9-28, the expression for $Z(t)$ may be rewritten as

$$Z(t) = (kS + N_1)\psi_1(t) + \sum_{k=2}^{\infty} N_k\psi_k(t) \qquad (9\text{-}29)$$

in which the N_k are statistically independent zero-mean gaussian random variables of variance N_0. We would intuitively assume that, since all the noise terms are independent, we would only need to observe $Z_1 = (kS + N_1)$ in order to make a good estimate of S. This is indeed true, as we show by slightly extending our knowledge about sufficient statistics beyond the situation of Sec. 8-1 in which the message was discrete-valued and our criterion of transmission was minimum probability of error.

Suppose we observe some vector-valued random variable $\mathbf{Z}$ which may take on values $\mathbf{z}$ and we wish to estimate the value of some related random variable S. If there exists a function $\tilde{S}(\mathbf{z})$ such that the conditional density function $f_{\mathbf{Z}|S}$ factors into the form

$$f_{\mathbf{Z}|S}(\mathbf{z} \mid s) = g(s; \tilde{S}(\mathbf{z}))w(\mathbf{z}) \qquad (9\text{-}30)$$

in which $w(\mathbf{z}) \geq 0$, we say that $\tilde{S}(\mathbf{z})$ is a *sufficient statistic for* S. The significance of this concept lies in the following fact. Suppose we wish to find the estimate; $\hat{S}(\mathbf{z})$, based on the observation $\mathbf{z}$, that minimizes the mean value of the weighted error

$$\mathscr{E}_q = E\{q[S - \hat{S}(\mathbf{Z})]\} \qquad (9\text{-}31)$$

in which q is some *non-negative* weighting function (e.g., $q(x) = x^2$, $q(x) = |x|$, etc.). *If a sufficient statistic $\tilde{S}(\mathbf{z})$ exists, then the estimate that minimizes the mean-weighted error is a function only of $\tilde{S}(\mathbf{z})$ and not of $\mathbf{z}$ itself.*

To prove this, let us write $\mathscr{E}_q$ in the form

$$\mathscr{E}_q = \int_{-\infty}^{\infty} \cdots \int_{-\infty}^{\infty} d\mathbf{z} \int_{-\infty}^{\infty} ds \, q[s - \hat{S}(\mathbf{z})]f(s, \mathbf{z})$$

and use Eq. 9-30, yielding

$$\mathscr{E}_q = \int_{-\infty}^{\infty} \cdots \int_{-\infty}^{\infty} d\mathbf{z} \, w(\mathbf{z})\left[\int_{-\infty}^{\infty} ds \, q[s - \hat{S}(\mathbf{z})]g(s; \tilde{S}(\mathbf{z}))f_s(s)\right]$$

Now, since w and q are non-negative, $\mathscr{E}_q$ is minimized if for each value of $\mathbf{z}$ the quantity inside the brackets is minimized; furthermore, the quantity inside the brackets can be minimized by a quantity $\hat{S}$ that is a function only of $\tilde{S}(\mathbf{z})$, since the rest of the integrand inside the brackets is only a function of $\tilde{S}(\mathbf{z})$.

Now consider our problem of estimating S from an observation of $Z(t)$ in this light. If we let the vector $\mathbf{Z}$ be an n-dimensional vector whose components are the first n-coefficients of $Z(t)$

$$\mathbf{Z} = (Z_1, Z_2, \ldots, Z_n)$$

then Z_1 will constitute a sufficient statistic for S.   To see this, simply note that we can write $f_{Z|S}$ as

$$f(\mathbf{z} \mid s) = \underbrace{\exp -\left\{\frac{(z_1 - ks)^2}{2N_0}\right\}}_{g(s,\, z_1)} \underbrace{\left(\frac{1}{2\pi N_0}\right)^{n/2} \prod_{k=2}^{n} \exp\left\{\frac{-z_k^2}{2N_0}\right\}}_{w(\mathbf{z})} \quad (9\text{-}32)$$

Thus to estimate S, we need only look at

$$Z_1 = \int_0^{T_d} Z(t)\psi_1(t)\, dt = \int_0^{T_d} Z(t)\phi(t)\, dt = kS + N_1 \quad (9\text{-}33)$$

and not at the process $Z(t)$ itself.   In order to specify what the best estimate of S is, given the observation Z_1, we have to specify our criterion of best: If we take the "best" estimate S to be the one that minimizes the mean-square error

$$\mathscr{E}_{\mathrm{sq}} = E\{(\hat{S} - S)^2\} \quad (9\text{-}34)$$

then, as we saw in Problem 3-11, the best estimate, $\hat{S}$, is the conditional expectation of S knowing Z_1

$$\hat{S}(z_1) = E\{S \mid Z_1 = z_1\} = E\{S \mid z_1\} \quad (9\text{-}35)$$

In order to compute what $E\{S \mid z_1\}$ is, we have to know the distribution of S.   If we assume that S is gaussian, then, since N_1 is also gaussian and statistically independent of S, $Z_1 = kS + N_1$ and S are jointly gaussian. In Problem 3-23 we observed that if Z_1 and S are jointly gaussian and S zero mean, then the *conditional distribution* of S, given that $Z_1 = z_1$, is *gaussian* with mean

$$\hat{S}(z_1) = E\{S \mid z_1\} = \frac{E\{SZ_1\}}{E\{Z_1^2\}}\, z_1 \quad (9\text{-}36)$$

and variance

$$\mathscr{E}_{\mathrm{sq}} = E\{(\hat{S} - S)^2\} = \sigma_s^2 - \frac{E^2\{Z_1 S\}}{\sigma_{Z_1}^2} \quad (9\text{-}37)$$

Using Eq. 9-33, evaluating these quantities in terms of

$$E\{S^2\} = \overline{S^2} \quad \text{and} \quad E\{N_1^2\} = N_0$$

yields

$$\hat{S}(z_1) = E\{S \mid z_1\} = \frac{k\overline{S^2}}{k^2\overline{S^2} + N_0}\, z_1 \quad (9\text{-}38)$$

and

$$\mathscr{E}_{\mathrm{sq}} = \overline{S^2} - \frac{(k\overline{S^2})^2}{k^2\overline{S^2} + N_0} \quad (9\text{-}39)$$

If we note that the average energy of the transmitted pulses is

$$E_{av} = E\left\{\int_0^T k^2 S^2 \phi^2(t)\, dt\right\} = k^2 \overline{S^2} \qquad (9\text{-}40)$$

then Eqs. 9-38 and 9-39 become

$$\hat{S}(z_1) = \left(\frac{z_1}{k}\right)\left(\frac{1}{1 + (N_0/E_{av})}\right) \qquad (9\text{-}41)$$

and

$$\mathscr{E}_{sq} = \overline{S^2}\left[\frac{1}{1 + \dfrac{E_{av}}{N_0}}\right] \qquad (9\text{-}42)$$

The above two equations have been derived upon the assumption that S is gaussianly distributed with zero mean. It is worth pointing out that the optimum estimator given by Eqs. 9-33 and 9-41, namely,

$$\hat{S}[Z(t), 0 \le t \le T_d] = \frac{1}{k(1 + N_0/E_{av})}\int_0^{T_d} Z(t)\phi(t)\, dt \qquad (9\text{-}43)$$

represents a linear operation upon the received signal. We have shown in Chapter 7 that if we *require* for ease of implementation that $\hat{S}$ be a linear operation on $Z(t)$, then $\hat{S}$ is the same estimate given by Eq. 9-43 for a known value of $\overline{S^2}$ but an otherwise arbitrary distribution for S.

Let us now reflect upon the situation in which the distribution of S is unknown. Regardless of the distribution for S, Z_1 is still a sufficient statistic. The a-posteriori density for S having observed Z_1 is given by

$$f_{S|Z_1}(s \mid z_1) = f_S(s)\frac{f(z_1 \mid s)}{f(z_1)} = f_S(s)\frac{\left[\dfrac{1}{\sqrt{2\pi N_0}}\right]\exp\left[-\dfrac{(z_1 - ks)^2}{2N_0}\right]}{f(z_1)} \qquad (9\text{-}44)$$

The quantity $f_{Z_1|S}(z_1 \mid s)$ regarded as a function of z_1 for a fixed value of s is a conditional probability density function. When this same quantity is regarded as a *function of s for a fixed value of* z_1, it is no longer a density function but is termed the *likelihood function*. The value of s that maximizes $f_{Z_1|S}(z_1 \mid s)$ for a given value of z_1 is referred to as the *maximum likelihood* estimate of S based on observation of Z_1 and is denoted by $\hat{S}_{ml}(z_1)$. In the absence of knowledge of the a-priori distribution of S, $f_S(s)$, the maximum likelihood estimate is often used. The reason behind this may be stated as follows. If $f_{S|Z_1}(s \mid z_1)$ is *unimodal* (having a single maximum) and *symmetric* about its maximum, then for any symmetric error-weighting function, this maximum value is a good estimate of S. Furthermore, if any information about the value of S can be obtained from an observation of Z_1, then $f_{S|Z_1}(s \mid z_1)$ will be more sharply peaked (as a function of s) than $f_S(s)$. In such a situation the function $f_S(s)$ varies only gradually compared to the function $f_{S|Z_1}(s \mid z_1)$; as a consequence the value of s for which the function

$$f_{S|Z_1}(s \mid z_1) = f_S(s) \frac{f_{Z_1|S}(z_1 \mid s)}{f_{Z_1}(z_1)}$$

has its maximum will be approximately $\hat{S}_{ml}(z_1)$, the value of s that maximizes $f_{Z_1|S}(z_1 \mid s)$. Thus, under the above conditions, the estimate $\hat{S}_{ml}(z_1)$ is a good estimate of the value of S given the observation z_1.

In the case at hand, the value of s that maximizes the factor in brackets in Eq. 9-44 for any given value of z_1 is $s = z_1/k$, thus

$$\hat{S}_{ml}(z_1) = \frac{z_1}{k} \tag{9-45}$$

Let us compare the mean-square error obtained by using this estimate with the error for the optimum estimate under the assumption that S was gaussian. We have

$$E\{[S - \hat{S}_{ml}(z_1)]^2\} = E\{[S - (Z_1/k)]^2\}$$

$$= E\{(N_1/k)^2\} = \frac{N_0}{k^2}$$

$$= \overline{S^2}\left(\frac{N_0}{E_{av}}\right) \tag{9-46}$$

Let us note that with no observation at all ($E_{av} = 0$) the estimate of Eq. 9-41 gives a mean-square error of $\overline{S^2}$ just by always estimating $S = 0$. Thus we are only interested in the case in which the observation allows us to substantially reduce the error, namely the case in which $E_{av}/N_0 \gg 1$. In this case we see by comparing Eqs. 9-42 and 9-46 that the maximum likelihood estimate performs nearly as well as the estimate of Eq. 9-41 which is optimum under the gaussian assumption.

Whether the estimate of Eq. 9-41 or the maximum likelihood estimate is used, the overall PAM system is of the form shown in Fig. 9-5.

Properties of PAM

Let us now point out several facets of PAM. First, for large signal-to-noise ratios, the mean-square error is given by

$$\mathcal{E}_{sq} = E\{(\hat{S} - S)^2\} \approx \overline{S^2}(N_0/E_{av})$$

This expression is exact for maximum likelihood estimation and approximate for the estimate of Eq. 9-43. Thus with PAM the only way of improving performance is to increase the transmitted pulse energy.

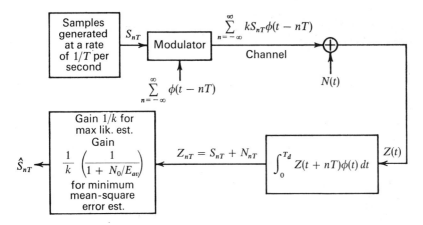

Figure 9-5 Pulse amplitude modulation transmission and receiving system.

Second, note that the optimum receiver essentially uses a filter matched to the pulse $\phi(t)$; that is, the estimate of the sample S_{nT} is

$$\hat{S}_{nT} = \frac{1}{k} \int_{nT}^{nT+T_d} Z(t)\phi(t-nT)\,dt = \frac{1}{k} \int_0^{T_d} Z(t+nT)\phi(t)\,dt \quad (9\text{-}47)$$

The corresponding transmitted portion of $Z(t)$ is

$$kS_{nT}\phi(t-nT) \qquad nT \le t \le nT + T_d$$

If there is to be no interference between pulses used to transmit different samples, this requires

$$\int_0^{T_d} \phi(t)\phi(t-kT)\,dt = 0 \qquad k = \pm 1, \pm 2, \dots \quad (9\text{-}48)$$

One way of achieving this would be to have the pulse $\phi(t)$ be of duration less than or equal to T. In this case most of the energy of the pulse $\phi(t)$ could be confined to a band of (two-sided) width $2W = 1/T$. Another possibility would be for $\phi(t)$ to be the perfectly band-limited pulse of infinite duration [$\phi(t)$ nonzero for all time $-\infty < t < \infty$]:

$$\phi(t) = \operatorname{sinc}[2Wt]$$

Since

$$\int_{-\infty}^{\infty} \operatorname{sinc}[2Wt]\operatorname{sinc}[2W(t-kT)]\,dt = 0 \qquad \begin{array}{l} T = 1/2W; k \text{ any nonzero} \\ \text{integer} \end{array}$$

Eq. 9-48 is satisfied for this choice of $\phi(t)$. This pulse is strictly limited to the band of (two-sided) width $2W$. In either case, the (two-sided) band-width occupied by the pulse-system is at least $2W$ c.p.s., the approximate bandwidth of the signal being sampled.

If N signals, all sampled at a rate of $1/T$ samples per second, are to be multiplexed onto the pulse channel, we require that Eq. 9-48 hold for shifts of T/N seconds

$$\int_0^{T_d} \phi(t)\phi[t - (kT/N)] \, dt = 0 \qquad k = \pm 1, \pm 2, \ldots \qquad (9\text{-}49)$$

In this case the duration of the pulses must be less than or equal to T/N or we must use sinc pulses of (two-sided) bandwidth $2NW$, so that the bandwidth occupied is $2NW$, the same as the total bandwidth occupied by all the signals being multiplexed onto the pulse channel. Thus the transmitted PAM signals occupy approximately the same bandwidth as the unmodulated message signals.

In the above we have not specified whether the pulse $\phi(t)$ is low-pass or band-pass. The propagation characteristics of many physical channels would require $\phi(t)$ to be an r-f pulse. In this case, $\phi(t)$ results by modulating some carrier by a low-pass pulse $g(t)$ of duration T seconds. Ordinary modulation would result in a (two-sided) bandwidth occupancy of $4W$; for the (two-sided) bandwidth occupancy of $\phi(t)$ to be only $2W = 1/T$ instead of $4W$ would require SSB modulation. Whether the complexity of SSB modulation would be worth avoiding doubling the bandwidth occupancy would depend upon the application. Second, note that our estimate

$$\hat{S}_{ml} = \frac{1}{k} \int_0^{T_d} Z(t)\phi(t) \, dt$$

requires coherent demodulation in the case in which $\phi(t)$ is a narrow-band pulse. If this is not practical, the transmitted pulse would have to be of the form

$$p(t, S) = [A + kS\phi(t)] \cos 2\pi f_0 t \qquad (9\text{-}50)$$

in which the signal $\phi(t)$ is a low-pass pulse. The signal $kS\phi(t)$ would have to be less in magnitude than A so that it could be recovered without distortion by envelope detection. The sample S can then be estimated by

$$\hat{S}_{ml} = \frac{1}{k} \int_0^{T_d} \phi(t) Y(t) \, dt$$

in which $Y(t)$ represents the output of the envelope demodulator. This system would suffer a loss of efficiency because of the wasted power transmitted in the carrier component $A \cos 2\pi f_0 t$.

Problem 9-3. Consider the transmitted pulse to be

$$p(t, s) = A[1 + cs\phi(t)] \cos 2\pi f_0 t \qquad 0 \le t \le T$$

in which $\phi(t) = \sqrt{2/T} \cos 2\pi f_m t$, $0 \le t \le T$, $f_m \ll f_0$. Assume that S is uniformly distributed between -1 and $+1$

$$f_S(s) = \begin{cases} \frac{1}{2} & -1 \le s \le +1 \\ 0 & \text{elsewhere} \end{cases}$$

Pick c so that S can be estimated by first envelope demodulating $Z(t) = p(t, S) + N(t)$ and calculate $\mathscr{E}_{sq}$ in terms of the average transmitted energy and N_0. Compare this with coherent transmission. Assume a high signal-to-noise ratio in determining the output of the envelope demodulator.

Problem 9-4. In this problem we wish to consider the bandwidth occupancy of PAM more precisely. Consider the pulse train

$$X(t) = \sum_{k=-\infty}^{\infty} S_k \phi(t - \Theta + kT)$$

generated by a PAM system. The random variables S_k are samples of a stationary message process, $S_k = S(kT)$; $\phi(t)$ is a known pulse of unit energy and Fourier transform

$$\Phi(f) = \mathscr{F}[\phi(t)]$$

and Θ is a random variable uniformly distributed between 0 and T:

$$f_\Theta(\theta) = \begin{cases} \dfrac{1}{T} & 0 \le \theta \le T \\ 0 & \text{elsewhere} \end{cases}$$

The random variable Θ is independent of the samples S_k and the correlation of the samples is

$$E\{S_k S_j\} = e^{-a|k-j|} \qquad \text{(note the absolute magnitude sign)}$$

(a) Find the correlation function of the transmitted signal

$$R_x(\tau) = E\{X_{t+\tau} X_t\}$$

Hint: Consider a way of generating $X(t)$ by means of an intermediate process and make use of any pertinent results in Sec. 9-1. If you do this the problem is trivial.

(b) For purposes of bandwidth allocation and filter design, the power spectral density, $S_x(f)$, is more useful than $R_x(\tau)$. Find a closed form (i.e., not an infinite series) expression for $S_x(f)$.

(c) Re-evaluate your answers to (a) and (b) for the special case

$$E\{S_k S_j\} = \begin{cases} 1 & j = k \\ 0 & j \ne k \end{cases}$$

9-3 Nonlinear Modulation—Geometric Interpretation

In this section we study the behavior of pulse modulation systems by means of a geometric interpretation which was first introduced by Kotelnikov [2] and which has recently been more fully developed by Wozencraft and Jacobs [3]. This geometric interpretation clearly points out the added potential of a nonlinear pulse modulation system over a PAM system; that is, the potential for trading increased bandwidth occupancy for improved signal-to-noise ratio. The geometric interpretation also clearly shows why a system exploiting this potential must exhibit a threshold effect. Let us first point out that PAM is linear; that is, for $p(t, s)$ given by

$$p(t, s) = ks\phi(t)$$

we have

$$p(t, \alpha s_1 + \beta s_2) = k\alpha s_1\phi(t) + k\beta s_2\phi(t) = \alpha p(t, s_1) + \beta p(t, s_2)$$

We wish to eventually extend our analysis to nonlinear pulse modulation systems. To do this, it will be useful to start by forming a geometric interpretation of PAM. Note that the transmitted signal is described only in terms of the function $\phi(t)$ and our estimate of S:

$$\hat{S} = \frac{1}{k}\left(\frac{1}{1 + (E_{av}/N_0)}\right)Z_1 \quad \text{or} \quad \hat{S}_{ml} = \frac{1}{k}Z_1$$

$$Z_1 = \frac{1}{T_d}\int_0^{T_d} Z(t)\phi(t)\,dt$$

is defined only in terms of Z_1, the $\phi(t)$ component of $Z(t)$. Let us thus plot a one-dimensional vector space whose single coordinate axis is z_1 as shown in Fig. 9-6. The heavy line represents the locus of possible transmitted signals. In plotting this, we have assumed for convenience that the samples have been normalized so that the possible range for S is $-1 < s < +1$. If S is a random variable which can take on all values (such as a gaussian random variable), it would be truncated in practice so that when S exceeds, say, $\pm 3\sigma_s$, the transmitted value is $\pm 3\sigma_s$. Thus in this case we would take S to be normalized so that $3\sigma_s = 1$. A typical transmitted vector, noise vector, and received vector are shown in Fig. 9-6.

Now let us generalize on PAM modulation in two respects. First, let us assume that the transmitted signal need not just be a multiple of some single unit energy function $\phi(t)$ but instead can be in the linear space spanned by the N orthonormal functions $\psi_k(t)$, $k = 1, 2, \ldots, N$. Second, we do not require that the modulated pulse be a linear function of the

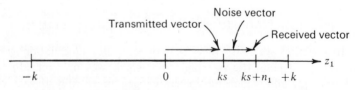

Figure 9-6 One-dimensional vector space portraying PAM.

sample s but rather we allow the dependence to be arbitrary. These two considerations lead to a transmitted pulse of the form

$$p(t, s) = \sum_{k=1}^{N} a_k(s)\psi_k(t) \qquad 0 \le t \le T \qquad (9\text{-}51)$$

Here we have assumed that in order to keep pulses corresponding to different samples from interfering, the duration of the pulse $p(t, s)$ is restricted to be less than or equal to T seconds, where $1/T$ is the rate at which samples are to be transmitted. The received signal

$$Z(t) = p(t, s) + N(t) \qquad (9\text{-}52)$$

can be described in terms of a complete orthonormal set of functions, of which the N $\psi_k(t)$ appearing in Eq. 9-51 comprise the first N such functions. The received process then is expressed as

$$Z(t) = \sum_{k=1}^{\infty} Z_k \psi_k(t) \qquad (9\text{-}53)$$

in which

$$Z_k = \begin{cases} a_k(s) + N_k & 1 \le k \le N \\ N_k & k > N \end{cases} \qquad (9\text{-}54)$$

the N_k again being statistically independent zero-mean gaussian random variables of variance N_0.

Problem 9-5. Show that the first N Z_k constitute a sufficient statistic for estimating the value of S.

With the result of Problem 9-5 in mind, it is again natural to describe the transmission by a set of N-dimensional vectors

$$\mathbf{a}(s) = [a_1(s), a_2(s), \ldots, a_N(s)] \qquad (9\text{-}55)$$

$$\mathbf{N} = (N_1, N_2, \ldots, N_N) \qquad (9\text{-}56)$$

$$\mathbf{Z} = (Z_1, Z_2, \ldots, Z_N) \qquad (9\text{-}57)$$

representing respectively the transmitted signal, the noise, and the received signal.

This vector representation is illustrated in Fig. 9-7, in which, for ease of representation, the dimension of the signals involved is taken as $N = 2$. The heavy line again represents the locus of possible transmitted signals. We assume in Fig. 9-7 and henceforth that $\mathbf{a}(s)$ is a continuous, differentiable function of s. We also continue to assume that the samples are normalized such that the range of possible sample values is $-1 \le s \le +1$.

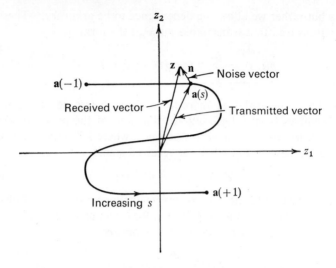

Figure 9-7   Locus of a two-dimensional transmitted pulse signal.

We now wish to use this geometric vector interpretation to study the following facets of nonlinear pulse modulation:

1. What represents a reasonable receiver rule for estimating the value of S from $\mathbf{Z}$?
2. How does the choice of modulation locus affect the mean-square error performance of the system?
3. How does the choice of modulation locus affect the threshold performance of the system; that is, the occurrence of large anomalous errors?

Estimation of the sample value

Let us focus our attention on the rule by which the receiver estimates S. First, note that if we wished to minimize the mean square error between S and the estimate $\hat{S}(\mathbf{z})$, the best estimate would be the conditional mean, which we could write as

$$\hat{S}(\mathbf{z}) = E\{S \mid \mathbf{Z} = \mathbf{z}\} = \int_{-\infty}^{\infty} sf(s \mid \mathbf{z}) \, ds$$

$$= \frac{1}{f(\mathbf{z})} \int_{-\infty}^{\infty} sf(\mathbf{z} \mid s)f(s) \, ds \tag{9-58}$$

Note that in evaluating this expression it is necessary to evaluate the density functions

$$f(\mathbf{z} \mid s) = f_{\mathbf{N}}[\mathbf{z} - \mathbf{a}(s)] \tag{9-59}$$

and

$$f(\mathbf{z}) = \int_{-\infty}^{\infty} f_N[\mathbf{z} - \mathbf{a}(s)]f(s)\,ds \tag{9-60}$$

To solve for $\hat{S}(\mathbf{z})$ as given by these three equations would be exceptionally difficult for any nonlinear modulation locus of interest. Moreover, this approach requires a knowledge of $f_S(s)$, which may not always be available.

For this reason, we will consider maximum-likelihood estimation. In the case at hand the conditional probability density for s given $\mathbf{z}$ is

$$f(s \mid \mathbf{z}) = f_S(s)\frac{f_{\mathbf{Z}|S}(\mathbf{z} \mid s)}{f_{\mathbf{Z}}(\mathbf{z})} = f_S(s)\frac{f_N[\mathbf{z} - \mathbf{a}(s)]}{f_{\mathbf{Z}}(\mathbf{z})} \tag{9-61}$$

The likelihood function, $f_{\mathbf{Z}|S}(\mathbf{z} \mid s)$, is given by

$$f_{\mathbf{Z}|S}(\mathbf{z} \mid s) = f_N[\mathbf{z} - \mathbf{a}(s)] = \left(\frac{1}{2\pi N_0}\right)^{N/2} \exp\left\{-\frac{\|\mathbf{z} - \mathbf{a}(s)\|^2}{2N_0}\right\} \tag{9-62}$$

It is easily seen that the likelihood function is maximized by the value of s that minimizes $\|\mathbf{z} - \mathbf{a}(s)\|$

$$\hat{S}_{ml} = \text{value of } s \text{ for which } \|\mathbf{z} - \mathbf{a}(s)\| \text{ is a minimum} \tag{9-63}$$

That is, *the maximum-likelihood estimate of S is the value of s corresponding to the point on the locus, $\mathbf{a}(s)$, which is closest to the received point.*

The advantages of the maximum-likelihood estimate are:

1. $\hat{S}_{ml}$ is given by the relatively simple relation of Eq. 9-63.
2. No assumptions regarding $f_S(s)$ are necessary.
3. If the peak of $f_{\mathbf{Z}|S}(\mathbf{z} \mid s)$ about $s = \hat{S}_{ml}$ is narrow compared to $f_S(s)$, and if $f_{\mathbf{Z}|S}(\mathbf{z} \mid s)$ is unimodal and roughly symmetric about $\hat{S}_{ml}$, the performance of $\hat{S}_{ml}$ will be nearly as good as that of any other possible estimate.

In support of this third point, let us recall from the previous section the relative performance for PAM of the maximum-likelihood estimate and the estimate based on the conditional mean, assuming gaussian statistics. The ratio of the mean-square error for the maximum-likelihood estimate to the mean-square error for the optimum estimate was $[1 + (N_0/E_{av})]$. *As the signal-to-noise ratio, E_{av}/N_0, becomes large, this ratio approaches one, and the performance of the maximum-likelihood estimates approaches that of the optimum estimate.* Although we are not in a position to prove it here,[1] this property holds true in general; as the signal-to-noise ratio

---

[1] The reader interested in this point should consult a reference on parameter estimation for a discussion of the properties of maximum-likelihood estimation. One such reference is Chapter 12 of Wilks [4].

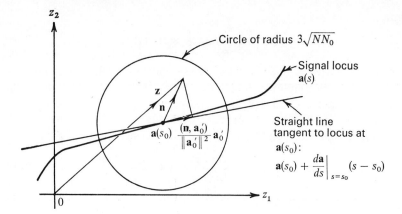

Figure 9-8   Signal locus about $\mathbf{a}(s_0)$ and linearized locus.

becomes large, the performance of a maximum-likelihood estimate approaches that of the estimate which yields minimum possible mean-square error.   Thus the maximum-likelihood estimate of Eq. 9-63 will be a very nearly optimum method of demodulation for arbitrary (nonlinear) modulation *when* the signal-to-noise ratio is high.

Performance of the Receiver at Low Noise Levels

Now let us turn to analyzing the performance of the maximum-likelihood estimator.   Note that the distribution of $f_{\mathbf{N}}(\mathbf{n})$ is spherically symmetric and that

$$E\{\|\mathbf{N}\|^2\} = NN_0 \tag{9-64}$$

With a probability very close to one, N will lie within a sphere of radius 3 or 4 times $\sqrt{NN_0}$.   Let us consider s_0, a particular value of S, and assume that $\sqrt{NN_0}$ is sufficiently small that the signal locus, $\mathbf{a}(s)$, is approximately a single straight line within a sphere of radius $3\sqrt{NN_0}$ about $\mathbf{a}(s_0)$. A two-dimensional cross section of this situation is shown in Fig. 9-8.

Under the condition that $\mathbf{a}(s_0)$ may be approximated by the straight line

$$\mathbf{a}(s) \approx \mathbf{a}(s_0) + \frac{d\mathbf{a}(s)}{ds}\bigg|_{s=s_0} (s - s_0) \tag{9-65}$$

it is quite easy to find the error due to the noise when maximum-likelihood estimation is used.   Note that the derivative

$$\frac{d\mathbf{a}(s)}{ds}$$

denotes the vector

$$\frac{d\mathbf{a}(s)}{ds} = \left(\frac{da_1(s)}{ds}, \frac{da_2(s)}{ds}, \ldots, \frac{da_N(s)}{ds}\right) \tag{9-66}$$

For notational convenience, we will use the abbreviated notation

$$\mathbf{a}' = \frac{d\mathbf{a}(s)}{ds}; \qquad \mathbf{a_0}' = \frac{d\mathbf{a}(s)}{ds}\bigg|_{s=s_0}$$

Now consider the error caused by the noise $\mathbf{n}$. The maximum-likelihood estimate picks the point on the locus closest to the received vector $\mathbf{z} = \mathbf{a}(s_0) + \mathbf{n}$. Under the conditions stated above, this is to a good approximation the point on the straight line closest to $\mathbf{z}$. But this point is $\mathbf{a}(s_0)$ plus the projection of $\mathbf{n}$ onto the straight line. The projection of a vector $\mathbf{n}$ onto a vector $\mathbf{a_0}'$ has length $(\mathbf{n}, \mathbf{a_0}'/\|\mathbf{a_0}\|)$ in the direction of the vector of unit length $\mathbf{a_0}'/\|\mathbf{a_0}'\|$. Thus $\mathbf{a}(s_0)$ plus the projection of $\mathbf{n}$ onto the tangent line is given by

$$\mathbf{a}(\hat{S}_{ml}) = \mathbf{a}(s_0) + \frac{(\mathbf{n}, \mathbf{a_0}')}{\|\mathbf{a_0}'\|^2} \mathbf{a_0}' \tag{9-67}$$

Comparing Eqs. 9-65 and 9-67, we see that

$$(\hat{S}_{ml} - s_0)\mathbf{a_0}' = \frac{(\mathbf{n}, \mathbf{a_0}')}{\|\mathbf{a_0}'\|^2} \mathbf{a_0}'$$

or

$$(\hat{S}_{ml} - s_0) = \frac{(\mathbf{n}, \mathbf{a_0}')}{\|\mathbf{a_0}'\|^2} \tag{9-68}$$

This gives the error for the particular noise vector $\mathbf{n}$. Given that s_0 is the sample value, the conditional mean-square error averaged over the noise ensemble is

$$E\{(\hat{S}_{ml} - S)^2 \mid S = s_0\} = \frac{E\{(\mathbf{N}, \mathbf{a_0}')^2\}}{\|\mathbf{a_0}'\|^4} \tag{9-69}$$

Problem 9-6. Show that $(\mathbf{N}, \mathbf{a_0}')$ is a gaussian random variable with zero mean and variance

$$\sigma^2 = N_0\|\mathbf{a_0}'\|^2 \tag{9-70}$$

Combining Eqs. 9-69 and 9-70 yields

$$E\{(\hat{S}_{ml} - S)^2 \mid S = s_0\} = \frac{N_0}{\|\mathbf{a_0}'\|^2} \tag{9-71}$$

Our vector representation has allowed us to visualize the transmission process and derive the above expression for the mean-square error. If this expression is to be useful, however, it must be expressed in terms of our pulse function

$$p(t, s) = \sum_{k=1}^{N} a_k(s)\psi_k(t) \tag{9-51}$$

Problem 9-7. Show that

$$\|\mathbf{a}'(s)\|^2 = \left\|\frac{d\mathbf{a}(s)}{ds}\right\|^2 = \int_0^T \left[\frac{d}{ds}p(t, s)\right]^2 dt \tag{9-72}$$

Combining Eqs. 9-71 and 9-72 yields

$$E\{(\hat{S}_{ml} - S)^2 \mid S = s_0\} = \frac{N_0}{\displaystyle\int_0^T \left[\frac{d}{ds}p(t, s)\Big|_{s=s_0}\right]^2 dt} \tag{9-73}$$

This equation gives an explicit rule for evaluating the error associated with a system using a given pulse function $p(t, s)$ when maximum-likelihood estimation is used and observation of $p(t, s)$ is interfered with by additive gaussian noise. Although Eq. 9-73 was derived on the assumption that $p(t, s)$ could be expressed in terms of N orthonormal functions, $\psi_k(t)$, our derivation could have been carried out for $N = \infty$ using a complete orthonormal set of $\psi_k(t)$ providing only that $p(t, s)$ obey certain regularity conditions that would always be satisfied in practice. *Thus* Eq. 9-73 *applies for a general form of pulse modulation; our restriction to finite N is to help develop a geometric picture of the transmission process.*

Optimum Sample Assignment for a Given Modulation Method

We have as yet only an incomplete answer, inasmuch as Eq. 9-71 or 9-73 gives the mean-square error conditioned by the transmitted sample having the value $S = s_0$. In actuality, we are interested in the average over all values that S may take on

$$\mathscr{E}_{sq} = E\{(\hat{S}_m - S)^2\} = N_0 \int_{-1}^{1} f_S(s) \left\|\frac{d\mathbf{a}}{ds}\right\|^{-2} ds \tag{9-74}$$

In this expression we have again assumed that the range of possible values for S is $-1 \le s \le +1$. The derivative $\|d\mathbf{a}/ds\|^2$ could be evaluated from Eq. 9-72.

With Eq. 9-74 in mind, let us now ask the following question. Suppose we are given a particular modulation method, such as pulse position modulation. This corresponds geometrically to a given signal locus whose length we denote by $2L$. We now ask how we should assign values of s to points on this locus in order to minimize the mean-square error of Eq. 9-74. To give this substance, let l denote length along the locus and express $\mathbf{a}$ as a function of l:

$$\mathbf{a} = \mathbf{a}(l) \tag{9-75}$$

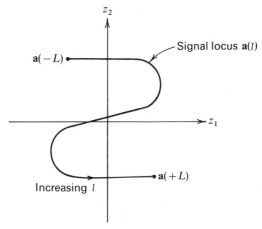

Figure 9-9   Signal locus defined in terms of length along the locus.

The locus will start at $\mathbf{a}(-L)$ and as l increases end up at the point $\mathbf{a}(+L)$. This situation is shown in Fig. 9-9.   Note that since l represents length along the locus, then by definition

$$\left\|\frac{d\mathbf{a}(l)}{dl}\right\| \equiv 1 \tag{9-76}$$

Assigning values of s to points on this locus amounts to assigning length along the locus as a function of s

$$l = l(s) \qquad \begin{cases} -1 \leq s \leq +1 \\ -L \leq l \leq +L \end{cases} \tag{9-77}$$

This mapping of sample values s into an intermediate variable l can be achieved by a circuit with nonlinear gain; in practice such a device is referred to as a *compander*.   Note that in order that there be a unique relation between points on the curve and values of s, we require that

$$\frac{dl}{ds} \geq 0 \qquad -1 \leq s \leq 1 \tag{9-78}$$

Now let us express the mean square error of Eq. 9-74 in terms of $l(s)$. Using Eq. 9-76 we have

$$\left\|\frac{d\mathbf{a}}{ds}\right\|^2 = \left\|\frac{dl}{ds}\frac{d\mathbf{a}}{dl}\right\|^2 = \left|\frac{dl}{ds}\right|^2 \left\|\frac{d\mathbf{a}}{dl}\right\|^2 = \left|\frac{dl}{ds}\right|^2 \tag{9-79}$$

Substituting from Eq. 9-79 into Eq. 9-74 yields

$$\mathscr{E}_{sq} = N_0 \int_{-1}^{1} f_s(s) \left|\frac{dl}{ds}\right|^{-2} ds \tag{9-80}$$

Noting that the locus is of total length $2L$ puts the following constraint on dl/ds

$$\int_{-1}^{1} \frac{dl}{ds}\, ds = 2L \tag{9-81}$$

We thus wish to pick dl/ds in such a manner as to satisfy the constraints of Eqs. 9-78 and 9-81 while minimizing $\mathscr{E}_{sq}$ as given by Eq. 9-80.

To find the function that minimizes $\mathscr{E}_{sq}$ we will need to make very rudimentary use of what is known as the calculus of variations.[1] Although the function dl/ds which satisfies the given constraints and minimizes $\mathscr{E}_{sq}$ is unknown, let us agree to denote it by $g_0(s)$. We know that

$$g_0(s) \geq 0 \qquad -1 \leq s \leq +1 \tag{9-82}$$

$$\int_{-1}^{+1} g_0(s)\, ds = 2L \tag{9-83}$$

and that $\mathscr{E}_{sq}$ has a smaller value when $g_0(s)$ is substituted for dl/ds than for any other choice of dl/ds satisfying the constraints of Eqs. 9-78 and 9-81. Let us now consider the following choice for dl/ds

$$\frac{dl}{ds} = g_0(s) + \epsilon\eta(s) \tag{9-84}$$

We will let $\eta(s)$ be arbitrary with the single exception that dl/ds as given by Eq. 9-84 satisfy Eq. 9-81 for all values of ϵ. This will require that

$$\int_{-1}^{1} \eta(s)\, ds = 0 \tag{9-85}$$

Now consider the value of $\mathscr{E}_{sq}$ that is obtained using the function dl/ds as given by Eq. 9-84. Let us specifically note that this will be a function of ϵ and $\eta(s)$; substituting from Eq. 9-84 into Eq. 9-80, we obtain

$$\mathscr{E}_{sq}[\epsilon, \eta(s)] = N_0 \int_{-1}^{1} f_S(s)[g_0(s) + \epsilon\eta(s)]^{-2}\, ds \tag{9-86}$$

Now if $g_0(s)$ is truly the function which minimizes $\mathscr{E}_{sq}$, then $\mathscr{E}_{sq}[\epsilon, \eta(s)]$ will have to be a minimum for $\epsilon = 0$; this will require that

$$0 = \frac{\partial \mathscr{E}_{sq}[\epsilon, \eta(s)]}{\partial \epsilon}\Bigg|_{\epsilon=0} = -2N_0 \int_{-1}^{1} f_S(s)[g_0(s) + \epsilon\eta(s)]^{-3}\,\eta(s)\, ds\Bigg|_{\epsilon=0}$$

$$= -2N_0 \int_{-1}^{1} f_S(s)[g_0(s)]^{-3}\,\eta(s)\, ds \tag{9-87}$$

[1] For an intermediate treatment of this subject the reader is referred to Chapter 2 of Hildebrand [5].

Note that $\eta(s)$ was arbitrary except that it satisfies Eq. 9-85; *thus* Eq. 9-87 *must hold for any function* $\eta(s)$ *satisfying* Eq. 9-85. Let us reinterpret Eqs. 9-85 and 9-87 as inner products in a vector space; the inner products of the vector $\eta(s)$ with the respective vectors $1(s) = 1$, $-1 \le s \le 1$, and $h(s) = f(s)[g_0(s)]^{-3}$:

$$0 = (\eta(s), 1(s)) = \int_{-1}^{1} \eta(s)\, ds \qquad (9\text{-}85')$$

$$0 = (\eta(s), h(s)) = \int_{-1}^{1} \eta(s)h(s)\, ds \qquad (9\text{-}87')$$

A requirement that $(h(s), \eta(s)) = 0$ for *all* $\eta(s)$ for which $(1(s), \eta(s)) = 0$ states that $h(s)$ is perpendicular to *all* functions that are perpendicular to $1(s)$. The only way this can occur is for $h(s)$ to be parallel to $1(s)$; that is, $h(s) = C' \cdot 1(s) = C'$, $-1 \le s \le 1$ for any constant C'. Thus the only way in which 9-87 can be satisfied for *all* $\eta(s)$ satisfying Eq. 9-85 is to have

$$f_s(s)[g_0(s)]^{-3} = C' \cdot 1 \qquad -1 \le s \le 1 \qquad (9\text{-}88)$$

in which C' may be any constant. Thus $g_0(s)$, the optimum choice of dl/ds, is given by

$$g_0(s) = \left(\frac{dl}{ds}\right)_{\text{optimum}} = [Cf_s(s)]^{\frac{1}{3}}; (C = 1/C') \qquad (9\text{-}89)$$

The constant C must be picked to satisfy Eq. 9-83. It should be noted that in looking for the optimum solution we have not yet invoked the constraint of Eq. 9-82. Since $f_s(s)$ is non-negative, the solution of Eq. 9-89 satisfies this constraint.

Problem 9-8. Show that the constant C in Eq. 9-89 is given by

$$C^{1/3} = \frac{2L}{\int_{-1}^{1} f_s^{\frac{1}{3}}(s)\, ds} \qquad (9\text{-}90)$$

and that the resultant minimum mean-square error obtained by using $g_0(s)$ is given by

$$\mathscr{E}_{\text{sq min}} = \frac{N_0}{(2L)^2}\left[\int_{-1}^{1} f_s^{\frac{1}{3}}(s)\, ds\right]^3 \qquad (9\text{-}91)$$

Problem 9-9. Show, for the uniform distribution

$$f_s(s) = \tfrac{1}{2} \qquad -1 \le s \le +1 \qquad (9\text{-}92)$$

that the optimum choice for dl/ds is

$$g_0(s) = [Cf_s(s)]^{\frac{1}{3}} = L \qquad -1 \le s \le 1 \qquad (9\text{-}93)$$

and that the resultant error is

$$\mathscr{E}_{\text{sq min}} = \frac{N_0}{L^2} \qquad (9\text{-}94)$$

Threshold Effect

Let us now reflect upon the results of Eq. 9-91 and 9-94 which state that $\mathscr{E}_{sq}$ is proportional to N_0/L^2. This would indicate that we could make $\mathscr{E}_{sq}$ as small as desired, and hence achieve any desired performance, by making L, the length of the signal locus, sufficiently large. Our immediate reaction is that there must be a catch somewhere. This is indeed the case. Let us first note that $\|\mathbf{a}(s)\|^2$ is equal to the energy in the pulse $p(t, s)$; thus a requirement that the energy of the transmitted pulse, $p(t, s)$, be less than E for all values of s places a restriction that

$$\|\mathbf{a}(s)\|^2 \le E \tag{9-95}$$

Second, as we have mentioned in Sec. 8-5, if the orthonormal functions $\psi_k(t)$ are chosen judiciously, the bandwidth occupied by the pulse $p(t, s)$ will be proportional to N, the number of $\psi_k(t)$ in the expression

$$p(t, s) = \sum_{k=1}^{N} a_k(s)\psi_k(t) \qquad 0 \le t \le T$$

or equivalently the number of components of $\mathbf{a}(s)$. A constraint that $p(t, s)$ occupy only a (one-sided) bandwidth of W_c c.p.s. would require that N be less than or equal to $2W_cT$. Thus *the signal locus $\mathbf{a}(s)$ is constrained to lie in a sphere of radius $\sqrt{E}$ and dimension $N = 2W_cT$.*

However, these requirements by themselves would not prevent us from making L arbitrarily large. It is easy to envision a curve of any length that lies in a two-dimensional sphere. Simply by making a large number of "folds" in the curve, as shown in Fig. 9-10, it is possible to make the

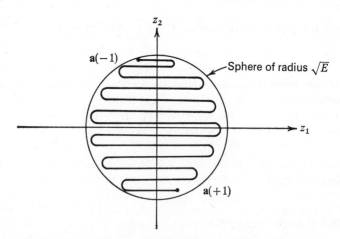

Figure 9-10   Curve of constrained energy but long length.

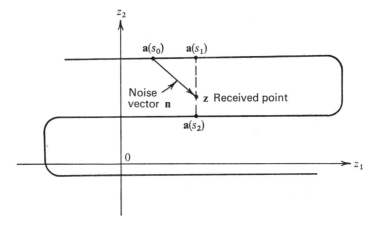

Figure 9-11   Occurrence of an anomalous or large error.

curve as long as desired.   The point that is still being overlooked is that
the derivation of our expression for the mean-square error was based on
the assumption that within a sphere of radius $3\sqrt{NN_0}$ about the transmitted point, $\mathbf{a}(s_0)$, the signal locus could be approximated by a *single
straight line*.   Although we did not emphasize before the requirement that
the locus be approximated by a *single* line within this sphere, it can easily
be appreciated why this is necessary.   Figure 9-11 shows an expanded
view of a portion of the locus of Fig. 9-10, centered about the transmitted
point $\mathbf{a}(s_0)$.   With high probability the noise vector will be of length less
than or equal to $3\sqrt{NN_0}$.   Let us assume that the folds of the curve of
Fig. 9-11 are closer together than $2\sqrt{NN_0}$.   Thus with non-negligible
probability the received point will lie closer to a different fold of $\mathbf{a}(s)$ than
the one on which $\mathbf{a}(s_0)$ lies; a noise vector for which this occurs is shown in
Fig. 9-11.   In this case our linear analysis would predict that the maximum
likelihood estimate is the value s_1; in fact, the maximum-likelihood
estimate would be the value s_2.   The error $s_2 - s_0$ is obviously considerably greater than the error $s_1 - s_0$ predicted by our linear analysis.
A large error caused by the receiver picking a point on the *wrong fold of
the curve* is referred to as an *anomaly* or *anomalous error* (or in radar
terminology an *ambiguity*).   The occurrence of these large errors prevents
making $\mathscr{E}_{sq}$ very small by placing the folds of the curve arbitrarily close
together and thus making the locus arbitrarily long.   For a discussion of
just how long a locus may be efficiently packed into the allowed signal
sphere when the dimension N is large without having anomalous errors,
the reader is referred to Sec. 8.4 of Wozencraft and Jacobs [3].

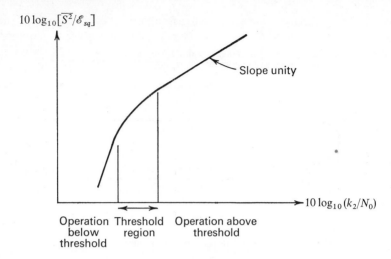

Figure 9-12   Threshold performance of a nonlinear pulse modulation system.

It is common to describe this phenomenon of the occurrence of anomalous errors in another way.   Consider the ratio of the mean-square value of S to the mean-square error.   When N_0 is sufficiently small, the linear approximation is valid and the form of behavior predicted by Eq. 9-91 applies

$$\frac{\overline{S^2}}{\mathscr{E}_{sq}} = k_1 \frac{L^2}{N_0} = \frac{k_2}{N_0}$$

The second equality assumes a fixed transmission system; i.e., a fixed locus of length L.   The expression is valid as long as N_0 is sufficiently small that the probability of an anomaly is negligible.   However, as N_0 increases, the probability of an anomaly becomes non-negligible and with a certain probability the errors will be much larger than predicted by the linear analysis.   Thus as N_0 increases beyond a certain point, the value of $\overline{S^2}/\mathscr{E}_{sq}$ will drop drastically below the value K_2/N_0.   This type of behavior is shown in Fig. 9-12 in which the output signal-to-noise ratio, $(S/N)_o = \overline{S^2}/\mathscr{E}_{sq}$, is plotted as a function of E/N_0.   The knee of this curve where anomalies begin to occur is referred to as the *threshold region* of the pulse modulation system.   Satisfactory operation occurs above *threshold* when the probability of an anomaly is negligible.   Below threshold, large errors are frequent and the operation of the system is unsatisfactory.

To calculate the behavior of a nonlinear modulation system in the region near threshold is an exceedingly difficult task.   Our discussion so far has been only qualitative, aimed at imparting an understanding of the occurrence of the threshold phenomenon in nonlinear pulse modulation systems. In the next section we give an approximate method of calculating the probability of occurrence of anomalies in pulse position modulation.

9-4   Pulse Position Modulation

Description of PPM

The most widely used method of nonlinear pulse modulation is pulse position modulation (PPM). In PPM the position or time origin of the pulse is shifted in accordance with the sample to be transmitted

$$p(t, s) = \sqrt{E}\,\phi(t - sT_0) \qquad (9\text{-}96)$$

A sequence of samples S_{kT}, $k = 0, \pm 1, \pm 2, \ldots$, would then produce the transmitted signal

$$X(t) = \sqrt{E} \sum_{k=-\infty}^{\infty} \phi(t - S_{kT}T_0 - kT) \qquad (9\text{-}97)$$

One way of implementing PPM is shown in Figs. 9-13 and 9-14. The message signal $S(t)$ is first sampled and then passed through a device with impulse response

$$h_1(t) = \begin{cases} \alpha & 0 \le t \le T \\ 0 & \text{elsewhere} \end{cases}$$

to yield a signal that is constant between sample times. This signal is then added to a sawtooth signal of period T. Next a detector measures the time at which the sum signal down-crosses 0 volts and produces a sharp pulse (approximately an impulse) at the time of this zero-crossing. As can be seen from Fig. 9-14, this pulse would occur at time $T/2$ if the corresponding sample value were zero. Thus, for this method of

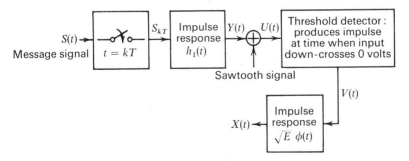

Figure 9-13   Block diagram of a method for generating PPM.

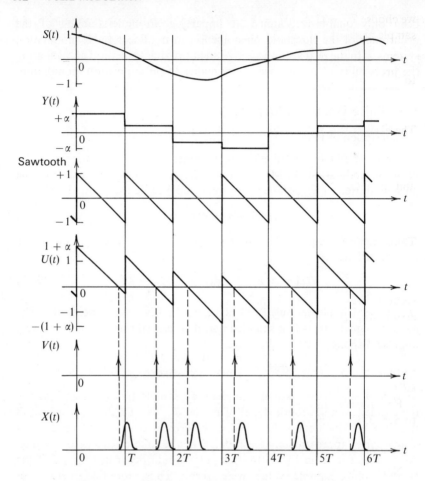

Figure 9-14   Signals occurring in the generation of PPM.

implementation, the transmitted signal would actually be

$$X(t) = \sqrt{E} \sum_{k=-\infty}^{\infty} \phi[t - S_{kT}T_0 - (T/2) - kT] \qquad (9\text{-}97')$$

In Fig. 9-14 it has been assumed that the range of possible sample values is $-1 \leq s \leq +1$, and the amplitude of the sawtooth signal is 1. The quantity T_0 in Eq. 9-97′ is given by

$$T_0 = \alpha \frac{T}{2} \qquad (9\text{-}98)$$

α being the gain of the impulse response $h_1(t)$. We denote by T_1 the duration of $\phi(t)$ and assume that $\phi(t)$ is nonzero from $t = 0$ to $t = T_1$. If we choose $T_1 = (1 - \alpha)T = T - 2T_0$, then the pulse corresponding to the sample at $t = kT$ would be "on" from

$$t = kT + (S_{kT}\alpha + 1)\frac{T}{2}$$

to

$$kT + (S_{kT}\alpha + 1)\frac{T}{2} + (1 - \alpha)T$$

The earliest this pulse could come on would be

$$kT + (1 - \alpha)\frac{T}{2}$$

and the latest it could turn off would be at

$$kT + (1 - \alpha)\frac{T}{2} + T$$

Thus each pulse falls in a time slot of duration T seconds starting

$$(1 - \alpha)\frac{T}{2}$$

seconds after the corresponding sample of $S(t)$. In what follows, we assume that the sample times occur at

$$t = kT - (1 - \alpha)\frac{T}{2}$$

so that the pulse corresponding to the kth sample will fall in the time slot kT to $(k + 1)T$.

For a more thorough discussion of the generation of PPM, refer to Sec. 3, Chapter V of Rowe [6].

Structure of the PPM Receiver

Next, let us consider implementation of the maximum-likelihood receiver. Recall that in terms of our vector representation, the maximum-likelihood estimation rule picks the value of s for which

$$\|z - a(s)\|^2 = \|z\|^2 - 2(z, a(s)) + \|a(s)\|^2$$

is a minimum. Since $\|z\|^2$ is independent of s, this is equivalent to picking the value of s for which

$$(z, a(s)) - \tfrac{1}{2}\|a(s)\|^2$$

is a maximum. For pulse position modulation, the energy in the transmitted pulse is independent of the sample value s, for assuming the timing arrangement described above, we have

$$\|a(s)\|^2 = \int_0^T p^2(t, s)\, dt = \int_0^T E\phi^2[t - (s + 1)T_0]\, dt = E$$

Thus for pulse position modulation the maximum-likelihood estimation rule is to *pick that value of s which maximizes the quantity*

$$(\mathbf{z}, \mathbf{a}(s)) = \int_0^T z(\tau)p(\tau, s)\, d\tau = \sqrt{E} \int_0^T z(\tau)\phi[\tau - (s + 1)T_0]\, d\tau \quad (9\text{-}99)$$

Although this estimation rule is conceptually simple, it is difficult to implement.

Problem 9-10. Let $h(\tau)$ be a filter with impulse response

$$h(\tau) = \begin{cases} \phi[T_1 - \tau] & 0 \leq \tau \leq T_1 \\ 0 & \text{elsewhere} \end{cases}$$

$[T_1$ again denoting the duration of $\phi(t)]$. Show that $\hat{S}_{ml}$, the value of s for which Eq. 9-99 is maximized is given by

$$\hat{S}_{ml} = \frac{1}{T_0} [t_{\max} - T_1 - T_0] \quad (9\text{-}100)$$

in which $t_{\max}$ is the time at which the filter output

$$Y(t) = \int_0^T Z(\tau)h(t - \tau)\, d\tau \quad (9\text{-}101)$$

is a maximum.

The maximum-likelihood estimate could thus be realized as shown in Fig. 9-15.

Referring to Eq. 9-99 which specifies the maximum-likelihood estimate of S, let us note that if pulses corresponding to samples at times separated by mT seconds are not to interfere with one another we must have

$$\int_0^T \phi[t + mT - (s + 1)T_0]\phi[t - (s' + 1)T_0]\, dt = 0 \qquad T_0 = \alpha \frac{T}{2} \quad (9\text{-}102)$$

for *all* values of s' and s, $-1 \leq s, s' \leq +1$, and all nonzero integral values of m. The only way this condition can be met is for $\phi(t - T_0 s)$ to lie

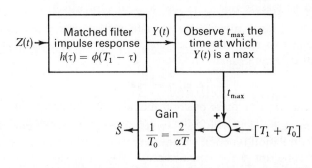

Figure 9-15   Implementation of a maximum-likelihood receiver for PPM.

wholly within a time slot of duration T seconds for *all values of s*, $-1 \leq s \leq +1$. This is the case for the implementation described by Figs. 9-13 and 9-14 in which T_1 and T_0 were taken such that $T_1 + 2T_0 = T$.

Problem 9-11. Take the transmitted pulse to be

$$p(t, s) = \sqrt{E}\, \phi[t - (s + 1)T_0]$$

in which $\phi(t)$ is a pulse of unit energy with Fourier transform $\Phi(f)$. Show that under the high signal-to-noise ratio assumption for which Eqs. 9-69 and 9-73 are valid, the mean-square error for maximum-likelihood reception is given by

$$\mathscr{E}_{\mathrm{sq}} = \frac{N_0}{ET_0{}^2 \int_0^T [\phi'(t)]^2\, dt} = \frac{N_0}{E}\frac{1}{T_0{}^2(2\pi)^2\overline{f_\phi{}^2}} \tag{9-103}$$

in which E is the energy of the pulse $p(t, s)$ and $\overline{f_\phi{}^2}$ is the mean square bandwidth of $\phi(t)$:

$$\overline{f_\phi{}^2} = \frac{\int_{-\infty}^{\infty} |\Phi(f)|^2 f^2\, df}{\int_{-\infty}^{\infty} |\Phi(f)|^2\, df} \tag{9-104}$$

It is interesting to compare Eq. 9-103 with Eq. 9-46 which gives the performance of PAM. Assume for the sake of argument that S is uniformly distributed in the interval $-1 \leq s \leq +1$ so that $\overline{S^2} = \frac{1}{3}$. Then $\mathscr{E}_{\mathrm{sq}}$ for PPM differs from PAM by the factor $[3(2\pi)^2\overline{f_\phi{}^2}/T_0{}^2]$. The time duration T_0 must be less than the sample interval T, but $\overline{f_\phi{}^2}$ can be made large compared to $1/T_1$, $T_1 = (T - 2T_0)$, by making the bandwidth occupancy of $\phi(t)$ large. Thus PPM, like FM, allows us to exchange bandwidth for signal-to-noise ratio. However, we cannot make $\overline{f_\phi{}^2}$ arbitrarily large without introducing large or anomalous errors, as we shall soon see.

The receiver implementation shown in Fig. 9-15 has one practical difficulty: it requires a method of observing at what time $y(t)$ is a maximum. It is difficult to design a circuit to measure at what time a voltage is at an absolute (as opposed to local) maximum. We thus wish to consider a more practical form of receiver implementation. Before doing so, it will be convenient to recall the definition of the correlation function of two (deterministic) signals made in Chapter 2

$$C_\phi(\tau) = \int_{-T}^{T} \phi(t)\phi(t + \tau)\, dt \qquad -T \leq \tau \leq +T \tag{9-105}$$

In the remainder of this chapter we refer to $C_\phi(\tau)$ very frequently; since the only correlation function we deal with is that of the pulse $\phi(t)$, we will drop the subscript ϕ for convenience. Note that since $\phi(t)$ is of unit energy, $C(0) = 1$.

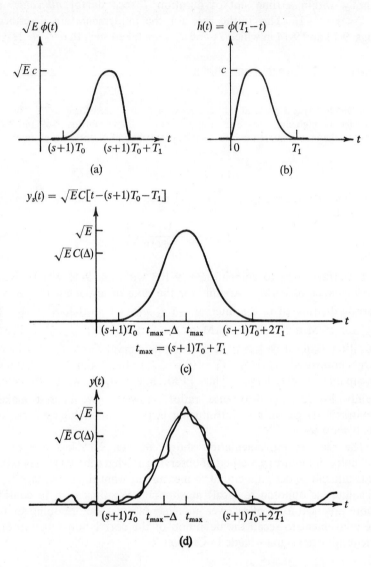

Figure 9-16   Response of $h(t)$ to $\phi(t)$:
(a) Pulse $E\phi(t)$.
(b) Impulse response $h(t)$.
(c) Filter response, signal only.
(d) Filter response, signal plus noise.

Problem 9-12. Show that $C(\tau)$ is symmetric

$$C(-\tau) = C(\tau) \qquad (9\text{-}106)$$

and that

$$|C(\tau)| \leq C(0) \qquad (9\text{-}107)$$

Hint: Use the Schwartz inequality discussed in Problem 8-3.

Now let us consider the response of the matched filter in Fig. 9-15, $h(\tau) = \phi(T_1 - \tau)$, to the input signal $\sqrt{E}\,\phi[t - (s + 1)T_0]$. This is the signal component of $y(t)$, and is given by

$$y_s(t) = \sqrt{E} \int_0^T \phi[\sigma - (s + 1)T_0]\phi[T_1 - t + \sigma]\,d\sigma$$

$$= \sqrt{E} \int_0^T \phi[\beta]\phi\{\beta - [t - (s + 1)T_0 - T_1]\}\,d\beta$$

$$= \sqrt{E}\,C[t - (s + 1)T_0 - T_1] \qquad (9\text{-}108)$$

A typical pulse $\phi(t)$ and the response $y_s(t)$ are shown in Fig. 9-16. Note that, by Eq. 9-107, $y_s(t)$ must have its maximum at $C(0)$ or $t = (s + 1)T_0 + T_1$. The observed signal $y(t)$ would consist of $y_s(t)$ plus a component due to the noise input to $h(\tau)$; a typical waveform for $y(t)$ under high signal-to-noise ratio conditions would thus be as shown in Fig. 9-16d. Recall now that our objective is to find a practical way of estimating the time at which $y(t)$ is a maximum. From Figs. 9-16c and 9-16d we can see that a good way to estimate $t_{\max}$ would be to take $t_{\max} = t_1 + \Delta$, in which t_1 is the time at which $y(t)$ first upcrosses $\sqrt{E}\,C(\Delta)$. Referring to Eq. 9-100, we see that the corresponding estimate of S would be

$$\hat{S}_{\text{upcross}} = \frac{1}{T_0}[t_1 + \Delta - T_1 - T_0] \qquad (9\text{-}109)$$

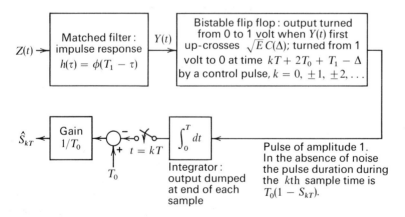

Figure 9-17 Implementation of the up-crossing receiver.

A possible system for implementing this estimate is shown in functional form in Fig. 9-17; all of the operations shown can easily be realized by electronic circuits.

Problem 9-13.   Calculate the mean-square error of the upcrossing receiver described above. Express your answer in terms of the pulse energy E, the noise spectral density N_0, the time shift T_0, and $C'(\Delta) = \dfrac{dC(\tau)}{d\tau}\bigg|_{\tau=\Delta}$. Assume a high signal-to-noise ratio condition. You may wish to make use of Eq. 9-114.

Probability of an Anomalous Error

The above analysis has all been concerned with the high signal-to-noise ratio case in which there are no large anomalous errors caused by the estimate $\hat{S}$ lying on a different fold of the signal locus than that of the transmitted sample value s. Let us now focus our attention on calculating the probability of an anomaly.

To be more specific, let us say that an anomaly occurs whenever $|S - \hat{S}| > \epsilon$ where ϵ^2 is the order of ten times the mean-square error predicted by the linear analysis leading up to Eq. 9-103. If we denote by A the event that such an anomalous error occurs, then for maximum-likelihood reception

$$P(A) = P\{Y(t_{\max}^*) \leq Y(t_{\max}^{**})\} \tag{9-110}$$

in which $t_{\max}^*$ and $t_{\max}^{**}$ are defined as follows. Let $t_{\max}$ denote the time at which the filter output $Y(t)$ would be a maximum in the absence of noise; then

$$t_{\max}^* = \text{time at which } Y(t) \text{ is a maximum for}$$
$$t_{\max} - \epsilon T_0 \leq t \leq t_{\max} + \epsilon T_0$$
$$t_{\max}^{**} = \text{time at which } Y(t) \text{ is a maximum for}$$
$$t < t_{\max} - \epsilon T_0 \quad \text{or} \quad t > t_{\max} + \epsilon T_0$$

To calculate $P(A)$ as given by Eq. 9-110 is literally an unsolved mathematical problem. We thus cannot hope to calculate $P(A)$ exactly and must be content to calculate an approximate expression. We will consider here an approximate method of calculation first suggested by Kotelnikov [2] and later extended by Wozencraft and Jacobs [3].

Let us denote by $Y_n(t)$ the response of the matched filter $h(\tau) = \phi(T_1 - \tau)$ to the noise $N(t)$ and again use $y_s(t)$ to denote the response of the filter to the pulse signal. We assume that $S = s$ is the transmitted sample value and that the maximum of $y_s(t)$ occurs at $t_{\max}$ for this sample value. Suppose there were a number of time instants $t_1, t_2, \ldots, t_q$ such that the noise samples $N_k = Y_n(t_k)$, $k = 1, 2, \ldots, q$, and $N_{\max} = Y_n(t_{\max})$ were all *jointly* statistically independent and that $|t_k - t_{max}| > \epsilon T_0$ for all of the t_k. Now an anomaly will certainly occur if

$$Y(t_k) > Y(t^*_{max})$$

for any t_k. The output of the matched filter will fluctuate only slowly; we thus assume that the maximum of $Y(t)$ in the small interval about $t = t_{max}$ is approximately equal to the value of $Y(t_{max})$

$$Y(t_{max}) \approx Y(t^*_{max}) \tag{9-111}$$

Under this approximation, an anomaly will occur if

$$Y(t_{max}) < Y(t_k)$$

for any of the t_k, or

$$P(A) \approx 1 - P[Y(t_{max}) > Y(t_k), k = 1, 2, \ldots, q] \tag{9-112}$$

Since $Y(t_k) = y_s(t_k) + N_k$, Eq. 9-112 can be rephrased as

$$P(A) \approx 1 - P[N_k - N_{max} < y_s(t_k) - y_s(t_{max}), k = 1, 2, \ldots, q]$$

Finding the probability of the event in this equation by conditioning on a particular value of N_{max}, making use of the assumed independence of the N_k and N_{max}, and integrating over all values taken on by N_{max} yields

$$P(A) \approx 1 - \int_{-\infty}^{\infty} f_{N_{max}}(n) \prod_{k=1}^{q} P[N_k < n + y_s(t_{max}) - y_s(t_k)]\, dn \tag{9-113}$$

The above expression is a lower bound; it is optimistic in that it compares $Y(t_{max})$ with only a finite number of points in the anomalous region instead of all points in this region. However, in certain cases it can provide a good estimate of $P(A)$ and yield some insight into how $P(A)$ is affected by certain factors in the system design, such as the shape of $\phi(t)$.

The correlation function $C(\tau)$ provides a means for setting up the calculations required for the bound of Eq. 9-113.

Problem 9-14. The process $Y_n(t)$ is the output of the matched filter $h(\tau) = \phi[T_1 - \tau]$ to white gaussian noise, $N(t)$, of spectral density N_0. Show that the correlation function of $Y_n(t)$ is given by

$$R_{y_n}(\tau) = E\{Y_{n,t+\tau} Y_{n,t}\} = N_0 C(\tau) \tag{9-114}$$

Problem 9-15. Let s denote the transmitted value; the response of $h(\tau)$ to $p(t, s)$ is then a maximum at t_{max}. Let s' denote the value corresponding to t_k; that is, the filter response to $p(t, s')$ is a maximum at t_k. Let E denote the energy of the transmitted pulse $p(t, s) = \sqrt{E}\, \phi[t - (s + 1)T_0]$.   Show, if $N_{\max} = Y_n(t_{\max})$ and $N_k = Y_n(t_k)$ are independent, that

$$P[N_k < n + y_s(t_{\max}) - y_s(t_k)] = 1 - Q\left\{\frac{n}{\sqrt{N_0}} + \sqrt{\frac{E}{N_0}}[C(0) - C[T_0(s - s')]]\right\}$$

$$= 1 - Q\left\{\frac{n}{\sqrt{N_0}} + \sqrt{\frac{E}{N_0}}\right\} \qquad (9\text{-}115)$$

in which

$$Q(x) = \frac{1}{\sqrt{2\pi}} \int_x^\infty e^{-\theta^2/2}\, d\theta$$

Let us now assume that $C(\tau)$ has zeros that are equispaced

$$C(\tau) = 0 \qquad \tau = m\Delta T \qquad m = \pm 1, \pm 2, \ldots, \pm \frac{T_1}{\Delta T} \qquad (9\text{-}116)$$

Thus any set of samples of the noise component of the filter output that are spaced ΔT seconds apart will be *jointly* independent since the process $Y_n(t)$ is gaussian.   Furthermore, $C(\tau)$ will be identically zero for $|\tau| > T_1$ if the pulse $\phi(t)$ is of duration T_1.   Thus we can apply the above analysis to the time instants

$$t_k = \begin{cases} t_{\max} + k\,\Delta T & k = 1, 2, \ldots, (1 - s)\dfrac{T_0}{\Delta T} \\[2ex] t_{\max} - k\,\Delta T & k = 1, 2, \ldots, (1 + s)\dfrac{T_0}{\Delta T} \end{cases}$$

We note that there are

$$q = \frac{2T_0}{\Delta T} \qquad (9\text{-}117)$$

such instants in the range of possible time shifts corresponding to the range of possible sample values $-1 < s < +1$.   We can combine Eqs. 9-113 and 9-115 in this situation to yield

$$P(A) \approx 1 - \int_{-\infty}^\infty f_{N_{\max}}(n)\left\{1 - Q\left[\frac{n}{\sqrt{N_0}} + \sqrt{\frac{E}{N_0}}\right]\right\}^q dn$$

Substituting the appropriate gaussian distribution for $f_N(n)$ and making the change of variable $x = n/\sqrt{N_0}$ then yields

$$P(A) \approx 1 - \frac{1}{\sqrt{2\pi}} \int_{-\infty}^\infty e^{-x^2/2}[1 - Q(x + \sqrt{E/N_0})]^q\, dx \qquad (9\text{-}118)$$

If we assume that $Q(x + \sqrt{E/N_0})$ is small for those values of x for which $e^{-x^2/2}$ is non-negligible we can approximate $[1 - Q]^q$ by $1 - qQ$.

This will result in a more pessimistic estimate since $[1 - Q]^q \geq 1 - qQ$ for $0 \leq Q \leq 1$ and $q > 1$. Using this approximation in Eq. 9-118 yields

$$P(A) \approx q \frac{1}{\sqrt{2\pi}} \int_{-\infty}^{\infty} e^{-x^2/2} Q(x + \sqrt{E/N_0}) \, dx \qquad (9\text{-}119)$$

The integral in this expression is easily evaluated by comparing two different equations for the probability of error for two orthogonal signals. Equating Eq. 8-75 with Eq. 8-77 and simplifying yields

$$\frac{1}{\sqrt{2\pi}} \int_{-\infty}^{\infty} e^{-x^2/2} Q(x + \sqrt{E/N_0}) \, dx = Q(\sqrt{E/2N_0}) \qquad (9\text{-}120)$$

so that Eq. 9-119 becomes

$$P(A) \approx q Q(\sqrt{E/2N_0}) = \frac{2T_0}{\Delta T} Q(\sqrt{E/2N_0}) \qquad (9\text{-}121)$$

Having derived this expression, we are now in a position to reflect on its validity. Since it is based on comparing the matched filter output at t_{max} to the filter output *only* at time shifts for which $C(\tau)$ is zero, the expression is useful when these time shifts are the principal sources of large errors. This situation prevails *only* when $C(\tau)$ has no positive peaks comparable in size to the central peak at $\tau = 0$. This point is explored in Problems 9-17 and 9-18.

Performance Calculation—An Example

Let us now consider a specific example in order to study the trade off between $\mathcal{E}_{sq}$, the mean-square error calculated on high signal-to-noise ratio assumptions, and $P(A)$, the probability of an anomaly. We shall take the pulse $\phi(t)$ to be

$$\phi(t) = \begin{cases} \sqrt{2W_1\beta} \text{ sinc } [2\beta W_1 t] & 0 \leq t \leq T_1 \\ 0 & \text{elsewhere} \end{cases} \qquad (9\text{-}122)$$

in which

$$W_1 = 1/2T_1 \qquad (9\text{-}123)$$

If β is $\gg 1$, then this sinc function is small at the end points where it is truncated and its transform is approximately the same as that of the untruncated sinc function

$$\Phi(f) \approx \begin{cases} \dfrac{1}{\sqrt{2W_1\beta}} & |f| < \beta W_1 \\ 0 & |f| > \beta W_1 \end{cases} \qquad (9\text{-}124)$$

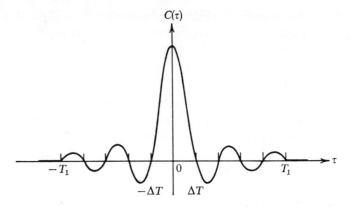

Figure 9-18   Correlation function of the pulse $\phi(t)$ defined by Eq. 9-122.

Problem 9-16.   Evaluate Eq. 9-103, using Eq. 9-124 for this pulse, and show that under the high signal-to-noise ratio assumption

$$\mathscr{E}_{sq} = \frac{N_0}{E} \frac{3T_1^2}{\pi^2 T_0^2 \beta^2} \qquad (9\text{-}125)$$

The function $C(\tau)$ is easily evaluated for the choice of $\phi(t)$ of Eq. 9-122. From the correlation property, we have

$$\mathscr{F}[C(\tau)] = \Phi(f)\Phi^*(f) \approx \begin{cases} \dfrac{1}{2W_1\beta} & |f| \le \beta W_1 \\[2mm] 0 & |f| > \beta W_1 \end{cases} \qquad (9\text{-}126)$$

and hence,

$$C(\tau) \approx \operatorname{sinc}[2\beta W_1 t] \qquad (9\text{-}127)$$

Note that $C(\tau)$ must in actuality be zero for $|\tau| > T_1$ since $\phi(t)$ is of duration T_1. The function $C(\tau)$ is shown in Fig. 9-18. Its zeros occur at $\tau = k(T_1/\beta)$, $k = \pm 1, \pm 2, \pm 3, \ldots$, and these are the points used in the approximate analysis of $P(A)$. The quantity ΔT of Eqs. 9-116 and 9-117 is T_1/β for this example and Eq. 9-121 becomes

$$P(A) \approx \frac{2T_0}{T_1} \beta Q(\sqrt{E/2N_0}) \qquad (9\text{-}128)$$

Wozencraft and Jacobs [3] have compared this expression with measured results (see pp. 629–631 and the reference given therein) and found the agreement quite good.

Let us now summarize the performance of this system and examine how $P(A)$ and $\mathscr{E}_{sq}$ are affected by the choice of the parameters describing the pulse. It will be convenient again to express T_0 and T_1 as fractions of the sample time

$$2T_0 = \alpha T$$

and

$$T_1 = (1 - \alpha)T$$

Let us note from Eq. 9-124 that the (one-sided) bandwidth occupancy of the transmitted pulse is

$$W_p = \beta W_1 = \frac{\beta}{1 - \alpha} \frac{1}{2T} = \frac{\beta}{1 - \alpha} W \qquad (9\text{-}129)$$

From this equation, we see that the quantity $\beta/(1 - \alpha)$ represents the ratio of the bandwidth occupied by the PPM system to the bandwidth of the message process being sampled. It will thus be convenient to denote this ratio by γ

$$\gamma \triangleq \frac{\beta}{1 - \alpha} \qquad (9\text{-}130)$$

In terms of this notation, Eqs. 9-125 and 9-128 become

$$\mathscr{E}_{\text{sq}} = \frac{12}{\pi^2} \frac{N_0}{E} \frac{1}{(\alpha\gamma)^2} \qquad (9\text{-}125')$$

and

$$P(A) = \alpha\gamma Q(\sqrt{E/2N_0}) \qquad (9\text{-}128')$$

The performance of the system is determined both by the frequent small errors, whose mean-square value is given by Eq. 9-125', and by $P(A)$, the probability of a large or anomalous error. It would be convenient to express the performance in terms of a single quantity. We might do this by estimating the value of an error when an anomaly occurs and including this in an overall expression for the mean-square error. If we denote the mean-square value of an anomalous or large error by $\mathscr{E}_{\text{large}}$, then the overall expression for the mean-square error is

$$\mathscr{E}_{\text{sq total}} = [1 - P(A)]\mathscr{E}_{\text{sq}} + P(A)\mathscr{E}_{\text{large}} \qquad (9\text{-}131)$$

It is not clear how to estimate the term $\mathscr{E}_{\text{large}}$, since the distribution of large errors is very difficult to calculate. A possible approximation is to simply assume that S and $\hat{S}$ are independent and uniformly distributed between $s = -1$ and $s = +1$. This yields

$$\mathscr{E}_{\text{large}} = \tfrac{2}{3} \qquad (9\text{-}132)$$

This approximation will be somewhat conservative, since the more probable values of error occur for values of $s - \hat{s}$ corresponding to positive peaks of $C[T_0(s - \hat{s})]$ (see Problem 9-18).   Substituting from Eq. 9-132, 9-125′, and 9-128′ into Eq. 9-131, we obtain

$$\mathscr{E}_{\text{sq total}} = (1 - \alpha\gamma Q\sqrt{E/2N_0})\frac{12}{\pi^2(\alpha\gamma)^2}\frac{N_0}{E} + \frac{2}{3}(\alpha\gamma)Q(\sqrt{E/2N_0}) \quad (9\text{-}133)$$

It should be noted that this quantity has a unique minimum as a function of $\alpha\gamma$ for any given value of E/N_0.   However, the performance of interest is the behavior of $\mathscr{E}_{\text{sq total}}$ for a *fixed system* (fixed values of α and γ) as a function of the signal-to-noise ratio, E/N_0, in which the system must operate.   The value of α might be determined by practical considerations; the transmitter, for example, might be limited in its *peak power* output, so that the energy in the pulse would be proportional to the pulse duration $(1 - \alpha)T$.   The value of γ might then be chosen to minimize the value of $\mathscr{E}_{\text{sq total}}$ for the nominal operating signal-to-noise ratio, E/N_0, consistent of course with a bandwidth restriction which places an upper limit on the value of γ.

The performance given by Eq. 9-133 is plotted in Fig. 9-19 as a function of the signal-to-noise ratio *per sample*, E/N_0, for $\alpha = \frac{1}{2}$ and a number of values of γ.   Rather than plotting $\mathscr{E}_{\text{sq total}}$ itself, the *output* signal-to-noise ratio

$$\left(\frac{S}{N}\right)_o = \frac{\overline{S^2}}{\mathscr{E}_{\text{sq total}}} \quad (9\text{-}134)$$

is plotted, assuming that S is uniformly distributed between $s = -1$ and $s = +1$, so that $\overline{S^2} = \frac{1}{3}$.

In our discussion, we have tacitly assumed that our transmitted pulses are low-pass.   The pulses to be transmitted may have to be r-f pulses to propagate over the physical transmission channel.   Our analysis of PPM would be directly pertinent to r-f pulses only if coherent demodulation were employed.   This is rarely used in PPM; Problem 9-18 explores this. Our analysis in the incoherent case should be applied to the envelope of the r-f pulse and the remarks made about PAM on this point apply here. In particular, we should note that in using Eq. 9-103, we want to evaluate $\overline{f_\phi^2}$ for the pulse envelope; this would be the variance of the bandwidth of the r-f pulse about its center frequency f_0:

$$\overline{f_\phi^2}_{\text{ envelope}} = \frac{\int_0^\infty |\Phi(f)|^2(f - f_0)^2\, df}{\int_0^\infty |\Phi(f)|^2\, dt} \quad (9\text{-}135)$$

Problem 9-17.   Let s denote the value of the sample corresponding to the transmitted pulse

$$p(t, s) = \sqrt{E}\, \phi[t - (s + 1)T_0]$$

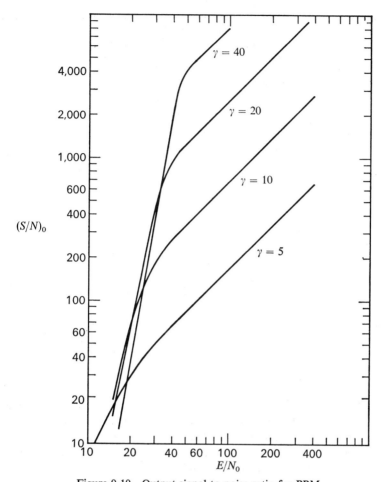

Figure 9-19   Output signal-to-noise ratio for PPM.

Consider $Y(t)$, the output of the matched filter $h(\tau) = \phi[T_1 - \tau]$ when the input is $p(t, s)$ plus white gaussian noise of spectral density N_0.   Let s' denote *any* other possible sample value, $-1 \leq s' \leq 1$.   Show that

$$P[Y(t') > Y(t_{\max})] = Q\left\{\sqrt{\frac{E}{2N_0}} \sqrt{1 - C[(s - s')T_0]}\right\} \qquad (9\text{-}136)$$

in which $t_{\max}$ is the time at which the filter response to $p(t, s)$ is a maximum and t' the time at which the response to $p(t, s')$ is a maximum.

Problem 9-18.   Let us consider using the pulse

$$\phi(t) = \begin{cases} \sqrt{2/T_1} \cos\left[\dfrac{2\pi mt}{T_1}\right] & 0 \leq t \leq T_1 \\ 0 & \text{elsewhere} \end{cases}$$

in the pulse modulation system described in Problem 9-17.

(a) Assuming the signal-to-noise ratio is sufficiently high that the linear analysis is valid, what is $\mathscr{E}_{sq}$ for maximum likelihood reception?

(b) Sketch the ambiguity function for $m = 5$. Explain what choice of time instants you might pick to apply the approximate expression for $P(A)$ given by Eq. 9-121, assuming $E/N_0 \approx 10$ and $2T_0 = T_1$; write the expression.

(c) In the light of Problem 9-17, would you expect the expression of (b) above to be accurate for this pulse for large values of m (say, 50 or more)? State why or why not. What does this say about using coherent demodulation for PPM when the transmitted pulse is an r-f pulse?

Problem 9-19. Show that the mean-square error for a PPM system in the high signal-to-noise ratio case using maximum-likelihood reception is given by

$$\mathscr{E}_{sq} = -\frac{N_0}{ET_0{}^2 C''(0)} \tag{9-137}$$

in which E is the energy of the pulse and

$$C''(\tau) = \frac{d^2}{d\tau^2} C(\tau)$$

Make use of any useful expressions derived in the process of working Problem 9-11.

In closing this section, we should point out that our discussion of the correlation function of the pulse $p(t, s)$ has only been in the context of PPM. However, if we defined this function as

$$C(s, s') = \int_0^T p(t, s)p(t, s')\, dt$$

then it would be pertinent to an arbitrary pulse modulation system. This generalized correlation function is useful in analyzing the same aspects of arbitrary pulse modulation systems that were analyzed in this section using $C(\tau)$. However, it should be pointed out in this regard that the analysis is considerably simplified for those systems for which $C(s, s')$ is a function only of the difference $s - s'$ (as in the case with PPM).

9-5   Pulse Code Modulation

In *pulse code modulation* (abbreviated *PCM*) each sample is quantized into one of q possible finite values. The value the quantized sample takes on is then transmitted by a method used to transmit digital information. Thus the only new topic here is the process of quantization. We shall consider this process and then consider the system performance obtainable with certain obvious methods of digital information transmission.

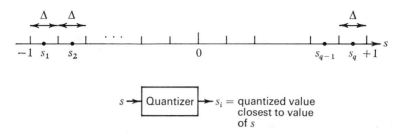

Figure 9-20   Illustration of the quantization process, assuming uniform quantization.

Quantization

In the process of quantization the random variable S obtained by sampling the message process $S(t)$ is to be represented by one of a finite number of possible values.   This process is shown in Fig. 9-20.   It has been assumed in this figure that uniform or equispaced quantization intervals are used.   The quantity Δ denotes the width of each quantization interval, q the number of such intervals, and s_i the value in the center of the interval.   If the random variable S is uniformly distributed between -1 and 1

$$f_S(s) = \begin{cases} \tfrac{1}{2} & -1 \le s \le +1 \\ 0 & \text{elsewhere} \end{cases}$$

then, since all values of the random variable are equally important, such a uniform quantization procedure is the best possible.   In this case the q intervals must each be of length

$$\Delta = \frac{2}{q} \tag{9-138}$$

If S takes on the value s, then the quantization error is $s_i - s$ in which s_i is the quantization point closest to s.   In the uniformly distributed case of q intervals of length $2/q$, the mean square quantization error is

$$\mathscr{E}_{\text{quant}} = \sum_{i=1}^{q} \int_{-\Delta/2\,=\,-1/q}^{\Delta/2\,=\,1/q} f_S(s_i + s)s^2 \, ds = \sum_{i=1}^{q} \tfrac{1}{2} \int_{-1/q}^{1/q} s^2 \, ds = \frac{1}{3q^2} \tag{9-139}$$

Even when S is not uniformly distributed, the quantization intervals are usually made equal in practice (referred to as *uniform quantization*) for ease of implementation.   It can be seen that uniform quantization does not necessarily yield the smallest average quantization error.   If, for example, S were gaussian, then it would be better to space the q quantization intervals so that the quantization was quite coarse out on the tails of S and quite fine for the values of S near the mean that occur with high probability.   In such a case a better practical solution than nonuniform quantization would be to precede a uniform quantizer with a nonlinear gain that compresses the larger values of S; such a nonlinear gain is termed a compander.   The problem of choosing this gain to minimize the average quantization error is equivalent to the problem of choosing the function $l(s)$ in Sec. 9-3.   For a discussion of this point see Algazi [7].

We now calculate the mean-square quantization error for uniform quantization and an arbitrary distribution for S:

$$\mathscr{E}_{\text{quant}} = \int_{-\infty}^{+\Delta/2} f_S(s_1 + s)s^2 \, ds + \int_{-\Delta/2}^{\infty} f_S(s_q + s)s^2 \, ds$$

$$+ \sum_{i=2}^{q-1} \int_{-\Delta/2}^{+\Delta/2} f_S(s_i + s)s^2 \, ds \qquad (9\text{-}140)$$

If the number of quantization intervals is large, then Δ, the width of the intervals, will be small enough that $f_S(s)$ is approximately constant over each interval and

$$\mathscr{E}_{\text{quant}} \approx \int_{-\infty}^{+\Delta/2} f_S(s_1 + s)s^2 \, ds + \int_{-\Delta/2}^{\infty} f_S(s_q + s)s^2 \, ds$$

$$+ \sum_{i=2}^{q-1} f_S(s_i) \int_{-\Delta/2}^{+\Delta/2} s^2 \, ds$$

$$= \int_{-\infty}^{+\Delta/2} f_S(s_1 + s)s^2 \, ds + \int_{-\Delta/2}^{\infty} f_S(s_q + s)s^2 \, ds$$

$$+ \frac{\Delta^2}{12} \sum_{i=2}^{q-1} f_S(s_i)\Delta \qquad (9\text{-}141)$$

The initial and final quantization points, s_1 and s_q, are usually picked sufficiently far out (s_1 to the left and s_q to the right) that the areas under the tails of the distribution

$$\int_{-\infty}^{-\Delta/2} f_S(s + s_1) \, ds \qquad \text{and} \qquad \int_{+\Delta/2}^{\infty} f_S(s + s_1) \, ds$$

are negligible.   Thus the errors contributed by the two tail terms in Eq. 9-141 will usually be small compared to the sum of the rest of the terms; furthermore, the sum in this equation will very nearly represent the total probability mass of the distribution, so that

$$\mathscr{E}_{\text{quant}} \approx \frac{\Delta^2}{12} = \frac{1}{3q^2} \qquad \Delta \text{ sufficiently small}; \, q \text{ sufficiently large} \quad (9\text{-}142)$$

In PCM the index of the quantized point is usually transmitted via a highly reliable digital communication system capable of transmitting one of q possible signals with a very small probability of error. Thus the quantization error discussed above is essentially the only error in such a system. This is one of the original reasons for the conception of PCM. If transmission must occur over a series of noisy transmission channels (such as over a microwave system with many repeaters), then the noise in each link would add in either a series of PAM or PPM links. However, if PCM is used and each link is capable of highly reliable digital communication, then errors do not accumulate and the quantization is the only cause of error regardless of the number of links in the system. This point will be investigated in Problem 9-20. In this context, a more important application occurs in transmission over cable systems where the distortion and slurring of a pulse by the cable is a more important limitation to high-rate pulse transmission than noise. In such a transmission system, PCM allows accurate detection and regeneration of pulses by repeaters spaced sufficiently closely that the distortion of a pulse due to transmission between one repeater and the next is tolerable. Another advantage of PCM is that, being nonlinear, it allows us to exchange bandwidth for signal-to-noise ratio. We consider this matter next.

Methods of Digital Transmission

Assuming that the message signal is sampled once every T seconds, any method of digital transmission capable of transmitting one of q possible values every T seconds may be used to transmit the value of the quantized sample. Here we will consider three methods of particular interest; the first two because they are easy to implement and thus encountered in practice and the last because it indicates the inherent performance capabilities of PCM.

Suppose we first consider transmitting a pulse of given form and duration T, the amplitude or level of the pulse being used to indicate the value of the quantized sample. Thus one might transmit

$$p_i(t) = \sqrt{3E}\, s_i \phi(t) \qquad i = 1, 2, \ldots, q \qquad (9\text{-}143)$$

in which $\phi(t)$ is a unit energy pulse of duration T. Such a system would occupy a (one-sided) bandwidth of approximtaely $1/2T$ (the same bandwidth as the message signal) if $\phi(t)$ is chosen to have minimum bandwidth occupancy. If S is uniformly distributed between -1 and $+1$, it is easily computed that the average transmitted energy is E. We assume that the quantization values s_i are spaced Δ apart as described earlier, and that $p_i(t)$ is transmitted over a single channel with additive white gaussian noise of spectral density N_0. The optimum receiver then observes the $\phi(t)$ component of the received signal and picks the quantization level closest to the value of this received component. The probability of an error in transmission is thus simply the probability that a gaussian random variable of variance N_0 falls outside the interval $\pm(\Delta/2)\sqrt{3E}$, or

$$P(A) = 2Q\left(\frac{\Delta}{2}\sqrt{\frac{3E}{N_0}}\right) \qquad (9\text{-}144)$$

This probability must be kept small for proper system operation. Since a digital error would cause a large error in the quantized sample reconstructed by the receiver, we can think of such an occurrence as an anomalous error: this is our reason for the choice of notation, $P(A)$. This transmission system is essentially just a quantized PAM system. Its behavior is considered further in Problem 9-20.

Next let us consider a system in which q, the number of quantization levels, is taken to be two raised to an integer power

$$q = 2^\gamma \qquad \gamma \text{ an integer} \qquad (9\text{-}145)$$

Describing the q possible levels can then be thought of as specifying a γ digit binary number. The T-second sample interval can be broken up into γ subintervals of duration T/γ seconds and the γ binary digits specifying the quantization level transmitted using binary signaling on each of these subintervals. This method of transmission is frequently referred to as *binary PCM*. If binary antipodal signals of energy E/γ are used (so that the energy per sample is E), the probability of an error in any given bit is

$$P(\text{bit error}) = Q\left(\sqrt{\frac{E}{\gamma N_0}}\right) \qquad (9\text{-}146)$$

The probability that one or more of the bits is in error is thus

$$P(A) = 1 - \left[1 - Q\left(\sqrt{\frac{E}{\gamma N_0}}\right)\right]^\gamma \qquad (9\text{-}147)$$

The (one-sided) bandwidth occupied by such a system is approximately $1/(2T/\gamma) = \gamma/2T$ or γ times the bandwidth occupancy of the original signal being sampled.

If the q quantized values of s_i are simply associated in sequence with the $q = 2^\gamma$ γ-digit binary numbers, then an error in one digit causes an erroneous quantized value that is almost uniformly distributed between -1 and $+1$ so that the resulting error would have an average value given approximately by Eq. 9-132

$$\mathscr{E}_{\text{large}} = \tfrac{2}{3} \qquad (9\text{-}132)$$

The total error that occurs is then the error due to quantization plus the large error that occurs when one or more of the bits is in error

$$\mathscr{E}_{\text{sq total}} = [1 - P(A)]\mathscr{E}_{\text{quant}} + P(A)\mathscr{E}_{\text{large}}$$

Substituting from Eqs. 9-132, 9-142, and 9-144 and noting that $P(A)$ will be much smaller than one, we have approximately

$$\mathscr{E}_{\text{total}} \approx \mathscr{E}_{\text{quant}} + \tfrac{2}{3}P(A) = \tfrac{1}{3}[2^{-2\gamma} + 2P(A)] \qquad (9\text{-}148)$$

Assuming again that S is uniformly distributed between -1 and 1, the output signal-to-noise ratio is just

$$\left(\frac{S}{N}\right)_o = \frac{\overline{S^2}}{\mathscr{E}_{\text{total}}} = \frac{\tfrac{1}{3}}{\mathscr{E}_{\text{total}}} = \frac{1}{[2^{-2\gamma} + 2P(A)]} \qquad (9\text{-}149)$$

Finally, substitution for $P(A)$ from Eq. 9-146 yields

$$\left(\frac{S}{N}\right)_o = \left[2^{-2\gamma} + 2 - 2\left[1 - Q\left(\sqrt{\frac{E}{N_0}}\right)\right]^{\gamma}\right]^{-1} \qquad (9\text{-}150)$$

This performance is plotted in Fig. 9-21 as a function of E/N_0 for values of γ of 5, 6, 7, and 8. It should be noted that for sufficiently large values of E/N_0 the curves simply flatten off to the value caused by quantization error. Furthermore, comparison with the PPM curves indicate substantially improved performance for binary PCM over PPM.

Now let us consider the performance that could be obtained if the type of coding considered in Sec. 8-5 were used to transmit the quantized values. If we have available a channel with average power,

$$P = \frac{E}{T} \qquad (9\text{-}151)$$

and (one-sided) bandwidth

$$W_{\text{channel}} = \gamma W = \gamma \frac{1}{2T} \qquad (9\text{-}152)$$

then Shannon's coding theorem states that it is possible to transmit in a nearly error-free manner

$$\frac{\gamma}{2T}\log_2\left(1 + \frac{E}{\gamma N_0}\right)$$

binary digits per second. This would allow

$$\frac{\gamma}{2}\log_2\left(1 + \frac{E}{\gamma N_0}\right)$$

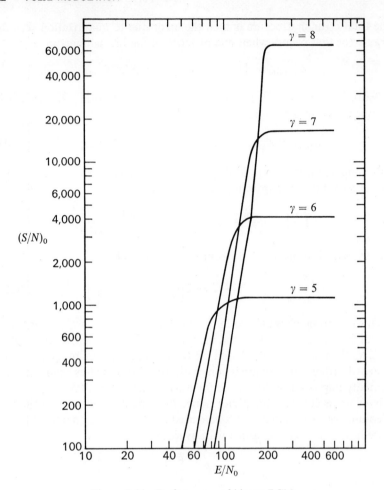

Figure 9-21   Performance of binary PCM.

binary digits per sample, or

$$q = \left(1 + \frac{E}{\gamma N_0}\right)^{\gamma/2} \tag{9-153}$$

quantization levels.   This equation, coupled with the appropriate equation giving the quantization error in terms of the number of quantization levels, yields the maximum performance that can be obtained with PCM. Assuming that the sample S is uniformly distributed, we obtain by combining Eqs. 9-139 and 9-153,

$$\mathscr{E}_{\text{quant}} = \frac{1}{3}\left(1 + \frac{E}{\gamma N_0}\right)^{-\gamma} \tag{9-154}$$

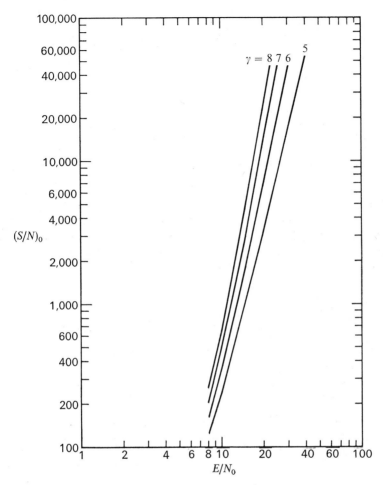

Figure 9-22   Performance of coded PCM.

or

$$\left(\frac{S}{N}\right)_o = \frac{\frac{1}{3}}{\mathscr{E}_{\text{quant}}} = \left(1 + \frac{E}{\gamma N_0}\right)^{\gamma} \tag{9-155}$$

This performance is plotted in Fig. 9-22 as a function of E/N_0 for $\gamma = 5, 6,$ 7, and 8.   It should be noted that a *single curve does not* correspond to a *single system*, since, as E/N_0 changes, the quantization level and digital signaling method must change in order to achieve error-free transmission at the quantization level given by Eq. 9-153.   It should also be pointed out that the performance of coded PCM is substantially greater than that

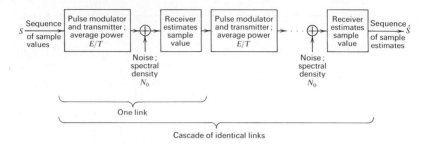

Figure 9.23   Cascade pulse modulation transmission.

of binary PCM.   The bandwidth occupancy of the system is again γ times that of the signal being sampled.

The reader interested in PCM may find the early paper by Shannon, Pierce, and Oliver [8], describing the philosophy and performance of PCM, to be of interest.

Problem 9-20.   Consider the situation shown in Fig. 9-23 in which information is transmitted over a cascade of ten identical repeater links.

(a) Assume that S is uniformly distributed between -1 and $+1$.   Consider using the quantized PAM system described in conjunction with Eqs. 9-143 and 9-144, and assume that the *average* signal-to-noise ratio in *each* link is $(E/N_0) = (16/3)10^2$.   Calculate the mean-square quantization error that results if we accept a probability of anomaly (digital error) of

(i) $P(A) = 10^{-2}$

(ii) $P(A) = 10^{-3}$

in the *cascade* system.   *Use any reasonable approximations.*

(b) Assume that PAM is used on each link and calculate the overall transmission performance.

REFERENCES

[1]   Woodward, P. M., *Probability and Information Theory, with Applications to Radar*, Pergamon Press, New York, 1953.

[2]   Kotelnikov, V. A., *The Theory of Optimum Noise Immunity*, McGraw-Hill Book Co., New York, 1959, R. A. Silverman, translator; see especially part III.

[3]   Wozencraft, J. M., and I. M. Jacobs, *Principles of Communication Engineering*, John Wiley and Sons, New York, 1965; see especially Chapter 8.

[4]   Wilks, S. S., *Mathematical Statistics*, John Wiley and Sons, New York, 1962; see especially Chapter 12.

[5] Hildebrand, F. B., *Method of Applied Mathematics*, Prentice-Hall, Englewood Cliffs, N.J., 1952; see Chapter 2.

[6] Rowe, H. E., *Signals and Noise in Communication Systems*, D. Van Nostrand, Princeton, N.J., 1965; see Chapter V.

[7] Algazi, V. R., "Useful Approximations to Optimum Quantization," *IEEE Trans. on Comm. Tech.*, **Com 14**, 297–302, June, 1966.

[8] Oliver, B. M., J. R. Pierce, and C. E. Shannon, "The Philosophy of PCM," *Proc. IRE*, **36**, 1324–1331, Nov., 1948.

Chapter 10

The Phase-Lock Loop

In Chapter 5, in discussing single-sideband modulation we assumed that we had available at the receiver a sinusoidal signal of the same frequency and phase as the carrier for synchronously demodulating the SSB signal. Again in Chapter 8, the optimum detector for reception of digital information required multiplying the received signal by exact replicas of the possible transmitted signals; this also presupposed that at the receiver the frequency and phase of the transmitter are known. In this chapter, we study a device called the phase-lock loop that can be used for tracking the phase of the carrier component of the received signal; this device thus generates a signal suitable for synchronous demodulation. Furthermore, this device can be used for demodulation of angle modulated signals (PM and FM); in the presence of strong noise, its performance as an FM demodulator surpasses that of the simple frequency-slope discriminator discussed in Sec. 6-2. The discussion of the performance of the FM discriminator demodulator in Chapter 6 was limited to the case of weak noise. Although Rice [1] has analyzed the strong noise performance of the FM discriminator, the methods of analysis are somewhat involved. In this chapter we use the relatively straightforward methods of analysis developed in Chapter 7 to determine for what values of channel signal-to-noise ratio the phase-lock loop demodulator is above threshold and the weak noise performance calculations are valid. This allows us to more completely calculate the performance of FM and PM for arbitrary message spectra. For an exhaustive treatment of the phase-lock loop, refer to Viterbi [2].

10-1 The Phase-Lock Loop and its Linear Model

We consider a received signal which, in the absence of noise, is given by

$$S(t) = \sqrt{2P} \sin [2\pi f_1 t + \Theta_1(t)] \qquad (10\text{-}1)$$

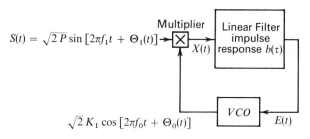

Figure 10-1 Block diagram of the phase-lock loop.

We have taken the amplitude of the sinusoid to be $\sqrt{2P}$, so that P represents the average power in the received signal. The changing phase angle $\Theta_1(t)$ may be an unwanted phase shift introduced by fluctuations in the transmission medium or by relative radial motion between the transmitter and receiver, as in transmission via a satellite. In this event we wish to track $\Theta_1(t)$ to produce a signal of the same angle or phase for synchronous demodulation purposes. If the changing phase is due to modulation by a message process, we wish to recover $\Theta_1(t)$ to estimate this message signal. The signal actually observed at the receiver will be the signal $S(t)$ plus receiver noise

$$Z(t) = S(t) + N(t) \qquad (10\text{-}2)$$

Also in this chapter, we assume that the noise $N(t)$ is a zero-mean white gaussian process. This noise will prevent perfect tracking of $\Theta_1(t)$.

Now consider the signal $S(t)$ as the input to the device shown in Fig. 10-1. This feedback system is referred to as a phase-lock loop. The device labeled VCO is a voltage-controlled oscillator which produces an output whose frequency is proportional to its input; if the input signal is denoted by $E(t)$, the output is then $\sqrt{2}\,K_1 \cos[2\pi f_0 t + \Theta_0(t)]$ in which

$$\frac{d\Theta_0(t)}{dt} = K_2 E(t) \qquad (10\text{-}3)$$

The frequency f_0 is the frequency of the oscillator with zero input. Normal design would make this frequency equal to the nominal transmitted carrier frequency. The block denoted with a cross indicates a multiplier; although good electronic multipliers are difficult to build when the two input signals are low-pass signals, it is not so difficult to build accurate multipliers for two band-pass input signals, particularly when one of the signals is of constant amplitude.

The object of the loop is to generate a VCO output which has the same phase angle (except for a fixed difference of $\pi/2$) as the input signal. Our goal is to be able to analyze the behavior of the loop in the presence of noise. Toward this end, we now consider the equations that describe the operation of the loop.

Operation of the Phase-Lock Loop

By using a standard trigonometric identity, the multiplier output $X(t)$ can be expressed as

$$X(t) = \sqrt{P}\, K_1\{\sin\,[2\pi(f_1 - f_0)t + \Theta_1(t) - \Theta_0(t)]$$
$$+ \sin\,[2\pi(f_1 + f_0)t + \Theta_1(t) + \Theta_0(t)]\} \quad (10\text{-}4)$$

The response of the linear filter to the input $X(t)$ is given simply by the appropriate convolution integral

$$E(t) = \int_{-\infty}^{t} b(t - \tau)X(\tau)\,d\tau \quad (10\text{-}5)$$

Equations 10-3, 10-4, and 10-5, describe analytically the operation of the loop. However, Eq. 10-4, relating $X(t)$ to $\Theta_1(t)$ and $\Theta_0(t)$, is non-linear. This greatly increases the difficulty of analyzing the given set of equations. It would thus be very useful to develop an approximate linear model which will be much easier to analyze and yet will give a good approximate description of the loop in certain modes of operation.

Linear Model of the Loop

To this end, let us first note that $X(t)$ consists of a double frequency term $(f_0 + f_1)$ and a difference frequency term $(f_1 - f_0)$. The filter $b(\tau)$ in the loop is a low-pass filter and its response to the double frequency term will be negligible. Thus, to a very good approximation, we could replace the filter input $X(t)$ with the input

$$X_{Lp}(t) = \sqrt{P}\, K_1 \sin\,[2\pi(f_1 - f_0)t + \Theta_1(t) - \Theta_0(t)] \quad (10\text{-}6)$$

Now, for convenience of notation, let us absorb the phase due to the difference in the transmitter frequency and the quiescent VCO frequency into a single term and denote the quantity $2\pi(f_1 - f_0)t + \Theta_1(t)$ simply by

$$\Theta(t) \triangleq 2\pi(f_1 - f_0)t + \Theta_1(t) \quad (10\text{-}7)$$

Equation 10-6 then becomes

$$X_{Lp}(t) = \sqrt{P}\, K_1 \sin\,[\Theta(t) - \Theta_0(t)] \quad (10\text{-}8)$$

As we have stated, the object of the loop is to generate a VCO output which has the same phase angle (except for the fixed difference of $\pi/2$) as the input signal.   Thus, in normal operation, $\Theta_0(t)$ would provide a good estimate of the process $\Theta(t)$:

$$\Theta_0(t) \approx \Theta(t) \qquad (10\text{-}9)$$

For small angles ϕ, $\sin \phi$ is well approximated by ϕ, the approximation being within 4.2% if the magnitude of ϕ is less than $\frac{1}{2}$ radian.   Let us thus assume that $\Theta_0(t)$ and $\Theta(t)$ are stationary, and also that

$$P\{|\Theta_{0,t} - \Theta_t| > 0.5 \text{ radian}\} < \epsilon; \qquad \epsilon \ll 1 \qquad (10\text{-}10)$$

Using the Chebyshev inequality, we know that this requirement will be satisfied if

$$E\{(\Theta_{0,t} - \Theta_t)^2\} \le \frac{\epsilon}{4} \qquad (\Theta \text{ expressed in radian measure}) \quad (10\text{-}11)$$

Under the conditions of Eq. 10-10, we can approximate Eq. 10-8 by

$$X_{Lp}(t) \approx \sqrt{P}\, K_1[\Theta(t) - \Theta_0(t)] \qquad (10\text{-}12)$$

Furthermore, our remarks about the response of the filter to the double frequency term allow us to rewrite Eq. 10-5 as

$$E(t) = \int_{-\infty}^{t} b(t - \tau) X_{Lp}(\tau)\, d\tau \qquad (10\text{-}13)$$

Equations 10-3, 10-12, and 10-13 describe a linear system which produces the signal $\Theta_0(t)$ in response to the signal $\Theta(t)$.   This system is shown in block diagram form in Fig. 10-2.

In the sections to follow, we will use the linear model of Fig. 10-2 to examine the dynamic response of the loop to different inputs, the errors in phase tracking caused by receiver noise, and the use of the loop as a demodulator.

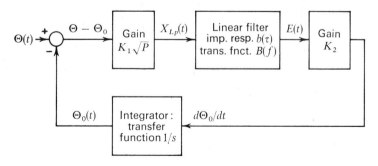

Figure 10-2   Block diagram of the approximate linear model of the phase-lock loop.

10-2   Dynamic Response of the Linear Model

When the phase-lock loop is used for synchronous demodulation of a carrier of varying phase and frequency, it must first lock-on to the input signal and then follow the angular variations of the signal. The process of locking-on is usually referred to as *acquisition* and the ensuing process is called *tracking*. In the acquisition mode, and possibly in the tracking mode, the phase error between the received carrier and VCO output will be large and the linear model of the loop will *not* be appropriate. Not only does the linear model give a poor quantitative description of the actual loop in this case, but *the loop may even exhibit some types of behavior not predicted by the linear model*. Thus our treatment in this section, which is based on the linear model, can give only a partial and imperfect idea of the dynamic behavior of the loop. For a thorough discussion of the nonlinear analysis of the loop dynamics, see Chapter 3 of Viterbi [2].

The linear model may still afford some insight into the dynamic response of the loop, for if the actual loop error eventually becomes small, this behavior must be predicted by the linear model. It is thus of interest to see for what inputs and loop filters the linear model predicts that the error response will settle to a small value. In analyzing this behavior, the final value theorem associated with the one-sided Laplace transform discussed in Sec. 2-6 is quite useful. Recall that if $x(t)$ is a time function which is identically zero for $t < 0$, and $\tilde{X}(s)$ is its Laplace transform,

$$\tilde{X}(s) = \int_{0_-}^{\infty} x(t)e^{-st}\, dt \qquad (10\text{-}14)$$

and $s\tilde{X}(s)$ has no singularities for $\sigma \geq 0$, then

$$\lim_{t \to \infty} x(t) = \lim_{s \to 0} s\tilde{X}(s) \qquad (10\text{-}15)$$

The importance of this relation is that it allows us to deduce the limiting behavior of a time function from its transform *without* having to go through the difficulty of taking the inverse transform. We will now apply this relation to study the dynamic behavior of our linear model of the phase-lock loop.

Returning to the linear model of Sec. 10-1, we note that the block diagram of Fig. 10-2 may be reduced to the form shown in Fig. 10-3 in which the single transfer function $\tilde{G}(s)$ is given by

$$\tilde{G}(s) = \sqrt{P}\, K_1 K_2 \frac{\tilde{B}(s)}{s} \qquad (10\text{-}16)$$

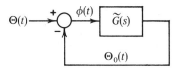

Figure 10-3   Reduced block diagram of the loop model.

In Fig. 10-3 the phase error has been denoted by the signal

$$\phi(t) = \theta(t) - \theta_0(t) \tag{10-17}$$

We assume that the signals $\theta(t)$ and $\theta_0(t)$ are Laplace transformable. The equations describing the loop of Fig. 10-3 may then be written

$$\tilde{\Theta}_0(s) = \tilde{G}(s)[\tilde{\Theta}(s) - \tilde{\Theta}_0(s)] \tag{10-18}$$

If we solve this equation for $\tilde{\Phi}(s) = \tilde{\Theta}(s) - \tilde{\Theta}_0(s)$, in terms of the input $\tilde{\Theta}(s)$, we obtain

$$\tilde{\Phi}(s) = \tilde{\Theta}(s) \frac{1}{1 + \tilde{G}(s)} \tag{10-19}$$

Substituting from Eq. 10-16, Eq. 10-19 becomes

$$\tilde{\Phi}(s) = \tilde{\Theta}(s) \frac{s}{s + \sqrt{P}\, K_1 K_2 \tilde{B}(s)} \tag{10-20}$$

Let us now consider the response of the loop to a constant offset in frequency. We take the phase angle of the received signal to be $2\pi f_1 t + \theta_1$ so that

$$\theta(t) = u(t)[2\pi(f_1 - f_0)t + \theta_1] \tag{10-21}$$

The transforms of the time functions appearing in Eq. 10-21 are easily found:

$$\mathscr{L}[u(t)] = \int_0^\infty u(t)e^{-st}\, dt = \frac{1}{s}; \qquad \sigma > 0 \tag{10-22}$$

and since

$$\frac{d}{dt}[u(t)t] = \frac{du(t)}{dt} \cdot t + u(t) = \delta(t) \cdot t + u(t) = u(t) \tag{10-23}$$

we have

$$\mathscr{L}[u(t)] = \frac{1}{s} \qquad \mathscr{L}[u(t)t] = \frac{1}{s^2} \tag{10-24}$$

Thus $\tilde{\Theta}(s)$ is given by

$$\tilde{\Theta}(s) = \frac{2\pi(f_1 - f_0)}{s^2} + \frac{\theta_1}{s} \tag{10-25}$$

Combining Eqs. 10-20 and 10-25 yields

$$\tilde{\Phi}(s) = \frac{2\pi(f_1 - f_0) + \theta_1 s}{s[s + \sqrt{P}\, K_1 K_2 \tilde{B}(s)]} \tag{10-26}$$

Let us now consider several choices of filters and investigate the behavior of $\phi(t)$. We will not be interested in finding an explicit expression for $\phi(t)$ for all time, because, as we pointed out earlier, the linear model gives an accurate description of the loop only when the phase error is small. We will thus confine ourselves to finding under what conditions and for what choices of filters the asymptotic value of the error, $\lim_{t \to \infty} \phi(t)$, becomes small.

If we first consider no filter at all, i.e., $\tilde{B}(s) = 1$, then Eq. 10-26 becomes

$$\tilde{\Phi}(s) = \frac{2\pi(f_1 - f_0) + \theta_1 s}{s[s + \sqrt{P}\, K_1 K_2]} \tag{10-27}$$

From the final value theorem we then have

$$\lim_{t \to \infty} \phi(t) = \frac{2\pi(f_1 - f_0)}{\sqrt{P}\, K_1 K_2} \tag{10-28}$$

Thus only if the initial frequency offset is sufficiently small will a loop with no filter settle to a satisfactory steady-state error.

If we consider a filter which contains an integration

$$\tilde{B}(s) = \frac{s + a}{s} \tag{10-29}$$

then the expression for $\tilde{\Phi}(s)$ becomes

$$\tilde{\Phi}(s) = \frac{2\pi(f_1 - f_0) + \theta_1 s}{s^2 + (\sqrt{P}\, K_1 K_2)(s + a)} \tag{10-30}$$

The final value theorem then yields

$$\lim_{t \to \infty} \phi(t) = 0 \tag{10-31}$$

A system with an integrating filter can thus asymptotically track a constant frequency offset with zero asymptotic error.

In reality, a perfect integrator whose input and output are dimensionally the same (such as an electrical filter whose input and output are both voltages) is impossible to realize. With actual components we might build a filter which approximated the integrating filter with a transfer function of the form

$$\tilde{B}(s) = \frac{s + a}{s + \alpha} \tag{10-32}$$

Note that the high-frequency gain of this filter is 1 so that it does not amplify high-frequency noise. For this filter we find that the final value theorem yields

$$\lim_{t \to \infty} \phi(t) = \frac{2\pi(f_1 - f_0)\alpha}{\sqrt{P} K_1 K_2 a} \qquad (10\text{-}33)$$

so that the asymptotic error is smaller by the factor α/a than a loop with no filter at all.

Problem 10-1. Consider an input in which the frequency offset increases linearly with time so that

$$\theta_1(t) = u(t)[\tfrac{1}{2}rt^2 + \theta_p]$$

This corresponds to an initial phase offset of θ_p, an initial frequency offset of $(f_1 - f_0)$, and a constant radial acceleration between the transmitter and receiver of $rc/2\pi f_1$, c being the propagation velocity of light. Find the steady-state error predicted by the linear model for the filter transfer functions of Eqs. 10-29 and 10-32 and the second-order integrating filter given by

$$\tilde{B}(s) = \frac{s^2 + as + b}{s^2} \qquad (10\text{-}34)$$

10-3   The Linear Model in the Presence of Noise

We next consider the effect of noise in the input. The situation of Fig. 10-1 now becomes changed by the presence of noise $N(t)$ in the input as shown in Fig. 10-4. We assume that the noise $N(t)$ is a zero-mean gaussian process that is independent of the phase process $\Theta_1(t)$. We also assume that $N(t)$ is the result of white noise of spectral density N_0 being passed through an r-f filter. The spectrum of $N(t)$ is thus given by

$$S_n(f) = N_0|H_{\text{rf}}(f)|^2 = N_0[|H(f + f_0)|^2 + |H^*(-f - f_0)|^2] \qquad (10\text{-}35)$$

The function $H(f)$ represents the positive frequency part of the r-f filter function translated down to 0 frequency. If we write the noise process $N(t)$ in the form

$$N(t) = \sqrt{2}\,[N_c(t) \cos 2\pi f_0 t - N_s(t) \sin 2\pi f_0 t] \qquad (10\text{-}36)$$

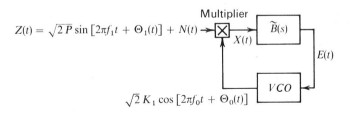

Figure 10-4   The phase-lock loop with input noise.

then, as we have seen in Sec. 5-2, the noise processes $N_c(t)$ and $N_s(t)$ are uncorrelated if $H(f)$ is symmetric about $f = 0$ and their spectral densities are given by[1]

$$S_{n_c}(f) = S_{n_s}(f) = N_0|H(f)|^2 \qquad (10\text{-}37)$$

In what follows, we assume that the gain of the r-f filter is one in its pass-band and that its pass-band is much greater than the pass-band of the loop; thus for purposes of computation, we approximate Eq. 10-37 by

$$S_{n_c}(f) = S_{n_s}(f) \approx N_0 \qquad (10\text{-}38)$$

or

$$R_{n_c}(\tau) = R_{n_s}(\tau) \approx N_0\delta(\tau) \qquad (10\text{-}39)$$

The noise processes $N_c(t)$ and $N_s(t)$ are thus independent white gaussian noise processes.

Let us now consider the output of the multiplier. On expanding the sine and cosine terms, this process is expressed as

$$X(t) = \sqrt{P}\, K_1\{\sin[\Theta(t) - \Theta_0(t)] + \sin[4\pi f_0 t + \Theta(t) + \Theta_0(t)]\}$$
$$+ K_1 N_c(t)\cos[\Theta_0(t)] - K_1 N_s(t)\sin[\Theta_0(t)]$$
$$+ K_1 N_c(t)\cos[4\pi f_0 t + \Theta_0(t)] + K_2 N_s(t)\sin[4\pi f_0 t + \Theta_0(t)]$$
$$(10\text{-}40)$$

We have already discussed the signal terms appearing in this equation; let us now focus on the noise terms. The double frequency terms will not be passed by the loop filter $B(f)$; we are thus interested in the term

$$N'(t) \triangleq N_c(t)\cos[\Theta_0(t)] - N_s(t)\sin[\Theta_0(t)] \qquad (10\text{-}41)$$

Let us note that $N_c(t)$ and $N_s(t)$ are white in the sense that $R_{n_c}(\tau)$ and $R_{n_s}(\tau)$ are virtually zero for time shifts τ greater than some time ΔT which is much, much smaller than the time constant of the loop. If we approximated the convolution denoting the response of $\tilde{B}(s)/s$ to $X(t)$ by a sum with time increments of width Δt, then $\Theta_0(t)$ would depend on $\Theta(\tau)$, $\tau \le t$, and a *large* number of *independent* random variables, $N_c(t)$, $N_c(t - \Delta T)$, $N_c(t - 2\Delta T), \ldots; N_s(t),\ N_s(t - \Delta T),\ldots$. Note that by prior assumption the processes $N_c(t)$ and $N_s(t)$ are independent of $\Theta(\tau)$. Due to the smoothing effect of the filter $B(f)$ whose time constant is much larger than ΔT, the effect on the loop and the consequent dependence of $\Theta_0(t)$ on any *single* one of these independent variables would be negligible. We thus assume that $\Theta_0(t)$ is independent of $N_c(t + \tau)$ and $N_s(t + \tau)$ for

[1] Note the factor of $\sqrt{2}$ appearing in Eq. 10-36 which was not used in the derivations in Sec. 5-2; this results in a factor of 2 not appearing in Eq. 10-37.

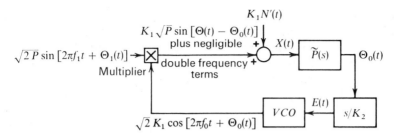

Figure 10-5   Model of the loop with an equivalent noise source inside the loop.

all τ.   From Eq. 10-41 it then follows that $N'(t)$ will be zero-mean, since $N_c(t)$ and $N_s(t)$ are both zero mean.   Furthermore, we have for the correlation function of $N'(t)$:

$$R_{n'}(\tau) = E\{[N_{c,t} \cos(\Theta_{0,t}) - N_{s,t} \sin(\Theta_{0,t})]$$
$$\times [N_{c,t+\tau} \cos(\Theta_{0,t+\tau}) - N_{s,t+\tau} \sin(\Theta_{0,t+\tau})]\}$$
$$= R_{n_c}(\tau)E\{\cos(\Theta_{0,t}) \cos(\Theta_{0,t+\tau})\} + R_{n_s}(\tau)E\{\sin(\Theta_{0,t}) \sin(\Theta_{0,t+\tau})\}$$
$$+ R_{n_c n_s}(\tau)E\{\cos(\Theta_{0,t}) \sin(\Theta_{0,t+\tau}) + \cos(\Theta_{0,t+\tau}) \sin(\Theta_{0,t})\}$$

Recognizing that $R_{n_c}(\tau) = R_{n_s}(\tau) = N_0\delta(t)$ and that $N_c(t)$ and $N_s(t)$ are independent, this expression for $R_{n'}(\tau)$ becomes

$$R_{n'}(\tau) = N_0\delta(\tau) \qquad (10\text{-}42)$$

The response of $\tilde{B}(s)$ to $X(t)$ is virtually equal to the response of $\tilde{B}(s)$ to the low-pass terms in $X(t)$; namely, the terms due to the noise process $N'(t)$ discussed above and the sine of the difference angle:

$$X_{Lp}(t) = \sqrt{P}\,K_1 \sin[\Theta(t) - \Theta_0(t)] + K_1N'(t) \qquad (10\text{-}43)$$

The phase-lock loop of Fig. 10-4 with noise in the input may thus be modeled by the block diagram shown in Fig. 10-5.   In this schematic diagram we have factored the filter $\tilde{B}(s)$ into two terms

$$\tilde{B}(s) = \tilde{P}(s)(s/K_2) \qquad (10\text{-}44)$$

The reason for this separation will soon become clear.

Let us now focus our attention on the mode of operation in which $\Theta_0(t)$ is accurately tracking $\Theta(t)$ so that the condition of Eq. 10-10 is satisfied. We may then approximate $\sin[\Theta(t) - \Theta_0(t)]$ by $\Theta(t) - \Theta_0(t)$; making this approximation and following the same procedure used in Sec. 10-1, the model of Fig. 10-5 may be replaced by the linear block diagram model of Fig. 10-6a.   Since we are not interested analytically in the variable $E(t)$, we may do away with this variable in our model.   Moreover, since the loop of Fig. 10-6a is linear, the noise source may be moved to the input of the loop.   These changes are shown in the model of Fig. 10-6b. Finally, the model of Fig. 10-6b may be replaced by the equivalent model of Fig. 10-6c in which a feedback loop does not appear explicitly.

This last model will allow us to consider the design of the loop to minimize the tracking error when $\Theta_1(t)$ is a random process.   Let us assume that $\Theta_1(t)$ is a stationary random process with known spectral

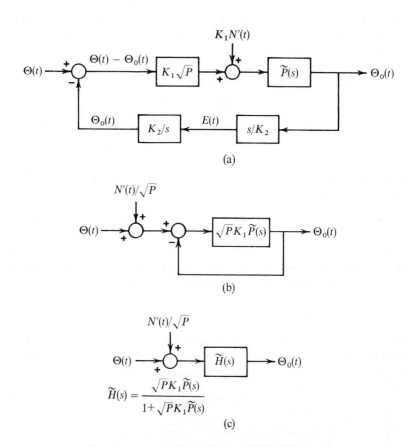

(a)

(b)

$$\tilde{H}(s) = \frac{\sqrt{P}K_1\tilde{P}(s)}{1+\sqrt{P}K_1\tilde{P}(s)}$$

(c)

Figure 10-6   Linear model of the loop with input noise:
(a) Linear model with noise in the loop.
(b) Linear model with noise in the input.
(c) Equivalent open loop system.

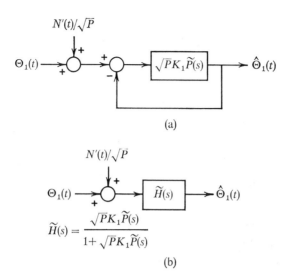

(a)

(b)

Figure 10-7 Loop model showing only the modulation term in the input:
(a) Feedback model.
(b) Equivalent open loop model.

density $S_{\theta_1}(f)$. If the transmitter carrier frequency is f_1 and the zero input VCO frequency f_0, then $\Theta(t)$ is given by

$$\Theta(t) = \Theta_1(t) + 2\pi(f_1 - f_0)t \qquad t > 0 \qquad (10\text{-}45)$$

in which we assume that the loop is turned on at $t = 0$. Note that $\Theta(t)$ is *not* a stationary process. However, we can split the input to our linear model into two components, $\Theta_1(t) + N'(t)/\sqrt{P}$ and $2\pi(f_1 - f_0)t$. Since the model is linear, the response to these two signals can be computed separately and $\Theta_0(t)$ is their sum. Let $\hat{\Theta}_1(t)$ denote the response of the model to $\Theta_1(t) + N'(t)/\sqrt{P}$ and $\theta_2(t)$ the response to $2\pi(f_1 - f_0)t$. The signal $\hat{\Theta}_1(t)$ will be the response of the model to the stationary process $\Theta_1(t) + N'(t)/\sqrt{P}$ and hence (ignoring starting loop transients) a stationary process. The signal $\theta_2(t)$ will be a deterministic signal which can be calculated by the methods discussed in Sec. 10-1. If $\Theta_1(t)$ and $N'(t)$ are zero-mean processes, then the mean-square error in the phase, $\Theta(t) - \Theta_0(t)$, will be given by

$$E\{(\Theta_t - \Theta_{0,t})^2\} = E\{(\Theta_{1,t} - \hat{\Theta}_{1,t})^2\} + [2\pi(f_1 - f_0)t - \theta_2(t)]^2 \qquad (10\text{-}46)$$

In order for the linear model to be valid, the sum of these two terms would have to be of the order of $(\tfrac{1}{2}$ radian$)^2$ or less. If our interest were in

$\Theta_1(t)$ (because it represented a message-bearing signal), the signal $\hat{\Theta}_1(t)$ could be obtained from $E(t) = (1/K_2)(d\Theta_0/dt)$, the VCO input. Since after the loop transients die out the signal $\theta_2(t)$ is a constant, $E(t)$ will approach $(1/K_2)(d\hat{\Theta}_1(t)/dt)$. This signal could be then multiplied by K_2 and integrated to obtain $\hat{\Theta}_1(t)$.

In calculating $\Theta_1(t) - \hat{\Theta}_1(t)$, the situation is the same as shown in Figs. 10-6b and 10-6c except that the input and output are now $\Theta_1(t)$ and $\hat{\Theta}_1(t)$, respectively. For clarity this situation is shown in Fig. 10-7.

In designing a filter $\tilde{P}(s)$ or $\tilde{H}(s)$, we want the design to minimize the sum of the two terms on the right-hand side of Eq. 10-46. When the system is used as a demodulator in an angle modulation transmission system, the frequency offset would be carefully controlled so that the second term would be the less important. In the following section we consider the loop as a demodulator in an angle modulation system and consider designing the filter to minimize the term $E\{(\Theta_{1,t} - \hat{\Theta}_{1,t})^2\}$.

10-4   The Phase-Lock Loop as a Demodulator

In this section we consider the mean-square error obtained when the phase-lock loop is used as a demodulator for angle modulation. We assume that frequency offset errors are negligible, and thus consider design of the loop to minimize only the error in tracking the message portion of the phase

$$\mathcal{E}_{\theta_1} = E\{(\Theta_{1,t} - \hat{\Theta}_{1,t})^2\} \qquad (10\text{-}47)$$

Let us first remark that regardless of the form of angle modulation used, PM, FM, or FM with pre-emphasis, the loop must still track the phase accurately and keep the error $\mathcal{E}_{\theta_1}$ small so that the loop operates in the linear mode. We thus consider design of the loop filter $\tilde{H}(s)$ [or equivalently $\tilde{P}(s)$] to minimize $\mathcal{E}_{\theta_1}$. Should the message not be strictly proportional to $\Theta_1(t)$, the phase-lock loop can be followed by another filter to recover the desired message process.

We note from Fig. 10-7b that designing the loop filter is equivalent to designing the filter $\tilde{H}(s)$ to estimate $\Theta_1(t)$ from the observed process $\Theta_1(t) + N'(t)/\sqrt{P}$, in which the noise $N'(t)$ is independent of the phase $\Theta_1(t)$ and has spectral density

$$S_{n'}(f) \equiv N_0 \qquad (10\text{-}48)$$

The quantity N_0 is also the spectral density of the noise at the input to the r-f stage of the receiver. Note that the filter $\tilde{H}(s)$ must be causal since it must be realizable in the form of the feedback loop of Fig. 10-7a. This situation is thus exactly the one to which Eqs. 7-89 and 7-90 are applicable. Noting only the factor of $1/\sqrt{P}$ in the noise term, these expressions can be directly applied in the present situation

$$\tilde{H}_0(s) = 1 - \frac{\sqrt{N_0/P}}{[(N_0/P) + \tilde{S}_{\theta_1}(s)]^+} \qquad (10\text{-}49)$$

and

$$\mathscr{E}_{\theta_1} = \frac{N_0}{P} \int_{-\infty}^{\infty} \ln\left[1 + PS_{\theta_1}(f)/N_0\right] df \qquad (10\text{-}50)$$

The filter $\tilde{P}(s)$ appearing in the phase-lock loop can be expressed directly in terms of $\tilde{H}_0(s)$, since the relationship between the feedback system and its open loop equivalent is

$$\tilde{P}(s) = (1/\sqrt{P}\, K_1) \frac{\tilde{H}_0(s)}{1 - \tilde{H}_0(s)} \qquad (10\text{-}51)$$

Substituting from Eq. 10-49 into Eq. 10-51 yields

$$\tilde{P}(s) = (1/K_1\, \sqrt{P}) \frac{[(N_0/P) + \tilde{S}_{\theta_1}(s)]^+}{\sqrt{N_0/P}} \qquad (10\text{-}52)$$

thus $\tilde{P}(s)$ is a stable, causal filter, as it must be since it appears in a real-time feedback loop.

The expression of Eq. 10-50 giving the mean-square error for the loop is very useful, for it provides a way of determining under what conditions Eq. 10-10 is satisfied and the loop is operating in a linear manner. Linear operation will require

$$\mathscr{E}_{\theta_1} \leq \mathscr{E}_c \qquad (10\text{-}53)$$

in which $\mathscr{E}_c$ is a suitable small value. Van Trees [3] reports that the threshold region dividing satisfactory and unsatisfactory loop operation occurs in the range $\mathscr{E}_c = 0.16$ to 0.33 (radians/sec)^2.

Problem 10-2. Let

$$S_{\theta_1}(f) = \frac{\beta^2}{2\pi} \frac{2f_0}{f^2 + f_0^2}$$

Note that the corresponding correlation function is

$$R_{\theta_1}(\tau) = \beta^2 e^{-2\pi f_0 |\tau|}$$

Use Eq. 10-49 to find $\tilde{H}_0(s)$ and then solve for the corresponding closed loop filter, $\tilde{B}(s) = s\tilde{P}(s)/K_2$.

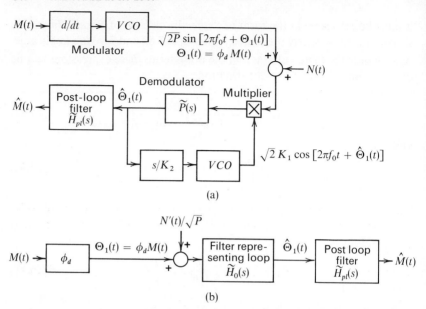

(a)

(b)

Figure 10-8   (a) Block diagram of phase modulation transmission system.
(b) Equivalent linear model of the phase transmission system.

Phase Modulation

We now consider the performance of phase modulation. The block diagram of the complete transmission system is shown in Fig. 10-8a and an equivalent linear model showing only the signals of direct interest is given in Fig. 10-8b.

We assume that the message process $M(t)$ is normalized so that it has unit power

$$E\{M_t^2\} = R_m(0) = \int_{-\infty}^{\infty} S_m(f)\, df = 1 \qquad (10\text{-}54)$$

If the modulation index is denoted by ϕ_d, the phase of the transmitted signal is

$$\Theta_1(t) = \phi_d M(t) \qquad (10\text{-}55)$$

The one-sided r.m.s. bandwidth occupancy is, from Eq. 6-54

$$[\overline{f_G^2}]^{1/2} = \left(\frac{\phi_d}{2\pi}\right)[R_m''(0)]^{1/2}$$

$$= \phi_d\left[\int_{-\infty}^{\infty} f^2 S_m(f)\, df\right]^{1/2} \qquad (10\text{-}56)$$

Under the assumption of Eq. 10-54 that the power is normalized so that $R_m(0) = 1$, the term in brackets is just the r.m.s. bandwidth of the message. Thus the r.m.s. bandwidth occupancy about $f = \pm f_0$ is

$$[\overline{f_G^2}]^{1/2} = \phi_d \cdot \text{r.m.s. bandwidth of the message} \qquad (10\text{-}57)$$

The post-loop filter, $\tilde{H}_{pl}(s)$, operates on $\hat{\Theta}_1(t)$ to yield $\hat{M}(t)$, an estimate of the message process $M(t)$. If $\tilde{H}_{pl}(s)$ is to be causal, then since $\hat{\Theta}_1(t)$ is the best causal linear estimate of $\Theta_1(t) = \phi_d M(t)$, $\tilde{H}_{pl}(s)$ is simply

$$\tilde{H}_{pl\,\text{causal}}(s) = 1/\phi_d \qquad (10\text{-}58)$$

and the mean-square error in the message estimate is

$$\mathscr{E}_{m\,\text{causal}} = E\{(M_t - \hat{M}_t)^2\} = (1/\phi_d)^2 \mathscr{E}_{\theta_1} \qquad (10\text{-}59)$$

It is of interest to calculate the performance for the set of Butterworth message-spectra

$$S_m(f, k) = \frac{(k/\pi f_0)\sin(\pi/2k)}{1 + (f/f_0)^{2k}} \qquad (10\text{-}60)$$

considered in Sec. 7-5. By identifying ϕ_d with β, and N_0/P with N_0, we can directly make use of Eqs. 7-95 and 7-96 to calculate $\mathscr{E}_{\theta_1}$

$$\mathscr{E}_{\theta_1,\,\text{causal}}(k) = \frac{2\pi f_0 N_0}{P \sin(\pi/2K)} \left[\left(1 + \frac{kP\phi_d^2 \sin(\pi/2k)}{\pi N_0 f_0}\right)^{1/2k} - 1\right] \qquad (10\text{-}61)$$

$$\mathscr{E}_{\theta_1,\,\text{causal}}(\infty) = 2f_0 N_0/P - \ln[1 + \phi_d^2 P/2N_0 f_0] \qquad (10\text{-}62)$$

Since the message power was taken to be unity, the output signal-to-noise ratio is given by

$$\left(\frac{S}{N}\right)_o = \frac{E\{M_t^2\}}{\mathscr{E}_{m\,\text{causal}}} = \frac{\phi_d^2}{\mathscr{E}_{\theta_1\,\text{causal}}} \qquad (10\text{-}63)$$

Using Eqs. 10-61, 10-62, and 10-63, $(S/N)_o$ has been plotted for $k = 1$ and $k = \infty$ in Figs. 10-9 and 10-10 respectively; $(S/N)_o$ is shown for various values of ϕ_d as a function of the channel signal-to-noise ratio,

$$\left(\frac{S}{N}\right)_o = \frac{P}{2f_0 N_0} \qquad (10\text{-}64)$$

This signal-to-noise ratio is just the modulated signal power divided by the noise power in a band of one-sided bandwidth f_0. The dashed lines on the figures indicate the region where threshold occurs ($\mathscr{E}_{\theta_1} = 0.16 - 0.33$). The solid curves for $(S/N)_o$ are not plotted to the left of these dashed lines since for lower values of channel signal-to-noise ratio the linear model of the loop is no longer valid and performance deteriorates rapidly below the value given by Eqs. 10-61, 10-62, and 10-63.

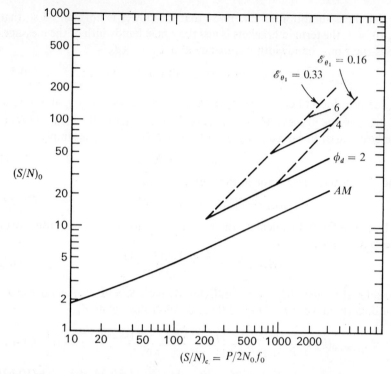

Figure 10-9   Performance of PM; first-order spectrum, causal filter.

In Fig. 10-9, the performance of an AM system has been plotted for comparison. Noting the remarks following Problem 7-11, it is easily shown that the performance for AM is the same as that for PM with $\phi_d = 1$, the only distinction being that for AM with synchronous demodulation there is no threshold.

If we are willing to tolerate a delay in the system, the post-loop filter is not simply a gain of $(1/\phi_d)$. From Fig. 10-8b, we see that the cascade $\phi_d \tilde{H}_0(s)\tilde{H}_{pl}(s)$ should be the optimum filter with delay for filtering $M(t)$ from the noise $N'(t)/\phi_d\sqrt{P}$. If we allow the delay to become long compared to the "correlation time" of $M(t)$, the time over which $R_m(\tau)$ is non-negligible, then the performance will be virtually the same as that of the noncausal filter discussed in Sec. 7-3. The resulting mean-square error is easily calculated from Eq. 7-97 by noting that the observed signal can be considered to be $M(t) + N'(t)/\phi_d\sqrt{P}$ and then associating N_0 with $N_0/\phi_d^2 P$. The result is

$$\mathscr{E}_{m,\infty \text{ lag}}(k) = \left[\frac{P\phi_d^2 \sin(\pi/2k)}{f_0 N_0 \pi/k} + 1 \right]^{-1 + 1/2k} \tag{10-65}$$

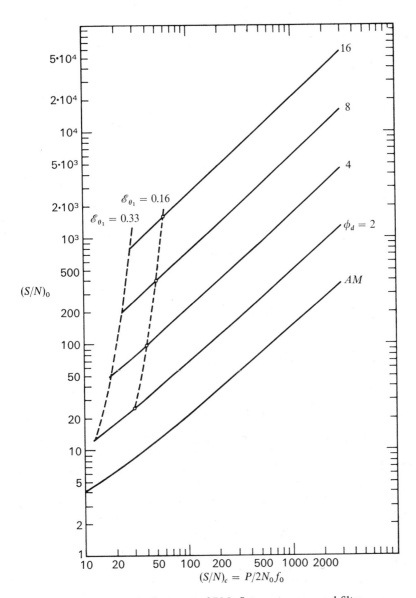

Figure 10-10   Performance of PM; flat spectrum, causal filter.

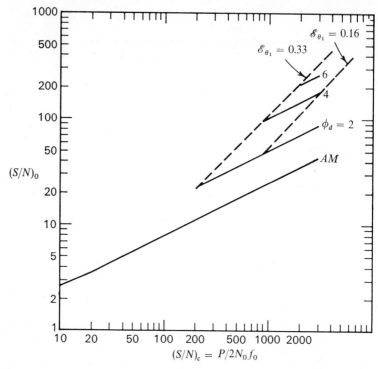

Figure 10-11   Performance of PM: First-order spectrum, infinite lag or noncausal filter.

The output signal-to-noise ratio is then simply

$$\left(\frac{S}{N}\right)_o = \frac{1}{\mathscr{E}_{m,\infty \, \text{lag}}(k)} = \left[\frac{P\phi_d^2 \sin{(\pi/2k)}}{2f_0 N_0 \pi/2k} + 1\right]^{1-1/2k} \tag{10-66}$$

This performance is plotted in Figs. 10-11 and 10-12, using the same format as Figs. 10-9 and 10-10.   Again, these calculated values are only valid to the right of the threshold curves $\mathscr{E}_{\theta_1} = 0.16 - 0.33$.   Since the loop filter must be causal, these values of $\mathscr{E}_{\theta_1}$ are not affected by the use of a noncausal post-loop filter.   The performance of AM using an infinite lag filter is drawn in for comparison.   In comparing Figs. 10-9 through 10-12, notice that the performance of the infinite lag filter is superior to that of the causal filter by a factor of approximately 2 for the first-order spectrum and approximately 10 for the flat spectrum.

Frequency Modulation

Figure 10-13a shows a frequency modulation transmission system and Fig. 10-13b shows the equivalent linear model.   In analyzing the

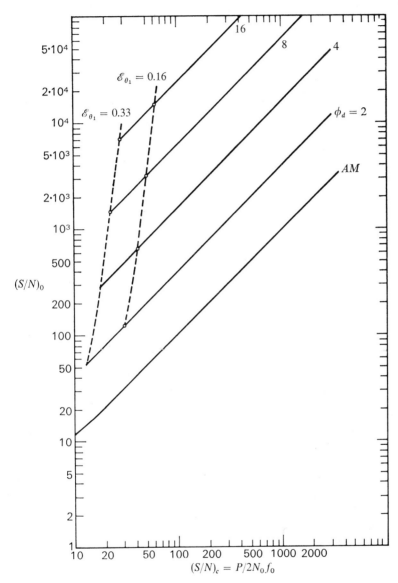

Figure 10-12   Performance of PM: Flat spectrum, infinite lag or noncausal filter.

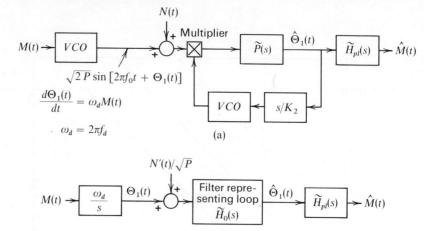

Figure 10-13   (a) Block diagram of an FM transmission system.
(b) Equivalent open-loop linear model.

performance of the FM system, we must again evaluate $\mathscr{E}_{\theta_1}$ by using the optimum loop filter, and $\mathscr{E}_m$ by using an optimum post-loop filter.   The quantity $\mathscr{E}_m$ or $(S/N)_o = 1/\mathscr{E}_m$ gives us a measure of the system performance when the constraint

$$\mathscr{E}_{\theta_1} \leq \mathscr{E}_c \approx 0.16 - 0.33 \qquad (10\text{-}67)$$

is satisfied.

In FM we encounter a mathematical difficulty not encountered in PM. The process $\Theta_1(t)$ is the response of a perfect integrator to the process $M(t)$.   It can be verified by simple calculation that if $\Theta_1(t)$ is the response of an ideal integrator that is "turned on" at $t = 0$ and whose input is a stationary random process, then $E\{\Theta_{1,t}^2\}$ increases indefinitely with time for certain input correlation functions.   In such an instance $\Theta_1(t)$ is not stationary, and the simple and useful theory that we have built up for filtering stationary processes is not valid.

Problem 10-3.   Let $X(t)$ be zero mean and wide sense stationary.   Let

$$Y(t) = \begin{cases} 0 & t < 0 \\ \int_0^t X(\tau)\, d\tau & t > 0 \end{cases}$$

and

$$\sigma_T^2 = E\{Y_T^2\}$$

(a) Show that

$$\sigma_T^2 = 2 \int_0^T dt \int_0^t d\tau R_x(\tau)$$

(b) Evaluate σ_T^2 for

$$R_x(\tau) = e^{-|\tau|} \leftrightarrow \frac{1}{(2\pi f)^2 + 1} = S_x(f)$$

Does σ_T^2 approach a limit as $T \to \infty$?

(c) Repeat (b) for

$$R_x(\tau) = e^{-|\tau|}(1 - |\tau|) \leftrightarrow \frac{4(2\pi f)^2}{[(2\pi f)^2 + 1]^2} = S_x(f)$$

The easiest way to resolve the difficulty arising from the nonstationarity of $\Theta_1(t)$ is to confine our attention to those message processes which lead to stationary phase processes. The result illustrated in Problem 10-3 can be generalized. If the spectrum of $M(t)$ goes to zero as f goes to zero, then $\Theta_1(t)$ will have a finite mean-square value and can be considered a stationary process once the transient terms in the integrator response die out. The fact that these spectra go to zero for f approaching zero does not prevent them from being useful models for message spectra. To the contrary, any message process that has been passed through an R-C coupled amplifier with d-c blocking capacitors will have this property. We consider the performance of FM for the two message spectra

$$S_{m_1}(f) = \frac{1}{2\pi} \frac{2f_0 f^2}{(f^2 + f_i^2)(f^2 + f_0^2)} \tag{10-68}$$

and

$$S_{m_\infty}(f) = \begin{cases} \dfrac{1}{2f_0} \dfrac{f^2}{f^2 + f_i^2} & |f| \le f_0 \\ 0 & |f| > f_0 \end{cases} \tag{10-69}$$

The constants in these spectra have been chosen such that for $f_i \ll f_0$, the integrated power is nearly one. The phase spectra corresponding to these two message spectra are respectively

$$S_{\theta_1}(f, 1) = \frac{1}{2\pi} \frac{2f_d^2 f_0}{(f^2 + f_i^2)(f^2 + f_0^2)} \tag{10-70}$$

and

$$S_{\theta_1}(f, \infty) = \begin{cases} \dfrac{1}{2f_0} \dfrac{f_d^2}{(f^2 + f_i^2)} & |f| \le f_0 \\ 0 & |f| > f_0 \end{cases} \tag{10-71}$$

We now proceed to consider the minimum phase error $\mathscr{E}_{\theta_1}$ that results from optimizing the loop filter. We are interested in the case in which $f_i \ll f_0$. Although we require $f_i > 0$ in order that the variance of $\Theta_{1,t}$ does not grow with time, $\mathscr{E}_{\theta_1}$ approaches a finite limiting value as f_i approaches zero. It is this limiting value that we calculate.

Let us consider $\mathscr{E}_{\theta_1}(\infty)$ first. Substituting from Eq. 10-71 into Eq. 10-50 yields

$$\mathscr{E}_{\theta_1}(\infty) = \frac{N_0}{P} \int_{-f_0}^{f_0} \ln\left[1 + \frac{P f_d^2}{2 f_0 N_0 (f^2 + f_i^2)}\right] df \tag{10-72}$$

Problem 10-4. Show, using the hint in Problem 7-10, that for $f_i = 0$ the integral in Eq. 10-72 can be evaluated as

$$\lim_{f_i \to 0} \mathscr{E}_{\theta_1}(\infty) = \frac{4 f_0 N_0}{P} \left[\sqrt{c} \tan^{-1} (1/\sqrt{c}) + \tfrac{1}{2} \ln (c + 1) \right] \tag{10-73}$$

in which

$$c = \frac{P}{2 f_0 N_0} \left(\frac{f_d}{f_0} \right)^2 \tag{10-74}$$

We next turn to the spectrum of Eq. 10-68. Unfortunately, we cannot directly evaluate the integral occurring in Eq. 10-50 for this spectrum and we must actually find $\tilde{H}_0(s)$ and use Eq. 7-87. Substituting into Eq. 10-49, after some unpleasant algebra we obtain

$$\tilde{H}_0(s) = \frac{(q_{11} + q_{21} - \omega_l - \omega_0)s + q_{11}q_{21} - \omega_l \omega_0}{s^2 + (q_{11} + q_{21})s + q_{11}q_{21}} \tag{10-75}$$

in which $\omega_l = 2\pi f_l$, $\omega_0 = 2\pi f_0$, $\omega_d = 2\pi f_d$, and q_{11} and q_{21} are respectively the left-hand-plane square roots of

$$(q_1)^2 = \frac{\omega_0{}^2 + \omega_l{}^2}{2} - \sqrt{\frac{(\omega_0{}^2 - \omega_l{}^2)^2}{4} - \frac{2\omega_0 \omega_d{}^2 P}{N_0}} \tag{10-76}$$

and

$$(q_2)^2 = \frac{\omega_0{}^2 + \omega_l{}^2}{2} + \sqrt{\frac{(\omega_0{}^2 - \omega_l{}^2)^2}{4} - \frac{2\omega_0 \omega_d{}^2 P}{N_0}} \tag{10-77}$$

Substitution from Eq. 10-75 into Eq. 7-87 yields

$$\mathscr{E}_{\theta_1}(1) = \frac{2\omega_0 \omega_d{}^2}{2\pi j} \int_{-j\infty}^{j\infty} F(s)F(-s)\, ds + \frac{N_0}{P} \frac{1}{2\pi j} \int_{-j\infty}^{j\infty} G(s)G(-s)\, ds \tag{10-78}$$

in which

$$F(s) = \frac{1}{s^2 + (q_{11} + q_{21})s + q_{11}q_{21}} \tag{10-79}$$

and

$$G(s) = \frac{(q_{11} + q_{21} - \omega_l - \omega_0)s + q_{11}q_{21} - \omega_l \omega_0}{s^2 + (q_{11} + q_{21})s + q_{11}q_{21}} \tag{10-80}$$

Evaluating the integrals in Eq. 10-78 from the tables in Appendix E of reference [4] and letting $\omega_l = 0$ yields

$$\mathscr{E}_{\theta_1}(1) = \frac{2\omega_0 \omega_d{}^2 + \tfrac{1}{2}(N_0/P)[q_{11} + q_{21} - \omega_0]^2 \sqrt{2\omega_0 \omega_d{}^2 P/N_0}}{\sqrt{2\omega_0 \omega_d{}^2 P/N_0}(q_{11} + q_{21})} \tag{10-81}$$

$$\omega_l = 0$$

If

$$\frac{2}{\pi} c \geq 1 \tag{10-82}$$

then $(q_{11} + q_{21})$ can be evaluated explicitly. In this event, Eq. 10-81 can be expressed as

$$\mathscr{E}_{\theta_1}(1) = \frac{\pi}{2} \frac{2N_0 f_0}{P} \frac{2\sqrt{2c/\pi} + [\sqrt{2\sqrt{2c/\pi} + 1} - 1]^2}{\sqrt{2\sqrt{2c/\pi} + 1}} \tag{10-83}$$

In these two equations, c is again the quantity given by Eq. 10-74. It is of interest to interpret the quantity c in terms of quantities of direct physical meaning. We note from Eq. 6-59 that since $R_m(0) = 1$, the quantity f_d is just the r.m.s. bandwidth occupancy of the modulated signal about $f = \pm f_0$. From Eq. 10-74 we see that

$$c = \left(\frac{S}{N}\right)_c \left(\frac{f_d}{f_0}\right)^2 \tag{10-84}$$

The term f_d/f_0 is the ratio of the r.m.s. bandwidth of the transmitted signal to the bandwidth of the message signal. The other term appearing in this expression for c is the ratio of the transmitted power to the power of the channel noise in a band of one-sided bandwidth f_0; this is the quantity that we have previously referred to as the channel signal-to-noise ratio

$$\left(\frac{S}{N}\right)_c = \frac{P}{2N_0 f_0} \tag{10-85}$$

Equations 10-73 and 10-83 give the mean-square phase tracking error of the loop for the spectra of interest. We now turn to design of the post-loop filter and the value of the message error. From Fig. 10-13b, we see that we are faced with the problem of observing

$$X(t) = \Theta_1(t) + N'(t)/\sqrt{P} \tag{10-86}$$

and estimating

$$S(t) = \frac{1}{\omega_d} \frac{d}{dt} \Theta_1(t) = M(t) \tag{10-87}$$

Thus the spectra appearing in the formulation of the Wiener filter are

$$S_x(f) = [N_0/P + S_{\theta_1}(f)] \tag{10-88}$$

$$S_{sx}(f) = \frac{jf}{f_d} S_{\theta_1}(f) \tag{10-89}$$

We consider only the case in which the post-loop filter is noncausal. In this case we want the cascade of the loop and post-loop filters to have the transfer function

$$\frac{S_{sx}(f)}{S_x(f)} = \frac{jfS_{\theta_1}(f)}{f_d[N_0/P + S_{\theta_1}(f)]} \tag{10-90}$$

The post-loop filter is thus given by

$$H_{pl}(f) = \frac{jfS_{\theta_1}(f)}{f_d[N_0/P + S_{\theta_1}(f)]H_0(f)} \tag{10-91}$$

in which $H_0(f)$ represents the closed-loop transfer function of the phase-lock loop.   The mean-square error

$$\mathscr{E}_{m,\infty\,\text{lag}} = E\{(M_t - \hat{M}_t)^2\}$$

involved in using the optimum unrealizable filter can be evaluated from Eq. 7-83.

Problem 10-5.   Evaluate Eq. 7-83 for the spectrum $S_{m_1}(f)$ of Eq. 10-68 and show that for $f_l \to 0$ and $(8c/\pi) > 1$ the corresponding output signal-to-noise ratio is given by

$$\left(\frac{S}{N}\right)_o = \frac{1}{\mathscr{E}_{m,\infty\,\text{lag}}(1)} = \left[\sqrt{\frac{8c}{\pi}} + 1\right]^{1/2} \tag{10-92}$$

Problem 10-6.   Evaluate Eq. 7-83 for the spectrum $S_{m_\infty}(f)$ of Eq. 10-69 and show that for $f_l \to 0$ the corresponding output signal-to-noise ratio is given by

$$\left(\frac{S}{N}\right)_o = \frac{1}{\mathscr{E}_{m,\infty\,\text{lag}}(\infty)} = \frac{1}{1 - \sqrt{c}\,\tan^{-1}(1/\sqrt{c})} \tag{10-93}$$

Equations 10-83 and 10-92 describe the performance of an FM system for the message spectrum $S_{m_1}(f)$.   Figure 10-14 shows $(S/N)_o$ plotted versus $(S/N)_c$ for various values of (f_d/f_0).   The dashed lines again indicate the loop threshold region where $0.16 \le \mathscr{E}_{\theta_1} \le 0.33$.   Equations 10-73 and 10-93 similarly describe the performance for the message spectrum $S_{m_\infty}(f)$ and this performance is plotted in Fig. 10-15 in the same format as Fig. 10-14.   In both figures the performance of an AM system with infinite lag is plotted for comparison by making use of the results of Problem 7-11.   In comparing Figs. 10-11, 10-12, 10-14, and 10-15, we note that for either AM, PM, or FM the system is markedly superior for the flat spectrum than for the first-order spectrum.   For the first-order spectrum, the performance of the PM system is noticeably superior to that of the FM system, whereas for the flat spectrum the converse is true.

Our treatment of angle modulation in this chapter has considerably extended the discussion in Chapter 6 in several important respects.   First, the demodulator considered here, the phase-lock loop, is useful as a demodulator for arbitrary angle modulation, including PM, FM, or FM with pre-emphasis.   In contrast, the discriminator of Chapter 6 was useful only for FM or FM with pre-emphasis.   Second, the phase-lock loop has better performance than the discriminator in the sense that its threshold occurs at a lower level of channel signal-to-noise ratio.   Third, and perhaps most important, we were able to calculate where threshold occurs for the phase-lock loop demodulator.   Finally, by making use of the background of Chapter 7, we extended our discussion of performance to arbitrary message spectra.

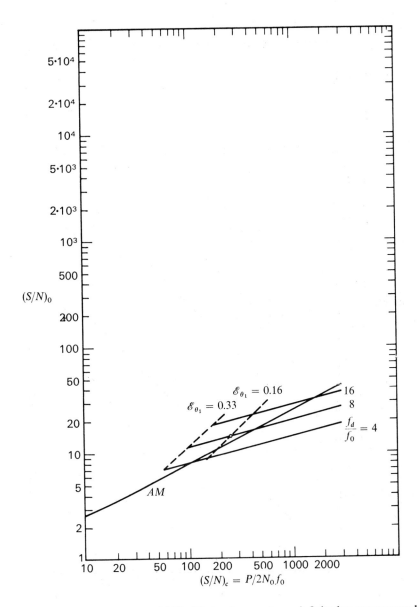

Figure 10-14   Performance of FM: First-order spectrum, infinite lag or noncausal filter.

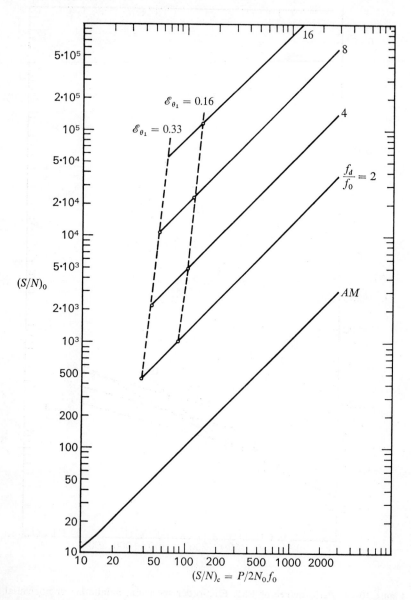

Figure 10-15   Performance of FM: Flat spectrum, infinite lag or noncausal filter.

Problem 10-7. For the spectrum $S_{m_\infty}(f)$, find the best output signal-to-noise ratio that can be obtained with FM, assuming that the post-loop filter is noncausal and $f_i = 0$. Do this for the four cases determined by:

(a) The r.m.s. bandwidth of the modulated signal about the carrier frequency $\pm f_0$ must be $\leq 8f_0$.

(b) No constraint on the bandwidth of the modulated signal.

For both (a) and (b) consider the values of channel signal-to-noise ratio given by

(i) $P/2N_0 f_0 = 40$

(ii) $P/2N_0 f_0 = 60$

Assume that the condition for satisfactory loop operation is $\mathscr{E}_{\theta_1} \leq 0.33$.

REFERENCES

[1] Rice, S. O., "Noise in FM Receivers," Chap. 25 in *Time Series Analysis*, M. Rosenblatt, Ed., John Wiley and Sons, New York, 1963.

[2] Viterbi, A. J., *Principles of Coherent Communication*, McGraw-Hill Book Co., New York, 1966; see especially Chaps. 1 through 6.

[3] Boardman, C. J. and H. L. Van Trees, "Optimum Angle Modulation," *IEEE Trans. on Communication Technology*, **COM 13**, No. 4, 452–469, Dec. 1965.

[4] Newton, G., L. Gould, and J. Kaiser, *Analytic Design of Linear Feedback Systems*, John Wiley and Sons, New York, 1958; see Appendix E.

Appendix I

Matrix Notation

In handling linear transformations of vectors or equivalently in describing sets of linear equations, it is extremely convenient to reduce the notational problems by making use of matrix notation. The purpose of this brief appendix is only to acquaint the reader with matrix methods as a convenient *notation* for concepts with which he is already familiar. For a treatise on the *theory* of linear vector spaces and matrix analysis, consult texts in this field [1–4].

By *an* (*n-dimensional*) *vector* we mean an ordered *n*-tuple of real or complex valued components $x_1, \ldots, x_n$, which we denote by

$$\mathbf{x} = (x_1, x_2, \ldots, x_n) \qquad (A\text{-}1)$$

We define a *matrix*, A, to be an $m \times n$ array of numbers:

$$A = \begin{bmatrix} a_{11} & a_{12} & \cdots & a_{1n} \\ a_{21} & a_{22} & \cdots & a_{2n} \\ \vdots & \vdots & \ddots & \vdots \\ a_{m1} & a_{m2} & \cdots & a_{mn} \end{bmatrix} \leftarrow \text{2nd } \textit{row} \text{ of } A \qquad (A\text{-}2)$$

$\uparrow$
2nd *column* of A

A shorter way of indicating the relation of the matrix A to its elements is

$$A = [a_{kj}] \qquad (A\text{-}3)$$

the quantity a_{kj} denoting a general element of A, the element in the kth *row* and jth *column*.

Let A and B *both* be $m \times n$ matrices. We then define the *sum* of these two matrices to be the matrix whose elements are the sum of the elements of A and B; i.e.,

$$C = A + B = [a_{kj}] + [b_{kj}] = [a_{kj} + b_{kj}] = [c_{kj}] \qquad (A\text{-}4)$$

Note that the sum matrix C is also an $m \times n$ matrix.

355

Let A be an $m \times n$ matrix and B an $n \times p$ matrix.   We then define the product matrix

$$C = AB = [c_{ij}] \qquad \text{(A-5)}$$

to be the matrix whose i-jth element is given by

$$c_{ij} = \sum_{k=1}^{n} a_{ik}b_{kj} \qquad \begin{cases} i = 1, 2, \ldots, m \\ j = 1, 2, \ldots, p \end{cases} \qquad \text{(A-6)}$$

In the product of Eq. A-5 we say that A *premultiplies* B or that B *postmultiplies* A.   Note that C is an $m \times p$ matrix and also note that it was necessary to have the *number of columns of A* be equal to the *number of rows of B* (n for both matrices in the above example).   Thus both of the matrix products AB and BA cannot be defined unless A and B are square matrices (possessing the same number of rows as columns) with the same number of rows.   Even when A and B are square so that both products AB and BA are defined, it is *not* true in general that

$$AB = BA \qquad \text{(A-7)}$$

(We say that the two matrices are equal if *all* their elements are equal.)

EXAMPLE.
  Let

$$A = \begin{bmatrix} 1 & 2 \\ 3 & 4 \end{bmatrix}; \qquad B = \begin{bmatrix} 1 & 0 \\ 1 & 2 \end{bmatrix}$$

then

$$AB = \begin{bmatrix} 3 & 4 \\ 7 & 8 \end{bmatrix}$$

while

$$BA = \begin{bmatrix} 1 & 2 \\ 7 & 10 \end{bmatrix}$$

When we consider an n-dimensional vector $\mathbf{x}$ as a matrix, we regard it as an $n \times 1$ matrix (sometimes referred to as a *column vector*, because it is a matrix with only one column)

$$\mathbf{x} = \begin{bmatrix} x_1 \\ x_2 \\ \vdots \\ x_n \end{bmatrix} \qquad \text{(A-8)}$$

The multiplication of an $m \times n$ matrix A times an n-dimensional vector $\mathbf{x}$ thus yields an m-dimensional vector $\mathbf{y}$

$$\mathbf{y} = A\mathbf{x} \qquad \text{(A-9)}$$

whose kth component is

$$y_k = \sum_{q=1}^{n} a_{kq} x_q \qquad k = 1, 2, \ldots, m \qquad \text{(A-10)}$$

Since multiplication of a vector by a matrix yields another vector, we can regard multiplication by a matrix as a transformation of one vector into another.   Such a transformation is in fact a linear transformation; i.e., if

$$\mathbf{y}_1 = A\mathbf{x}_1; \qquad \mathbf{y}_2 = A\mathbf{x}_2$$

then

$$A(a\mathbf{x}_1 + b\mathbf{x}_2) = a\mathbf{y}_1 + b\mathbf{y}_2$$

in which $\mathbf{x}_1$ and $\mathbf{x}_2$ are any vectors and a and b arbitrary constants (scalars). We leave the proof of the fact that this linearity follows from our definitions of matrix addition and multiplication as an exercise for the reader.

The $n \times n$ square matrix with ones along its diagonal and all other entries zero is denoted by I:

$$I = \begin{bmatrix} 1 & & & & \\ & 1 & & \mathbf{0} & \\ & & 1 & & \\ & \mathbf{0} & & \ddots & \\ & & & & 1 \end{bmatrix} \qquad \text{(A-11)}$$

and termed the *identity matrix*.   The reason for this term is that it transforms every n-dimensional vector into itself

$$\mathbf{x} = I\mathbf{x} \qquad \text{all } \mathbf{x} \qquad \text{(A-12)}$$

Moreover, I multiplied by or multiplying any $n \times n$ matrix A yields back this same matrix

$$IA = AI = A \qquad \text{all } A \qquad \text{(A-13)}$$

It is left to the reader to verify Eqs. A-12 and A-13 by making appropriate use of Eq. A-6.

Consider any $n \times n$ *square* matrix A.   If there exists another $n \times n$ matrix A^{-1} satisfying

$$AA^{-1} = A^{-1}A = I \qquad \text{(A-14)}$$

we refer to A^{-1} as the inverse of A.   Note that A^{-1} regarded as a transformation of an n-dimensional vector is the inverse transformation of A; i.e.,

$$A^{-1}(A\mathbf{x}) = \mathbf{x} \qquad \text{all } \mathbf{x} \qquad \text{(A-15)}$$

We can find an expression for the elements of A^{-1} by means of Cramer's rule. Let $\mathbf{y}$ and $\mathbf{x}$ be n-dimensional vectors and consider the vector or matrix equation

$$\mathbf{y} = A\mathbf{x} \tag{A-16}$$

Written out component by component, this equation is equivalent to the set of linear equations

$$y_k = \sum_{j=1}^{n} a_{kj}x_j \qquad k = 1, 2, \ldots, n \tag{A-17}$$

It is known that the solution to these equations can be obtained by Cramer's rule [5] as

$$x_j = \sum_{k=1}^{n} c_{jk}y_k \qquad j = 1, 2, \ldots, n \tag{A-18}$$

in which the c_{jk} can be expressed as follows. Let $|A|$ denote the determinant of the matrix A and

$$A_{ij} = (-1)^{i+j} \cdot \text{[Determinant of the array formed by deleting}$$
$$\text{the } i\text{th row and } j\text{th column from } A] \tag{A-19}$$

then

$$c_{jk} = \frac{A_{kj}}{|A|} \tag{A-20}$$

(Note the interchange of row and column indices between c_{jk} and A_{kj}.)

Now return to the matrix equation A-16; premultiplying both sides of this equation by A^{-1} yields

$$A^{-1}\mathbf{y} = A^{-1}A\mathbf{x} = \mathbf{x} \tag{A-21}$$

However, Eq. A-18 written in vector form is

$$\mathbf{x} = C\mathbf{y} \tag{A-22}$$

Comparing Eqs. A-21 and A-22 and noting that both equations hold for an arbitrary choice of the vector $\mathbf{x}$, we have that

$$A^{-1} = C = [c_{jk}] \tag{A-23}$$

in which the c_{jk} are given by Eq. A-20.

EXAMPLE. Let $A = \begin{bmatrix} 1 & 2 \\ 3 & 4 \end{bmatrix}$. To find A^{-1} we first compute

$$|A| = 1 \cdot 4 - 2 \cdot 3 = -2$$

in this case

$$A_{11} = a_{22} = 4; \qquad A_{12} = (-1)a_{21} = -3$$
$$A_{21} = (-1)a_{12} = -2; \qquad A_{22} = a_{11} = 1$$

so that

$$A^{-1} = \frac{1}{-2}\begin{bmatrix} 4 & -2 \\ -3 & 1 \end{bmatrix} = \begin{bmatrix} -2 & 1 \\ \frac{3}{2} & -\frac{1}{2} \end{bmatrix}$$

We leave it to the reader to verify that the inverse of a diagonal matrix

$$A = \begin{bmatrix} a_{11} & & & \\ & a_{22} & & \mathbf{0} \\ & & \ddots & \\ \mathbf{0} & & & a_{nn} \end{bmatrix} \qquad a_{jk} = 0 \text{ if } j \neq k$$

is simply

$$A^{-1} = \begin{bmatrix} 1/a_{11} & & & \\ & 1/a_{22} & & \mathbf{0} \\ & & \ddots & \\ \mathbf{0} & & & 1/a_{nn} \end{bmatrix}$$

The *transpose* of an $m \times n$ matrix A is the $n \times m$ matrix A' whose rows are the columns of A; i.e., the element in the kth row and jth column of A' is a_{jk}, the element in the jth row and kth column of A. In particular, for an n-dimensional vector $\mathbf{x}$ we have

$$\mathbf{x} = \begin{bmatrix} x_1 \\ x_2 \\ \vdots \\ x_n \end{bmatrix}; \qquad \mathbf{x}' = [x_1, x_2, \ldots, x_n] \qquad \text{(A-24)}$$

We leave it to the reader to verify from the definition of Eq. A-6 for the product of two matrices that the transpose of the product $C = AB$ is given by

$$C' = (AB)' = B'A' \qquad \text{(A-25)}$$

Given a space of n-dimensional vectors whose components are all real valued, the *inner product* of any two such vectors $\mathbf{x}$ and $\mathbf{y}$ is usually taken to be

$$(\mathbf{x}, \mathbf{y}) = \sum_{k=1}^{n} x_k y_k \qquad \text{(A-26)}$$

(For a discussion of this definition, see Sec. 8-2.)   Note that in matrix notation this can be written

$$(\mathbf{x}, \mathbf{y}) = \mathbf{x}'\mathbf{y} \qquad \text{(A-27)}$$

If **y** is the result of premultiplying some vector **z** by the matrix A, the scalar quantity $(\mathbf{x}, \mathbf{y}) = (\mathbf{x}, A\mathbf{z})$ can be expressed in the following different notations

$$(\mathbf{x}, A\mathbf{z}) = \mathbf{x}'A\mathbf{z} = \sum_{j,k=1}^{n} x_j a_{jk} z_k \tag{A-28}$$

An $n \times n$ matrix A is said to be *positive definite* if

$$(\mathbf{x}, A\mathbf{x}) = \mathbf{x}'A\mathbf{x} > 0 \qquad \text{for } all\ \mathbf{x} \neq 0 \tag{A-29}$$

and *positive semi-definite* if the strict inequality is weakened to include equality

$$(\mathbf{x}, A\mathbf{x}) = \mathbf{x}'A\mathbf{x} \geq 0 \qquad \text{for } all\ \mathbf{x} \tag{A-30}$$

In some cases we wish to consider simultaneously a number of random variables, $X_1, X_2, \ldots, X_n$. The *vector random variable* **X** is defined to be the n-dimensional vector whose kth component is the random variable X_k. The expected value of this vector random variable is the *mean vector*

$$\mathbf{m} = E\{\mathbf{X}\} = (m_1, \ldots, m_n) \tag{A-31}$$

whose kth component is

$$m_k = E\{X_k\} \qquad k = 1, 2, \ldots, n \tag{A-32}$$

For references, see page 363.

Appendix 2

The Central Limit Theorem

In this appendix we wish to prove the so-called equal components case of the *central limit theorem*.[1] Let X_i, $i = 1, 2, \ldots$, be a sequence of independent identically distributed random variables with mean m and finite variance σ^2. We make no further assumptions about the distribution of the X_i. Let us define a set of normalized random variables

$$Y_k = (X_k - m)/\sigma \qquad \text{(A-33)}$$

then

$$E\{Y_k\} = 0; \qquad \text{var}\,\{Y_k\} = 1 \qquad \text{(A-34)}$$

We consider the random variables

$$U_N = \sum_{n=1}^{N} X_n \qquad \text{(A-35)}$$

and

$$V_N = \frac{1}{\sqrt{N}} \sum_{n=1}^{N} Y_n \qquad \text{(A-36)}$$

Note that by combining Eqs. A-33 and A-35 we have

$$U_N = \sigma \sqrt{N}\, V_N + Nm \qquad \text{(A-37)}$$

Our objective is to show that the distribution of U_N approaches a gaussian distribution as N approaches ∞. From Eq. A-37 we see that if we can establish that the distribution of V_N approaches that of a zero mean unit variance gaussian random variable, then the distribution of U_N approaches that of a gaussian random variable with mean Nm and variance $N\sigma^2$.

It is sufficient to show that

$$\lim_{N \to \infty} M_{V_N}(\nu) = e^{-\nu^2/2} \qquad \text{(A-38)}$$

[1] Our discussion follows closely that of Davenport and Root [6].

361

From Eq. 3-53, it follows that the characteristic function of $\sqrt{N}\, V_N$ is $[M_Y(\nu)]^N$; from Eq. 3-55 it then follows that

$$M_{V_N}(\nu) = [M_Y(\nu/\sqrt{N})]^N \tag{A-39}$$

Now from Taylor's theorem with remainder [7]

$$M_Y(\nu) = M_Y(0) + \nu M_Y'(0) + \frac{\nu^2}{2} M_Y''(\theta\nu) \qquad |\theta| < 1 \tag{A-40}$$

But

$$M_Y(0) = E\{1\} = 1$$

and

$$M_Y'(0) = (j)E\{Y\} = 0$$

thus

$$M_Y(\nu) = 1 + \frac{\nu^2}{2} M_Y''(\theta\nu) \tag{A-41}$$

From Eq. A-39 it then follows that

$$\ln M_{V_N}(\nu) = N \ln M_Y(\nu/\sqrt{N}) = N \ln \left[1 + \frac{\nu^2}{2N} M_Y''(\theta\nu/\sqrt{N}) \right] \tag{A-42}$$

Let us now take an aside and consider $\ln (1 + x)$.

$$\ln (1 + x) = \int_0^x \frac{dt}{1 + t} = x + \int_0^x \frac{dt}{1 + t} - \int_0^x dt$$

$$= x + \int_0^x \left[\frac{1}{1 + t} - 1 \right] dt$$

$$= x - \int_0^x \frac{t}{1 + t}\, dt \tag{A-43}$$

Let us use the notation

$$B(x) = \int_0^x \frac{t}{1 + t}\, dt \tag{A-44}$$

then

$$\ln (1 + x) = x - B(x) \tag{A-45}$$

We note that for $|x| < \frac{1}{2}$,

$$\left| \frac{1}{x} B(x) \right| = \left| \frac{1}{x} \int_0^x \frac{t}{1 + t}\, dt \right| \le \left| \frac{2}{x} \int_0^x t\, dt \right| = |x| \tag{A-46}$$

Thus

$$\lim_{x \to 0} \frac{1}{x} B(x) = \lim_{N \to \infty} NB(1/N) = 0 \tag{A-47}$$

Let us now combine Eqs. A-42 and A-45 to yield

$$\ln M_{V_N}(\nu) = \frac{\nu^2}{2} M_Y''(\theta\nu/\sqrt{N}) - NB\left[\frac{\nu^2}{2N} M_Y''(\theta\nu/\sqrt{N})\right] \qquad \text{(A-48)}$$

The function B defined by Eq. A-44 is continuous; also the fact that σ^2 is finite implies that M_Y'' is continuous at $\nu = 0$.[1] Furthermore,

$$\lim_{N \to \infty} M_Y''(\theta\nu/\sqrt{N}) = -\sigma_Y^2 = -1 \qquad \text{(A-49)}$$

Taking the limit as N approaches infinity in Eq. A-48 and using Eqs. A-47 and A-49 thus yields

$$\lim_{N \to \infty} \ln M_{V_N}(\nu) = -\nu^2/2 \qquad \text{(A-50)}$$

or, since exp ( ) is a continuous function

$$\lim_{N \to \infty} M_{V_N}(\nu) = \exp\left[-\nu^2/2\right] \qquad \text{(A-51)}$$

It should be pointed out in passing that, for most distributions of the random variable X, the distribution of V_N approaches a gaussian distribution rather quickly, i.e., for only modest values of N. However, for modest values of N, the approximation of $f_{V_N}(v)$ by a gaussian distribution will be accurate *only* for values of v near the mean of V_N, while the approximation is poor for values of v out in the tails of the distribution.

REFERENCES

[1] Hildebrand, F. B., *Methods of Applied Mathematics*, Prentice-Hall, Englewood Cliffs, N.J., 1952; Chapter 1.

[2] Bellman, R., *Introduction to Matrix Analysis*, McGraw-Hill Book Co., New York, 1960.

[1] The continuity of $M_Y''(\nu)$ can be reasoned as follows. Twice differentiating $M_Y(\nu)$ and interchanging differentiation and integration yields

$$M_Y''(\nu) = (j)^2 \int_{-\infty}^{\infty} y^2 f_Y(y) e^{j\nu y}\, dy$$

In finding the limit of $M''(\nu)$ from this expression we can interchange limiting and integration; the continuity of $M_Y''(\nu)$ then follows from the continuity of $e^{j\nu y}$. The interchange involved is valid because $|y^2 f_Y(y) e^{j\nu y}| \le y^2 f_Y(y)$ for all ν and

$$\int_{-\infty}^{\infty} y^2 f_Y(y)\, dy = \sigma^2 < \infty$$

For a discussion of this point, see property G, Sec. 2-5.

[3] Shilov, G. E., *An Introduction to the Theory of Linear Spaces*, Prentice-Hall, Englewood Cliffs, N.J., 1961.

[4] Halmos, P. R., *Finite Dimensional Vector Spaces*, 2nd ed., D. Van Nostrand, Princeton, N.J., 1958.

[5] Hildebrand, *op. cit.*, pp. 1–12.

[6] Davenport, W. B., and W. L. Root, *Random Signals and Noise*, McGraw-Hill Book Co., New York, 1958; pp. 81–84.

[7] Courant, R., *Differential and Integral Calculus*, I, rev. ed., Interscience Publishers, New York, 1937; Chap. VI, Art. 2, Sect. 3.

Index